I0879893

Embracing Our Complexity

SUNY series in Chinese Philosophy and Culture

Roger T. Ames, editor

Embracing Our Complexity

Thomas Aquinas and Zhu Xi on Power and the Common Good

CATHERINE HUDAK KLANCER

SUNY
PRESS

Cover Image: Smokey background from Fotolia.

Published by State University of New York Press, Albany

Printed in the United States of America

For information, contact State University of New York Press, Albany, NY
www.sunypress.edu

Production, Diane Ganeles
Marketing, Michael Campochiaro

Library of Congress Cataloging-in-Publication Data

Klancer, Catherine Hudak.
Embracing our complexity : Thomas Aquinas and Zhu Xi on power and the common good / Catherine Hudak Klancer.
pages cm. — (SUNY series in Chinese Philosophy and Culture)
Includes bibliographical references and index.
ISBN 978-1-4384-5841-0 (hc : alk. paper)—978-1-4384-5840-3 (pb : alk. paper)
ISBN 978-1-4384-5842-7 (e-book)
1. Authority. 2. Power (Philosophy) 3. Common good. 4. Thomas, Aquinas, Saint, 1225?–1274. 5. Zhu, Xi, 1130–1200. I. Title.

BD209.K55 2015
303.3'6—dc23 2014045869

10 9 8 7 6 5 4 3 2 1

For my mother and father

Give ear, you that rule the people, and that please yourselves in multitudes of nations: For power is given you by the Lord, and strength by the most High, who will examine your works, and search out your thoughts: Because being ministers of his kingdom, you have not judged rightly, nor kept the law of justice, nor walked according to the will of God. Horribly and speedily will he appear to you: for a most severe judgment shall be for them that bear rule. For to him that is little, mercy is granted: but the mighty shall be mightily tormented.

—*The Book of Wisdom*, 6:3–7

King Xuan of Qi asked, "Is it true that Tang banished Jie and King Wu assaulted Zhou?" Mencius replied, "This is contained in the records." "For a minister to slay his ruler—can this be countenanced?" Mencius said, "One who injures humaneness is called a thief; one who injures righteousness is called a brute. Someone who is a thief and a brute is called a mere fellow. I have heard of the execution of the mere fellow Zhou, but I have not heard of the killing of a ruler."

—*The Book of Mencius*, 1B:8

Contents

Acknowledgments

I must begin by thanking the teachers who have been so essential to the production of this book. I have always benefited from wonderful teaching: throughout my life, I have trusted, respected and loved the women and men who have guided my education, from kindergarten to college. Their collective influence may be seen in the fact that I have stayed in school as long as I have. Although neither of us knew it at the time, Professor T. James Kodera was doing me a wonderful favor, with lifelong consequences, by introducing me to the thought of Zhu Xi while I was a student at Wellesley College. In my postgraduate career, I was truly fortunate to study with Wm. Theodore de Bary at Columbia University; Professor de Bary's year-long seminar on Neo-Confucianism was in many ways the beginning of the doctoral project that became this book.

At Boston University, I was privileged to work with many fine professors, and to find three readers whose comments and guidance have contributed so much to this book. I must thank John Berthrong for his care and enthusiasm in directing my study of Zhu Xi, his advice concerning the direction of this project, and his insights, shared both personally and in print, concerning the Confucian tradition. Without his assistance, this project simply would not have been possible. I also owe an enormous debt of gratitude to Adam Seligman, who has been one of the most challenging teachers I have ever had, pushing me to attain higher levels of clarity and depth in my thinking and writing. I must also thank James Keenan, who welcomed me into his theology seminars at Boston College, supervised my study of Aquinas, and provided generous and constructive feedback on every stage of this project, which began to take shape in a term paper I wrote for one of his classes. Finally, I am very grateful to Gina Cogan and Diana Lobel for graciously agreeing to serve on my defense committee, and for providing valuable advice concerning how to develop this project for publication.

Being in Boston has meant that I have been surrounded not only by wonderful professors, but also by brilliant fellow students. In particular, I would like to thank Derek Michaud and Nicholas Austin for giving me the benefit of their valuable insight on preliminary drafts of this project, and for their intellectual generosity and friendship throughout my time as a doctoral candidate. I would also like to thank Bede Bidlack, Karen Enriquez, and Erik Ranstrom for organizing and participating in the 2007 Engaging Particularities Conference at Boston College, at which the ideas in this book had their first public hearing. Special thanks are also due to my fellow members of the Friends of the Way, or *Daoyoumen* (道友們), whose comments helped me to reconsider and improve aspects of my argument at a very early stage: Michael Ing, Jason Clower, Misha Tadd, Matt Stefon, Lucas Bender, Brian Loh, and Fanfan Wang. I am also grateful to the three anonymous reviewers of the manuscript, who provided valuable feedback on the project as it neared completion. Of course, any errors or omissions that remain in the finished product are my own.

Finally, it is the case that projects like this are rarely, if ever, completed without sacrifices, oftentimes made not only by the writer, but also by the innocent bystanders in her immediate vicinity. I give heartfelt thanks to my husband, Richard Klancer, whose patience and encouragement are implicitly present in every page of this book. Similarly present is the influence of my entire family, especially that of my parents, Kathleen D. Hudak and Samuel A. Hudak III, who have unfailingly and lovingly supported me throughout all the ups and downs of my life. I am glad to fulfill a dream of long standing by dedicating this book to my mother and father.

An earlier version of Chapter 5 was published in the *Heythrop Journal*, vol. 53, no. 4 (July 2012): 662–677.

Introduction

Tensions Timeless and Contemporary

One of the more mesmerizing aspects of our technologically advanced society is the way in which it enables direct communication between people who intensely dislike each other. The World Wide Web, for example, makes it possible for people with diametrically opposed views on health care, energy policy, and gay marriage to come together for the express purpose of lambasting each other's grammar, morals, and probable socioeconomic background. Ranging over a wide variety of topics, Internet debates can draw on everything from scriptural passages to personal anecdotes to statistical polls. In the midst of all this diversity it is often easy to come to the depressing conclusion that the discussions have nothing in common but their conspicuous lack of civility.

However, looking beneath the less-than-courteous surface reveals another commonality: many of these conversations focus on issues of power. People are asking—and bluntly answering—questions such as: Is the government justified in legislating and enforcing universal access to health care? How much autonomy does the White House have vis-à-vis oil companies, and how much should it have? Do the courts have the right to define what constitutes a legal marriage, or should the voters settle this question? In short, people are arguing about how to define authority, or power, understood as fairly exercised or justly wielded.[1] As countless pages across the Internet show, the twin projects of figuring out how to fairly exercise power, and mapping out the boundaries within which such exercise must be contained, are often quite contentious. Moreover, these projects are also ubiquitous: even online conversations about one celebrity's apparent inability to keep the pounds off, or another's failure to put pounds on, touch on highly complex and interwoven issues of personal autonomy, moral agency, and community responsibility—issues that are quite significant in our lives away from the computer.

Dealing with these already knotty affairs can be further complicated by the fact that oftentimes, mutually exclusive options will appear equally attractive to us as we attempt to make the most mundane of decisions about how to think or behave over the course of an ordinary day. Should we stick to our diet or temporarily forget about it? *Self-discipline is important, but what are the chances I'll ever be offered a freshly baked red velvet cupcake in my classroom again?* Should we turn our plans upside down when our parents, siblings, children, or spouse ask us to do so? *Family is family, but my life is my life.* Should we try to keep our spirits up as we look for work in a stubbornly bleak job market? *A positive attitude helps, but no amount of optimism can alter the unemployment rate.*

In the end, all but the best integrated of us will find that to be human is to live in a state of sometimes trivial, sometimes momentous, but nearly always nagging tension. We wish for hard and fast rules on which we can depend, but also the flexibility to meet new challenges as they arise. We desire to remain independent of our fellows, yet we also keenly desire communion with others. During difficult times, we can find ourselves fluctuating, often wildly, between the firm belief that we are doomed and the impassioned conviction that the good and the right will prevail. Different voices in our hearts and minds urge us in different directions—toward rigidity or relativism, self-regard or solidarity, defeatism or delusional optimism—sometimes all at once.

It is often very difficult to know which voice to listen to at which instant. If we are to be moved by more than the spur of the moment, we need to have a stable idea of how we should exercise our own power, when we should submit to that of others—whether personal or institutionalized—and where the boundaries of rightfully exercised power lie. The theory that provides us with these positions will in turn be based on certain understandings of the world, human nature as it is, and human nature as it should be.

Throughout history, sacred texts and traditions have provided this trifold context. In so doing, they have set the terms for both exercising and limiting power, making relevant demands on their followers in the process. These demands have always encouraged certain tensions of their own—if people were not inclined to use power for selfish and narrow purposes, for example, Jesus would not have had to almost ceaselessly admonish his listeners to help the unfortunate. Likewise, if people were not given to using their personal talents in service of gaining material goods over cultivating virtue, there would not be so many recorded instances of Confucius inveighing against them doing so. Nonetheless, the fact that we still know who Jesus and Confucius were thousands of years after they lived tells us something about an inherent receptivity in the human psyche to their ideas. Investigating their traditions for ways of navigating these tensions hence makes a great deal of *prima facie* sense. This book thus looks into the work of the Christian saint Thomas Aquinas (c. 1225–1274) and the Confucian master Zhu Xi (朱熹, 1130–1200)[2] on power. These two thinkers were not chosen in an attempt to indulge in what Aaron Stalnaker calls the "simplistic tradition/modernity dichotomy."[3] Rather, they were chosen because they invite their readers to consider the moral, practical, emotional, and spiritual resources available to those who (a) conceive of wisdom as including, yet surpassing, human intelligence, and (b) engage with an explicit faith in the moral order of the cosmos and the ethical potential of human beings. As readers familiar with Thomas might know little or nothing about Zhu, and vice versa, the sections below provide brief historical background on both figures, as well as an explanation of the methodological reasoning employed in comparing them.

Introduction to Zhu Xi and Thomas Aquinas

An elementary note before beginning: this book refers to both thinkers by the names most often given them in English. Nonetheless, it should be noted that Zhu, in particular, used several names. In addition to his given name (*ming*, 名) of Xi, Zhu also had several courtesy names and pseudonyms. Although the practice is no longer common in Chinese society, courtesy names (*biaozi*, 表字) were traditionally given to Chinese males at the age of twenty, marking their coming of age (courtesy names were sometimes given to females in marriage). The given name was reserved for oneself and one's elders, while the *biaozi* would be used by adults of the same generation to refer to one another on formal occasions or in writing—hence the term "courtesy name." A person might have more than one *biaozi*; such "additional" names were usually referred to as "pseudonyms" (*hao*, 號). A *hao* was usually self-selected, and it was possible to have more than one. The *hao* was often a very personal, sometimes whimsical, choice, oftentimes highly poetic; in other cases, it might be the name of one's residence. Zhu Xi had several courtesy names and pseudonyms as well, so that he was known variously as Yuanhui (元晦), Zhonghui (仲晦), Hui'an (晦庵), Shenlang (沈郎),

Jiyan (季延), Huiweng (晦翁), Dunweng (遯翁), and Yun'gu Laoren (雲谷老人). Finally, after his death, he was made a duke (*gong*, 公) and posthumously referred to by the honorary title Wen (文), thus giving him yet another name: Wengong. As for Thomas: Thomas Aquinas is the Anglecized version of *Tommaso d'Aquino*.

According to the twentieth-century Confucian scholar Ch'ien Mu (錢穆 [Qian Mu]), "in the history of China, in the ancient past there is the Master Kong [Confucius]; in the nearer past there is the Master Zhu. In the intellectual as well as the cultural history of China, these two men were of the utmost prestige and exercised the greatest influence."[4] Ch'ien Mu's claim that Zhu is second only in importance to Confucius (551—479 BCE) is not merely rhetorical in nature, but rather is based on a comparison of the roles they played in their respective historical periods. In Ch'ien's estimation, "the great achievement of Confucius [was to] gather together ancient scholarship and thought, establishing the School of the Literati (儒學, *Ruxue*), [Confucianism], which became a backbone of Chinese culture and tradition."[5] (The problem of terminology is a vexed one. What I have translated here as "school of the literati" is often translated as the more familiar "Confucianism." My general approach to the use of the latter term may be summed up in the words of Wm. Theodore de Bary: "for our purposes it is enough to identify as Confucianists those who accept the authority of the Confucian classics as providing the most reliable guide to the conduct of life and government."[6]) A millennium and a half later, Zhu performed a similar task in service to the tradition: "when Master Zhu rose up, not only was he able to accomplish the great achievement of gathering together [into a cohesive whole] the study of principle that had begun in the Northern Song [Dynasty]: it may also be said that he accomplished the great achievement of bringing together all scholarship and thought since Confucius."[7] In Ch'ien's eyes, both men were unsurpassed in fostering and expanding the tradition, in gathering together and synthesizing new ideas in new ways.

While Wing-tsit Chan does not go quite so far in his assessment of Zhu's importance in the Confucian tradition, identifying Mencius as a more significant thinker (a view more representative of the general consensus than Ch'ien's),[8] he is willing to compare Zhu quite favorably with great thinkers of the West: "if Chu Hsi's [Zhu Xi's] accomplishment were limited to completing Neo-Confucian philosophy, he would have been but a Chinese Spinoza or a St. Thomas Aquinas with whom he has been compared."[9] This judgment of Zhu as greater than Thomas has some merit. While, as Julia Ching points out, "as an orthodoxy, Chu's [Zhu's] system represented perennial truth, as did Aquinas's for the Catholic Church,"[10] it is nonetheless true that Thomas Aquinas's writings were never the basis of multinational curricula and civil service examinations. When Zhu's work was enshrined as the state orthodoxy by successive Chinese imperial houses, the stage was set for his influence to reach Korea, Japan, and Vietnam. On the other hand, while papal documents have extensively promoted the study of Thomas's work, particularly in the last two centuries, it was never elevated to the position of Church orthodoxy. As John Paul II explains, "the Church has no philosophy of her own nor does she canonize any one particular philosophy in preference to others."[11]

At the very least, it is tempting to surmise that no good Christian would ever rank Saint Thomas above Saint Paul in importance. This may seem an unfair comparison: after all, Saint Paul's letters form part of the Christian New Testament, the canon of which was closed long before Thomas was born. Nonetheless, Thomas's importance is seen as less than that of other thinkers in the tradition as well. Thus, for example, according to philosopher of religion Brian Davies, OP, Thomas's "influence on Christian thinking is *second only to* writers like St Paul and St Augustine."[12]

Nonetheless, even if Saint Thomas appears to have a slight disadvantage in comparison with the Master Zhu, there are quite palpable similarities between the two scholars. Both came from what we might call upper-class families: at a time when social class was intricately related to placement in the imperial bureaucracy of the Song Dynasty, Zhu was born to a scholar-official father in Yuxi, Fujian province, whereas Thomas was born to a family belonging to the minor aristocracy, in Roccasecca, halfway between Rome and Naples. Both were successful at a young age: after attracting the attention of Albert the Great (c. 1200–1280) while in his early twenties, Thomas became a professor or Master of theology at the University of Paris by the time he was thirty-one. Rather more spectacularly, Zhu passed the highest level of the civil service examinations and earned his *jinshi* (進士) degree, not only qualifying as a scholar-official (*shi dafu*, 士大夫) but also reaching the first rank of civil officialdom, at the age of eighteen. Both were also born into tumultuous times, and both suffered accusations of heresy in their home traditions before achieving the status of heroes of orthodoxy.

Zhu Xi

To begin with, Zhu lived during a time of national upheaval: after a mortifying loss of territory to Jurchen invaders, whom the Chinese considered to be uncivilized barbarians, the Song Dynasty (960–1279) fled its original seat in the northern city of Kaifeng and established its capital in southern Hangzhou in 1127.[13]

Moreover, the militarily and politically successful Jurchen were not the only antagonists: the new Confucian movements of the Song also identified a philosophical adversary in Buddhism, which had reached China about the second century CE. There is no question but that the Buddhists had been as successful in their sphere as the Jurchen had been in theirs, and, unfortunately, the long rise of Buddhism was accompanied by the drawn-out fall of Confucianism as a viable intellectual force.[14] However, in the long run, Buddhism proved to be a vital factor in the growth and expansion of the Confucian tradition.

First of all, the sheer need to defend the tradition against the encroachment of Buddhism provided the Neo-Confucian movement of the Song with a great deal of energy and focus.[15] Zhu Xi, for example, was well known for denouncing Buddhism.[16] In a more positive sense, Zhu also responded to the challenge posed by Buddhist doctrines of emptiness (*xu*, 虛; or *kong*, 空) by reaching back into his own historically practical tradition to explore and develop the metaphysical notion of an ontological principle, or *li*, undergirding and pervading the cosmos. As Carsun Chang has noted, "the greatest stimulus Buddhism gave to the Chinese mind was that it induced Chinese scholars to go back to the base of Confucianism and build their own system there. When they found in Buddhism a gigantic system, they soon conceived the idea that they too must have a cosmology, a theory of human nature, and attitude towards human life, family and government. In other words, they must have metaphysics, ethics, epistemology, etc."[17]

Moreover, it may be argued that Buddhism influenced Neo-Confucianism in other ways as well. While the skepticism with which Zhu and his Song predecessors viewed human feelings certainly does not amount to a thinly disguised Buddhist teaching of the wisdom of becoming detached from the world, it does show a spirit more attuned to Buddhist thought than to Mencian. In any case, convinced that he was providing a powerful solution to both political and philosophical crises, Zhu claimed to have rediscovered the Confucian truths that would not only counteract Buddhism, but also bring prosperity back to the state.

Zhu's claims to such powerful truths hardly went unchallenged. In fact, as distinguished scholar of Confucianism Wm. Theodore de Bary points out,

> . . . five years before his death in A.D. 1200, Chu Hsi [Zhu Xi] was officially condemned as a heretic and propagator of false teachings. For several decades thereafter the official status of his teachings remained unsettled . . . Even when he was rehabilitated in the 1230s by the Sung [Song] court, it was in a manner that did little credit to either Chu [Zhu] or the court—a series of face-saving maneuvers and empty honors that accomplished little. After making ritual obeisance to the memory of Chu Hsi [Zhu Xi] and other Neo-Confucian patriarchs, the Emperor Li-tsung (r. 1225–1264) went back to the business of enjoying himself in his palace and letting the dynasty run off to its doom. Nothing significant was done to institutionalize Chu's [Zhu's] teachings in the one form essential to the implementation of state orthodoxy: prescribing it for the civil service examinations, which tended also to determine the school curriculum.[18]

Nonetheless, even though Zhu's canonization as the orthodox Confucian thinker *par excellence* would have to wait for the enshrinement of his Four Books by the Mongol Yuan dynasty (1279–1344),[19] in the end, Zhu's teachings remained the state orthodoxy during the two dynasties that succeeded the Yuan—the Han-controlled Ming (1368–1644), and the Manchu-led Qing (1644–1911)—falling from grace only when the imperial system was abolished by Republican revolutionaries in the early twentieth century.

Thomas Aquinas

Like Zhu Xi, Thomas Aquinas faced social upheaval and philosophical challenges. In his time, the religious landscape of Europe was changing, and with it notions of how members of a consecrated Christian order should study and live. As Marie-Dominique Chenu explains, pedagogical and educational changes were afoot, and these changes had wide-ranging implications for the religious orders of the times:

> . . . the fact alone that schoolmen now enjoyed the privileges of free association and of an elective system is enough to show

> how far the university college had gotten away from the old monastic schools with their restriction to the enclosure of their domain, with their commitment to a class of people who knew no traveling, with their abbatial rule based on paternalism, monastic schools, in short, that were closely dependent upon that majestic feudal system on which monastic life had laid its earthly foundations.[20]

Thomas's own life provides a portrait in miniature of such sweeping cultural change. As a child, Thomas lived in the great Benedictine abbey at Monte Cassino, intended by his mother and father to one day become its abbot. Much against the wishes of his family, as a young man, he left the Benedictines to join the new order of Dominican friars. In the fall of 1245, Thomas came to Paris to the convent of Saint James, then the most prominent scholastic center of the Dominican order, situated right at the heart of the university. Thomas's decision to strike out on this less cloistered path not only meant that his life would be more active and mobile, it also had a significant impact on the intellectual material with which he would be engaged. Rather than focusing solely on the tradition of Christian Neo-Platonism, especially as transmitted through the great Saint Augustine (354–430), Thomas would also have—and take—the opportunity to develop a genuine admiration for the work of Aristotle (384–322 BCE), only recently recovered in the Latin West. Unlike Zhu Xi, who viewed Buddhist philosophers and theologians as a threat to his tradition, Thomas saw the pagan Aristotle as correct and insightful in his views concerning humanity—so far as the latter went. More than Zhu Xi—and much more so than his [Thomas's] venerated predecessor Saint Augustine—[21]Thomas is willing to appeal to philosophers who do not share his beliefs for intellectual insights, and to give the moral nonbeliever his or her due. (N.B.: this is not to say that he reads Aristotle in a way that the Philosopher himself would recognize. Rather, Thomas is doing his work in a highly Christian context, and most often for the purpose of reconciliation of the non-Christian philosophers with this context. Thus it is well to note at the outset that "the manner in which he uses his preferred authors does not leave them intact; the inspiration of his own synthesis profoundly transformed those borrowed elements."[22])

The process of such synthesis is not always a smooth one; bringing the likes of the naturally bound Aristotle and the supernaturally inclined Augustine together in one system represents quite a challenge.

As Bonnie Kent felicitously puts it, "Thomas operates very much like a host laboring to produce congenial, fruitful conversation among guests deeply at odds with each other. Like all good hosts, he conceals how hard he must work to ensure that conflicts are defused and the party goes well."[23] While Thomas's efforts to be a congenial host eventually proved successful, it is nonetheless the case that the party did not seem to be going particularly well during his lifetime or in the years immediately thereafter.

During the mid-thirteenth century, Aristotelian claims concerning the eternity of the world and the immortality of the soul were the cause of many theological battles. For some time, the tide appeared to be turning in favor of the Philosopher's critics. According to Ralph McInerny, "the urgency of the situation cannot be overstated. If the spirit of the condemnations [of Aristotle] had prevailed, the university would have turned its back on the enormous philosophical achievement of Aristotle and even more seriously called into question the assumption that faith and reason are complementary, not inimical, to each other."[24] During the last years of Thomas's life, and for decades after his death, the outcome of this vital project was by no means certain. Luckily enough, efforts to discredit Thomas and his Aristotelian leanings were ultimately unsuccessful: in Brian Davies's rather laconic turn of phrase, "as things turned out, Thomas was canonized in 1323."[25]

Thus, a great synthesis of two traditions was not only achieved, but allowed to endure. As Alasdair MacIntyre puts it, "Aquinas provided a new and richer conceptual and theoretical framework, without which anyone whose allegiance was given to both the Aristotelian and Augustinian traditions would necessarily have lapsed either into incoherence, or, by rejecting one of them, into a sterile one-sidedness."[26]

Thomas and Zhu in Conversation

This ability to successfully synthesize disparate philosophical elements is certainly a trait Thomas shares with Zhu Xi.[27] Both of these thinkers respond to an epistemological challenge neither by closing their ears to it nor by shouting it down: Thomas supplies us with an explicitly positive model of productively weaving unfamiliar ideas into an established framework, while Zhu shows us a more indirect way of accommodating foreign insights, namely, by widening the parameters of his home tradition to include new topics of discussion, and hence providing opportunities for the development of new insights. As I will discuss in more detail in the conclusion to this Introduction, familiarity with both of these approaches is to be desired in our pluralistic global society, in which someone in Beijing can e-mail, call, or Skype people in Vancouver, Rome, and Tokyo, with all the intercultural exchange such communication implies.

Moreover, not only do Thomas and Zhu show us how different metaphysical ideas can be harmonized, but they also show us how to balance tensions inherent in the human condition with their theories of power. As this book will endeavor to demonstrate, both Thomas and Zhu provide us with valuable insights into the context within which human authority is exercised, the kind of person fit to exercise authority, and the ways in which we can become that kind of person. It turns out that the wide-ranging curricula of Zhu and Thomas share significant elements in common. First, instead of investigating any one object in isolation, both sought to provide an understanding of reality as a whole. Second, in developing their doctrines of *gewu* (格物, "the investigation of things"), and of the perfection of the intellect by Trinitarian grace, Zhu and Thomas exhibited a profound belief in two separate but intertwined truths. These involve the sacred character of existence, and the ability of human beings to cooperate with the world around them, to its betterment and their own. This book argues that their inclusive and idealistic approach provides all of the elements necessary for a satisfactory answer to the intertwined questions of how best to exercise and limit authority.

The argument has five main components:

(1) *The exploration of a moral order inhabited rather than made by human beings*. Zhu's teaching of *li yi fen shu* (理一分殊, "one principle, many manifestations"), and Thomas's work on the Creator God who is present in (but not conflated with) all things, provide an ontological character to goodness and morality. Such a character successfully combats the grosser forms of relativism that can result from systems that recognize no will but that of the human individual or collective, chiefly by providing standards of goodness and rules of engagement that must be respected, regardless of personal or communal desires to the contrary. Their teachings also provide a safeguard against relying on rigid and static interpretations of these standards and rules, as they both understand that the cosmos is ultimately mysterious, beyond the power of human reason to fully comprehend or interpret once and for all.

(2) *The presentation of human beings as inextricably rooted in this order, as intelligent agents with moral potential*. Here, Thomas's doctrine of

Aristotelian virtue perfected by grace, and Zhu's belief in the efficacy of human effort in *xiushen* (修身, self-cultivation), emphasize a universal human nature that must be respected wherever it is found, while providing standards of achievement against which individual persons may be measured. Moreover, their conception of human beings as born with moral potential that must be developed in concert with the objective ethical demands of the universe and in communion with others includes a consideration of the purposes for which human authority must be developed, and where such authority should end—hence precluding an excessive focus on either self-regard or solidarity.

(3) *The description of how human beings develop their moral potential in human and cosmic community.* In Thomas's system, human beings are meant to be God's stewards on Earth before participating in the beatific vision of the afterlife, while in Zhu's, they are uniquely positioned to bring about the flourishing of the *wanwu* (萬物, ten thousand things). Every human being, whether against her will or in concert with it, is called to this role of stewardship, to the extent of whatever power she possesses. Thomas's work concerning the development of the virtues in a Christian context, and Zhu's veneration for the proper *LI* (禮, ritual; propriety)[28] for all facets of life, provide not only a sense of the sacred as something with which humans are meant to be in communion and accord, but also ways in which the will, desires, and interests of a person are to be shaped and formed before they are asserted—ways that are difficult, but nonetheless doable. In other words, neither despair nor delusional optimism regarding human prospects is promoted by either thinker.

(4) *The examination of authority properly exercised.* Both philosophers' ideas concerning the human endowment and the common good, as well as their shared recognition of differences in the moral development of specific individuals, provide grounds both sacred and mundane for the rightful exercise of authority by and within the human race. These ideas, in combination with their theories of the common good, demonstrate ways and frameworks within which authority may be virtuously exercised, with reference to the moral demands of the universe and the human race, and the dignity and worth of each.

(5) *The investigation of the proper limits of authority.* The "common sense" of both philosophers, as well as their work on the finitude of the human mind and the infinity of the cosmos, provide a framework within which human authority can never be absolute, given the impossibility of knowing all that there is to know. In addition, Thomas's work

on the virtue of humility, and Zhu's teachings concerning the humility and open-mindedness of the sage, as well as both thinkers' ideas regarding tyranny, are presented to chart the rightful boundaries of authority within the framework laid out in previous chapters.

These five components are presented in support of the central thesis of this book: that the proper exercise and limitation of authority requires a particular virtue, hitherto latent in the work of both Thomas and Zhu.[29] A person with this virtue, which I call *humble authority*, is described in the conclusion as "properly grounded in the moral order, and fully cognizant, theoretically and practically, of the parameters of human nature and the responsibilities attendant upon the human role."

Notwithstanding all that Thomas and Zhu have to offer to contemporary debates, this book does not argue that Zhu and Thomas provide complete, *prêt-à-porter* answers to current issues. In fact, as will be noted throughout the discussion, more reductionist views of the self encourage certain questions not directly addressed by thinkers such as Thomas and Zhu. For example, their shared belief in the existence of a good for humans qua humans, grounded in a universal and sacred order, made it difficult for them to conceive of individual rights as they are understood today. This does not mean that individual rights are wholly incompatible with their systems of thought, but rather that elements in their traditions must be systematically developed in order to address the practical needs and theoretical queries of the present. So, for example, in meditating on the justice or lack thereof of executing individuals, Thomas says: "If we consider a man in himself, it is unlawful to kill any man, since in every man though he be sinful, we ought to love the nature which God has made, and which is destroyed by slaying him." Although "the slaying of a sinner becomes lawful in relation to the common good, which is corrupted by sin," Thomas insists that "it is in no way lawful to slay the innocent."[30] This line of thought leads very easily into teachings concerning not only the dignity of the innocent as a group, but also the worth of individual human beings.

Meanwhile, while Zhu thought more in terms of socially necessary roles than individual rights, in assigning dignity to the role he also assigned dignity to the person who held it: "most people today are careful about choosing sons-in-law but careless in selecting daughters-in-law . . . The choice [of a daughter-in-law] is very important. How can it be neglected?"[31] Turning to Chinese imperial history, we find that such role-centered dignity could be as empowering as the most individual of rights. As the *Dictionary of Ming Biography* tells us, "when the emperor

[Ming Taizu (1328–1398)] once rebuked [the Empress Ma (1332–1382)] for inquiring about the prosperity and contentment of the people, saying that this was not her province, she countered by reminding him that she was as much the mother of the people as he was their father."[32] Moreover, in the case of Empress Ma, this line of reasoning was both successful and politically consequential: "all records agree that Empress Ma was a woman of much native good sense, who exercised considerable influence on the first emperor."[33]

Clearly, both traditions have elements that harmonize with facets of the contemporary individual rights movement, and that can be developed to be useful in the present. According to MacIntrye, it is only through such development that traditions are able to maintain themselves over time: "it is in respect of their adequacy or inadequacy in their responses to epistemological crises that traditions are vindicated."[34]

It is clear that both Thomas and Zhu played the role of vindicator. In fact, their willingness to engage with foreign ideas did more than vindicate their traditions: Thomas's successful marriage of Aristotelianism and Christianity, and Zhu's response to the metaphysical challenges presented by Buddhism, helped their respective traditions to grow. While my aims are considerably more modest, as an adherent and practitioner of Thomas's tradition, and a respectful student of Zhu's, I wish to do my small part in helping both to advance, by engaging in the same kind of inter-traditional conversation. The section below provides a statement of the methodology employed in this project of dialogue, comparison, and development.

Methodology

The basic methodology of this project is to engage two great minds in answering one highly complex question, namely, what should authority look like? In attempting to provide the solution to a problem as opposed to the description of a virtue, the project differs in content from a comparative work such as Lee Yearley's remarkable *Mencius and Aquinas: Theories of Virtue and Conceptions of Courage* (1990). Nonetheless, the *form* of the book owes a great deal to the field of comparative virtue ethics. For example, in a discussion of cardinal virtues, moral theologian James Keenan asks, "could we not make the description of the cardinal virtues formal enough so that each culture could fill in each virtue with its specific material context and apply it practically?"[35] Thus, his cardinal virtues "express what minimally constitutes a virtuous person"[36] and are "thinly described. There is no flesh on this skeleton. But [these cardinal virtues] actually provide us with a way of talking across cultures."[37] Similar methods include Robert Neville's "vague categories," which, in being constituted by possibly contradictory specifications, are flexible tools for discussing commonalities and differences among ideas from different cultural and historical contexts,[38] and Aaron Stalnaker's "bridge concepts," which "provide limited, thematic links to guide comparison, and yet are still open to greater specification in particular cases."[39] This book follows in the footsteps of these scholars as it asks a very formal question, and attempts to provide a response that will be pertinent to two very different cultures.

This formal question is asked of texts. The specific written texts to be observed in this book include Thomas Aquinas's *Summa theologiae*, the massive systematic study of God, creation, and Christian redemption he began in the last of decade of his life. Generally speaking, I rely on the excellent translation provided by the Fathers of the English Dominican Province, although the original Latin is provided for key terms.[40] I also look to the Notre Dame translation of Thomas's other great theological synthesis, the *Summa contra gentiles*, when the SCG more directly engages with the issue I am raising, although in such cases I provide reference to similar passages and ideas in the *Summa theologiae*. On occasions when I deviate from these two texts, in order to discuss ideas not explicitly addressed in either, I provide the entire passage in Latin, along with my own translation thereof. (N.B.: To my knowledge, none of the passages I select from texts such as the *De regno* or the *Compendium theologiae* contradict material in either of the *Summas*, whether directly or indirectly.)

Selecting a main text from Zhu is not quite so straightforward a task. As Wing-tsit Chan points out,

> . . . systematic treatises are almost unknown in [the Confucian] tradition. The customary means of carrying on philosophical discussion were conversational dialogue among philosophers and their students or phrase-by-phrase commentary on the classics. Thus an over-all view of a school of philosophy could be obtained only by painstaking study of voluminous commentaries or wide reading in recorded conversations.[41]

As Chan goes on to explain, Zhu Xi did attempt to remedy this situation, but not through developing a systematic treatment: "instead of taking it upon himself to write his own summation of Neo-Confucian teaching—too egotistical an approach for the Confucian—he produced a convenient anthology drawn from the sayings of others." This "convenient anthology," the *Jinsilu* (近思錄), co-authored with his friend Lü Ziqian (呂祖謙, 1137–1181), was indeed exceptionally important, but it does not hold the same central place in studies of Zhu that the *Summa theologiae* holds in studies of Thomas. Therefore, following in Zhu's footsteps, this book relies on a wide range of Confucian texts, including the *Jinsilu*, Zhu's *Yulei* (語類, the conversations recorded by his students), his commentaries on ancient Confucian classics, and his essays, all of which are collected in *The Complete Works of Master Zhu* (*Zhuzi quanshu*, 朱子全書).

To borrow Lee Yearley's terms, my project is one of *emendation* of these texts, not of *elaboration*:

> . . . elaboration utilizes modern historical and textual scholarship to understand the language and context of texts. It is especially important with ideas that appear in forms that either make them easily misunderstood or allow their challenge to be easily overlooked. Emendation utilizes modern theoretical analyses and formulations to clarify, test and reformulate the ideas the texts present.[42]

To be clear: I do not argue that Thomas and Zhu recognized the virtue of humble authority as such. Rather, this book seeks to *develop* their ideas in directions neither thinker ever thought to explore, and in a way that adequately addresses contemporary issues they were unable to foresee.

On a related note, recognizing the historical limitations of Zhu Xi and Thomas Aquinas may well—and often does—extend to criticizing some of the values they did or did not espouse given their cultural and historical situations. Such criticism may be undertaken without slights on either of the authors, while still retaining its edge. As sinologist Thomas Metzger puts it, "[I] would not blame Confucius for failing to lead a movement against sexism, since in his historical context, there was no 'good reason' to lead one. In evaluating Confucius, however, I want to know not only whether he is blameless but also whether I should affirm any of his views. A theory of evaluation, in other words, has to tell me how, in this world of clashing cultures and philosophies, I should go about figuring out what is nonsense and what makes sense."[43] (Naturally, teachings or proclamations deemed to be mean-spirited or intentionally unjust will not be judged "blameless" in this type of evaluation.) While this book is a primarily constructive project, and seeks to explore the positive contributions Zhu Xi and Thomas Aquinas can make to contemporary discourse rather than to criticize either one of them, in the Conclusion to this book, I do address the question of what in their hierarchical teachings is nonsense and what makes sense in our more egalitarian time.

Difficulties such as these should remind us that, as Yearley warns, "the actual process of emendation is a complicated and, at time, dangerous, activity. Emendation, that is, might so change the original that a disinterested observer could well wonder what role the traditional text played."[44] Throughout the book, I attempt to forego this problem by constant reference to the texts themselves, as well as to responsible and widely respected contemporary work on these texts.

Inevitably, such a close reading of two figures from such different backgrounds will also raise questions of cultural translation. As Yearley notes, "with truly different cultures the questions people think it important to ask, the issues they think they must solve, or the concepts and secondary theories they believe they must utilize all differ radically."[45] John Berthrong concurs, pointing out that, in interreligious dialogue, "just making sure that the partners are talking about the same things takes up a great deal of time."[46] In the many cases where it turns out that they are not talking about the same things, the people speaking to one another across religious divides need not despair: as May Sim argues, "explainability, not translatability, is the pivotal issue for mutual understanding [across traditions]."[47]

This book proceeds in a spirit similar to that of Sim's work. Rather than attempting to base its discussion on perfectly matched terms in the two traditions under discussion, it attempts to "articulate the possibility of social and conceptual diversity without collapsing into either naïve universalism or pernicious relativism"[48] by looking for areas of complementarity and harmony between Zhu and Thomas. Throughout the following chapters, very real differences between the two thinkers under discussion will emerge. For example, Zhu's *li* (理, principle), which permeates and suffuses all of existence, is neither a Creator God nor His goodness and love. When human beings receive this *li*, they have not received a divinely created and wholly unique soul, but rather their own personal allotment (*fen*, 分) of the same principle shared by everyone and everything else. Then again, Thomas considers that the entire universe in all of its glory was created for human beings—a belief that Zhu, who conceives of a more eternal and inclusive human partnership with nature, certainly does not share. Finally, as aforementioned, the thinkers sharply diverge in their emotional reactions to challenges to their traditions, with Thomas enthusiastically welcoming the insights of Aristotle, and Zhu responding to Buddhist teachings by building up his own Confucian resources as in defense against an enemy. Nonetheless, it remains the case that there is genuine consonance between the two thinkers—consonance that is revealed by asking the highly formal question at hand.

The question, in addition to being formal, is also complex, requiring a specific kind of skeleton for an adequately comprehensive response. Thus the book is supported by certain structural themes that are both distinct and intimately connected. Such themes are to be found in the work of both thinkers, and they concern the kind of world in which we live (*ontologically moral and not wholly under our control*), the kind of beings we believe ourselves to be (*intelligent agents obligated to develop our moral potential*), the kind of beings we believe we *should* be (*loving stewards of ourselves, others, and the world*), and the process by which we become so (*self-cultivation in community*). These themes are all interrelated with regard to the question of what authority should look like: according to both thinkers, before a human being is qualified for a position of power, she must be cognizant of the rightful uses to which authority must be put, and know the boundaries beyond which she must not tread. In presenting a morally charged environment within which human power is to be exercised, and in accordance with whose demands the human being is required to develop herself, as well as the methods and means of such self-development, Zhu Xi and Thomas Aquinas provide a context, content, and curriculum of the study of legitimate power that may not be available in more secular systems of thought. In so doing, they resolve not only conflicts specific to their respective intellectual cultures, but more universal tensions in human nature as well. The following section outlines the book's treatment of both thinkers' understanding of the deepest truths of cosmic and human existence, as well as its discussion of the methods and personal models for better aligning ourselves with these truths.

Chapter Outline

The first chapter, entitled "An Objectively Moral Universe," deals with harmonizing the tension between rigidity and relativism, chiefly through establishing objective moral demands that must be creatively met. Opening with a consideration of a more secular approach, it consists of an investigation of parallel themes in both cosmologies, namely, the fundamental goodness of the universal order and the moral demands of objective reality. The chapter closes by considering the kind of response such an order and demands may be reasonably expected to elicit in human beings, one characterized not only by reverence but also by love, the latter here understood to be synonymous with feeling and expressing concern for others. Such a response is particularly significant for the proper exercise and limitation of authority, for it contains within it the seeds of a desire for the flourishing of all that is, and the resultant commitment to use power only to the extent that such flourishing is encouraged.

Chapter 2, "Intelligent Agents with Moral Potential," addresses the tension between urges toward self-regard and solidarity, making the case that the ethical and intellectual promise of individual human beings may be fully developed only in loving communion with others. It commences with an exploration of secular notions of the self before turning to the belief common to Thomas Aquinas and Zhu Xi that the morally charged cosmos houses a human being similarly charged, exploring the work of Zhu and Thomas for a view of people as intelligent agents with moral potential. While both scholars emphasize the necessity for outside assistance in the project of moral development, this chapter contrasts the opinions of the two scholars concerning what kind of assistance is required, exploring on the one hand Thomas's doctrine of the need for supernatural grace, and Zhu's belief in the efficacy of human effort on the other. It closes by considering what is to be gained by a theory of human nature that focuses primarily on attaining moral goals, as opposed to one that focuses on maximizing interest: namely, a sense of loving community that provides impetus for both exercises and limitations of power. Thomas's and Zhu's reading of human beings is inextricably bound up with their ideas about authority, for only those who have developed their selves in accordance with the demands of the cosmos, and who display loving concern for the flourishing of the common good, are prepared to exercise authority within its proper bounds.

Having discussed sacred order and humanity, the book proceeds to explore the ways and means of developing a positive relationship between the two in Chapter 3, opening with a comparison of secular and religious conceptions of human roles. With regard to the tension between despair and delusional optimism, Zhu and Thomas avoid the twin extremes of either promising utopia or threatening dystopia, choosing instead to focus on the lifelong effort needed to first create and then maintain good relationships with others and the world. Before turning to a discussion of how humans are equipped to meet these challenges (through education in social etiquette and ritual (*LI*, 禮) in Zhu's system, and through focusing on the virtue of the individual in Thomas's), the chapter explains the methodological reasoning for focusing on socialization in Zhu's work, and on the virtues themselves in Thomas's. The chapter concludes by addressing how the understanding of the importance and substance of roles shared by both thinkers, as well as their belief that roles both social and cosmic should be played in a spirit of love, constrains them to counsel a positive engagement with power that is nonetheless self-limiting.

The fourth chapter builds on this trinity of cosmos, humankind, and the relationship between them, and begins to look at power *per se*. The chapter opens by providing examples of how many people today conceive of reasonable interference by the government in cultural matters before looking to Zhu and Thomas for an alternative view. It goes on to consider their shared notion of the sacred calling of humanity in general to exercise authority, before discussing their similar convictions that certain individuals are more specifically called to exercise authority over their peers. The chapter examines the qualifications for such leadership provided by both thinkers, which include virtues of both wisdom and love, before closing with a consideration of the importance of positively engaging with the notion of authority in contemporary politics and daily life.

Having established the grounds for authority, the book proceeds to map out its rightful boundaries. Chapter 5 first examines the contemporary distrust of humility before turning to Thomas and Zhu for their more positive treatments of this disposition. The chapter then looks to see how humility is grounded in our finite natures and limited abilities for knowledge, before surveying how this humility is meant to be lovingly expressed in our relationships with our neighbors. The chapter considers what Thomas and Zhu have to say about excessive pride in the powerful before closing with reflections on the viability of humility as a virtue for the strong, and its especial importance for people in positions of leadership today.

The Conclusion begins by confronting the complexity of the world before moving on to discuss embracing paradoxes in power, showing how apparently contradictory terms such as "humility" and "authority" can be brought together in cooperation, as they do in the lives and work of Thomas Aquinas and Zhu Xi. It is here that I define the virtue of humble authority, arguing that, while this virtue (explicit or implicit) is necessary to the proper functioning of power structures at any time, it is especially suited to and required by the contemporary era. Insofar as it upholds and even enhances the dignity of the individual person, in part by (a) referring to objective standards of value that must be continuously re-interpreted, (b) requiring his or her loving engagement with society and the world at large, and (c) providing neither utopian promises nor apocalyptic threats but rather reasonable hope for human flourishing, humble authority is a particularly vital contribution to contemporary discussions of power. The book concludes with an exploration of some of the wider implications of this comparative project and its thesis, and a brief consideration of the moral and spiritual value of religious belief and virtue.

The Wider Context

In my experience, one of the most painful and difficult questions that an academic can face is also one of the simplest: *Why should anyone care about my project?* In this particular case, the question may come in the form of: *Why should we listen to either Aquinas or Zhu, both of whom are long dead and gone?* However brilliant they may have been in their own eras, their shared premise that one can make definitive and intellectually defensible statements without empirical proof may disqualify them for serious consideration in our own pluralistic age. Rather than ducking this question, I propose to address it in this section.

As I noted in the beginning of this Introduction, being human is often synonymous with confronting tension both within and without ourselves, and this has always been the case. What has not always been the case is that our opinions are now held and our decisions made in a context that challenges every premise we rest on, and every goal we strive toward, from achieving personal peace and quiet to saving the world with triumphal fanfare. To clarify: I do not mean to suggest that ours is the first epoch in which people have intimately confronted such challenges. After all, the Christian narrative begins with the ancient

Hebrews, who quite consciously defined themselves in opposition to the peoples around them. The continued presence of the Jewish community, the advent of Islam in both the East and the West, and the more or less constant appearance of teachings deemed "heretical" throughout Christian history—not to mention the debates that took place within the bounds of orthodoxy—all put paid to the notion of a monolithic Christendom of the past. Meanwhile, East Asian culture has always been a meeting ground for many different religious traditions—Buddhism, Daoism, Shinto, and Confucianism among them.

Nonetheless, the sheer breadth of diversity in the contemporary era, both in terms of content and reach, is arguably unparalleled in human history. Today, regardless of whether we embrace a "spiritual" position, from which we look for an experience of fullness that ordinary life does not provide on its own, or a "materialist" one, from which we don't,[49] we know that we might have chosen otherwise. In fact, no matter how close knit or closed off our coterie may be, the briefest moment of reflection should make us aware that more people on the planet disagree than agree with our views on life and death, the sacred and the profane.

This state of affairs can be profoundly uncomfortable because, as Charles Taylor puts it, multiple understandings of the nature of reality tend to "fragilize"[50] each other by presenting alternatives to and critiques of each other's most privileged assumptions. As Taylor's work meticulously demonstrates, a view from within a religious tradition will encourage understandings of the world that may make little sense from without, and vice versa. In other words, whatever we find metaphysically compelling is intimately tied up with where we are standing. The problem is that, in the contemporary world, people keep coming along to knock us over—sometimes through violently disagreeing with our user comments online, but perhaps even more often by quietly, and with no particular ill will, charting a course that ends up running right into us.

Our inability to settle these issues once and for all should call our attention to the fact that our most basic conceptions of the world and human striving always require belief concerning which elements of the world and the self are most fundamental, characteristic, or important. Who is to definitively say that pursuing scientific knowledge is better or nobler than pursuing spiritual wisdom, or vice versa? If postmodernism has taught us anything, it is that no incontestable case exists for either position. Perhaps more subtly, but just as significantly, nor is there anything even approaching a universal consensus on which methodology should be used to evaluate these or other similar issues.

Here we begin to see that the commonsensical divide between "religious" and "secular" is built on sand, as both positions are based on radically questionable assumptions about or attitudes toward reality. To the extent that religion is about believing certain propositions about how best to engage with the world, an empiricist's belief in and devotion to the scientific method is no less religious than a Christian's disposition concerning contemplative prayer, or a Confucian's concerning the practice of quiet sitting. In fact, despite the popularity of narratives of secularization and the triumph of science over religion, religious conviction broadly construed is central to life in the contemporary world: even dedication to explicitly humanist themes of social justice, equality, or scientific skepticism requires a very rugged *faith* that these are the values that really matter, if this dedication is to survive in a sea of alternative views.

It should be clear that faith in the sense I am using it here has nothing intrinsically in common with the "evil" that "requires no justification and brooks no argument" heartily disparaged by Richard Dawkins and others.[51] Rather, it involves a commitment (successful or otherwise) to live and learn within a particular tradition or system of thought.[52] Today, this commitment will likely be a conscious matter of choice between different alternatives.

One of our most fundamental choices as members of contemporary society will involve that between religion and secularism. To clarify an issue of terminology: it is my position that any metaphysical stance about the world, whether articulated or unconscious, is religious in character insofar as it involves belief, and that secularism is hence a variant of religion as opposed to an alternative to it.[53] Nonetheless, it is also the obvious case that a religious belief is usually understood to be qualitatively different from a scientific hypothesis or theory. For the purposes of this book, religious belief in this narrower sense refers to a commitment to a tradition that (a) holds that the deepest truths about existence are not reductively materialist in character, and (b) provides methods and personal models for better aligning ourselves with these truths. Such traditions include but are not limited to the monotheistic religions of the West, Hinduism, Buddhism, Daoism, and Confucianism. Religious faith, as will be discussed in far more detail in Chapter 1, tends to focus on things unseen, unproven, or to be hoped for, and, as discussed especially in Chapters 2 and 3, to demand specific types of responses to said things.

My definition of a religious tradition thus places me somewhere in between Huston Smith, who emphasizes the ethical and spiritual similarities between each of the traditions he discusses in his classic *The World Religions: Our Great Wisdom Traditions* (1991), and Stephen Prothero, who focuses very robustly on the different goals and practices of each of the religions he discusses in his more recently published *God is Not One: The Eight Rival Religions That Run the World—and Why Their Differences Matter* (2010). As I will further discuss in the section on Methodology below, this book is grounded in the understanding that there is a great deal of core complementarity in the two traditions discussed, but takes care to address the very real differences between them.

On the other hand, secular thinkers will reject the kind of traditions discussed here, and may well turn to ways of being in the world that depend more exclusively on empiricism and/or rationality. I do not mean to imply an impermeable barrier between these two basic approaches, as the well-known dispute between science and religion concerning the beginnings of the universe and life on this planet all too often does. Given the highly charged rhetoric on both sides, eagerly reported on by a media that thrives more on sensationalism than sober, plodding, and arguably boring coverage of well-reasoned points of view, it can be rather difficult to remember that most forms of religion are not locked in a duel to the death with most forms of science. To the contrary, the lines between the two camps can be very fuzzy: there are scientists who experience a reverent sense of wonder before the material universe they survey, and Christians who forego flights of ecstasy insofar as they dryly and methodically analyze the Bible and the work of systematic theologians. In fact, fundamentalist Christianity and fundamentalist scientism are so similar that Charles Taylor speaks of a strangely "intra-mural quality" to the Creationism/natural selection debate, in which both sides agree that the question to be settled is how best to squeeze the mystery out of the ongoing story of the universe.[54]

Nonetheless, the secularist's rejection of the transcendent still stands as a boundary-defining issue between the two basic perspectives, which is, in the end, irresolvable. The careful reader may have noted that the religious thinker, as yet, has no reason to celebrate. Granting that no incontestable case for a secular perspective exists does not provide us with any intrinsic reason for investigating religious ways of being in the world; to the contrary, it can convince us to walk away from religious positions as being similarly contestable, and, in fact, often does. (See the Conclusion to this Introduction for a brief discussion of "consumer exhaustion" in the religious marketplace.) Hence, in addition to those who place themselves firmly in a religious or a secular campground, there are also those who define themselves as "spiritual." Such people are interested in connecting with the sources of deepest cosmic and human meaning, but unwilling to give up personal freedom in seeking it by joining a community with dogma, rules, and regulations.[55] While spiritual seekers as such do not come into this discussion, it is well to keep in mind that, in today's culture of personal autonomy, even believers will conceive of their religious affiliation in ways that might surprise their forebears. As Catherine Bell observes, "while many people affiliate with religious institutions, they are less concerned with issues of—doctrinal orthodoxy and more with issues of personal fulfillment. Although community-based forms of religion may be seen as affirming moral values and supporting one's personal search, the meaning people are looking for is ultimately understood as an intrinsically personal form of spirituality."[56] Finally, the Conclusion of this Introduction addresses a fourth group of people, who have no particular spiritual doctrine or practice at all.

Thus, cases need to be made for the wisdom of religion in general and for particular traditions, always with the understanding that these will rely on the art of persuasion—which is understood in this context to involve rational argument—as opposed to the technique of proof.[57]

To commence such a project: due to their belief in a deeply moral ontological order, Thomas and Zhu are committed to living in a way that expresses respect, even reverence, for the same. For Thomas, the cosmos is hallowed by the omnipresence of a benevolent God beyond the power of human reason or imagination to fully conceive.[58] Meanwhile, Zhu's universe is pervaded by a moral principle (*li*, 理) that has neither shape nor substance, the full import of which is only attainable through a burst of enlightenment.[59] In both cases, the cosmos as such make ethical demands on them that must not be ignored, and provides the context within which power is to be reasonably exercised and rationally limited.

As these references to reason indicate, the entire person—intellectual, emotional, physical, and spiritual—is understood to be involved in the process of a good and well-ordered life. Thomas, as indicated by his lifelong study of the decidedly un-Christian Aristotle, places a very high value on reason, and is most emphatically not a proponent of uncritical acceptance of religious truth by anyone who is fortunate enough to have the social resources and the personal capacity to advance in understanding. Indeed, as will be seen throughout this book, he himself explored his beliefs to the best of his considerable intellectual capabilities.

While the Confucian tradition never developed strong doctrines of reason or faith as such (topics discussed more fully in Chapter 1), Zhu's thinking turns out to be quite compatible with Thomas's when it comes to questions of the universe and how to respond to it. Like Thomas, who uses his faith in God as a starting point for exercising the mind, Zhu uses his belief in principle as the foundation for his intellectual development, and counsels a great deal of academic study to achieve progress in understanding this principle. Crucially, such principle is not to be taken on the kind of faith that does not ask questions: according to Zhu, "before anything else, the student must know how to doubt."[60]

The openly embraced and articulated belief of Zhu and Thomas in their respective orders helps them to envisage and encourage a society in which faith, intelligence, and love operate in open harmony rather than working at submerged and unacknowledged cross-purposes. As the following chapters will endeavor to show, their theories of authority are based on their sense of the sacred worth of every element of existence, and their practices of exercising and limiting power involve robustly investigating the best ways in which to contribute to the cause of universal flourishing. Moreover, the collaborative nature of the entire enterprise encourages a system of checks and balances, in which intelligence, faith, and concern for others work to keep each other in line and on track.

To paint this rosy picture of religious tradition and life is not to make the claim that the efforts of Zhu and Thomas to promote properly exercised and limited authority never fail or backfire, nor that religious people never rationalize their way into committing heinous crimes against others or wreaking horrendous damage on the world—of course they do. To my knowledge, there is no social project, moral theory, or religious position that does not contain within it a horrific blueprint for disaster. Even the briefest survey of human history leads to the bleak conclusion that there is no idea or invention so good or perfect that human beings cannot pervert it to truly ghastly ends.

Nonetheless, the temptation to throw the faithful baby out with the fanatical bathwater must be resisted. As one team of philosophers puts it, "neither traditional Chinese culture nor Confucianism reduce to foot binding, any more than the richness of Western art and music reduce to breast implants."[61] This is not to say that foot binding did not emerge out of the Confucian tradition, nor that breast implant surgery does not take place in the West. Rather, it is imperative to remember the simple truth that traditions and scriptures mean different things to different people. Great teachings about the complementary roles of the sexes, or about care of the body, are susceptible to all kinds of interpretations and developments: good, bad, and indifferent. Given the continued influence of the great religious traditions, it is imperative to address their teachings in way that promote both justice and flourishing rather than their opposites.

It also makes a great deal of practical sense to consider what the religious traditions have to say because, unlike the nascent New Atheist movement,[62] they offer centuries of accumulated advice and wisdom as to how we can productively harmonize the tensions inherent in the human condition: how we can balance our desires for abstract rules and recognition of concrete contingencies in our moral decision making, how we can negotiate between our urges for independence and fellowship, and how we can achieve a state of hope rather than despair or foolish presumption in our dealings with the world at large. In short, these traditions can give us insight as to how, when, and why to exercise whatever power has been given us, and the boundaries beyond which we must not tread.

The particular traditions under discussion here were also chosen because of their continued significance. While a book comparing Fuke Buddhist and Sabian teachings on authority might be of substantial academic interest to specialists in either field, short of a highly improbable chain of events, its conclusions would be unlikely to move anyone outside of a graduate student seminar. Thomas Aquinas and Zhu Xi are representatives from two traditions that continue to influence the intellectual and spiritual lives of millions in the world today, not least through the work being done in both to respond to and influence contemporary global culture. The New Confucian movement launched in the twentieth century, headed by such scholars as Mou Zongsan and Tu Weiming, and the reforms set in motion by the Catholic Vatican II council of the 1960s, are well known—and arguably successful—ongoing attempts to combat the tendency to view religious traditions as belonging to a less scientifically and politically enlightened past.

Of course, while including two voices is better than only listening to one, the reality of our diverse religious landscape strongly suggests that more perspectives should be considered: a daunting proposal. How can we ever create a conversation that accommodates all of the diverse perspectives and beliefs available? The answer to this question may be frustrating for those who like quick fixes: our only hope of success involves our taking one slow step at a time. Precisely because of the dizzying array of perspectives available, we must be careful not to sacrifice depth for breadth: more superficial treatments may blind us to the very real fact that traditions are not set in stone, but are rather kept alive by people who often agree on nothing except the questions worth arguing about. Limiting the present discussion to Confucian and Christian ideas aids in achieving a faithful and accurate portrayal of the relevant teachings, one that would be difficult to sustain in a wider-ranging conversation.

In fact, such methodological concerns encourage further constraint, as reflected in the choice to look at two thinkers rather than two traditions at large. Focusing on the recorded words of Zhu Xi and Thomas Aquinas allows me to escape the inevitable pitfalls of claiming that I have identified *the* Neo-Confucian or *the* Catholic approach to human authority. Nonetheless, an implicit argument of this book is that the texts of Zhu Xi and Thomas Aquinas are *representative* of their sacred cultures. This case may be made on the basis of their orthodox status and their widespread influence even among those in their traditions who do not agree with their premises or who find fault with their preeminence, as well as on the basis of other factors.

For example, one reason for categorizing them as characteristic representatives of their respective traditions involves their ability to move with the times. Christianity has been adaptive since its very inception: Paul is recorded as using Greek narrative and belief in his attempts to convert the people of Athens in Acts 17:22–28, and claims to adopt the perspectives of the people with whom he works (Jews, Gentiles, and the weak) in 1 Cor. 9:19–22. While this kind of tactic was originally developed in the interests of more effective evangelization, such openness to other viewpoints meant that Christianity ended up absorbing a great deal from the cultures with which it came into contact (for example, Greek philosophy, Easter Eggs, and Christmas trees). Meanwhile, the Confucian tradition, which is famously practical, records that Confucius himself would put aside ancient ritual practices in favor of contemporary economy (see *Analects* 9:3), and its followers have often been preoccupied with making ritual relevant to the times, as we will see in Chapter 3.

Hence, perhaps most important for the purposes of this project, having duly recognized them as iconic figures in their prominent traditions, we find that both Thomas and Zhu are quite adept themselves at dealing productively with positions that have the capacity to destabilize their own. This project aims at being genuinely relevant, not only in its exploration of each scholar, but also in the way in which it puts these scholars into conversation with each other: an important project, given the contemporary proliferation of religious perspectives. This book is patterned on their multi-perspectival work in its attempt to harmonize their ideas concerning how authority must be balanced with, not replaced by, humility—a theme more fully explored in the section below.

Finally, as will be discussed more fully in the book's Conclusion, I propose that, if my comparison of Zhu and Thomas is successful, it should (a) call attention to the positive role that religious traditions can play in contemporary society, (b) provide a case study of how common ground may be found between religious cultures, and, in doing the latter, (c) present two constructive ways of dealing with religious difference.

Conclusion

Many people react defensively to the cacophony of contemporary society by refusing to listen. We are all familiar with reports of the fundamentalists who find it necessary to establish vigilantly protected and sheltered communities, whether in Montana or the deserts of Afghanistan, for the express purpose of closing their ears to the themes threatening to overcome their own. Less candidly discussed is the fact that disenfranchised monotheists are not the only people to retreat to carefully guarded ghettos: the modern European or North American academy is a fairly safe place to go if one does not wish to be challenged on his or her secular perspectives.[63]

Nonetheless, as anyone reading the user comments on Yahoo! News or the *Boston Globe* website knows all too well, this sort of guarded retreat is hardly the end of the story: more aggressive tactics for dealing with difference are certainly available as well. At the other end of the spectrum, we can watch as people attempt to defend their own position by drowning out those who oppose them: as Michael Sandel has put it, public debate now typically takes place either in "shouting matches on cable TV" or "intellectual food fights on the floor of Congress."[64]

Of course, most of us are familiar with a third option as well. A commonplace of contemporary society is that an unprecedented number of people today fail to strike out an explicit position vis-à-vis the great questions of life: the condition of many of my engineering students, who neither know nor care about the religious options available to them, but don't bother to read Daniel Dennett, either. Nor is this condition limited to those who have no truck with spiritual or metaphysical issues: even those people who seek some kind of spiritual meaning or objective truth often find themselves unable to commit to one tradition or another due to a kind of consumer exhaustion. As psychologist Barry

Schwartz explains in *The Paradox of Choice: Why More is Less*, people tend to be overwhelmed by an abundance of alternatives, and many opt out of making a decision when confronted with too robust a display of options.[65] Such people may close themselves off to the possibility of taking on a position of faith, and ignore calls, from both within and outside themselves, to commit to a particular tradition or set of values.[66]

In all of these cases, the theory of authority in place, whether explicit or implicit, will be tightly linked with stifling any opposition, whether through groupthink, a shock-and-awe campaign of sheer relentless noise, selective personal deafness, or some combination of the three. For those of us who may take enjoyably self-righteous pleasure in distancing ourselves from these sorts of nonintellectual tactics, it is important to remember we all participate in them at one point or another. Given the difficulty of achieving and maintaining personal equilibrium, it should come as no surprise that we are frequently disposed to find peace in a quiet that refuses to truly consider what other voices may have to say. Regardless of how much some of us may value open-mindedness or intellectual curiosity, all of us are forced by the demands of daily living to habitually close our ears to the often terrifying multitude of voices that throw our necessary arrangements and order into destabilizing question.[67]

However, the attempt to make our environments uniformly pure or bland will simply not be successful all of the time. To quote a wise elf in Tolkien's *The Lord of the Rings*, "the wide world is all about you: you can fence yourselves in, but you cannot forever fence it out."[68] In addition, efforts to expand our territory can expect only partial success. While evangelizing secularists (or followers of religious traditions, for that matter) is always an option for those who wish neither to ignore nor shout down their opponents, such work will be, by definition, unsuccessful a significant percentage of the time. Unfortunately for those who dream of resurrecting Christendom or traditional Confucian society, or for those who cling to visions of a culture based solely on reason and science, or even for those who wish only to be left alone, it is the case that the people who remain untouched or unconvinced by proselytism, polemics, or passive rejection must still be lived with, in all their stubborn inconvenience. After all, contemporary Western societies, and, increasingly, societies in other parts of the world, are composed of individuals who are free to think and speak as they choose: it is a commonplace of human rights theory that no individual or group should be forced to take on the views of another. *We don't want to have to agree with everyone we have to live with.* This mindset means that we need to be able to converse and cooperate with people who disagree with us, on issues both big and small. Moreover, even on a strictly personal level, we must deal with the fact that there are different voices *within ourselves* that need to be attended to, and which cannot be stifled indefinitely.

Thus, rather than looking for peace by attempting to silence the voices that challenge us, it may be fruitful to turn to more musical terminology and ask how we may orchestrate these different voices into the performances that are our lives. Thinking in these terms does not cancel out the possibility of cacophony, as any number of twentieth-century symphonies should remind us. For example, if the major theme of our lives is Christian in character, we may decide that the themes played by astrophysics or evolutionary biology will blare with minor sevenths as they futilely crash up against the implacable mysteries of God, only to be resolved through development into wholly different tunes. On the other hand, thinking in terms of orchestration opens us up to the possibility for more melodious ways of interacting with perspectives different from our own, and we may decide that contemporary science helps us to develop ever-richer harmonies praising the wonders of the Divine plan and fecundity.

The musical metaphor helps us to realize that, whatever our own personal theme, we can choose between welcoming unexpected insights and information with bright major keys, or reacting to the same with more somber minor chords; that we may assert our own themes *fortissimo* in the face of new material, or retreat, *piano*, before the melodies of others, eventually to take them on as our own. In short, the orchestral metaphor helps us to come to terms with the fact that a great variety of expression is available in the world around us, and that it is not always a priori obvious how to deal with it when it enters our personal performance space. This metaphor provides us with ways of imagining both the limitation and exercise of authority, for it reminds us that, not only do we have to deal with new voices, but we also should also be playing a theme of our own.

Further on this note, the metaphor can also remind us of how important faith is in *sustaining* any kind of theme over time. While certainly leaving the door open to the possibility of an atonal or discordant personal symphony, thinking in terms of orchestration reminds us that harmoniously incorporating new material into our performances can deepen our faith commitments. Just as Zhu Xi's willingness to engage with Buddhist metaphysics led him to a keener sense of the morality of the world order in which we live, and Thomas Aquinas's openness to the brilliance of Aristotle helped him to cultivate insightful theories about human moral potential, so too can we learn from others and in so doing enrich the ways in which we understand the world and live our lives.

A point deserving of emphasis here is that, while open minded, the orchestral approach is not relativistic. Indeed, rather than prescribing a dilution, weakening, or aggressive ghettoization of religious beliefs and values, this book suggests that it is possible to exercise and even develop our religious faith in a pluralistic global community, and in the cooperative company of others who disagree with us. In fact, its entire discussion is based on the premise that it is only those people who can draw upon their deepest convictions who will be able to retain the commitment and inspiration necessary to do all the endless work of productively responding to a diverse and ever-changing world. Through revealing consonances between Confucianism and Christianity, this book shows how different religious conceptions of authority can work together in harmony: a valuable prospect in a global society that needs ethical meaning and motivation when it comes to questions of power, but cannot rely on just one source of either.

Chapter 1

An Objectively Moral Universe

> The world is a looking-glass, and gives back to every man the reflection of his own face. Frown at it, and it will in turn look sourly upon you; laugh at it and with it, and it is a jolly kind companion; and so let all young persons take their choice.
>
> —William Makepeace Thackery, *Vanity Fair*

As I noted in the Introduction, people are often torn between the desire for hard and fast rules on which they can depend, and the wish to be able to meet new and sometimes unprecedented challenges as they arise. These often conflicting desires can pull people toward the extreme of either clinging to the rules they know, even when doing so subverts the very values the laws were put in place to promote and uphold, or, in confusion, exasperation, or weariness, of refusing to acknowledge any fundamental values at all. As this chapter will make clear, the religious traditions of Confucianism and Christianity provide lessons about how to harmonize the tensions between these opposing urges, as they explicitly recognize not only objective and enduring standards of value deeply embedded in the world around us, but also the need to continuously re-interpret these standards. Moreover, the attitude that they counsel toward this dual process of recognition and re-interpretation encourages the kind of intense and ongoing effort necessary to ethically meet the challenges and surprises that a complex world has to offer: a strength of their approach that is arguably missing from secular attempts to understand the natural world, and that informs their theories of what authority should look like.

What's Your Proof? Limitations of the Scientific Model

When I presented the basic ideas of this book to an audience of area scholars of Chinese philosophy, one of my listeners persistently demanded to know why any reasonable person would buy into my project. Even given that we need an intelligent and moral way of dealing with questions of power, what reason is there for subscribing to Thomas's and Zhu's views of reality? Where was my *proof* that either was right about his conviction that the universe is morally and sacrally charged?

My colleague's reaction, of course, was not all that surprising. The idea that all claims must be rationally or empirically proven is commonsensical in contemporary society. As the poet and author Kathleen Norris has pointed out, in today's society,

> . . . religious narratives, images, and metaphors, such as those used to convey the Christian mysteries, [seem] suspect, unsuitable for rational adults, the province of the gullible, the overemotional, immature, ignorant or stupid. This attitude is so prevalent in American society that when the Episcopalian church recently ran some newspaper advertisements to attract baby boomers, one of them depicted the face of Christ with the slogan, "He Died To Take Away Your Sins, Not Your Mind."[1]

Clearly, although a significant number of Americans still report regularly attending religious services,[2] for the many people outside of religious communities, it may well seem that the acceptance of the former entails the loss of the latter. Moreover, the relationship between faith and reason may also be viewed as fraught within religious communities themselves. Martin Luther (1483–1546), for example, claimed that "reason in no way contributes to faith . . . For reason is the greatest enemy that faith has; it never comes to the aid of spiritual things—but, more frequently than not—struggles against the Divine Word, treating with contempt all that emanates from God."[3] While Luther admitted in calmer moments that reason, when enlightened and informed by faith, can "further and advance" the latter,[4] his rhetoric has undoubtedly influenced the wariness of many in Fideist traditions toward human reason, most particularly when it seems to lead to positions that contradict those of the Christian Bible.

While there are many reasons for the often uneasy relationship between contemporary thought and religious belief, such as the collapse of the belief in a cosmological order discussed in Chapter 2, it may be argued that one of the most crucial involves Sir Isaac Newton's (1643–1727) work in the natural sciences. In the first of his classic four rules of philosophy, Newton says, "*we are to admit no more causes of natural things than such as are both true and sufficient to explain their appearances.*"[5] Such a rule *prima facie* excludes trusting or placing faith in authoritative religious teachings supported by scriptural claims or subjective personal experience when other causes are manifestly available. Rather, according to Newton, the way forward to understanding the world around us is empirical and objective in character: "the whole burden of philosophy seems to consist in this—from the phenomena of motions to investigate the forces of nature, and then from these forces to demonstrate the other phenomena."[6]

It is in texts such as Newton's that we find the birth of the scientific method, which is based on collecting data through observation of things and events, and experimentation, leading to the formulation and testing of hypotheses. While philosophers of science such as the great Karl Popper remind us that the practitioners of this method once had much more sweeping ambitions and views,[7] today, scientific observations are characteristically limited and focused in scope, for the aim is to come to a defensible hypothesis of one thing or event rather than one concerning reality at large. (This is arguably a significant enough project in itself, given that there remains an element of uncertainty in all scientifically generated results: the fourth of Newton's rules, "*in experimental philosophy we are to look upon propositions inferred by general induction from phenomena as accurately or very nearly true, notwithstanding any contrary hypothesis that may be imagined, till such time as other phenomena occur, by which they may either be made more accurate, or liable to exceptions,*"[8] points to the provisional nature of all scientific knowledge.) In short, with its specialized character and demand for empirical proof, the scientific method has neither room nor use for belief in the sacred nature of the universe as a whole.

As we all know, this mode of framing the epistemological project has proven to be highly effective. Narrowly focusing on one problem or question can and has led to real improvements in the daily lives of millions of human beings around the world, and the knowledge produced by the scientific method has benefited the human race in a dazzling variety of ways. From advances in pharmaceutical research, to progress in agricultural production, to new technologies of communication and transportation, the gains produced by applying the scientific method, while by no means solely positive (we must remember here, for example, developments in military technology that make it easier to kill far more people far more quickly than ever before), have nonetheless helped to make the human experience a less perilous and oftentimes richer prospect.

Hence, it is hardly surprising that industrialized science has become, as sociologists of science Richard Harvey Brown and Elizabeth L. Malone put it, "the dominant mode of knowledge production."[9] This is true not only in explicitly scientific disciplines, but also in some areas of religious study. So, for example, a century ago, William James explored the individual and social psychology of religious feeling and belief in *The Varieties of Religious Experience*. Today, efforts of creationists to scientifically prove the literal accuracy of the Genesis account of the beginning of the world are representative of this trend (for an online example, see the Edinburgh Creation Group, "an active forum where scientifically minded people meet to discuss evidence supporting the biblical account of creation.")[10] On a related note, many philosophers display the tendency to believe that the existence of God can and moreover *should* be rationally, if not empirically, proven without a doubt.

Nonetheless, the scientific method, like all other forms of engagement with the world, has its limitations. As philosopher of science Steven Toulmin points out, "how we view any aspect of nature or 'domain', as scientists–in what terms (using what 'concepts') we frame our questions about it—decides what questions we shall ask about it, and so predetermines what propositions we can put forward at all for verification/falsification/corroboration or whatever. (Recall Kant on 'putting Nature to the question' . . . but it is always our question!)"[11] This state of affairs has an impact not only on the answers we seek but also on those we don't: in a society that places great emphasis on the scientific method, emotional or spiritual knowledge can come to seem rather insubstantial or untrustworthy. I do not mean to suggest that this is always the case: as noted in the Introduction, fundamentalist religion is as much a part of the contemporary era as secularist science. Moreover, the success of New Age publications, bookstores, and workshops point to a strong valuation of alternative forms of knowledge in American society. Nonetheless, to the extent that the scientific method as traditionally understood is held up as the ultimate paradigm of human knowledge retrieval and production, emotional or spiritual knowledge will continue to be slighted. Moreover, as discussed below, even rationality itself can become too narrowly defined.

First, the scientific method promotes an exclusive focus on those rational powers that observe and deduce, and attempts to control for personal bias based on previous experience, expectations, emotions, and even hope.[12] While this is certainly a defensible project, it does tend to have a pinched understanding of rationality, one that cuts off knowledge that can be gained through other venues. For example, as the sociologists Colin Jerolmack and Douglas Porpora have argued, there is more than one kind of rationality: they differentiate between instrumental rationality (means-end rationality), normative rationality (deontological rationality, concerning conformity and commitment to a moral value or ideal), and epistemic rationality, the last of which they explain by saying that "it is [epistemically] rational to hold a belief if there are good conceptual and evidentiary grounds for considering the belief true."[13] Such rationality, moreover, is not limited to the intellect; in fact, with regard to the human person, it may be more "rational" to have a more comprehensive approach to information gathering and knowledge production:

> . . . there are both rational and irrational emotions, just as there are both rational and irrational beliefs. Rationality is itself in turn dependent on certain emotional postures. Emotions therefore are not apart from rationality but inseparable from it . . . Insofar as human chess masters, unlike computers, rely primarily on intuition, neither can intuition be regarded as something other than rationality. It is different from calculation, but that is the point. It is only an outmoded positivism—still peculiarly strong in the sociology of religion—that equates rationality solely with calculation.[14]

While, as discussed above, such calculation has been of enormous benefit to humanity, embracing it requires neither slighting other forms and sources of rationality, nor deploring the fact that rationality is socially and physiologically conditioned—a fact increasingly obvious to intellectuals working in fields ranging from cross-cultural studies to medicine. So, for example, Thomas Metzger notes that rationality varies from culture to culture: "when I told a learned visitor from Taiwan that, for us Americans, it is irrational to expect a government to be uninfluenced by selfish interest groups, he replied that this American willingness to accommodate political immorality appeared to him as irrational."[15] Meanwhile, the neurologist Antonio Damasio has written extensively on the inseparability of emotion and reason within the human person.[16] To return to the Thackeray quote with which I opened this chapter: our proclivities, whether cultural, professional, physical, moral, intellectual, or emotional, and the ways in which we exercise and control them in relation to our surroundings, will certainly have an impact on what we select out of the world for consideration, and how we respond to it.[17] This basic premise granted, the world begins to look a lot more complex and even more interesting, as different people seek to answer different questions for different purposes.

This leads us to our second point: not only can we use other mental powers, but we can use them to address questions left aside by the scientific method and its cold, clear calculation. For example, in her work on the tragic poems of ancient Greece, Martha Nussbaum notes that "dealing, as they do, with the stories through which an entire culture has reflected about the situation of human beings and dealing, too, with the experiences of complex characters in these stories, they are unlikely to conceal from view the vulnerability of human lives to fortune, the mutability of our circumstances and our passions, the existence of conflicts among our commitments."[18] On a related note, the famed author and philologist J. R. R. Tolkien held that some truths may *only* be grasped by means of story.[19]

Such truths are of more than academic interest; according to some, coming to terms with them is the main and most characteristically human task of life. As Pope John Paul II puts it, "born and nurtured when the human being first asked questions about the reason for things and their purpose, philosophy shows in different modes and forms that the desire for truth is part of human nature itself. It is an innate property of human reason to ask *why* things are as they are."[20] Questions of meaning and purpose loom large enough in his imagination so that he claims, "one may define the human being, therefore, as *the one who seeks the truth*."[21]

Nor should this be viewed as a peculiarly religious way of conceptualizing things. For social theorists working in the symbolic interaction school, like Herbert Blumer, the study of social life rests on "three simple premises": "human beings act toward things on the basis of the meanings that the things have for them . . . the meaning of such things is derived from, or arises out of, the social interaction one has with one's fellows . . . these meanings are handled in, and modified through, an interpretative process used by the person in dealing with the things he encounters."[22] In this school of thought, "to ignore the meaning of the things toward which people act is seen as falsifying the behavior under study."[23] While realities such as social status are important to members of this school, they are nonetheless merely a subset of social meaning.

Moreover, paying attention to meaning and significance has hefty pragmatic value. The ability to interpret available information, assigning different weight to different data, so that disparate pieces of information may be organized into a cohesive and significant whole, is implicitly required by even the scientific method, which obliges its users to decide, for example, which experiments are worthwhile or reasonable to pursue. It is also of enormous importance in everyday life. As virtue ethicist Linda Zagzebski points out,

> . . . we each know in the propositional sense an enormous number of facts about a person with whom we are intimately acquainted, yet the knowledge of such facts does not constitute knowing the person. To understand a person's motivation or character we often need to be able to pick from the profusion of information about him stored in our memory certain facts that become salient in particular contexts. The juxtaposition of one bit of knowledge with another—say, his susceptibility to jealousy and fearfulness of other sorts—can produce insights that extend and deepen our understanding of his psychic makeup. And, of course, this same ability is crucially important in our knowledge of ourselves.[24]

She adds, "no specifiable procedures tell a person how to recognize the salient facts, how to get insight, or how to think up good explanations, much less how to use all three to get to a single end."[25] Rather, what is needed is a kind of learning that involves propositions but then goes beyond them. Such skills may be found among the members of musical ensembles,[26] sports teams, construction crews, or any group of people who successfully live and/or work together. In all these cases, more than rational knowledge is required for intra-group success; similarly, while empirical knowledge of other people's predilections, strengths, and weaknesses is crucial, knowledge of how to work smoothly within the context constituted by such elements is just as important.

Hence, the choice to explore questions outside the purview of science is inherently no more irrational than the choice to leave such questions aside in favor of more objectively verifiable prospects. In fact, making the decision to engage with reality as a whole, in a full-bodied way that requires the participation of the entire human person, is an inherently rational project, and provides the seeker with more forms and sources of rationality on his quest.[27]

Unlike many academics today, Thomas Aquinas and Zhu Xi made the rational decision to address questions of sacred value and meaning from a position of religious faith. In addition, unlike contemporary specialists in both the sciences and the humanities, rather than focusing on one aspect of reality in isolation, they grounded their wide-ranging work in the conviction that all of reality is worthy of study, and in so doing engaged not only their readers' intellects, but their desires and values as well. Their approach also takes into account both enduring realities and new insights, guarding against moral rigidity on the one hand and relativism on the other. The next section shall look at Thomas's and Zhu's religious faith, taking especial care to unpack this term, straightforward in a Christian context, in Zhu's Confucian milieu, before exploring the universe as they saw it and explaining what their comprehensive approach has to offer to discussions of human power.

A Different Way of Thinking: The Mind of Faith

Thomas Aquinas—Faith Informed by Reason, Reason Informed by Faith

Schisms between knowledge and faith, religion and science, are so familiar as to seem almost commonsensical. Well-publicized debates between fundamentalists and scientists over issues such as teaching evolution to schoolchildren, which have continued well into the twenty-first century, seem to underscore the incompatibility of informed logic and spiritual belief. Nonetheless, the conversation between religion and science, or faith and reason, does not necessarily have to be quite so contentious. Indeed, in Thomas Aquinas, discourse between the mind and the spirit turns out to be quite harmonious.[28]

According to James Weisheipl, "Thomas was very much a man of his age and his environment."[29] As even a cursory glance at any history of the period will demonstrate, the Europe of Thomas's lifetime was decidedly Christian, and in a way almost unimaginable today. While contemporary Western philosophers look at the world in a vast diversity of different lights, this was not the case in the medieval period.

At that time, as Frederick Copleston explains, "owing to the common background of the Christian faith, the world presented itself to the medieval thinker more or less in a common light. Whether a thinker held or denied a clear distinction between the provinces of theology and philosophy, in either case he looked on the world as a Christian and could hardly avoid doing so."[30] As Maurice de Wulf diplomatically puts it, "in the Middle Ages no one openly opposed dogma, but everyone explained it in his own way."[31]

Saint Thomas was certainly no exception to the rule: he was nothing if not a follower of Jesus of Nazareth. In addition to the markedly Christian character of much of his writing—found not only in the themes, but also in the source material on which he relies: in the *Summa theologica*, he cites Scripture more than any other source, and Biblical references are to be found in all of the questions[32]—stories of his intense spirituality and reliance on prayer abound. For example, Jacques Maritain tells us that

> . . . on his return to Naples after the death of Thomas, Reginald [his *socius*, or personal assistant] was to exclaim: 'As long as he was living my Master prevented me from revealing the marvels that I witnessed. He owed his knowledge less to the effort of his mind than to the power of his prayer. Every time he wanted to study, discuss, teach, write or dictate, he first had recourse to the privacy of prayer, weeping before God in order to discover in the truth the divine secrets, and, though he had been in uncertainty before praying, as a result of his prayer he came back instructed.' When doubtful points would arise, Bartolommeo di Capua likewise reports, he would go to the altar and would stay there weeping many tears and uttering great sobs, then return to his room and continue his writings.[33]

According to Brian Davies, Thomas "thinks as a Christian, and he uses his ability to think in a way which, in his view, does all that it can to show that the revelation given in Christianity is not just a creed for those who cannot think and give reasons for what they believe."[34] In fact, in Thomas's estimation, Christianity offers opportunities for the exercise and development of reason unavailable outside of it.

To begin with, Thomas, as is indicated by his lifelong study of the decidedly un-Christian Aristotle, places a very high value on reason.

Saint Thomas would simply not recognize the sort of picture often drawn by creationists and scientists battling over evolution, in which reason counteracts religion. In his *Summa contra gentiles*, traditionally understood to have been written for missionaries in the Muslim field, Thomas famously writes, "although the truth of the Christian faith which we have discussed surpasses the capacity of the reason, nevertheless that truth that the human reason is equipped to know cannot be opposed to the truth of the Christian faith."[35] Thomas has no doubt that the process of reasoning produces real knowledge: "man forms a sure judgment about a truth by the discursive process of his reason: and so human knowledge is acquired by means of demonstrative reasoning."[36] Moreover, the rational powers within the human intellect are understood to be very helpful in exploration of sacred doctrine:

> . . . [since] grace does not destroy nature but perfects it, natural reason should minister to faith as the natural bent of the will ministers to charity. . . . Hence sacred doctrine makes use also of the authority of philosophers in those questions in which they were able to know the truth by natural reason, as Paul quotes a saying of Aratus: "As some also of your own poets said: For we are also His offspring" (Acts 17:28).[37]

Given his understanding of the importance and power of the human intellect, it is hardly surprising that, for Thomas, reasonable arguments are valuable as they remove obstacles to faith,[38] and empirical observations are key in both developing faith and correcting errors.[39]

However, this does not mean that human intellectual power can of itself lead to the kind of truth Thomas is most interested in: "the researches of natural reason do not suffice mankind for the knowledge of Divine matters, even of those that can be proved by reason."[40] Surprising, in view of statements like these, is the commonly accepted notion that Thomas believes it possible to develop definitive rational proofs for the truths made known in Christian Revelation. According to Davies, "it has [recently] been suggested that, in his view, faith, at least for some, is a matter of being convinced by evidence. The idea is that those with faith, or at least some of them, are rationally convinced of the truths stated in the classical Christian creeds, and that this is enough to give them what Aquinas means by 'faith.' They are like a judge who is forced to admit that *X* murdered *Y* because the facts cannot be otherwise interpreted or because the balance of probability comes down in its favor. But this reading of Aquinas needs to be contested."[41]

Additional support for Davies's position is available in the *Summa contra gentiles*:

> the sole way to overcome an adversary of divine truth is from the authority of Scripture—an authority divinely confirmed by miracles. For that which is above the human reason we believe only because God has revealed it. Nevertheless, there are certain likely arguments that should be brought forth in order to make divine truth known. This should be done for the training and consolation of the faithful, and not with any idea of refuting those who are adversaries. For the very inadequacy of the arguments would rather strengthen them in their error, since they would imagine that our acceptance of the truth of the faith was based on such weak arguments.[42]

Moreover, such weak arguments pose more dangers than exposing Christian doctrines to ridicule by unbelievers: they may lead the unsuspecting Christian to thinking that he or she has all the answers.[43]

In the end, it turns out that faith, which Thomas defines as "the substance of things to be hoped for, the evidence of things that appear not,"[44] while never *opposed to* reason, is always *more important than* reason. For Thomas, faith is not opposed to knowledge; rather, it is a kind of knowledge[45] that is necessary for full development of the human person: "since man's nature is dependent on a higher nature, natural knowledge does not suffice for its perfection, and some supernatural knowledge is necessary."[46] The supernatural knowledge of faith raises the knower above the limitations of reason, logic, and intellect: "in many respects faith perceives the invisible things of God in a higher way than natural reason does in proceeding to God from His creatures. Hence it is written (Sirach 3:25): 'Many things are shown to thee above the understandings of man.' "[47] Thus, Thomas sees faith as *empowering* reason, and contributing to its full development. Hence, while revelation can indeed be rationally understood to a point, it can never be fully comprehended by any one individual or even institution. This doctrine flows very smoothly into the realization that, while not all of the answers have been provided to us, we have been given fundamental principles and values on which we can depend. When accepted, this realization supports the search for a middle ground of commitment and flexibility between the extremes of rigidity and relativism.

In all, the knowledge of faith is more comprehensive than that of intellectual reason alone, embracing more of the human experience and person. While Thomas did not consider the passions to be rational in themselves, nor did he believe that they were immune to reason as exercised by the intellect: rather, along with Aristotle, he is of the opinion that "it is manifest that the sensitive powers are rational, not by their essence, but only by participation" (Ethic. i, 13.)[48] In Thomas's understanding, coming to grasp the divine truth in any measure will require properly directed passions: in other words, a properly ordered will. "To believe is an act of the intellect inasmuch as the will moves it to assent. And this act proceeds from the will and the intellect, both of which have a natural aptitude to be perfected in this way. Consequently, if the act of faith is to be perfect, there needs to be a habit in the will as well as in the intellect."[49] One's desires, passions, intellect, and the will are all addressed by Saint Thomas's approach. Indeed, as Fergus Kerr points out, for Thomas, "theological activity is a form of sharing in God's being, a form of union with God, an anticipation of the divine beatitude."[50] With such an end in mind, Thomas, while never disparaging the intellectual exercise, or, for that matter, the human mind,[51] assigns a greater deal of significance to the virtue of faith than to the arguments that support it—"the light of faith makes us see what we believe"[52]—and far more agency to God than to the believer: "since man, by assenting to matters of faith, is raised above his nature, this must needs accrue to him from some supernatural principle moving him inwardly; and this is God. Therefore faith, as regards the assent which is the chief act of faith, is from God moving man inwardly by grace."[53]

This latter process is not conceived to be one of coercion, domination, or struggle. Rather, Thomas understands that divine grace, which he defines as "the effect of the Divine love in us . . . whereby a man is made worthy of eternal life,"[54] cooperates with the human mind and person: "grace does not destroy nature but perfects it."[55] Thus, rather than conceiving of a relationship in which divine grace struggles with and against a wholly alien human nature, Thomas conceives of grace as a wonderful gift that elevates the human person who accepts it. As Kerr explains, for Thomas, "the gift of grace that is God's self-disclosure, the basis of all theology then, as well of course of all prayer, means that not only are we not frustrated in our desire to know what lies infinitely beyond us but we are drawn to a destiny we could never of ourselves have imagined."[56] For Thomas, the human person is enabled by grace to behold the face of God after death, and to spend eternity in the rapt contemplation of the beatific vision: "final Happiness consists 'in the vision of the Divine Essence, Which is the very essence of goodness."[57] With grace, such a destiny becomes imaginable, if only faintly, to our powers of intellect, which themselves will be expanded and sharpened. That Thomas believes that our intellects are developed in this process is beyond a doubt. As Aidan Nichols points out, "to Thomas' way of thinking, human salvation and the perfection of man as an intellectual being are one and the same."[58]

Given this understanding of the precious, but finite, character of rational and intellectual inquiry, and the joys of contemplating the blessed infinity of God, it is hardly surprising that Thomas combines reason and feeling in his discussions of the divine. As Aidan Nichols notes, "in the course of giving a brief answer to a couple of objections to some thesis, Thomas is perfectly capable of switching from the most austere metaphysical analysis to some extravagant metaphor taken from a Greek Father or a Carolingian monk."[59] The Thomistic system provides us with more of a continuum of experience than that available in more scientific disciplines, or in more exclusively rational thinkers such as Kant—rather than divorcing faith from reason and setting each in a separate mental space, Thomas allows them to cooperate. In fact, it is eminently possible that Thomas would understand Kant's failure to approach the highest truths of creation with his intellect as a result of his refusal to allow his faith to work together with his reason.

Thomas looks beyond the intellect, beyond the material world, and beyond the realm of empirical observation, seeking that which is greater than all of these, yet without forsaking any of them: teaching those of us who read him today how to balance and harmonize the complexity of our own experience, rather than succumbing to the tone-deafness that can result from focusing solely on one aspect of our nature—such as our intellect—or one method of dealing with things—such as rule following or spontaneous intuition.

In closing, this section, rather than being an exercise in Christian apologetics or a defense of Thomas's understanding of reason, has been an exploration of the kind of thinking that leads him to conclusions of practical import and emotional relevance; the question of whether or not his religious faith is necessary to reach those conclusions will be explored in greater detail later in the book. For the present, we will turn to Zhu for his religious views.

Zhu Xi—An Intellectually Rigorous Faith

That Saint Thomas turns out to have a profound religious faith in that which surpasses human understanding is hardly surprising. But what about Zhu Xi? It is unquestionably the case that he does not see himself as a person of faith in the same sense that Thomas does, and that faith is not the cardinal concept for the former as it is for the latter. Nonetheless, as this section will endeavor to show, both he and his tradition subscribe to a particular kind of religious faith.

To commence: from the very beginnings of his tradition, it has been associated with a worldly, practical focus and lack of interest in the afterlife. Hence, it makes sense to ask the question: Is Confucianism a religion? The early Jesuit missionaries to China answered this question in the negative—as Julia Ching puts it, "where the Jesuits were concerned, Buddhists were idolaters whereas Confucians were potential allies and converts"[60]—but their reading of the Confucian tradition as more humanistic than religious cannot even be said to be the "early modern Catholic" analysis of the situation, as Rome rejected their interpretation. A similar lack of consensus surrounds the tradition today, one that involves differing definitions of religion. Below, I review some of the literature surrounding this question before arguing that Zhu and his tradition are in fact religious.

Given the theocentric nature of their own tradition, the Jesuits had good reasons for their construal of Confucianism as something "other" than a religion. Perhaps most important, none of the educated scholar-officials around them had anything to say about God. Obviously, in the Christian Trinity, knowledge of the Second Person is based on the divine Incarnation of Jesus; perhaps as obviously, Confucius was no Christ. (As I tell my students, while Jesus was reported to have been fathered by God himself, Confucius came into the world in the usual way. Where Jesus turned water into wine, Confucius turned ancient texts into something read by the young, and where Jesus miraculously rose from the dead, Confucius died.) Moreover, the First Teacher is well known for his reticence on speculative matters; for example, the *Analects* tells us that "Confucius never discussed the uncanny, feats of strength, disorders, or spirits,"[61] while the great Classic *The Doctrine of the Mean* records him as saying, "there are those who seek for the mysterious, and practice wonders. Future generations may mention them. But that is what I will not do."[62] Nonetheless, as further discussed in Chapter 2, Confucius did understand himself as having a relationship with divine elements in the cosmos, and, moreover, believed that these elements have revealed certain great truths to humankind. As Julia Ching points out, "one cannot just say that there has been no historical 'revelation' in the Confucian tradition. The truth is much more complex. While the knowledge of God as Lord-On-High and Heaven had come to the Chinese people through 'natural hierophanies', these in turn appear to have been largely mediated through sage-kings and other charismatic, almost prophetic, individuals."[63] However, as Ching is careful to emphasize: "Confucianism, even in its early form, only *came close* to being a prophetic religion."[64]

A further question then arises: Need a religion be prophetic in order to be called a religion? Xinzhong Yao says no, identifying Confucianism as a "humanistic religion." Such a religion

> . . . takes the world as a unity of human beings and spirits or Spirit. While it does not deny the existence and the importance of the Transcendent, it does insist that the human world and the spiritual world, this life and that life, are inseparable. Further, their unity can be understood only from the point view [*sic*] of this world and this life—that is, from the point of view of human endeavor to transcend the limitation of life—in contrast to a theistic religion, which insists that their true relation can be revealed only by God and though God's grace.[65]

The recognition of the possibility of "humanistic" religion makes it possible to recognize the religiosity of much of the Confucian tradition; for example, as Ren Jiyu notes, "'honoring the honorable and being kind to kindred,' and 'revering virtue and safeguarding the people' all bore the traces of the primitive religion. The Confucian Classics have always had a strongly religious character."[66] More expansively, Benjamin Schwartz claims that

> . . . there is no reason whatsoever to believe, in the case of Confucius, that a heaven which is immanent in the regularities, routines, and generative processes of nature may not also possess attributes of consciousness and spirit. Such a notion may be La Place's "superfluous hypothesis" from the point of view of the theoretical and technical concerns of modern science but not from the view of a Confucius eager to find in Heaven's way in the cosmos a model for human behavior.[67]

As Schwartz's reference to regularities and routines suggests, Confucianism also provides an example of a religion that is profoundly rational. As de Bary points out,

> Confucian rationalism does not involve a conscious exaltation of reason as opposed to faith or intuition (none of the early masters seems to have acknowledged such an explicit dichotomy). It derives rather from three basic attitudes found in Confucius and the classical Confucians: *first, that the universe is characterized by order, regularity, and a harmonious integration of its parts; second, that it is possible for man to discern this order underlying things and events*; and third, that to devote oneself to what the "Great Learning" calls the *systematic study* of "things" . . . is the high calling of the "noble man" (*chün-tzu* [*junzi*]).[68]

In fact, like the Christians who believed in the harmonious relationship between reason and revelation, the Confucians saw nothing incongruent about the happy coexistence of rationality and religion; indeed, they highly resented seeing the latter without the former. Again, de Bary:

> . . . over the long course of history the [Confucian] schools served the ruling elite better than the general populace, and its rationalism served scholarship better than popular religion, which Confucianism dealt with at arm's length with great skepticism and notable diffidence. Hence, for all the efforts of Confucians historically, and especially the Neo-Confucians, to revive the old-time religion of the Zhou aristocracy and resurrect the classic rituals, they had little success in winning over the general populace and experienced almost constant frustration, if not despair, over their failures to wean the masses from their seeming bewitchment by the magic of Buddhist and Daoist liturgies and religious spectacles.[69]

To return to Confucius's core goal, arguably both practical and rational—to find a model for human behavior—is to uncover perhaps one of the elemental differences between the Christian and Confucian traditions. According to Xinzhong Yao,

> . . . in Christian spirituality, ethical matters are expressed in theological terms and in a creational context. The source and resource of moral growth is therefore God and the fundamental question is the relationship of humans to God. In Confucian spirituality, however, [the] transcendental ideal is described by an ethical terminology and in a moral context. To be transcendental is to be moral and to cultivate one's virtue.[70]

In Ching's succinct reading: "Christianity would seem to be God-centered where Confucianism is man-centered."[71] (N.B.: this is not to say that Confucius was an atheist: a topic discussed later in the chapter, and in Chapter 2 as well.) Nonetheless, Ching identifies Zhu's Great Ultimate with the Christian God,[72] and is of the opinion that "for the dialogue between Christianity and Confucianism, an understanding of faith in man as openness to the transcendent remains the most promising starting point."[73]

That there is such an openness in both traditions gives credence to the definitions of Confucianism which address its religious elements, even if such definitions do not call Confucianism a religion per se. Peng Guoxiang prefers to call Confucianism "宗教性的人文主义, *zongjiaoxing de renwenzhuyi*," or "religious humanism." Pointing out that "religion" and humanism" are terms that have more to do with the history of modern Western philosophy than anything else,[74] Peng writes,

> . . . first of all, if we use the original meaning of the two words "humanism (人文, renwen)" and "religion (宗教, zongjiao)" in the historical linguistic background of Chinese as the standard, well, then we are able to say without harm that Confucianism is a kind of "humanism," that it gives expression to a focus on the "human spirit." We may also say that Confucianism is a kind of "religion," given that, historically, it was once regarded as a kind of "religion," without the slightest doubt, along with Buddhism and Daoism. Secondly, even if when we use the two words "*renwen zhuyi*" and "*zongjiao*" we are corresponding to the "humanism" and "religion" of the West, as long as we do not limit our understanding to modern mainstream "secular humanism (*shisu renwenzhuyi*)" or only use the monotheism of Western Asia

> as the standard for "religion," well, we can then look at the Confucian tradition equally as a kind of humanism, and also as a kind of religion. Thirdly, even if we use "*renwenzhuyi*" and "*zongjiao*" in situations where we are strictly corresponding to mainstream Western secular humanism and using only Western Asian monotheism as a standard, we will still be able to see that the Confucian tradition simultaneously possesses elements of "humanism" and "religion."[75]

Tu Weiming thinks that such an inclusive approach is the most useful of all, as it helps to prevent the danger of focusing on one or two elements of the tradition to the exclusion of others:

> . . . philosophically, as well as historically, Confucianism symbolizes a very complex spiritual phenomenon. The scope of its involvement defies simple categorization. Even broad terms such as *religion*, *social philosophy*, and *ethical system* are too narrow to encompass the diversity of Confucian concerns, especially if the terms are used in a restrictive sense. For example, if Confucianism is described as a religion and by religion is meant a kind of spiritualism purportedly detached from the secular world, the whole dimension of sociality in Confucianism will be left out. If Confucianism is described as a social philosophy, its central concern of relating the self to the most generalized level of universality, or *t'ien* [tian] (heaven), will be ignored. If the spiritual aspect of Confucian self-cultivation is emphasized exclusively, its intention of complete self-fulfillment, which must also embrace the whole area of corporality, will be misunderstood. On the other hand, if the Confucian insistence on man as a sociopolitical being is overstated, its ideal of self-transcendence in the form of being one with Heaven and Earth will become incomprehensible.[76]

In short, Confucianism is certainly religious, if not a religion in the sense that Christianity or Islam is a religion, because it recognizes and has faith in the moral relevance of the material universe, which, moreover, endures during the long ages when people ignore it. Confucius himself certainly did not believe that Heaven depended on him for its continued survival or relevance, saying, "'I do not wish to speak!' Zigong said, 'Master, if you do not speak, then what will we disciples pass on?'

Confucius replied, 'What does Heaven say? The four seasons pass one into the other, the hundred things are born; what does Heaven say?' "[77]

Having explored the question of the religiosity of the Confucian tradition as a whole, our next question is more specific in focus. Again, however, the issue of Zhu Xi's religious proclivities is complex.

To begin with, Zhu states that "the mind of heaven and earth is to produce things."[78] To those who would rush to identify this fecund mind with a creator God, Chung Tsai-chun offers the warning that "the concept 'the Mind of Heaven' must not be identified with God, for the Neo-Confucianists were never theists."[79] Zhu himself is very clear on what the mind of Heaven and Earth is *not* (a lord in the sky or elsewhere), although he is rather more unclear as to what it *is*: "someone asked: 'Is the mind of heaven and earth a spirit? Or is it just unresponsive and without action?' [The Master] answered: 'You cannot say that the mind of heaven and earth is *not* a spirit; however, it does not deliberate as a person does. Yi Chuan [Cheng Yi, 1033–1107] said, "Heaven and Earth do not have mind but transform things, the sage has a mind and does not act."' "[80] Unlike Thomas, who dedicates most of his life in an attempt to understand the mind of the Christian Heaven and Earth as clearly as possible (always with the caveat that such a project has inherent limitations, as discussed further below), Zhu Xi gives deliberately ambiguous and evocative answers to those who seek to expand their knowledge of this dimension of reality. As Yü Ying-shih points out, "as a matter of fact, the absence of theology in the Chinese tradition is something that no intellectual historian can possibly fail to notice. Chinese speculations on heaven or cosmos from the third century B.C.E. on led only to the rise of the *yin-yang* cosmology, not theology."[81] On the basis of similar thinking, Roger Ames goes so far as to claim that "Classical Confucianism is at once a-theistic and profoundly religious. It is a religion without a God, a religion that affirms the cumulative human experience itself."[82] While I certainly agree with Ames's premise that Confucianism affirms the human experience, I disagree with the atheistic conclusion that he draws from it, a theme I discuss in more detail in Chapter 2. I limit myself here to noting that scholars including Julia Ching[83] and Deborah Sommer[84] challenge Ames's reading of the early tradition, and, that, in any case, in the Neo-Confucian era of the tradition, such a lack of divine person(s) does not necessarily translate to what we might construe as a secular worldview.

In his *Recorded Conversations*, or 語類 *Yulei*, Zhu is quoted as saying, "Confucius said, 'Unable to serve people, how can you serve spirits! Not knowing life, how can you know death!' This says it all."[85] Reflecting a true Confucian spirit, he adds, "Nowadays we need to go to understand those affairs which are right in front of us. The affairs of ghosts and supernatural beings have no shape and no shadow; you don't want to vainly waste your mental energy [on them]."[86] Nonetheless, it is possible that Zhu protests too much: an entire chapter of the *Yulei* is devoted to the discussion of such affairs, and Zhu never denies the existence of supernatural beings; to the contrary, he defines their substance: "supernatural beings are merely *qi* [material force]."[87]

Zhu's practical or pragmatic attitude toward a more or less accepted supernatural realm is seen in his *Family Rituals [Jiali,* 家禮*].* As Patricia Ebrey notes in the preface to her translation of this work, "none of the ceremonies described in Chu Hsi's [Zhu Xi's] *Family Rituals* departed very far from ordinary life. They involved no weird symbolisms or improbable juxtapositions, no dancing, trances, or violence. No one did anything that could not be done in non-ritual contexts."[88] Nonetheless, despite the "ordinary" character of the rituals, they are designed to reach out to a realm unseen and unheard. For example, Zhu instructs his readers to make "grave goods" as if the dead would need them.[89] This task is not viewed merely as an expression of filial piety, or as psychologically fulfilling for the people left behind in grief, because Zhu's handbook also instructs people to offer goods to *gods* and *spirits* at certain times.[90] Such instructions, given without apparent irony in a ritual handbook, lend credence to the idea that Zhu was not a strict materialist: he believed in beings he could not see, and in an order about which he could not be certain.

Like Thomas, he counsels a robust intellectual searching of the moral deposits of the cosmos. As a follower of Confucius, Zhu believes in the presence of a moral element to the universe that is in no way dependent on the will of human beings and endures despite all human folly, pointing to the sacred, non-negotiable nature of this element when he muses that, in his own day, "although there are no sages to [explore the principle (*li*, 理) of the Way], this heavenly principle is still of itself in the midst of Heaven and Earth."[91] Rather than conceiving of morality and the sacred in anthropocentric terms—up to humans to conceive, construct, and lay to rest at will—Zhu clearly believes that principle stands outside of human control. Moreover, as will be discussed further below, he also, to use Rodney Taylor's phrasing, clarifies the relationship of the individual with the principle in which he believes:[92] in Zhu's understanding, *li* is forever available for communion and cooperation with humans, even when no one is accepting the perpetual invitation for engagement.

Like Thomas, who uses his belief in God as a starting point for exercising the mind, Zhu uses his faith in principle as the foundation for his intellectual development, counseling a great deal of academic study to achieve progress in understanding this principle. In this latter project he was hardly breaking new ground. The Confucians throughout the ages have been nothing if not committed to scholarly activities. As de Bary puts it, "there has probably been no other tradition so clearly committed to scholarship as the Confucian, and in the absence of sacerdotal, pastoral or monastic activities, it was book learning and literary activity which became for the Confucian even more central tasks than for the Christian, Jew, Muslim, Hindu or Buddhist."[93] Zhu himself certainly takes book learning seriously. He believes that the great *li* that fills the cosmos may be grasped through careful study of the Confucian Classics: "reading the classics [is done] in order to see the meaning of the sages and worthies; because [in] the meaning of the sages and worthies, natural principle may be seen."[94]

Nonetheless, such seeing is not blind, so to speak: Zhu's system requires people to think for themselves, and requires robust questioning from those engaging with its curriculum. In fact, Zhu claims that, "if one doubts where there is nothing to doubt, then there is real progress."[95] In his estimation, such careful consideration can lead not to the construction of new truths but to the discovery of insights hitherto hidden: "moral principle is infinite. What our predecessors said does not necessarily exhaust it. We must pick it up ourselves and resolutely look it in all its breadth, penetrating it deeply and exhausting all that is there."[96]

This method of constant questioning and exploration is different from Thomas's careful balancing of reason and faith. Nonetheless, to return to and build on May Sim's insight that it is "explainability, not translatability"[97] that matters in comparative work: it can often make more sense to look for complementary ideas than one-to-one correspondences in terminology, as such terminology is heavily influenced by concerns—soteriological, for example—that may not be shared across traditions. The lack of such correspondences can blind us to commonalities beneath the surface vocabulary—in this case, the fact that both Zhu and Thomas encourage intellectual development on the basis of commitment to a tradition that holds that the deepest truths of the universe are not reductively materialist in character. Moreover, their accounts of true learning and growth not only harmonize with each other, they can also enrich each other. Putting these figures into conversation leads to a more comprehensive vision of the life of the mind than would have been likely were we to focus on only one of them, as students of Zhu are invited to delve into the minutiae of their thought processes more systematically through reading Thomas, and students of Thomas may be moved to consider more deeply the role of doubt through reading Zhu.

Even before entering into such conversation, we find that Zhu's intellectual program is broader than that of the scientific method: Zhu's principle cannot be wholly grasped through deductive proof or empirical observation. (There is a theoretical exception to this rule: Zhu tells us it some are born "bright and clear, pure and unadulterated, and who do not have a hair's worth [of] cloudy and turbid [endowment]," and these "do not have to study but already can [know the truth], like [sage kings] Yao or Shun."[98] Nonetheless, as the last sage to be born was Confucius (551–479 BCE), it is wise to engage in the process of effort and learning! See Chapter 4, "Qualifications for Leadership," for further discussion of this issue.) Unlike Thomas's God, Who can reach out to the human being at any time,[99] principle does not reveal itself to those who do not strive to know it, and knowledge of it does not come easily to most people (a topic more fully discussed in Chapter 3).

The end goal, for Zhu, is the moment of enlightenment that may come after long toil and effort. "Master Hengqu [Zhang Zai] told Fang Zhi, 'our generation cannot attain the level of the ancients. What is the source of this malady?' Fang Zhi asked about this, and the Master replied: "This is not difficult to understand. The person who said this deeply desired students to dwell on this [problem] without forgetting, to immerse their hearts and minds in it as a matter of course, [so that] one day, they will suddenly awaken as if out of a deep sleep."[100] Of course, the student cannot force this moment or any other of enlightenment, for, as Zhu says, they will come unexpectedly, and neither the pupil nor the teacher can predict when they will arrive. Failure to reach such moments is a failure on the part of the student, not of the reality which he or she has not grasped: as noted above, principle remains, whether people are aware of it or not. Moreover, as also noted above, deduction and experimentation will only take one so far: religious faith in the reality of the moral substance of both the cosmos and the self is necessary to truly grasping it.

Thus, in Zhu's prescribed method of study, relativism is prohibited: the ancient sages did in fact catch glimpses of eternal truths, which continue to stand outside us. On the other hand, however, there is little room for rigidity, either: these truths have not been exhaustively studied or grasped, and each student is granted the possibility of suddenly intuiting a lesson hitherto unlearned even by the wise. Zhu's comprehensive teachings, which make room not only for rules but also for embracing the new, is important in a pluralistic world for other reasons as well. While his doctrine of *gewu*, the investigation of things, is in some respects similar to the empirically oriented scientific method, Zhu's religious consciousness of the moral and sacred nature of omnipresent principle expands his approach and grants it an emotional relevance not encouraged by the scientific method—topics discussed further below.

Thomas and Zhu in Conversation

To borrow Aaron Stalnaker's term, Zhu and Thomas share a tendency toward "chastened intellectualism," which means that they view "the task of learning not merely as gaining new information but primarily as the task of assimilating transformative knowledge into one's mode of existence."[101] Thus, rather than focusing exclusively on logical proofs or scientific method, Zhu and Thomas put these into conversation with other elements and concerns, exploring the cosmos as a whole in order to find the answers to metaphysical questions of meaning, motivation, and purpose.

Their answers to such questions are religious in the sense that both recognize a sacred character to the universe around us, which carries with it certain moral demands and obligations. Moreover, they both counsel a religious attitude of reverence and, especially, love before such realities. As we will see, Zhu's cardinal virtue of *ren* (仁) and Thomas's of *caritas*, while different in important respects, share the quality of love, which I define as synonymous with feeling and expressing concern for others. In the sections below, we will look at their teachings concerning the morally charged nature of the universe before considering the impact these have on discussions of human power.

An Ontological Morality

Zhu Xi's Ontology

According to Zhu Xi, "the student is required to engage with reality."[102] This apparently simple statement has a wealth of complicated and deep meaning behind and within it, because Zhu, unlike the Buddhists by whom he felt surrounded, believed in the fundamental concreteness and facticity of all that he saw around him, from the revolutions of the heavens to the most mundane affairs of everyday life. Even more important, he assigned a moral value to the cosmos, in both its furthest reaches and its closest manifestations. In so doing, he was following an ancient and revered tradition,[103] even as he used terminology that would have been unfamiliar to sages and worthies such as Confucius and Mencius (*Mengzi*, 孟子, ca. 371–289 BCE). His own claims in this regard are clear: "In the realm of heaven and earth it is this moral principle alone that flows and cycles everywhere. We should not say that if the sages do not speak of it moral principle does not exist. Moral principle exists of itself eternally in the midst of Heaven and Earth."[104] His understanding of this moral principle, as well as how it operates, is described below.

In the *Jinsilu*, the great Neo-Confucian anthology Zhu Xi compiled with his friend Lü Ziqian, the workings of the cosmos are described in the following way:

> . . . the Great Ultimate moves and generates *yang*. When its movement reaches its limit, it becomes tranquil. When it is tranquil, it generates *yin*. When tranquility reaches its limit, movement begins again. So movement and tranquility alternate and become the root of each other, giving rise to the distinction of *yin* and *yang*, and the two modes are thus established.
>
> [The Five Agents of] Water, Fire, Wood, Metal and Earth arise from the transformation of *yang* and its union with *yin*. When these five material forces are harmoniously ordered, the four seasons run their course.
>
> The Five Agents are one *yin* and one *yang*, and *yin* and *yang* are one Great Ultimate. The Great Ultimate is fundamentally the Ultimate of Non-Being.[105]

Finally, the *Jinsilu* tells us,

> . . . when the reality of the Ultimate of Non-Being and the essence of *yin*, *yang* and the Five Agents come into mysterious union, integration ensues. *Qian* [Heaven] becomes the male element, and *kun* [Earth] becomes the female element. The interaction of these two material forces engenders and trans-

> forms the ten thousand things. The ten thousand things produce and reproduce, and there is unending transformation.[106]

The question immediately arises: What is this Great Ultimate? In the *Yulei*, Zhu offers a definition, one that includes its omnipresent nature: "the Great Ultimate is merely the principle of Heaven and Earth, and the ten thousand things."[107] As Zhu expresses in his doctrine of *liyifenshu* (理一分殊), this principle is one, connecting and grounding all of existence, but its many manifestations are expressed in the fecund diversity of the *wanwu* (萬物), the ten thousand things.

Clearly, Zhu subscribes to the "general Chinese view regarding the root of all life [as] monistic and unity-oriented: all is ultimately one, and the one is manifest in all."[108] Nonetheless, as the *fenshu* portion of his doctrine implies, the empirically obvious differences between people, things, and affairs make it possible, on a practical level, to discuss the different "principles" within things.

According to Zhu, such "things" are not limited to organisms—the world is neither limited to living creatures nor even to the products of nature: "as soon as there is a thing, it has its principle. Heaven cannot produce a pen, but humans can make a pen out of rabbit hair. As soon as there is a pen, it has its principle."[109] A pen, of course, is used for writing, just as other objects and living beings have other purposes. For Zhu Xi and his school, principle "has both an ontological and a pragmatic dimension; it is ontological as it presupposes recognition of an ultimate order and structure in the ontological sense. It is pragmatic as it can apply through the agency of mind to practice for guidance of life."[110]

Moreover, as previously noted, this principle also has a moral dimension. As Zhu's student Chen Chun explains, ". . . if we look at things, there is in each of them the principle of what it *should* be."[111] Oftentimes, the principle within an object is waiting for us to activate it, as it were. Thus, for example, when Zhu says, "a bamboo chair has the principle of a bamboo chair,"[112] he does not mean merely that the chair is made to be sat on. As Galia Patt-Shamir points out, "in the same way that everything has a shape and size, so it has a moral value. Exactly in the way that when I see a chair I know it as having a certain color, a certain shape legs, and a surface to sit on, I also know it as something that can be offered to an elderly person when necessary."[113] Only when we act in accordance with the principle within the object will its moral potential be exploited. Moreover, that we have a responsibility to do so is never called into question. In the words of Chung Tsai-chun: "the world of Principle is immanent in the empirical world, and becomes 'the Way the empirical world should be.' In this sense our world may be regarded as a world of moral obligation."[114]

This world of moral obligation makes certain demands of us as human beings, not the least of which is to pay close and searching attention to our surroundings. In Zhu's understanding, "principle does not have form or shape."[115] The fact that principle has no shape of its own, but manifests itself in a variety of forms, leads Zhu to his famous exhortation to *gewu*, or "investigate things"—preferably as many things as humanly possible. Principle itself requires such effort for its understanding: as Zhu explains, "as for moral principle, each [manifestation of it] has its own place. You can't talk about only one aspect of it. When it's here, you should talk about it this way; when it's there, you should talk about it like that. Its relative conditions are different depending on where it is in each circumstance."[116] Moreover, such effort is required for gaining the kind of knowledge most valued by Zhu: "if you merely look at things and do not discern [the principle within them], although you spend your heart-and-mind's energy to the utmost in studying the words and sayings of the sages, in the end you will not still not understand their meaning. The *gewu* spoken of by the *Great Learning* simply requires people to look at things so that they may discern [principle]."[117]

Sometimes the moral obligation of a situation's principle is fairly straightforward. (N.B.: Principle adheres not only in people and things, but also in affairs (*shi*, 事).) Mencius's famous illustration of a child near a well is a good case in point. In Wing-tsit Chan's translation:

> . . . all men have the mind which cannot bear [to see the suffering of] others. . . . When I say that all men have the mind which cannot bear to see the suffering of others, my meaning may be illustrated thus: Now, when men suddenly see a child about to fall into a well, they all have a feeling of alarm and distress, not to gain friendship with the child's parents, nor to seek the praise of their neighbors and friends, nor because they dislike the reputation [of lack of humanity if they did not rescue the child].[118]

Most can agree that this circumstance calls for the observer to jump forward and catch the child before she falls—a fairly simple project at first glance. Nonetheless, even here the investigation of things is necessary, both in the moment and in the preparation for it. As Robert Neville points out, "the body needs to be educated so that we can perceive with sensitivity and discrimination and also so that we can act effectively on what we need. A person who does not pay attention would not notice the child on the lip of the well, and a klutz would tumble into the well with the child while trying to save it."[119]

Moreover, as the situation becomes more complicated, more investigation is required. While it is not necessary to know anything about the child or her situation in life in order to save her from immediate physical danger, helping her in other respects may well require such information, as well as knowledge of the correct principles to apply. As Neville further notes, "a person's cognitive skills need to be developed as well: it is one thing to understand the simple danger to the child, another to understand the problems of economic competition; whereas the remedy for the child's situation does not need much learning, the remedy for economic problems does."[120] A serious engagement with reality is called for indeed: as Zhu asks, "When has the Way ever stopped? It is only that people do not follow it."[121] The complicated nature of the world at the best of times means that a constant vigilance is necessary if principle is to be illuminated in the midst of all the elements and its Way put into practice. That such a Way is always there, Zhu does not doubt, and he calls on his followers to follow the Way with their whole beings. Neither a rigid reliance on the laws already revealed nor a relativistic rejection of them will suffice for the student wishing to genuinely engage with the world.

While a sharp intellect is certainly important in defining this Way, the will is important as well. For example, it is not up to any person to decide on his or her own whim what is "best" for another person or situation. Rather, the knowledge gained through *gewu* is meant to be used in the service of others: "there are only two things to consider [in learning]: understanding, and putting [understanding] into practice."[122] In this process, the will (*zhi*, 志), while not as central or developed a concept as it is for Thomas, is certainly important to Zhu, for, as he says, "the important thing for students to do is to firmly establish their wills"[123]—and even, "learning depends on firmly establishing the will."[124] It is notable that the will is an element that must be pointed in the right direction and developed in accordance with principle: moral decisions have to be made on the basis of the objective needs of the circumstances, and this fact is non-negotiable, woven into the very texture of the cosmos generated by the mind of Heaven and Earth, for there is not a single thing in which the invaluable principle inherent in the human mind does not adhere.[125] Moreover, to act in accordance with this principle is to act in accord with the originally good nature bestowed on us by Heaven, which, according to Zhu, is the core goal of the Confucian tradition as a whole: "all of the countless words of the sages and worthies: all these desire is merely to [help] people retain their original mind-and-heart."[126] What is good in us, in other words, is what ties us to the rest of existence. As de Bary puts it, as opposed to Buddhism,

> Neo-Confucianism reasserted in an even more far-reaching manner what Confucius and his followers had always taught—that the human sense of order and value does not leave one alienated from the universe but is precisely what unites one to it. The world of human ethics, of social relations, of history and political endeavor is a real one, an unfolding growth process, and not just a passing dream or nightmare from which people must be awakened to the truth of Emptiness or Nothingness.[127]

As Zhu says, "the mind of heaven and earth is to *produce things*."[128] According to Zhu, this mysterious spirit that produces the ongoing process of all that is might not have what we would recognize as a conscious thought process or sense of self, but is nonetheless characterized by *ren* (仁): a term analogous to the Christian *caritas* in its central location among the virtues and its association with love (topics discussed further below), and variously translated into English as benevolence,[129] humanity,[130] and humaneness.[131] In his *Treatise on* Ren, Zhu writes,

> . . . the mind of Heaven and Earth is to produce things. When people and things are produced, they each receive the mind of Heaven and Earth as their mind. Therefore when speaking of the virtue of this mind, although there is nothing it does not absorb or connect, still, one word is sufficient to cover [all of] it, and that word is *ren*.[132]

In the *Yulei*, "*ren* is categorized under affection."[133] Indeed, says Zhu, "when you speak of *ren*, you are referring to affection:"[134] "it is when *ren* issues forth that situations of affection are generated."[135] Thus, to the metaphysical value of *li* is added the emotional resonance of love.

In human beings, this *ren* becomes the most central of all the virtues (a topic discussed further in Chapter 2), yet, as the citation above suggests, *ren* has implications for all of existence, not merely human beings. The presence of this *ren* in even the smallest of things or affairs thus means that they are invested with a depth and meaning that is available to anyone who cares to notice. From the Neo-Confucian perspective of Zhu Xi, simply to be human, to live one's daily life in an upright and caring manner, is to participate in the one principle of love that pervades all of existence. It is this vision, which assigns sacred value to family life, community, and good government, that he offers up as an alternative to Buddhist teachings of emptiness, liberation, and detachment. His combined intellectual rigor, deep faith in the sacred deposits of the cosmos near and far, and valuation of love and its robust expression proved alluring not only to centuries of Chinese, but also to many Vietnamese, Koreans, and Japanese,[136] and may well prove attractive to those disillusioned by scientific methods that separate such concerns or dwell on one to the exclusion of the others. In the end, his *gewu* is meant to increase a person's own innate *ren*—the latter identified as the foundation of personal as well as communal morality—and that which brings human relationships beyond more scientific or calculating concerns, as will be discussed further in Chapter 2.

In short, Zhu's full-bodied embrace of the world can help us today in our pluralistic society. In dwelling on both the oneness of principle and its many manifestations, Zhu provides not only a model for harmonizing our desires for stability and dynamism, but also for intertwining the intellectual and emotional elements of human experience. Regarding the former, he gives us clues as to *how* we can genuinely cooperate with others; with the latter's focus on care and concern, he gives us insights about *why* we should do so.

Thomas Aquinas's Ontology

As the scholar of Western medieval philosophy Jan Aertsen surmises, "since 'good' is a basic concept both in ethics and metaphysics, we may expect that the analysis of the good somehow reflects the relation between the two sciences."[137] This is certainly true in Thomas's case. Unlike Immanuel Kant, who preferred to keep his religion and his reason separate, and who referred to divine matters as "things of which [the young] understand nothing and into which, moreover, *neither they nor anyone else in the world will ever have any insight*,"[138] Thomas sees the divine will as present—and accessible—in ordinary physical life and experience. Even more strongly, God is accessible through even inanimate objects. In Thomas's understanding, the whole point and purpose of every part of creation is the communication—and reception—of God's goodness:

> [God] brought things into being in order that His goodness might be communicated to creatures, and be represented by them; and because His goodness could not be adequately represented by one creature alone, He produced many and diverse creatures, that what was wanting to one in the representation of the divine goodness might be supplied by another. For goodness, which in God is simple and uniform, in creatures is manifold and divided and hence the whole universe together participates [sic] the divine goodness more perfectly, and represents it better than any single creature whatever.[139]

This is not to overromanticize his teaching. Thomas does not escape what Metzger calls the "problem of triage," whereby a theory, whether openly or not, decides that some kinds of suffering are more important than some others.[140] From Thomas's perspective, the order of existence has created within it certain inequalities between entities, with some subject to rightful destruction by others. Untroubled by the moral scruples that lead some people in our day to become the defenders of animal rights, he writes: "according to the Divine ordinance the life of animals and plants is preserved not for themselves but for man. Hence, as Augustine says (De Civ. Dei i, 20), 'by a most just ordinance of the Creator, both their life and their death are subject to our use.' "[141] However much vegans or vegetarians may disagree with him, Thomas does not see the consumption of meat and fish as problematic or disrespectful to the organisms consumed, and promotes omnivorousness even as he proclaims the worth of every element of creation. As Fergus Kerr puts it: "Thomas repeatedly insists on the goodness of the created order . . . The world, for Thomas, much against what was quite widely believed in his time, is simply the expression of divine bounty: freely shared, entirely unforced, 'unnecessary'—simply an expression of love."[142]

In Thomas's understanding, the order of such excellent beings is expressed in a great chain of being, one in which a likeness to God may be found in the humblest elements of creation:

> . . . we see that some things of the lowest degree share in the divine likeness only with respect to [having] existence, such as inanimate beings; others, however, share in the divine likeness with respect to existence and life such as plants; and yet others such as animals share in the divine likeness with respect to sense perception. But the highest degree is of the intellect, which makes us most similar to God.[143]

As in the Confucian tradition, the omnipresence of goodness has an impact on the way we move morally through the world. As Aidan Nichols explains,

> . . . the total good of the universe consists in the inter-relationship of things, *ordo rerum ad invicem*, "the ordering of things to one another." Ultimately this is not just an aesthetic question—a matter of the *pattern* of the world, the "rich and complex" tapestry God has made. More than this, it is a question of the *purpose* of the universe, and the way in which all the beings which constitute the world in their inter-relation conspire, whether consciously or not, to serve the final purpose of God, his saving plan.[144]

As this passage implies, it is the *order* that is principally important rather than the individual creatures that inhabit it. As Thomas himself says, "the slaying of a sinner becomes lawful in relation to the common good, which is corrupted by sin."[145] Further on this note: it is not the case that all "natural" thoughts, desires, and inclinations on the part of one human being are "excellent." As Gilson notes, "for Thomas and his Greek masters, nature is not a chaos—a juxtaposition of facts without order, structure or hierarchy. On the contrary, it is a system of nature, each of which is the concrete realization of some standard, and although no individual realizes it perfectly, all represent it in their own way . . . This standard is normal; any corruption of it is a deviation into the pathological. Whatever is in nature is natural, but not everything in nature is normal."[146] In Thomas's system, it is the part of the intellect to realize that "dominating any discussion of this kind is the fact that certain natural principles pertaining to a species can fail or be perverted in individual cases."[147]

Thus, for Thomas, as for Zhu, it is extremely important to pay attention to all the variations nature has to offer, both within and without the human community, but always with a consciousness of the one source of goodness supporting and suffusing them, and the order in which they have been set. Because "by the work of creation the Divine goodness is communicated to all creatures in a certain likeness,"[148] Thomas argues that "the consideration of creatures is necessary not only for instruction in the truth, but also for the elimination of errors."[149] In this investigation of things, in addition to a better knowledge of God Himself, Thomas is also attempting to find a kind of principle; in his case, the eternal law:

> . . . just as in every artificer there pre-exists a type of the things that are made by his art, so too in every governor there must pre-exist the type of the order of those things that are to be done by those who are subject to his government. And just as the type of the things yet to be made by an art is called the art or exemplar of the products of that art, so too the type in him who governs the acts of his subjects, bears the character of a law . . . Now God, by His wisdom, is the Creator of all things in relation to which He stands as the artificer to the products of his art. . . . Moreover He governs all the acts and movements that are to be found in each single creature. . . . Wherefore as the type of the Divine Wisdom, inasmuch as by It all things are created, has the character of art, exemplar or idea; so the type of Divine Wisdom, as moving all things to their due end, bears the character of law. Accordingly the eternal law is nothing else than the type of Divine Wisdom, as directing all actions and movements.[150]

Thus, the will of God may be found in contemplating the order He designed, in part via a consideration of the creatures He made to inhabit it. Given this emphasis on the workings and connections of the order as a whole, "it is perhaps not too much to say that Thomas sees the way that things are in terms of the way that they ought to be. Certainly, he does not picture knowing as the subject's projecting value and intelligibility on raw data. Rather, we exist at all only by participation in being (the doctrine of creation), and, since minds are what we are, we participate, by exercising our intellectual capacities, and of course to a very limited extent, in God's own knowledge of the world."[151] This participation, intellectual and moral, is ultimately directed toward our last end: "for Thomas the theological character of ethics is rooted in his fundamental belief that everything proceeds from and returns to God: God as the world's *principium et finis*."[152]

Here, we see that Thomas's cosmos is very different from Zhu's in a very important way: the world's principle is also the world's end, and is a personal God rather than an impersonal element of existence. However, God and *li* share the quality of omnipresence. For Thomas, the created world is good, not only because it communicates divine goodness, displays the divine will, or imitates God, but because it is permeated and suffused by *God Himself*. According to Thomas, God is at the innermost core of every thing or person that exists:

> God is in all things; not, indeed, as part of their essence, nor as an accident, but as an agent is present to that upon which it works. For an agent must be joined to that wherein it acts immediately and touch it by its power. . . . Now since God is very being by His own essence, created being must be His proper effect; as to ignite is the proper effect of fire. Now God causes this effect in things not only when they first begin to be, but as long as they are preserved in being; as light is caused in the air by the sun as long as the air remains illuminated. Therefore as long as a thing has being, God must be present to it, according to its mode of being. But being is innermost in each thing and most fundamentally inherent in all things since it is formal in respect of everything found in a thing . . . Hence it must be that God is in all things, and innermostly.[153]

Paying attention to creation, whether a stone or a child, thus means paying attention to God—the most important element in his thinking,[154] and solely for the greater understanding of whom he undertakes his careful study of the world and of human beings.[155]

Of course, Thomas, an orthodox—and canonized—Roman Catholic Christian, is no pantheist: he does not view creatures as pieces of God, so to speak, and he can see that evil exists in the world. Thus, he is careful to distinguish between that which is unquestionably and ontologically good on the one hand, and that which is more problematic on the other: "we may consider two things in man, namely that which is God's, and that which is man's. Whatever pertains to defect is man's: but whatever pertains to man's welfare and perfection is God's."[156] (This passage does not seem particularly kind to humans as such; still, as discussed in Chapter 2, Thomas's teachings regarding human nature are more forgiving than Augustine's.) The practical and moral implications of this stance may be easily inferred; Thomas himself draws the logical conclusion that "we must not only revere God in Himself, but also that which is His in each one."[157] Again, Thomas is no pantheist, and thus immediately qualifies the latter part of this statement: "although not with the same measure of reverence as we revere God."

More to the point, in connection with Zhu Xi, we must *do something* in order to activate the God within us, so to speak. As Nichols puts it: "without for a moment dissolving the wondrous particularity of creatures into a cosmic soup, Thomas was deeply concerned with the dynamic character of things, the way their being structured as they are passes over into congruent activity."[158] Hence, while giving substance its due,[159] in describing the *imago Dei* in human beings, Thomas writes,

> . . . if the image of the Divine Trinity is to be found in the soul, we must look for it where the soul approaches the nearest to a representation of the species of the Divine Persons. Now the Divine Persons are distinct from each other by reason of the procession of the Word from the Speaker, and the procession of Love connecting Both. But in our soul word "cannot exist without actual thought," as Augustine says (De Trin. xiv, 7). Therefore, first and chiefly, the image of the Trinity is to be found in the *acts of the soul*, that is, inasmuch as from the knowledge which we possess, by actual thought we form an internal word; and thence break forth into love.[160]

Just as Zhu counsels knowing principle so that one may properly love the ten thousand things, Thomas counsels knowing and loving God that we might become more like Him in so doing, on both individual and interpersonal levels. Such knowledge, again, is meant to engage with objective reality in a comprehensive way that includes but moves beyond intellectual capabilities. As paying attention to omnipresent *li* is vitally important for Zhu, noting the presence of God in all things and circumstances is necessary for moral success in Thomas's mind. Thus, every objective detail, no matter how small, must be paid its proper attention; a rather commonsensical ideas, for, as Wieland notes, "if intention alone were enough, the floodgates would be open for randomness and complete relativity. One therefore must locate individual intention within a more comprehensive moral context."[161]

Accordingly, Thomas follows Aristotle's insight that "to have [feelings] at the right times on the right grounds toward the right people for the right motive and in the right way is to feel them to an intermediate, that is to the best, degree; and this is the mark of virtue."[162] In a similarly complicated fashion, Thomas formulates a good act in the following way:

> . . . a fourfold goodness may be considered in a human action. First, that which, as an action, it derives from its genus; because as much as it has of action and being so much has it of goodness . . . Secondly, it has goodness according to its species; which is derived from its suitable object. Thirdly, it has goodness from its circumstances, in respect, as it were, of its accidents. Fourthly, it has goodness from its end, to which it is compared as to the cause of its goodness.[163]

It is going too far to say that feelings and the will "disappear" in Thomas's account; after all, Thomas also says that "a thing is said to be good or evil, from its relation to the end: thus the giving of alms for vainglory is said to be evil."[164] However, the way in which he frames the issue certainly takes the main focus off of the moral agent him- or herself, and his or her will is certainly not left to its own devices in moral activity.

As he further explains, "nothing hinders an action that is good in one of the ways mentioned above, from lacking goodness in another way."[165] How complicated all this can become is clear in his discussion of circumstance: "a circumstance, so long as it is but a circumstance, does not specify an action, since thus it is a mere accident: but when it becomes a principal condition of the object, then it does specify the action."[166] Thus, in Westberg's example, "if you are driving to work, then it usually makes no difference who actually owns the vehicle. But driving a car that you have no right to take constitutes theft, and this circumstance now becomes the main condition—you are no longer (primarily) driving to work, but stealing a car."[167] Such moral concerns are obviously important in relationships, which also loom large in Thomas's imagination.

Carefully considering the circumstances, material realities, and people around us, and their moral implications, is ultimately meant to help us grow in love, as Zhu urges us to grow in *ren* through *gewu*. Like Zhu's principle, the presence of God is inescapable, and inexpressibly good. Also like Zhu's principle, it calls on us to produce goodness in our turn, for in Thomas's understanding, goodness is by definition relational: "it belongs to the essence of goodness to communicate itself to others."[168] Such communication will require both reference to God as the source of goodness, and to the particular elements of the circumstances in which one finds oneself: here, as with Zhu's understanding of the world, neither excessive reliance on the rules nor rejection of them will do, as the eternal love of God manifests itself in unimaginably diverse ways throughout cosmic and human history.

This love holds as central a place in Thomas's philosophy as in Zhu's. Firstly, Thomas's Triune God is lovingly relational by nature, and this state of affairs has implications for interpersonal relations among humans as well. As Davies puts it, Thomas "does not see the doctrine of the Trinity as a complicated exercise in speculative celestial physics. He thinks of it as a wonderful truth which is full of implications for people."[169] According to Thomas, "every law aims at establishing friendship (*amicitia*), either between man and man, or between man and God. Wherefore the whole Law is comprised in this one commandment, 'Thou shalt love thy neighbor as thyself,' as expressing the end of all commandments: because love of one's neighbor includes love of God, when we love our neighbor for God's sake."[170] Indeed, such love is the substance of the greatest of all the virtues: *caritas*, or charity. While Zhu's *ren* is present in all things, as their most fundamental character, Thomas's *caritas* is more narrowly a virtue that can be bestowed on human beings by God (a topic further discussed in Chapter 2). Nonetheless, it is similar to Zhu's *ren* in its being paired with love: "to love belongs to charity as charity,"[171] and while not necessarily the character of all existence, is certainly a channel to the foundation of all that is: "charity attains God Himself that it may rest in Him."[172] Indeed, as *gewu* helps us to attain knowledge of principle, *caritas* enables us to have knowledge of and relationship with God.

Of course, God consciously calls us in a way that principle does not (a topic further addressed in Chapters 2 and 3). Nonetheless, the goodness shared by both concepts, and the love both are understood to involve, imply that the very nature of reality in both systems calls for moral recognition and response. Both thinkers call on us to not only identify the good, but also to cooperate with it for the betterment of the self, society, and the world at large: Zhu's threefold principle, and Thomas's rapturous vision of an omnipresent God, inspire efforts to properly recognize the sacred character of existence and to act accordingly, in a spirit of love: a quality shared by *caritas* and *ren*.

Conclusion

Thomas and Zhu share a belief in the truth that surrounds us, believing that this belief may be intellectually explored, but its object never fully comprehended. This understanding of the world precludes both rigidity and relativism, as it calls us to recognize that, while fundamental answers as to the nature of the universe have been provided to us, our right response to these principles is not passive acceptance, but rather active engagement. In fact, it is through our attempts to apply these eternal principles to diverse temporal circumstances that we will come to a greater understanding of both. This is no easy project, not least because it has no end in sight for individuals, societies, or humankind as a whole.

Thus, Zhu recognizes the sheer difficulty of the mental and moral task, even for the most virtuous of characters: "King Wen himself still [had to] work hard. Then what must the situation be for those with little virtue!"[173] So the *Yulei* tells students that, "if you have read something today, read it again tomorrow; if you have read something in the morning, read it again in the evening; if you have read something before eating, read it again after eating."[174] Nonetheless, if they can only manage to stay the course, they are sure to succeed, according to Zhu and his tradition as a whole, for, as he tells them, "in the Way of book learning, the more effort one puts in, the more profound is his achievement. In the beginning it is difficult, afterward there is achievement; in the beginning there is work, afterward there is gain: all this is the principle [of book learning]."[175] Nonetheless, the Confucian student who perseveres to success will remain finite, never holding all of the answers, for the great Way of the cosmos is beyond the comprehension of even the sage: according to the ancient *Doctrine of the Mean*, "in the utmost reaches [of the Way of the superior person], there is something which even the sage does not know."[176]

In a similar manner, Thomas always holds that "the same thing is opposed both to God and to reason, whose light flows from God."[177] Indeed, his high regard for intellectual development is fueled by his conception of God: "men are called the children of God in so far as they participate in the likeness of the only-begotten and natural Son of God . . . Who is Wisdom Begotten. Hence by participating in the gift of wisdom, man attains to the sonship of God."[178] Nonetheless, even though Thomas holds out the possibility of individual persons becoming more like God, we are not destined, in his understanding, to become gods ourselves.[179] Even after death, in the rapture of the beatific vision, we will remain finite creatures before the God who is infinite: "the happiness of God, Who, in understanding his Essence, comprehends It, is higher than that of a man or angel who sees It indeed, but comprehends It not."[180] As Kerr puts it, "it is important to remember that possession of God, being possessed by God, which human beings are understood to enjoy in the beatific vision, is not a grasp, or enclosing within their finite minds, of that which is unfathomable. On the contrary, it is an enjoyment in which one is enraptured—captured by, rather than capturing, the One by whom one is enraptured."[181] Even more than remaining finite creatures, we will remain *ourselves:* "as to that Good itself, Which is the object and cause of Happiness, one Happiness cannot be greater than another, since there is but one Sovereign Good, namely, God, by enjoying Whom, men are made happy. But as to the attainment or enjoyment of this Good, one man can be happier than another; because the more a man enjoys this Good the happier he is. Now, *that one man enjoys God more than another, happens through his being better disposed or ordered to the enjoyment of Him.*"[182]

Both Zhu and Thomas thus both encourage a humble posture in the face of cosmic reality, which is both beyond our ability to fully grasp and impervious to our attempts to bend it to our own will. (Of course, this is not to say that the way of principle or God cannot be thwarted: for Zhu's and Thomas's treatment of evil in human nature, see Chapter 2.) Moreover, as discussed above, the sheer goodness of the fundamental character of the universe is meant to inspire love toward all who inhabit it: a significant stance with regard to both the exercise and the limitation of authority.

While larger questions of whether or not Confucianism is a "religion" are bound to be debated for some time, it is indubitably clear that both Zhu and Thomas share what may be called religious concerns: for them, the cosmos is a fundamentally sacred arena, every nook and corner suffused with moral significance and value. Also, for both, growing in the understanding of the world is a process that involves not only the mind, but also the will and the heart: both require religious commitments made in love. Thus, they share but transcend the questions that science can or wishes to answer, providing a more comprehensive idea of learning, and, indeed, life, that eschews falling into one-sided extremes in favor of a more harmonious approach.

In closing, we return to the question raised at the beginning of this chapter: with no finally decisive rational or empirical proofs for their claims about the morally charged nature of the cosmos, is there any reason, given the dangers, to further explore the religious ideas of Thomas and Zhu? After all, even the virtue that this book seeks to ground in their cosmologies may be placed upon other, less contentious foundations. It may be argued that it is in our best interests to be good, or even that we are simply hardwired to be so.[183] Or, the feeling of finitude encouraged by their notions of the cosmos might well be based on a rational assessment of our practical limitations. Even the most determined secular humanist might agree with Thomist scholar Ralph McInerney's insight that "few things are more conducive to the realization that we are creatures who have only an imperfect control over our lives than our constant openness to the unexpected and unintended consequences of our deeds."[184] Such a recognition can breed the humility necessary to properly limit authority, while positively recognizing the rights shared by all human beings can breed the authority necessary to protect them.

Nonetheless, something will be lost in this translation: much of the richness, beauty and wonder of Thomas's and Zhu's accounts will no longer be present. The risky endeavor of religious faith, which requires dealing with mutually exclusive truth claims, also has its rewards: in the words of Charles Taylor, "we will have least put an end to the stifling of the spirit and to the atrophy of so many of our spiritual sources which is the bane of modern naturalist thought."[185] Taking the religious claims of Thomas and Zhu seriously can awaken one to the kind of wonder that underlies the virtue of humble authority: and perhaps as well to the recognition of the sacred character of the world so obvious to Thomas and Zhu.

This is not to say that scientists do not love the world, or that a passion for their subject does not motivate them. Rather, it is to say that, as with many other modern secular paradigms—two of which will be discussed in the chapters immediately following—the kind of love that is characteristic of both *ren* and *caritas* is sidelined by the scientific method. This mushy, messy and in the end unquantifiable phenomenon of human experience does not have much of a place in either natural or social scientific discourse. But both Thomas and Zhu put their understandings of love at the very center of their systems of intellectual exploration, and from the center extend this love to all elements of existence. In not only acknowledging but also celebrating the diversity of the world, they provide the means to successfully deal with the tensions encountered both within ourselves and in the world around us.

At the very least, it is hoped that it has been demonstrated that holding such a view of the world is not an irrational prospect. In fact, if Thackery was correct in his estimation of the power of perception in the epigraph above, it may in the end simply make more sense to believe in a morally charged cosmos, for people tend to find what they seek, and to miss what they don't—the latter sometimes in cases where it is right before them. Finding moral and sacred worth within the cosmos lends itself to a properly exercised authority, for the love and reverence such discovery may be expected to kindle can simultaneously encourage the positive exercise of authority in the best interests of that which is loved, while also limiting authority in cases where its exercise does not best serve such interests.

In closing, Thomas and Zhu had a great deal of religious faith in a morality ontologically grounded in a sacred order that is in no way dependent on the arbitrariness of the human will, and that precludes both rigidity and relativism. For them, the morally charged order and interconnection of all of existence calls for human beings to continuously cause and assist the good, simultaneously providing the basis for both the exercise and the limitation of human power. Their shared emphasis on the objective nature of goodness, as present in the very cosmos itself, strongly influences their moral anthropologies: a topic further addressed in Chapter 2.

Chapter 2

Intelligent Agents with Moral Potential

> Our theory of human nature is the wellspring of much in our lives. We consult it when we want to persuade or threaten, inform or deceive. It advises us on how to nurture our marriages, bring up our children, and control our own behavior. . . . And because it delineates what people can achieve easily, what they can achieve only with sacrifice or pain, and what they cannot achieve at all, it affects our values: what we believe we can reasonably strive for as individuals and as a society.
>
> —Steven Pinker, *The Blank Slate: The Modern Denial of Human Nature*

As Stephen Pinker argues, our fundamental understanding of human nature profoundly affects the way in which we live our lives.[1] For example, people often find themselves in a "push me, pull me" kind of relationship with others. On the one hand, we want to pursue our own interests, without hindrance or interference from those around us, but, on the other, we also enjoy company and companionship. When we conceive of our individual selves as fundamentally separate from the communities in which we find ourselves, the tension between our desires for independence and fellowship can very quickly become competitive. Then, the project of how to live in community with others begins to be framed in terms of a zero sum game: should people pursue their own interests, *or* those of their society at large? Shall we practice self-regard, *or* solidarity?

Thomas Aquinas and Zhu Xi offer us a different way of conceiving of human nature, and hence human life and community. They see the right relationship between persons as one of cooperation rather than competition. In their view, the human being is essentially an intelligent agent with moral potential that can only be developed in loving engagement with society and the world at large. As this chapter will demonstrate, in the work of Zhu Xi and Thomas Aquinas, a universe filled with ethical significance and value houses a human being with similar characteristics. On the other hand, a notion of the individual as a self-interested actor—and reactions against this notion—can flow very naturally out of one in which there is no innate morality.[2]

Self-Interested Actors and Selfless Comrades

In democratic societies around the world today, it is a commonplace that, as human beings, we all act in our own individual interests and have the right to do so, and that we should be free to do so. From this secular, political perspective, people are fundamentally, for all intents and purposes, self-interested actors, even given various exceptions to the rule.[3] Hence, we are often wary of anything that might stop us from achieving our interests, even when framed in a positive sense. For example, the notion of a "common good" that may at times supersede the good of the individual is bound to raise red flags for many people in contemporary society. They may well ask such questions as: Whose goods are these, *really*? Who will have the power to decide such things? And how might they abuse this power once they have it?

It is illuminating in this regard to consider the insight of the medievalist and philologist Tom Shippey:

> . . . the opinion that "power corrupts" is a distinctively modern one . . . before [the modern age] the idea does not seem to be attractive. It might even have been thought perverse . . . There is in fact an Anglo-Saxon proverb analogous to Lord Acton's, but still significantly different. What it says is "man does as he is when he may do as he wishes," or more colloquially, "You show what you're like when you do what you like." This is certainly cynical about the ill-effects of power, but what it implies is "power *exposes*," not "power *corrupts*."[4]

Going back further into Western history, we find that Aristotle held a similar notion about power: "the saying, 'office will reveal the man' is felt to be valid."[5] Whence comes this difference? Why were medieval Anglo-Saxons and the ancient Greeks so much more comfortable with power-as-such than their modern descendent Lord Acton?

Part of the answer lies in the collapse of the belief in a cosmological order. People of Hobbes's time and after came to the conclusion that no moral order existed outside us, and that claims to the contrary were not only false, but also dangerous, as they made demands of human beings that simultaneously destroyed their peace of mind and hid from them the true way to happiness: the pursuit of personal interest. Such people had good reason for their new mindset. As political philosopher Pierre Manent points out, "whatever the intrinsic merits of classical antiquity and primitive Christianity, these two great doctrines existed in England only as *opinions*"[6]—and, according to many early modern European philosophers, bad ones at that. Their understanding was that "the deplorable political effects of [the classical and Christian doctrines] refuted their claim to reflect an experience authoritatively."[7]

Often, to the extent that the notion of an underlying order and its universal values disappeared, so too did the notion of human beings as morally perfectible creatures. In his discussion of the early modern era in the West, A. O. Hirschman highlights the tendency of thinkers like Spinoza to focus on human proclivities for depravity rather than on humankind's ability for virtue, and to call this new emphasis "realistic": "in the opening paragraph of the *Tractatus politicus* [Spinoza] attacks the philosophers who 'conceive of men not as they are but as they would like them to be' . . . That man 'as he really is' is the proper subject of what is today called political science continued to be asserted—sometimes almost routinely—in the eighteenth century."[8] Rather than focusing on the possibilities of human moral development, these influential thinkers focused on the evils latent in human beings and the world in which they lived: according to them, "men must no longer be guided by goods or by the good, but by the right that is born from the necessity of fleeing evil. In the political and moral language developed by Hobbes, and which is still ours today, the *right* replaced the *good*."[9]

In the minds of many early modern philosophers, man-as-he-is, once he had been properly defined, would no doubt prove easier to govern and organize than the chimera of man-as-he-should-be dreamed up by the deluded moralists of the past. Rather than aiming at impossibly lofty moral goals, governments would focus on giving the people what they wanted: "the belief that interest could be considered a dominant motive of human behavior caused considerable intellectual excitement: at last a realistic basis for a viable social order had been discovered."[10] Thus came the development lamented by Allan Bloom: "the turn in philosophy away from trying to tame or perfect desire by virtue, and toward finding out what one's desire is and living according to it," and through which "our desire becomes a kind of oracle we consult."[11]

One of the foremost exponents of this view was David Hume (1711–1776). In keeping with the scientific reasoning of his age, Hume empirically saw that people had passions on the basis of which they acted. Calling such passions "sentiments," he employed them as the foundation of his ethics, claiming, "all morality depends upon our sentiments; and when we say action, or quality of the mind, pleases us *after a certain manner*, we say it is virtuous; and when the neglect, or non-performance of it, displeases us *after a like manner*, we say it is vice."[12] Continuing to build on the centrality of the sentiments, he grants to reason—so important in previous ethical systems—a secondary function:

> . . . reason's first practical role is to answer a type of question which the passions provide motives for asking and answering . . . Second, reason provides means for the achievement of such ends set by the passions and judges these means as more or less efficient in terms not only of the particular end in view but also in terms of other ends which the agent is or may be moved to pursue. . . . So reason acts only at the command of passion.[13]

Reason's diminished function is reflected in its diminished power. While in the ancient and medieval schools of Aristotelianism and Thomism, reason is able to transform "disordinate" passions into "ordinate" proclivities, the Humean system holds out no such hope: "all [moralists or politicians] can pretend to, is, to . . . teach us that we can better satisfy our appetites in an oblique and artificial manner, than by their headlong and impetuous motion."[14] This, then, is the role of reason: to properly direct the passions so that they may be better fulfilled, for "the [natural and inherent principles and passions of human nature] are inalterable."[15] In the words of Charles Taylor:

> . . . the anatomization of moral sentiments is not undertaken to free ourselves of them, to stand outside them . . . to sus-

> pend them or change them . . . The aim was to show the house that we as humans had to live in. We anatomize the moral sentiments, in all their ultimate metaphysical arbitrariness, could-have-been-otherwiseness, in order to accept them, endorse them, know what address we are living at.[16]

Man-as-he-is, apparently, will stay as-he-is.

Clearly, Hume does not encourage people to transform or develop their passions through obeying a moral order that stands outside them. This inability or unwillingness to consider the possibility of moral development as traditionally understood was shared by many thinkers of his age. Their influence came to dominate modern politics. Whether primarily "liberal" or fundamentally "democratic," in the contemporary era, "the end of the political institution is to ensure the *security* of persons and goods. The more certain the security, the more recommendable the institution."[17]

At first glance, it may seem that such moves do not destroy the self as moral agent; after all, there is nothing to prohibit virtue from flourishing under a government that provides security and stability to its citizens. And Hume, for all his iconoclasm in the face of traditional ideas concerning moral development, does not have a quarrel with virtue itself. On the surface, in this respect, he has little in common with his theoretical predecessor Bernard de Mandeville (1670–1733), who openly argues that virtue and intelligence are mutually exclusive characteristics. In his poem *The Fable of the Bees: or, Private Vices, Publick Virtue*, Mandeville lectures those who would be good, saying: "Fools only strive/ To make a Great an honest Hive. / T'enjoy the World's Conveniencies,/ Be famed in War, yet live in Ease/ Without great Vices, is a vain/ Eutopia seated in the Brain."[18] While Hume certainly does not say anything like this, he is nevertheless working with and building on the vocabulary handed down to him from Adam Smith, whose classic *Wealth of Nations*, as Hirschman points out, "was wholly focused on the passion traditionally known as cupidity or avarice." However, "Smith was able to take a giant step in the direction of making the proposition palatable and persuasive: he blunted the edge of Mandeville's shocking paradox by substituting for 'passion' and 'vice' such bland terms as 'advantage' or 'interest.'"[19] Or "sentiment," we might add. The transformation of vices into virtues; the new recalcitrance and willful stolidity of human passions; a prevalent belief in Invisible Hands—all of these conspired to lead to a situation in which it was "as if God told us, 'Don't be afraid, my child, of apparently transgressing against my commands. I have so arranged everything that you are justified in neglecting morality in this particular case.' "[20]

Rather than the proper development of the raw materials or sentiments within the self, then, the agent and his interests, which are up to him to decide, came to center stage. Even concerns originally quite spiritual in character became commodified over time. The open identification of values as quasi-economic goods is obvious in the way religion is often treated in the West. In his aptly named book *The Divine Deli*, John Berthrong notes that, in contemporary America, "New Agers are not interested in definitional religious purity, they are interested in the spiritual quest and *what works for them*."[21] The focus on the self and personal values as opposed to God or tradition, and the idea of religion as a useful tool in personal fulfillment, upset the old-fashioned balance of things, to say the least. As Philip Rieff puts it: "whenever I hear that word ['value'], I know another god has died."[22]

This trend of focusing on the individual and his interests can persist even when he is concerned about other people. As sociologist James Coleman points out,

> . . . classical economic theory always assumes that an individual will "act in his interest;" but it never examined carefully the entity to which "his" refers . . . [when a man is willing to contribute much, even his life, to national defense] men act *as if* the "his" referred to some entity larger than themselves. That is, they appear to act in terms, not of their own interests, but of the interests of a collectivity or even of another person.[23]

An interested self is still interested, in other words, even if his notion of his self has expanded to include others. The will, and what it wants, remains paramount. Given this emphasis, reluctance to say what the will ought to want grew over time in the West: as Manent points out, the democratic idea of sovereignty and the liberal idea of the law, while contradictory in many aspects, nonetheless "have a common 'negative' matrix: they agree that man has no ends inscribed in his nature, and that the element of human action is not the good or goods."[24]

To return to themes discussed in Chapter 1, this purportedly "value-free" view of humankind was spurred by the magnificent advances ongoing in the physical sciences of the early modern era. During this period, people had increasingly solid grounds for thinking that "man-as-he-is" would be amenable to objective study and comprehension: as Hirschmann points out, "the advances of mathematics and celestial mechanics held out the hope that laws of motion might be discovered for men's actions, just as for falling bodies and planets."[25] It's hence not surprising that they turned to a reductionist way of thinking of humans—focusing narrowly on the will—that owed a great deal to the scientific method, nor that such thinking produced good results in many cases. The widespread emphasis on personal interests and desires allowed many to break free of societal and familial expectations. These beneficiaries of the new system went on to become very successful in spheres that would have been closed to them in the past, and without recourse to the kind of military violence that had often provided already established families with their pedigree and social position.

With such gains in mind, political liberalism leaves a great deal up to the individual to decide. While people living in politically liberal societies are not completely free to chart their own course—they understand that they must fulfill certain obligations (paying taxes, serving on juries) when instructed to do so—positive social requirements can be few and far between.[26] Unfortunately, as everyone knows, his or her decisions about self-interest and how to achieve it may not always be in concert with those of others. In practice, societies based on the individual gratification of interests can turn out to be quite volatile: a realization that led Émile Durkheim, living in the turmoil of late nineteenth-century France, to write, "there is nothing less constant than interest. Today, it unites me to you; tomorrow, it will make me your enemy."[27] The idea that men pursuing their interests would be forever harmless began to fray when the reality of capitalist development was on full view: "as economic growth in the nineteenth and twentieth centuries uprooted millions of people, impoverished several groups while enriching some, caused large-scale unemployment during cyclical depressions, and produced mass society, it became clear to a number of observers that those caught in these violent transformations would on occasion become passionate—passionately angry, fearful, resentful."[28] Of course, human beings at all times and in all places can and do find reasons to become angry and resentful, in societies organized around ideals of sacred order or more individualistic concerns. Nonetheless, as Durkheim points out above, the volatile and unpredictable nature of personal interests arguably provides a particularly unstable foundation for society.

Evidence for his claim can be found in twentieth-century China, where the backlash against the ideals of Western political liberalism—

following a period during which Western politics and technology were viewed by young Chinese intellectuals as holding the solutions to China's most critical problems—[29] was passionate indeed. Powerful Communist leaders like Mao Zedong dedicated their lives to uprooting any traces of the "bourgeois" mentality such liberalism encouraged, and strove to re-educate the Chinese people that they might achieve self-transformation into genuine comrades, or *tongzhi* (同志; the word literally means "same will" or "same purpose"), selflessly dedicated to the good of the nation. However, this proved to be a difficult project.

In 1937, after nearly two decades of nationwide Communist organization in China,[30] Mao was still fighting the "extremely harmful (*shifen youhaide*, 十分有害的)" force of liberalism (*ziyou zhuyi*, 自由主义) in his own party. He defined this force as a "type of corrosive that disrupts unity, weakens relationships, stops work, and causes differences of opinion [between comrades]."[31] According to Mao, such problems may all be traced to people's selfish interests: "the source of liberalism is in the selfishness of the petty bourgeois class (*xiao zichan jieji*, 小资产阶级), which puts individual interest in the first place [of importance]."[32]

Even after the Communists took power in 1949 and were free to promote their own agenda, such elements were not to be easily dispelled. Campaign after campaign was launched to combat the stubborn and tenacious proclivity to self-regard found throughout the Chinese population, culminating spectacularly in the Great Proletarian Cultural Revolution (*Wuchan jieji wenhua da geming*, 无产阶级文化大革命, 1966–1976), which was putatively designed to wipe out all traces of bourgeois society.[33] In the document establishing the commencement of this Revolution, Mao and his colleagues proclaimed:

> . . . although the bourgeoisie has been overthrown, it is still trying to use the old ideas, the old culture, the old customs, and the old habits of the exploiting classes to corrupt the masses and conquer people's mind-and-hearts. They are making every effort to achieve the goal of recovering their power. The proletariat must do exactly the opposite: it must meet every challenge of the bourgeoisie in the ideological arena head-on . . . At present our objective is to struggle against and crush those persons in authority who are taking the capitalist road, to censure the reactionary bourgeoisie academic "authorities" and condemn the ideology of the bourgeoisie and all other exploiting classes.[34]

This call to revolution, aimed primarily at the young, created a movement that quickly spun out of control: "the initial battle cry 'To rebel is justified' was taken from an early speech by Mao, but 'rebellion' came to mean almost anything, depending on whatever group was activated to engage in generalized 'class struggle,' and before long the movement deteriorated into an anarchy of cross-purposes and violent infighting."[35] This Mao should have been able to see in advance, based on his own personal philosophy.

While Mao disagrees with Hume in thinking that people's desires are subject to development, as evidenced by his embrace of a Cultural Revolution intended to "touch people's souls" in a "deepening of the development of the socialist revolution in our country,"[36] it is also clear that he understands such innate desires are extremely difficult to change. For example, students during the Cultural Revolution were put in one of three categories: red, black, or gray. As Jung Chang explains in her family memoir, "the 'reds' were from the families of 'workers, peasants, revolutionary officials, revolutionary officers, and revolutionary martyrs.' The 'blacks' were those with parents classified as 'landlords, rich peasants, counterrevolutionaries, bad elements, and rightists."[37] In her school, she writes,

> . . . together with a girl whose father was a shop assistant, the children of "office staff" were branded "grays." It was announced that they were to be kept under surveillance, sweep the school grounds and clean toilets, bow their heads at all time, and be prepared to be lectured by any Red Guard who cared to address them. They also had to report their thoughts and behavior every day. These pupils suddenly looked subdued and shrunken. Their vigor and enthusiasm, which they had had in abundance up to now, had deserted them.[38]

These students' revolutionary fervor and desire to serve the Party were not as important as their socioeconomic background, or perhaps even their genetic proclivities. In fact—as Mao's political experience would attest—he believes that struggles over these and other issues are to be the main characteristic of life. As he had written in 1957, "the unity of opposites is conditional, temporary and transitory, and therefore relative; struggle between opposites is absolute."[39]

In identifying struggle, as opposed to unity, as the true nature of existence, Mao might seem realistic, for it is inescapably the historical and empirical case that people are inclined to fight with one another. But it is also the case that people are inclined to come together and cooperate. Focusing on one or the other reality immediately begins to color one's realism. As Manent points out in a different context, "speaking of Machiavelli's 'realism' means having accepted his point of view: [that] 'evil' is politically more significant, more substantial, more 'real' than 'good.'"[40] The question of whether it is possible to have a wholly neutral stance on issues such as these is beyond the scope of this chapter.[41] For the present, it suffices to note that Thomas Aquinas and Zhu Xi disagree with both Machiavelli and Mao.

Deeply convinced that the good is more fundamental than evil, Thomas, adopting a classically Augustinian doctrine,[42] writes that "evil (*malum*) is the privation (*privatio*) of good (*bonum*)."[43] Moreover, nor can this evil ever *become* more fundamental than good: "if the wholly evil could be, it would destroy itself; because all good being destroyed (which it need be for something to be wholly evil), evil itself would be taken away, since its subject is good."[44]

In a like manner, Zhu believes that human goodness, however hidden, always remains: "nature is like water, it is always originally clear. If it is ladled into a clean receptacle, then it is clear; if it is ladled into a receptacle which is not clean, then it stinks; if it is placed in a filthy receptacle, then it is muddy (*zhuo*, 濁). The original clearness is always present. But since [the container] is smelly and turbid, it is suddenly difficult to [re]acquire the original clearness."[45] Just as with Thomas, evil, or turbidity, has nothing to be in without the originally good and clear water.

Moreover, Thomas and Zhu both see society fundamentally as a place within which the moral potential of people may be developed rather than as an arena of eternal struggle. One of the Four Books Zhu enshrined as Confucian doctrine, the *Great Learning* (*Daxue*, 大學), begins, "the Way of the Great Learning is in illuminating the luminous virtue, loving the people, and extending goodness to its utmost."[46] Zhu demonstrates his belief in the importance of these practices in his commentary on this text, in which he writes, "these three are the guiding principles of the *Great Learning*."[47] Meanwhile, the fundamentally cooperative nature of society for Thomas is demonstrated by his dictum that "every law aims at establishing friendship (*amicitia*), either between man and man, or between man and God."[48] For both Zhu and Thomas, the ideal society is characterized by a certain level of care and concern, of cooperation: luminous virtue and loving the people are inextricably linked for Zhu, and their realization is the realization of the Great Way

(*Dao*, 道) of the universe. Meanwhile, Thomas speaks of maximizing love via communal means such as laws.

Of course, both Thomas and Zhu are well aware that human beings, both individually and communally, do not always live up to the promise inherent in the human condition. Nonetheless, they do not choose to make the best of this reality with social contract theories that grant the individual protection of certain rights in exchange for his compliance with given rules, or strive to submerge problematic individuals into a collective far greater than they are. Instead, they present a portrait of the human being as requiring moral development in communion with others. In other words, their understanding of human nature leads them to develop ways of harmonizing the tensions that often erupt between our urges toward self-regard on the one hand and solidarity on the other, leaving us with a middle ground that is potentially far more fruitful than either the idea of selfish individual or selfless comrade.

The next section shall explore the moral anthropologies of Zhu Xi and Thomas Aquinas, which are rooted in their morally charged cosmologies, and which foster a sense of community by beginning with considerations of elements that all people share, rather than with the individual interests that may drive them apart. As we shall see, for both thinkers, loving relationships are necessary for the person to develop: they differ only in their conception of possible relationship partners.

Intelligent Agents with Moral Potential

Zhu Xi's Human Being: In Need of Communal Assistance

As suggested by the discussion in Chapter 1 about the moral nature of the cosmos,

> when we turn from Chu Hsi's cosmology and metaphysics of human nature to his practical moral philosophy, we shall find a certain continuity of thought. In his ethics and his theory of cultivation, Chu Hsi continues to speak of *T'ai chi* [*Taiji*] (Great Ultimate), of *li* (principle), and of *ch'i* [*qi*] (matter, energy). He does not abandon one realm, that of speculative thought, in order to enter into another, that of moral action and spiritual cultivation.[49]

This linking of metaphysics and morals is certainly sophisticated. As Yü Ying-shih points out, Zhu and others within the Neo-Confucian movement moved beyond the argument, dating back to the classical period, of whether human nature is essentially virtuous or vicious. Mencius was best known for his doctrine of the goodness of human nature, as explicated in his famous example of universal horror people feel on seeing a child about to fall into a well.[50] Nonetheless, he was not an ivory tower idealist. Living in a time of war and chaos, he was well aware of the depths to which people may sink. He blamed these on lack of proper training and socialization: "The way of human beings [is that], if they are well fed, warmly clothed, and comfortably lodged but without education, they will become almost like the birds and beasts."[51] So Mencius counseled kings to "establish seminaries, academies, schools, and institutes to teach the people."[52] Such advice blended his conviction that people *must* be taught with his confidence that they *can* be taught.

Mencius's rival Xunzi (荀子, ca. 310–215 BCE), who believed instead in the inherent immorality of human nature, notes, "straight wood does not await bending to become straight; it is straight by nature. But crooked wood awaits the apparatus for straightening timber; it must be heated before it becomes straight because by nature it is not straight."[53] In much the same way, people need to be tempered with morality before they can fulfill the Confucian ideal. Education is necessary for this process, for people must know what is right before they can do it, and the world will not necessarily furnish them with the correct knowledge. In fact, even the best and brightest may find themselves at a loss in a time of confusion: "as the forms of right and wrong are not clear, even the officials who guard the law and the scholars who recite [the Classics] are in a state of confusion."[54] Nonetheless, if given the proper principles, Xunzi proclaims that "the man in the street can become a Yu [sage king]."[55]

Regardless of the theoretical differences between the two thinkers, they share the characteristically optimistic appraisal of the Confucian tradition at large when it comes to the question of practice: both believed that human beings could become morally perfect through a proper program of education. As will be demonstrated in this section, and further in Chapter 3, Zhu Xi follows them both in this regard, while also providing a more nuanced account of our nature. In company with other Song and Ming (1368–1644) scholars, he

> admitted that human nature has its two sides of good and bad. The nature of the mind-and-heart is the nature of righteousness and principle [*li*]; it is the transcendent nature, and it

> is different from the nature of birds and beasts. The nature of *qi* is then the nature people share with the ten thousand things.[56]

For Zhu, just as everything in existence has *li*, or principle, so too does it have *qi*, or material force. (Here, I use Wing-tsit Chan's translation of *qi* in order to convey both the matter and the energy alluded to by this term. The inclusion of energy in its definition is one of the differentiating factors between it and the Western notion of matter; an issue taken up in more detail later in the chapter). According to Zhu, "there is no material force under Heaven without principle, and there is also no principle without material force."[57] It is certainly the case for Zhu that *qi* tends to be more problematic than *li*. To be clear: *li* is *always* good. As Zhu explains, "when there is *li*, then there is *qi*; when there is *qi*, then there must be *li*. But the clear endowment of *qi* goes to make a sage or worthy, [whose *li* is] like a pearl in the midst of clear water; the murky endowment of *qi* goes to make the stupid and unscrupulous person, [whose *li* is] like a pearl in the midst of dirty water."[58] While a person may have bad characteristics, they should not be imputed to the *li*, for the pearl remains the same in both cases: it is the *qi*, or water, which differs in the sage and the dishonest or stupid person. As Zhu further explains, a great deal depends on our endowment of *qi*. First, we all receive an allotment thereof:

> . . . of the years, months, days and seasons, there are none which do not have the *qi* of the Five Agents; all things are also categorized in terms of *yin* and *yang*: there is only the *qi* of the Five [Agents] and the Two [*yin* and *yang*]. When a person is born, he receives his *qi*; there are those who obtain a clear endowment, and there are those who obtain a murky endowment. Whether rich or poor, long-lived or dying young, all are the same [in receiving an endowment of *qi*].[59]

The metaphysical reality that all *qi* is not created equal has implications for the moral character of human beings. Cosmic forces and endowments have a great impact on good and evil in human beings:

> . . . there are those [people] who are born good, and those who are just born bad. This is because of differences in their endowment of *qi*. When the *qi* of the sun and moon is clear and bright, and the [weather] is appropriate [to the] season,

> the person born at this time will receive this *qi*; then [having] this *qi*, he or she will certainly become a good person. If the sun and moon are dim and darkened, and the [weather of] the season is abnormal, all this is the perverse *qi* of heaven and Earth. If a person obtains this *qi*, he or she will become a bad person. How can this be doubted?[60]

In his discussions with students recorded in the *Yulei*, Zhu Xi explains that a person's virtue—or lack thereof—has a great deal to do with his or her material endowment: "if a person obtains more wood *qi* [in his endowment], [his] humaneness will be greater; if someone receives more metal *qi* [in her endowment], [her] righteousness will be greater."[61] He also explicitly links the five main human virtues to the Five Agents of the cosmological account: "humaneness [*ren*] is wood, righteousness [*yi*] is metal, propriety [*LI*] is fire, wisdom [*zhi*] is water, and faithfulness [*xin*] is earth."[62] According to this theory, the virtues have a reality beyond the artifices of humankind. Indeed, for Zhu and his school, virtue is not *merely* human. In fact, the Master Cheng is reported as saying: "humaneness is the mind-and-heart of Heaven and Earth to produce things."[63] It should be noted that, in other contexts, the *Yulei* defines virtue more narrowly as a human attribute: "Heaven has spring, summer, autumn and winter; Earth has metal, wood, water and fire; and Humankind has humanity, righteousness, propriety and wisdom."[64] Nevertheless, even here there is a sense of relationship, if analogical; moreover, the emphasis on the ontological, natural givenness of human virtue is never lost or obscured in the *Yulei*. Nor is the emphasis on the goodness of human nature in general: outside of conversations that specifically mention the virtues, Zhu says, "that which has been decreed by heaven is the nature,"[65] and even "nature is merely principle."[66] Moreover, the human mind-and-heart is understood to have a cooperative role with Heaven-endowed nature: "Master Shaoyao said, 'The nature is the embodiment of the way; the mind-and-heart is that within which the nature is contained.' This is an excellent way of putting it."[67] In fact, the *Yulei* even goes so far as to claim that "[human] nature is *merely* humanity, righteousness, propriety and wisdom."[68]

Due, perhaps, to his inviolate faith in the unshakeable goodness of *li* in all human beings, as well as in their fundamentally virtuous nature, Zhu does not divide humanity into those with good and those with bad *qi*. Although it may be better in one person than in another, the human endowment in general is always of great value and worth: "only human beings receive [*qi*] in its highest refinement, and therefore they are most intelligent."[69] Thus, Zhu's emphasis falls on the moral potential of all human beings given to them by this refined *qi*. As Cheng Chung-ying puts it: "at the top of the ethical ladder, Man alone is endowed with complete perception and consciousness, which is the perquisite for the fulfillment of Principle. So Man is the only moral creature."[70] It is striking that humans are virtuous simply by virtue of being human.

Nonetheless, merely being human is not enough: if being human is the root of goodness, developing moral potential is the branch. Zhu understands that the vast majority of people will have an endowment that will need clarifying to some degree or another, and that a rigorous process of self-cultivation, or *xiushen* (修身), will be necessary. Therefore, as he tells his students, with regard to uncovering their moral principle within, "'although you are stupid, you must become bright; although you are weak you must become strong.' Use your energy to the utmost, then afterwards you will be able to arrive [at clarified *qi*]."[71]

The difficult process by which this endowment must be purified is one that involves the intellect in the study of the Confucian Classics. Zhu explains, "reading books is to observe the intentions of the sages and worthies, because observing the intentions of the sages and worthies is to observe natural principle."[72] He believes that this process will only inspire greater efforts at self-development: "when you begin down the path, then [you see that] you are dissimilar in respects to the sages and worthies—how can you not urge yourself on?"[73] The sages, though long gone into the mists of Chinese history even in Zhu's day, are nonetheless perceived as important partners in the process of self-cultivation: their timeless power to model and inspire moral truth is indispensable for the student, who cannot expect to reach any genuine heights without the guidance of such teachers.

However, nor are the works of the sages viewed as substitutes for real life experience in the world and society: according to Zhu, "reading books is a secondary concern for the student."[74] Rather than simply trying to understand intellectual propositions, Zhu says, students should bear in mind that the point of education is to improve one's entire self: "in studying, the wish of people is to change their endowment of *qi*; however it is extremely difficult to change."[75] In addition, he warns his students that the road to improvement is not only rocky, but also long: "you can't seek after or long for rapid accomplishment."[76] As noted above, the wisdom to be developed through study is a virtue that must be nourished over time and in a variety of ways. As Julia Ching explains,

> . . . in English, the world "virtue" tends to have moral connotations, so that one may be surprised to find wisdom among the virtues. In Chinese thought, wisdom is not merely an intellectual quality. In a society where all knowledge is oriented to moral action, it also refers to moral knowledge. And since this human mind is the source of *both* intellectual and moral dispositions, such knowledge or its accumulation is also considered a virtue.[77]

Zhu's inclusion of wisdom in his four cardinal virtues thus means that it is more than a merely intellectual concern (Thomas has a similar understanding of wisdom, which will be discussed below). While studying the words of the sages is undeniably important, Zhu tells his students: "when one knows something but has not yet acted on it, his knowledge is still shallow. After he has intimately experienced it, his knowledge will be increasingly clear, and it will have different significance than before."[78] While a kind of weak knowledge without action may be possible, Zhu, with his respect for the wisdom that comes with experience, claims that, "knowledge and action are always mutually dependent."[79] Indeed, he says,

> . . . you cannot be partial with regard to the effort that you put into extending knowledge and diligent practice [of what you have learned]. If you lean too much to one side, then the other side will suffer; you must realize that while they are separate, they are said to be like two feet. You just need to distinguish between which is first, and which is last; which is light and which is heavy. Speaking in terms of first and last, then you should say extending knowledge comes first; speaking in terms of lightness and weightiness, then you should say action is weightier.[80]

It seems that the complexity of the "one principle, many manifestations" doctrine requires a similar complexity in the learning process. As de Bary puts it, "the unity and the diversity of principle are equally real and irreducible. In the human order one cannot realize this unity without attending at the same time to one's proper function. Merely to intuit or grasp the 'unity' of all things in some 'transcendent' experience of enlightenment will not do; such unity could be genuine only if 'realized' through the practical; fulfillment of one's own particular functions."[81]

The Confucian valuation of both intellectual and practical human experience is mirrored in the tradition's balanced approach to the human person. In keeping with the valuation of harmony over strife or struggle, Confucians such as Zhu conceive of an ideal relationship between the mind and the emotions. In Thomas Berry's turn of phrase, "the Confucian ideal of knowledge was that of an understanding heart rather than a thinking brain."[82] This ideal makes a great deal of sense when one considers the role emotions, half-conscious thoughts, and "instinctive" reactions play in our everyday lives. David Wong invites us to

> . . . consider a situation in which the potential to feel compassion is there but has not yet developed. Suppose that we have no difficulty feeling compassion for a child about to fall in a well, but not for homeless persons we pass in the street, asking for change. As we approach such a person, as our eyes meet with his, and as we realize what he is asking us for, we may feel a vague feeling of discomfort, and emotional disturbance. But further suppose at this point we do not know what we are feeling: annoyance at being accosted, or fear of being attacked, or indignation that this person isn't working for a living, or compassion for him. It is quite possible that we are feeling the beginnings of more than one of these, and one of the possibilities is compassion . . . The other's suffering might not register clearly as the salient feature of the situation to which we are emotionally responding. Or we may perceive the other's suffering but are unclear on how we want to respond to that suffering. We might desire to try to help in some way, or alternatively to shut out the other's suffering and go about our business.[83]

The language used by Wong in the passage above—"vague feeling," "discomfort," "indignation," "compassion"—strongly suggests that much of our thinking and judgment takes place on a pre-rational level: as-yet-unrationalized indignation, if allowed to develop, may lead one to lecture the homeless person on the street, while the "automatic" response of compassion may similarly develop into the conscious decision to give the person money or buy him a sandwich. Cheng Chung-ying is prescient on this point: "the human mind is not simply human rationality as the rationalistic tradition would have it . . . the human mind is not simply the mind alone but comprises both the mind and the heart, both of which are rooted in the nature of being human."[84]

Moreover, the human being is not merely the human mind. Thus, the *Yulei* is also replete with admonitions concerning the body: "in reading, you want mind and body all to enter into the passage."[85] Zhu is quite specific in his instructions as to how to accomplish this: "in reading books, students must collect themselves and sit up straight, look unhurriedly at the text, and hum softly."[86] The full-bodied nature of learning is clear: "the words of the sages and worthies must often pass before your eyes; you must roll them over your tongue and turn them over in your mind-and-heart."[87] Zhu himself paid a great deal of attention to what he wore:

> Chu Hsi's dress seems to be a trivial matter, yet Huang Kan took special care in his "Hsing-chuang" to note that the Master dressed in a "deep" garment, in which the jacket and skirt were attached, headgear of a wide cloth, and square-toed shoes. Moreover, the chronological biographies (*nien-p'u*) emphatically state that as soon as his official status was terminated, Chu Hsi received guests in the simple dress (*yeh-fu*) of a commoner. Obviously, Chu Hsi took his dress very seriously.[88]

A man who dresses himself so carefully could not possibly believe in a "clear spirit/matter dichotomy in which the physical is denigrated. [For Zhu], the body as flesh is not something evil, something to be overcome."[89] Rather, the body is meant to be *improved* and *trained* in the art of making the sacred principle already within it manifest: as he puts it, "the books you read and the principle you explore should be *embodied* in your person."[90]

In fact, given the metaphysical claims he makes, Zhu could not recognize the spirit/matter dichotomy without lapsing into utter incoherency. His belief in the omnipresence of the Great Ultimate precludes the serious possibility of flesh being evil in itself; moreover, his belief in the physical grounding of the virtues would also make it difficult for him to call the flesh evil *qua* flesh. Rather, the theme of the ontological goodness of the universe is sustained through his teachings on virtue, ethics, experience, wisdom, and the body. The goodness of the cosmos at large is intimately linked to the moral potential of the human being. As Julia Ching points out,

> Chu Hsi's doctrine of personal cultivation belongs to the realm of practical moral philosophy while also going beyond it to embrace a spiritual and ascetic doctrine with mystical implications. It is also firmly grounded in the more speculative parts of his philosophy, namely, in his metaphysics of human nature, in his view of man as microcosm of the universe, participating in the cosmic process and assisting in the perfection of the universe through his efforts towards self-cultivation.[91]

Such effort is important, and must be maintained. Thus, truly being human requires the participation of one's entire person, including one's will. As Tu Weiming explains, for the Confucians, "the task of being human . . . involves not merely the exercise of universalizable rationality in moral situations but the antecedent commitment to and the actual activity of moral self-development."[92] Zhu agrees: "learning depends on firmly establishing the will."[93] The inclusion of the will in this rich and complex picture of the self, however, is not to grant it the same kind of primacy given it in a conception of the person as a self-interested actor, or for that matter the negative significance it has in the selfless comrade who has given up his personal desires in favor of following those of the collective. Rather than decreeing what is to be desired or being discarded, the will is taken up by Zhu as an element of the self in need of development, in concert with others and in loving consideration of their claims.

Following in the footsteps of Confucius, who taught that the best way to establish oneself was to establish others,[94] Zhu counsels concern not just for other human beings, but for all of existence. Calling on his followers to perform a truly Herculean task, Zhu promises epic results: "If we can eliminate selfishness and return to the Principle of Heaven, then the substance of this mind-and-heart [*ren*] will be everywhere, and its function will always be in operation."[95] That Zhu believes his students to be capable of moving toward this goal is clear in his results-oriented curriculum. For him, *ren* is not merely an interesting intellectual proposition, to be perused at leisure in a library or a study. As he says, "*ren* is in affairs. If you cannot see it in affairs, then how can you see it?"[96] Moreover, he also notes with a characteristically Confucian pragmatism, "doing a suitable thing: this is also *ren*."[97] Thus, all of his philosophical teachings about the mind, the body, and the will are to be put into actual practice out in society and in the world at large, in a spirit of *ren*. Only by extending themselves to others in a spirit of *ren* will individuals reach their full human potential: in other words, self-regard will only be truly satisfied in a context of solidarity, in which all people and all the ten thousand things are viewed as relationship partners, capable of not only being helped, but also of helping.

That all of this self-cultivation is an exhausting process is indubitable. In the end, there is so much to be done to develop the self, and in assist the development of others, that Zhu sees little point in leaving the subject at hand to engage with more speculative concerns: "nowadays we need to go to understand those affairs which are right in front of us. The affairs of ghosts and supernatural beings have no shape and no shadow; you don't want to vainly waste your mental energy [on them]."[98] Not only are such entities extremely difficult to understand or grasp, they are not going to be of much assistance in the moral journey.

This mindset is characteristically Confucian. Confucius himself was not in the habit of petitioning Heaven (天, *tian*) for assistance in his own moral development. This was certainly not because he was an atheist (see Chapter 1 for brief reference to Roger Ames's alternative view), or even because he thought that Heaven was indifferent to his character or behavior; in fact, he seemed to think that he would be renounced by Heaven were he to fall from virtue. According to the *Analects*, "When Confucius saw Nanzi [a woman of notorious character], Zilu was upset. The Master swore an oath, saying, 'If I have done anything wrong, may Heaven forsake me! May Heaven forsake me!'"[99] That he was convinced of Heaven's renunciation of the vicious is demonstrated by his dictum that, "One who commits an offense against Heaven has no one and nothing to pray to."[100]

Conversely, Confucius thought that Heaven would recognize his good efforts in such a way that prayer on his part would be purely superfluous: "When Confucius fell ill, Zilu asked him to pray . . . Confucius said, 'I have already been praying a long time.'"[101] In this passage, Confucius makes reference to his long life of service to the cause of Heaven on Earth, and expresses his belief that this life has already said all that is necessary.

Nonetheless, Confucius never claimed to fully comprehend the ways of Heaven. In his more poignant moments, he realized that nothing would *guarantee* preferential treatment by Heaven. This lesson was delivered to him most keenly with the fate allotted to Yan Hui, his most beloved and best student. "When Yan Hui died, Confucius cried out, 'Alas! Heaven has abandoned me! Heaven has abandoned me!' "[102] Despite Confucius's honorable, filial, and actively virtuous life—to say nothing of the excellence of Yan Hui himself—Heaven took Yan Hui from Confucius at a young age. Confucius suffered greatly, but he is not recorded as having deeply probed the mind of Heaven in search of answers as to *why* he suffered. Rather, he consistently implied that such questions will not tend to edification, often by way of silence: "Confucius never discussed the uncanny, feats of strength, disorders, or spirits."[103] Perhaps he felt that addressing such questions were ultimately exercises in futility: a theme more positively expressed in other early texts. The *Doctrine of the Mean* notes that, even after becoming a partner with Heaven and Earth, the most enlightened person of all will still be ignorant of some of the deepest secrets of the universe: "in the utmost reaches [of the Way of the superior person], there is something which even the sage does not know."[104] The underlying assumption that this something will not reach out to human beings is carried forward into the supernatural theories of Zhu Xi.

Just as Zhu did not anthropomorphize Heaven (see Chapter 1), he assigned an impersonal character even to the ghosts of human beings. This is borne out by looking at certain affairs that took place in the areas under his jurisdiction as a scholar-official. In one case, "a ghost was doing violence in a certain locality. After the people used explosives to destroy the tree on which the ghost depended, the violence ceased. As Chu Hsi [Zhu Xi] understood it, the force of an unjust death had not dispersed until the explosive shocked it into dispersion."[105] Impersonal Heaven, un-dispersed *qi*: these are hardly elements that encourage seeking supernatural or transcendent assistance in improving one's moral character or behavior.

Thus, hardly surprisingly, the Confucian tradition is prone to offer exhortations to "try again!" to those who fail in their ethical duties and obligations. If people can only manage to stay the course, they are *almost* sure to succeed, according to Zhu and his tradition as a whole: "there is no consistent feeling in Confucianism that the goals for which men strive are beyond their power to secure."[106] Confucians, famous for their practicality, have innately practical—and optimistic—explanations for the presence of evil in the human race. While it is certainly true that human evil is rampant, this is not because humanity is inescapably doomed to misery. Rather, as Confucius said, "I know why the Way is not put into practice. The intelligent go too far, while the stupid do not [go] far enough."[107] In other words, people simply do not know better. Confucius believed that the solution was simple: that people must be taught to know better. Rather than appealing to divine powers or Heavenly mercy, he counseled his students that the key to self-development lies in more prosaic arenas, in ordinary perseverance and dedication. "If another person succeeds by one effort, you will use a hundred efforts. If another person succeeds by ten efforts, you will use a thousand efforts. If one can go this way, even if he is stupid, he must become intelligent, and even if he is weak, he must become strong."[108] Confucius, along with Mencius, Xunzi, and Zhu Xi, subscribes to the belief that humanity is capable of solving its own problems, and does not appeal to Heaven for assistance in the moral quest.

Nonetheless, however, no one can actually *guarantee* success in this venture, just as no one can guarantee success or a long life for the virtuous. Zhu admits that there are those who just cannot seem to "get it": "ordinarily, if a person reads a book ten times and cannot [understand it], he will then read it twenty times. If he still cannot [understand it], he will then read it thirty to fifty times. [Then] there must be points he can perceive. If [on] the fiftieth time, it is still dark and unclear, then this is because his *qi* is not good."[109] As Julia Ching notes, although Zhu can explain *how* it is that one person is blessed with a good allotment of *qi*, he and other Neo-Confucians "did not attempt to explain *why* one man may receive a pure endowment, and another, a turbid one. This is just taken for granted."[110] Other questions which are less taken for granted than never raised include: What help is available to the person who has failed fifty times? Is there any hope for the person with hopelessly clouded *qi*? After generously allowing fifty tries with a text, Zhu apparently has no more advice—nor, perhaps, use—for the student who suffers from a tragically turbid endowment of *qi*. This raises uncomfortable issues for remorseful persons who wish to improve their behavior or character, but who often fail in their efforts.[111]

Such issues are particularly significant in the Confucian context, which is characterized by exceptionally challenging moral expectations and standards. Given the difficult, sacred call to envelop all that is with the cardinal Confucian virtue of *ren*, the ramifications of a limited stream of practical advice in self-development can be both serious and painful. According to Thomas Metzger, the kind of constant failure that we all experience as human beings, when coupled with the demanding expectations of the Neo-Confucians for moral self-perfection, led to a psychological crisis for many Chinese in the centuries following Zhu Xi: "the Confucian believed that the individual can and should summon a godlike flow of moral power within himself, but this belief was paradoxically combined with a fearful realization that he would be unable to do so, trapped in a fundamental predicament."[112] In practice, all too many people found that their personal efforts were not enough to achieve even a modicum of perfection, and, without other resources to fall back on, fell into despair—or rejected the Confucian tradition utterly. Metzger argues, "to a large extent, it was the indigenous, intense, centuries-old desire to escape from a metaphysical, psychological, political, and economic predicament which led many Chinese enthusiastically to devote their lives to the overthrow of traditionally revered institutions."[113]

While giving this reading the respect it deserves, it may also be argued that Confucian teachings concerning the naturalness of human morality and moral development can be inspiring. Zhu's fundamentally positive understanding of reality is strongly influenced by Mencius. For Mencius, morality is a part of nature: he sees the Four Beginnings, of humaneness (*ren*), righteousness (*yi*), propriety (*LI*), and wisdom (*zhi*) as "sprouts" (*duan*, 端) innate to the human individual rather than as artificial constructs.[114] While Mencius certainly believes that effort must be expended in order for the individual to reach his or her ethical potential,[115] he nonetheless does not consider the process of moral development to be unnatural.[116] In this and other areas, Zhu Xi unquestionably saw himself as a true heir of Mencius. In the understanding of Neo-Confucian orthodoxy, the transmission of the true message of Confucius ceased with the death of Mencius in 289 BCE, and was not revived until the Cheng brothers began writing and teaching in the eleventh century. This assessment is founded on claims made by Cheng Yi himself: after Cheng Hao's death in 1085, Cheng Yi began to claim that he and his brother had rediscovered the learning of the sages, and that no one after Mencius and before the Chengs had understood them properly.[117]

Zhu Xi's preface to the *Great Learning* makes it quite clear that he agrees with Cheng Yi's appraisal of the role played by himself and his brother. After lamenting the long popularity of heterodox (Buddhist and Neo-Taoist) doctrines, which he likens to a "chronic disease (*gu*, 痼)" bringing nothing but "decay and chaos (*huailuan*, 壞亂)," Zhu celebrates the return of the Confucian Way:

> Heaven moves in cycles: nothing goes forth that does not return. The virtue of the Song [Dynasty] was grand and

> flourishing, and teaching rested in clarity. At this time, the two Masters Cheng of Henan came forth, and found it within their capacity to take up again the tradition of Mencius. They were truly the ones who [first] began to give faithful reverence to this text. After putting it in order, they developed its points of interest which had been lost. After [their efforts], the ancient methods of teaching people the greater learning, which was the concern of the Sage's Classic and the worthies' commentary, were brilliantly illuminated in the world again.[118]

In this preface, moreover, he passes himself the torch: "Although I, Xi, am not clever, I was still fortunate to have learned [from the Cheng brothers'] virtuous [work], and so share in having heard [the tradition]."[119] For Zhu, knowledge of this tradition through education by teachers both past and present is necessary for the development of the person. Such education is defined widely indeed, encompassing not only study of the great Classics, but also of the virtuous behavior of others, whether sages and worthies long gone, or the upright moral figures to be found in one's community. As will be discussed more fully in Chapter 3, Zhu Xi places a great deal of importance on teaching people the proper ways to act and, indeed, *be*, in relationship with those around them.

In closing, from Zhu's perspective, moral development requires above all a commitment to personal and communal improvement, as opposed to the attainment of personal or communal interest. Zhu considers such a commitment, when acted on with and for the exercise of a true concern and love for others, sufficient cause for the perfection of the person. To an alternative view we now turn.

Thomas Aquinas's Human Being: In Need of Grace

To begin with, Thomas, like Zhu, has a very comprehensive view of the human person. Indeed, his understanding of the form and matter that are the most fundamental components of the human person (and the rest of the material universe) is much like Zhu's *li* and *qi*. For Thomas, all physical existence is composed of matter and form,[120] and the form is perfect in all cases. Faults in the operation of individual things are due to problems with their matter: "everything composed of matter and form owes its perfection and goodness to its form; therefore its goodness is participated, inasmuch as matter participates the form."[121] To this point, there is little substantive difference with Zhu's idea of *qi* and *li*. However, form and matter are not exactly the same as *li* and *qi*, for, unlike the latter, a combination of the two does not exhaust the entirety of what is. Not only are angels lacking in matter,[122] Thomas holds that "it is impossible that matter should exist in God."[123] Moreover, God as the perfect form[124] has a consciousness that *li* does not.

Nonetheless, as neither angelic nor perfect, human beings are by definition composed of form and matter. In his definition of the human person, Thomas writes, "it belongs to the notion of man to be composed of soul, flesh and bones . . . man is not a soul only, but a composition of soul and body."[125] The soul and the body are related as form is to matter: "it belongs to the notion of a soul to be the form of a body."[126] Something important to note here is that, not only are both body and soul *necessary* in the composition of a human person, both are *good*. As Gilson explains,

> . . . it would be completely foreign to the Thomistic perspective to regard the material universe as the result of some calamity, and the union of body and soul as the consequence of a fall. In a universe created by pure goodness all its parts are so many reflections of God's infinite perfection. Origen's teaching that God created bodies in order to imprison sinful souls in them is most alien to Thomas' thought. The union of body and soul is not the punishment of the soul, but a salutary bond through which the human soul will reach its full perfection.[127]

In fact, the body turns out to be quite indispensable not only in terms of basic intellectual development, but also in learning about God himself: "although our bodies are unable to enjoy God by knowing and loving Him, yet by the works which we do through the body, we are able to attain to the perfect knowledge of God."[128] As Robert Pasnau points out, in Thomas's understanding, this knowledge of final ends is inextricably linked to knowledge of our*selves*: "we can't know what the most significant human capacities are unless we know what the ultimate end of human life is."[129] As in Zhu Xi's thought, what is good in us is what ties us to what is good in the rest of existence.

As the body plays a significant role in our process of learning, and can participate in the enjoyment of the perfect knowledge of God, Thomas posits that the body as such must be loved: "Hence from the enjoyment in the soul there overflows a certain happiness into the body, viz., 'the flush of health and incorruption' as Augustine states (Ep. ad Dioscor. cxviii). Hence, since the body has, in a fashion, a share of happiness, it can be loved with the love of charity."[130] A clarification: Thomas should not be viewed as celebrating the body without inhibition. As his order of charity implies—one should love first God, then self, then neighbor, and then the body—[131] the body should not be one's primary concern: Thomas certainly does not grant it the importance that it receives in much contemporary feminist theology, where it often plays a central and pivotal role.[132] In fact, given that Thomas locates the passions in the soul,[133] the body can come to seem almost like a remainder concept.[134] Even in this reading, however, we find that the body is still fundamentally good, morally important, and simultaneously needed in a moral life and in need of moral development. Here we see a theme common to both Zhu and Thomas: we must exercise the goodness within us if we are to bring it to its proper fullness. For both Zhu and Thomas, the potential of any part of ourselves for goodness must be developed.

Also like Zhu, Thomas understands that learning and knowledge, broadly construed, are key components in this endeavor. Indeed, one of the most important ways in which we reach our full perfection is through learning and knowledge. And it is here that the body reveals itself to be indispensable. Although Thomas holds that the soul is form and wholly devoid of matter,[135] and that its intellect is incorporeal, he also holds that all knowledge a person has is ultimately based on the senses. He adopts Aristotle's explanation of the process of obtaining knowledge as his own:

> Aristotle held that the intellect has an operation which is independent of the body's cooperation. Now nothing corporeal can make an impression on the incorporeal. And therefore in order to cause the intellectual operation according to Aristotle, the impression caused by the sensible does not suffice, but something more noble is required, for "the agent is more noble than the patient," as he says (De Gener. i, 5). Not, indeed, in the sense that the intellectual operation is effected in us by the mere impression of some superior beings, as Plato held; but that the higher and more noble agent which he calls the active intellect . . . causes the phantasms [the images of particular things impressed on, or preserved in, bodily organs][136] received from the senses to be actually intel-

> ligible, by a process of abstraction. According to this opinion, then, on the part of the phantasms, intellectual knowledge is caused by the senses.[137]

Thomas adds by way of clarification: "but since the phantasms cannot of themselves affect the passive intellect, and require to be made actually intelligible by the active intellect, it cannot be said that sensible knowledge is the total and perfect cause of intellectual knowledge, but rather that it is in a way the material cause."

The knowledge caused by the senses is of primary importance for the human being as being the stuff of the intellectual virtue of wisdom. This position places Thomas in closer company with Zhu than with many today, for, as Eleonore Stump points out, "in contemporary culture it is more customary to think in terms of excellences, rather than virtues, of the intellect; and the paradigm excellence of mind currently valued is intelligence or smartness. We say admiringly of some academic whose philosophical positions strike us as utterly wrongheaded that although his views are widely agreed to be wildly mistaken, he himself is so smart."[138] Neither Thomas nor Zhu would admire the wayward academic, as both conceive of intellectual understanding as linked inextricably with moral character.

As Thomas writes in the *Summa contra gentiles*, "there is no question that intellectual agents act for the sake of an end, because they think ahead of time in their intellects of the things which they achieve through action; and their action stems from such preconception."[139] Moreover, this is not just something that particularly intelligent people do, but it is built into the human condition itself: "an agent does not move except out of intention for an end. For if the agent were not determinate to some particular effect, it would not do one thing rather than another: consequently in order that it produce a determinate effect, it must, of necessity, be determined to some certain one, which has the nature of an end."[140]

Thomas's venerated predecessor Aristotle goes further than this, however, and counsels knowledge not only of the ends of discrete actions, but also of the ends of life itself: "our activities have an end which we want for its own sake, and for the sake of which we want all the other ends—if we do not choose everything for the sake of something else (for this will involve an infinite progression, so that our aim will be pointless and ineffectual)—it is clear that this must be the good, the supreme good."[141] Aristotle defines this supreme good as happiness, which he says is a "virtuous activity of the soul,"[142] and identifies politics as the best discipline in which to study and achieve it.[143]

Thomas agrees with Aristotle both about the person's last end as perfect happiness and about the importance of the community in the development of one's nature. As regards the last end, McInerny notes, although "philosophers after Thomas divorced duty and nature, value and fact, and tried to talk about the moral duty as divorced from our desire for happiness . . . for Thomas the desire for happiness, the love of the good, is part and parcel of the action-guiding judgments that he calls precepts of natural law."[144] (Scholars of Thomas tend to contrast him in this regard against Kant, the latter of whom, in the words of Fergus Kerr, believed that "the last thing worthy of Christians was to want to be happy."[145]) Thomas's linking of desire with the good is enough to underscore this point: as he says, "desire is only of what is good or apparently good."[146]

As regards the importance of other people in the process of moral cultivation, Thomas writes about the role played by community organization in the development of the virtuous person. Law, which he defines as "nothing else than an ordinance of reason for the common good, made by him who has care of the community, and promulgated,"[147] also holds sway over the moral state of individuals: "a private person cannot lead another to virtue efficaciously: for he can only advise, and if his advice be not taken, it has no coercive power, such as the law should have, in order to prove an efficacious inducement to virtue, as the Philosopher says (*Ethic.* x. 9)."[148] Certainly, as in Zhu Xi's estimation, the moral student cannot be left to pursue his own devices: other people, and human institutions, are necessary to full and true development of the human person.

However, unlike both Zhu and Aristotle, Thomas believes that "man is not ordained to the body politic, according to all that he is and has . . . But all that man is, and can, and has, must be referred to God."[149] As it turns out, Thomas has an amplified idea of happiness:

> Happiness is the attainment of the Perfect Good. Whoever, therefore, is capable of the Perfect Good can attain Happiness. Now, that man is capable of the Perfect Good, is proved both because his intellect can apprehend the universal and perfect good, and because his will can desire it. And therefore man can attain Happiness. This can be proved again from the fact that man is capable of seeing God, as stated in I, 12, 1:

> in which vision, as we stated above (Question 3, Article 8) man's perfect Happiness consists.[150]

As he says throughout the *Summa theologiae*, "God is the last end of man and of all other things."[151]

Note here that Thomas considers God the *last* end of human beings—not the only end. Thomas's intense awareness of the divine does not "take away" from the worth of nature-as-such. Unlike Aristotle, who "linked all virtues to happiness in this life,"[152] Thomas, with his belief in a supernatural end surpassing the natural powers of human beings to attain, also felt that theological and divinely infused virtues, linked to happiness after this life, were necessary for all humans (a subject discussed in more detail in Chapter 3). Nonetheless, naturally "acquired" virtues (*virtus acquisita)* are real virtues to Thomas, a reflection of the fact that he is "convinced that Aristotle's outlook on the world and human life was incomplete and inadequate rather than simply wrong."[153] Indeed, one of Thomas's favorite and most fundamental formulations is that "grace does not destroy nature but perfects it."[154] This doctrine places him in between Aristotle and Saint Augustine (354–430), the latter of whom links all virtues to happiness in the afterlife.

As the Catholic philosopher John Langan puts it,

> Augustine's doctrine on the unity of virtues in charity results in an understanding of the moral life which makes the crucial division not between the sage who possesses virtue perfectly and the unwise who fall short of the ideal of apathy, but between those who possess charity even in a rudimentary degree and those who, whatever their other attainments, lack charity and so lack true virtue altogether. [This accords with] his notorious depreciation of the virtues of the pagan Romans . . .[155]

Thomas flatly disagrees with Augustine's teaching that all virtues need charity in order to be considered true virtues. The inclusivity of his take on human or acquired virtue is clear when read against the following passage from Augustine:

> We must declare war upon vices, and wage this war keenly, lest we be landed in damnable sins . . . And indeed this victory cannot be sincerely and truly gained but by delighting

> in true righteousness, and it is faith in Christ that gives this . . . Sometimes, indeed, patent vices are overcome by other and hidden vices, which are reckoned virtues, though pride and a kind of ruinous self-sufficiency are their informing principles. Accordingly vices are then only to be considered overcome when they are conquered by the love of God, which God Himself alone gives, and which He gives only through the Mediator between God and men, the man Christ Jesus, who became a partaker of our mortality that He might make us partakers of His divinity.[156]

Thomas, on the other hand, claims that "human virtue directed to the good which is defined according to the rule of human reason can be caused by human acts: inasmuch as such acts proceed from reason, by whose power and rule the aforesaid good is established."[157] Such valuation of rational—and diverse—goods also separates him from Augustine. As Stalnaker puts it: "for Augustine, we need to turn away from our 'carnal' orientation of private delight in lower, earthly goods, and turn toward God, the supreme good."[158] As Bonnie Kent notes, Thomas differs from Augustine in having

> . . . a healthy respect for human nature and the happiness attainable through people's natural resources in human society. His steadfast defense of pagan virtues as genuine virtues attests to this. But in insisting on the two ends of humankind, he sees more at stake than the moral credit that Christians should award non-Christians. The earthly happiness of Christians themselves deserves attention. Thomas firmly resists any attempt to reduce life to some dreary waiting room on the train route to heaven—as if its value were purely instrumental to salvation, or as if the loves, friendships and work Christians enjoy here and now were so many false goods. Purely human goods are still genuine goods, for Christians no less than other people.[159]

Nonetheless, as Thomas, in Gilson's felicitous phrase, "continues nature into supernature,"[160] he is far more in agreement with Augustine than with Aristotle not only with regard to the heights that may be reached by human beings, but also in deepening the depths to which they may sink. As we approach the boundaries of Aristotelian territory, we also begin to see a dramatic departure from Zhu's more or less cheery appraisal of the human self.

According to Aristotle, all problems with human behavior are caused by irrationality and disorderliness that are under the control of the agent. In the Philosopher's discussion of good behavior, he says that the mark of virtue is to "have [feelings] at the right times on the right grounds towards the right people for the right motive and in the right way is to feel them to an intermediate, that is to the best, degree."[161] This degree is set by reason: "virtue is a purposive disposition, lying in a mean that is relative to us and determined by a rational principle."[162] Vice, as opposing virtue, inherently involves either a failure or a refusal to make rational judgments and connections:

> . . . people get into this condition by their own fault, by the slackness of their lives; i.e., they make themselves unjust or licentious by behaving dishonestly or spending their time in drinking and other forms of dissipation; for in every sphere of conduct people develop qualities corresponding to the activities that they pursue. . . . *to be unaware that in every department of conduct moral states are the result of corresponding activities is the mark of a thoroughly unperceptive person.*[163]

Aristotle's faith in reason, once the latter is properly developed by the exercise of both moral and intellectual virtues, is almost absolute. He conceives of nothing like the Christian notion of original sin, as is evident when he blithely opines: "if, as we have said, the quality of a life is determined by its activities, no man who is truly happy can become miserable; because he will never do things that are hateful and mean. For we believe that the truly good and wise man bears all his fortunes with dignity, and always takes the most honourable course that circumstances permit . . . and if this is so, the truly happy man can never be miserable."[164] Unfortunately for the vicious, the reverse is also true.[165]

Thomas has an Aristotelian respect for reason—to a point. The definition of virtue he approves is as follows: "virtue is a good quality of the mind, by which we live righteously, of which no one can make bad use."[166] The Aristotelian nature of his virtue comes out most strongly when he defines the good in this context: "good, which is put in the definition of virtue . . . is the good as fixed by reason, with regard to which Dionysius says (Div. Nom. iv) "that the good of the soul is to be in accord with reason."[167] His virtues (to be discussed more fully in

Chapter 3) are to help the person to act in accord with reason, which is to rule over the person in a cooperative spirit:

> . . . as the Philosopher says (Polit. i, 2): "We observe in an animal a despotic and a politic principle: for the soul dominates the body by a despotic power; but the intellect dominates the appetite by a politic and royal power." For a power is called despotic whereby a man rules his slaves, who have not the right to resist in any way the orders of the one that commands them, since they have nothing of their own. But that power is called politic and royal by which a man rules over free subjects, who, though subject to the government of the ruler, have nevertheless something of their own, by reason of which they can resist the orders of him who commands . . . the intellect or reason is said to rule the irascible and concupiscible by a politic power: because the sensitive appetite has something of its own, by virtue whereof it can resist the commands of reason.[168]

This "something of its own" bothers Thomas more than it does Aristotle: human reason not only is unable to be "despotic," it is also not enough to save the person from viciousness, because Thomas's person has an innate tendency to sin.

According to Thomas, a sin "is nothing else than a bad human act."[169] Now, Thomas's bad human act is worse than the one conceived of by Aristotle, in which human reason is flouted. In Thomas's bad act lies an offense against reason *and* against God:

> . . . a human act is evil through lacking conformity with its due measure: and conformity of measure in a thing depends on a rule, from which if that thing depart, it is incommensurate. Now there are two rules of the human will: one is proximate and homogeneous, viz. the human reason; the other is the first rule, viz. the eternal law, which is God's reason, so to speak.[170]

Such sin is not only offensive to a higher force in Thomas than in Aristotle, it is also grounded more deeply in human nature. Unlike the Philosopher, who so cheerfully believes that, once we are far enough down the road to virtue, we are all set, as it were, Thomas identifies a fatal flaw that can pull us back and down at any time. Sin thus opens up a huge divide between the two philosophers. As Sweeney points out, "the opening question considering vice and sin brings out the tension between the two main categories organizing Aquinas's discussion: vice (the Aristotelian category) and sin (the religious category)."[171] An Aristotelian structure, for example, does not really have room for questions about whether the Devil can cause humans to sin[172] or whether original sin is passed down to us through our mother or our father.[173] The presence of the latter query in particular in the *Prima secundae* warns us that we are, to that extent, in un-Aristotelian territory. Moreover, this original sin is something that we all share:

> . . . there are two things in original sin: one is the privation of original justice; the other is the relation of this privation to the sin of our first parent, from whom it is transmitted to man through his corrupt origin. As to the first, original sin has no degrees, since the gift of original justice is taken away entirely; and privations that remove something entirely, such as death and darkness, cannot be more or less . . . In like manner, neither is this possible, as to the second: since all are related equally to the first principle of our corrupt origin, from which principle original sin takes the nature of guilt; for relations cannot be more or less. Consequently it is evident that original sin cannot be more in one than in another.[174]

Nor, more discouragingly, is it *less* in one than in another. The further he moves from an Aristotelian theory of human moral weakness, the further Thomas moves from Zhu's way of thinking. In Zhu's system, it is theoretically possible—and historically probable, in the case of the ancient sages—that some people may be born with a perfect bequest of *qi* (see Chapter 1). In sharp contrast, Thomas says that *everyone* is born with the problematic "endowment" of original sin. There is no doubt that "Aquinas is convinced that the human race inherited from Adam a kind of sickness tinged with guilt."[175]

According to James Keenan, who defines sin not as simply a "bad act" but rather as "the failure before God to try to acknowledge the opportunities for making ourselves, our neighbours and our world better,"[176] Thomas's definition can produce a great deal of pain for those who try to improve themselves and repeatedly fail: "[people with compulsions have never benefited] by the long-standing traditional (but not rooted in Scripture) identification of wrong action with personal badness or sin. On the contrary, that identification has caused, over the centuries, hurt, consternation and frustration."[177] While I agree with Keenan that Thomas's treatise on sin is defective in bearing "the [Aristotelian] imprint of his earlier deficient moral psychology,"[178] I also think that Thomistic teachings as a whole are positive for those who are struggling to be good. For one thing, while he approves of "shamefacedness," or what we might call "Catholic guilt," explaining that it is "sometimes called a virtue, since it is a praiseworthy passion"[179] in the sense that it "fosters honesty, by removing that which is contrary thereto,"[180] he explicitly warns his readers against despair as both intellectually and morally problematic, given Christian teachings about salvation and divine pardon.[181] In other words, incessant beating up of the self is both unnecessary and unwise, for hope for forgiveness and salvation is grounded in reality: according to Thomas, the object of hope, attainment of salvation, and the beatific vision that awaits the blessed, is "difficult but possible to obtain,"[182] even for those of us—from Thomas's point of view, everyone—who commit bad human acts.

Hence, in the words of the inimitable Chesterton, "it is profoundly true to say that the glad good news brought by the Gospel was the news of original sin."[183] Indeed, rather than seeing original sin and despairing, "following Saint Augustine, Saint Anselm, and many others whom Scripture turned in this direction, Thomas naturally invokes the need for the healing of the wound caused by sin (*remedium peccati*), for restoration (*reparatio*) of humanity to friendship with God, for satisfaction of sin, all of which appear as the most far-reaching motives."[184] In Thomas's understanding, there is hope for even the worst of sinners to develop his original moral potential, for God will give grace, defined as "the effect of the Divine love in us . . . whereby a man is made worthy of eternal life,"[185] to those who will accept it. Here again, we see that relationship is crucial to the development of the human person—in this case, with God Himself.

The grace poured out on human beings in right relationship with God produces several different results. Thomas explains that "there are five effects of grace in us: of these, the first is, to heal the soul; the second, to desire good; the third, to carry into effect the good proposed; the fourth, to persevere in good; the fifth, to reach glory."[186] Thus, with reference to the brokenness of original sin, the *Summa theologiae* says that original sin is incompatible with grace,[187] and that, moreover, God can and will heal it: "original sin is taken away by Baptism as to the guilt, in so far as the soul recovers grace as regards the mind."[188] Thus, according to Nichols,

> . . . for Thomas, two things are involved in that divine work of salvation that is made known to us not through the natural light of reason but by way of the prophetic light of revelation. Salvation entails the elevation of the entire natural order in which we live to a new supernatural end: we can call that salvation as transfiguration—our receiving that kind of wholeness, integrity, health that go with becoming transformed creatures. Salvation also entails the applying of medication to whatever in our natural condition needs doctoring: we can call that salvation as redemption, our receiving back the sort of wholeness, integrity, health that befits creatures of God who are (in this formal perspective, then) not so much transformed as healed. For Thomas, saving grace is both *gratia elevans*, grace that raises (from the natural level) and *gratia sanans*, grace that heals (heals, namely, the wounds of created human nature).[189]

For Thomas, "the gift of Christ surpasses the sin of Adam."[190] Not only does Thomas deal with a problem that Aristotle and Zhu do not address, he also describes a great wonder unthought of by both, and with great bounties to aid us in our development, surpassing the natural virtues we can develop through practice and habituation. This is not to declare the realm of natural virtue a God-free zone. The "certain seeds or principles of acquired virtue" which "pre-exist in us by nature,"[191] and which we bring to fruition or flower through moral and intellectual effort, are given us by God, Who is the author of our nature. Thus does Thomas differ again from Zhu Xi: while Thomas, like Zhu, believes that human beings are born with innate virtue waiting to be developed, he attributes this fortuitous state of affairs not to an impersonal principle or Way, but rather to a personal and loving God.

The bounties that divine generosity bestows upon us include the gifts of the Holy Spirit, described thusly:

> . . . now it is manifest that human virtues perfect man according as it is natural for him to be moved by his reason in his interior and exterior actions. Consequently man needs yet higher perfections, whereby to be disposed to be moved by

> God. These perfections are called gifts, not only because they are infused by God, but also because by them man is disposed to become amenable to the Divine inspiration, according to Isaiah 50:5: "The Lord . . . hath opened my ear, and I do not resist; I have not gone back." Even the Philosopher says in the chapter On Good Fortune (Ethic. Eudem., vii, 8) that for those who are moved by Divine instinct, there is no need to take counsel according to human reason, but only to follow their inner promptings, since they are moved by a principle higher than human reason. This then is what some say, viz. that the gifts perfect man for acts which are higher than acts of virtue.[192]

The work of Thomas thus assigns an incalculable value to the relationship with the divine, which enables the transmission of grace and the gifts and virtues that accompany it. This is not an either or relationship of competing interests, in which we either do what we wish or do what God wishes us to do, but rather one in which loving cooperation provides true self-growth.

The most important of all the virtues that relationship with God provides is *caritas*: "charity is more excellent than faith or hope, and, consequently, than all the other virtues."[193] This charity is of great importance not only with reference to God, but also to human relationships on Earth, for it is meant to be extended to all of one's neighbors. Such neighbors are widely defined. Drawing on the work of his great predecessor, Thomas writes, "Augustine says (De Doctr. Christ. i, 30) that 'when it is said: "Thou shalt love thy neighbor," it is evident that we ought to look upon every man as our neighbor.' "[194] Not surprisingly in such a Christian context, this injunction applies to relationships with sinners as well as the virtuous:

> Two things may be considered in the sinner: his nature and his guilt. According to his nature, which he has from God, he has a capacity for happiness, on the fellowship of which charity is based, as stated above (3; 23, 1, 5), wherefore we ought to love sinners, out of charity, in respect of their nature. On the other hand their guilt is opposed to God, and is an obstacle to happiness. Wherefore, in respect of their guilt whereby they are opposed to God, all sinners are to be hated, even one's father or mother or kindred, according to Luke

> 12:26. For it is our duty to hate, in the sinner, his being a sinner, and to love in him, his being a man capable of bliss; and this is to love him truly, out of charity, for God's sake.[195]

See Chapter 1 for further discussion of what is classified as "God's" and what is classified as "man's" in terms of human behavior.

In the end, just as Zhu's *ren* remains a central concern in all of his work on moral development, so too does *caritas* for Thomas: in the mind of the latter, *caritas* is the most excellent of all virtues, and it is meant to pervade all interaction between human beings, who are all to treat one another with the love appropriate for one's neighbors. In other words, people must always be in relationship in order to flourish—with other human beings and with God himself.

Thomas thus achieves a stupendous balancing act. His Christian doctrine of original sin, when combined with his Aristotelian reverence for human reason and virtue, ends up producing a picture similar to Zhu's in that human beings are called on to develop the moral potential within themselves, in communion with others. However, for Thomas, the most important partner in these efforts is not the sage who wrote a Classic, nor the teacher who imparts it, but rather the Lord God Who created all, and Who alone can provide the divine grace necessary for overcoming original sin. Moreover, such grace, as the "effect of God's love in us," inspires us to extend *caritas*, the virtue of love, to everyone we meet, and hence grow in love. This project harmoniously combines the self-regard of one who wants to attain full and true happiness with solidarity for others by making the success of the former dependent upon the exercise of the latter.

Conclusion

As Andrew Dell'Ollio notes in his brief comparison of Zhu Xi and Thomas Aquinas,

> . . . the ultimate aim of each philosopher's moral teachings is a spiritual one as both maintain that the ultimate end of human life involves a kind of embodiment of, or participation in, a supreme reality or principle. In other words, for Zhu Xi and Aquinas, moral development is at once a form of self-realization through human reason and a form of

> self-transcendence by conforming to the nature of what is ultimate or divine.[196]

Of course, differences still abound. In attempting to conform to the *ultimate* rather than the *divine*, "unlike the Christian approach, the Confucian line of thinking rejects the idea that the ultimate source of [moral] effort is God's grace. It argues that in the process of self-realization, the very foundation of such an act relies on the moral mind, or in Confucian terminology, the mind of *jen* [*ren*], which is intrinsic to every human being."[197] According to Tu Weiming, "despite the tension and conflict within the Neo-Confucian tradition, it seems that there is an agreement among virtually all of the Neo-Confucianists: man is a moral being who through self-effort extends his human sensitivity to all the beings of the universe so as to realize himself in the midst of the world and as an integral part of it, in the sense that his self-perfection necessarily embodies the perfection of the universe as a whole."[198] Livia Kohn points out that this Confucian tendency is a characteristic of Chinese culture and religion in general: "the human condition in this system is normatively seen in an overwhelmingly affirmative mode: it is good to be alive, it is most precious to be born human, it is not only desirable but possible to realize oneself humanly in and through this world."[199] Given this state of affairs, it is hardly surprising that

> Confucian teachings have focused more upon human perfectibility where Christianity appears to support the idea of human fallibility. Thus, Confucianism projects the image of a man in harmony with society and the universe, where Christianity appears to support the idea of a man at war with himself and his sinful nature, struggling to overcome a world estranged from God.[200]

Nonetheless, however peaceful and harmonious are Confucian teachings regarding the good, it remains a fact that many people struggle in the world, both against themselves and others. According to Ching, "the Confucian tradition has been one-sided, because it has not considered the darker, and sometimes demonic, side of human nature as have other Chinese philosophical traditions."[201]

Given that even good people demonstrably have such darker sides, it might be said that Thomas's faith in the existence of a loving Divine, and the attainability of the beatific vision, is matched by Zhu's faith in the self-perfectibility of humanity. In fact, it could be argued that, in promoting the existence of a "mind of *ren*" in every human being, and asking people to act upon it even when they can see it in neither others nor themselves, Zhu asks for even more faith than Christians like Thomas, who can rely on their personal loving God for help during moments of profound doubt and consciousness of personal weaknesses. In practice, the person with horribly turbid *qi*, the person born without the resources to study, the person born into an unhappy family that fails to give even the rudiments of moral wisdom and knowledge—all these are left behind.

A cautionary note: I do not mean to overstate my case. Zhu and his tradition, while certainly placing a very high premium on textual study, never conceived of the scholar-officials as possessing wisdom *substantively* different from what was possessed by uneducated people. Rather, the knowledge of the wise was understood to be different in *degree* from ordinary knowledge. As the *Doctrine of the Mean* reveals, "common men and women, however ignorant, may be granted [knowledge] of it . . . Common men and women, however ordinary, can carry it into practice."[202] Nonetheless, it cannot be denied that such ordinary men and women would have little hope—if any—of moral development as full as that of the well-read. This aspect of Confucian teaching jars not only against contemporary egalitarian sensibilities but also against Christian doctrine, which claims that all, no matter how disadvantaged, can become great saints due to the grace of God. Hence, we can imagine that Thomas would have "developed" Zhu in much the same way he "developed" Aristotle to fit within his Christian worldview, retaining Zhu's faith in the efficacy of human efforts toward improvement of the self and others, while reserving *perfection* for God himself.

On the other hand, there is no doubt that many people—both within and without the Christian tradition—find the doctrine of original sin disturbing, offensive, or even dangerous, and choose to set it aside. For example, the Christian Rev. Rick Warren, in his bestselling book, *The Purpose Driven Life: What On Earth Am I Here For?*, claims that the greatest problems of humankind are guilt, resentment, anger, materialism, fear, need for approval, and unused potential, stress, and unfulfilled life.[203] The term "original sin" does not come up in this recital of human tribulations, and in fact does not appear in the book at all. Indeed, Warren presents sin as a bad or irreverent choice rather than as a tragic component of the human condition: "all sin, at its root, is refusing to give God glory."[204]

With regard to people outside of the Christian communion, it is certainly the case that the stark and sobering doctrine of original sin was not very well received when it first came to China. As Weber notes, "in vain Christian missionaries tried to awaken a feeling of sin . . . an educated Chinese would simply refuse to be continually burdened with 'sin.' "[205] When first confronted with the teaching, many Chinese chose to set it aside, seeing little point in devoting time and worry to the question of human evil when so much was necessary to be done to develop human good, perhaps even regarding such a doctrine to be counterproductive.

The answer to whether it was Zhu or Thomas—or neither—who was correct in his appraisal of human good and human evil will never be finally decided, and religious faith is necessary to subscribing to either position. Regardless of their differences on the issue of how much improvement human beings need and the resources available to them in the process of moral development, Zhu and Thomas certainly share many perspectives in common: not least, they both believe that moral development of the original nature is necessary. In addition, they also share a propensity to focus primarily on the objective good in which they perceive humans to participate, rather than taking desires and interests as their starting point. For both men, "[the educated moral agent] does what is virtuous *because* it is virtuous."[206] The issue is not framed in terms of "virtue is its own reward," as it might be for the self-interested actor or the selfless comrade, but rather in terms of "doing the right thing." Doing the right thing, of course, is also seen as being in the moral agent's best interests, as well as those of his community, but such interests are subsumed, and certainly not given center stage. Both Zhu and Thomas would agree with MacIntyre, who warns against thinking of the virtues in terms of means to an end:

> . . . the virtues are precisely those qualities the possession of which will enable an individual to achieve *eudaimonia* and the lack of which will frustrate his movement towards that *telos*. But although it would not be incorrect to describe the exercise of virtues as a means to the end of achieving the good for man, that description is ambiguous . . . The exercise of the virtues is not *a* means to the end of the good for man. For what constitutes the good for man is a complete human life lived at its best, and the exercise of the virtues is a necessary and central part of such a life, not a mere preparatory exercise to secure such a life.[207]

Moreover, virtue is not the only constitutive element in such a life: other *people* are important. And these people are also intelligent agents with moral potential that must be developed in the context of loving relationships. As Aristotle states, in an opinion with which his student Thomas would concur: "it is a generally accepted view that the perfect good is self-sufficient. By self-sufficient we mean not what is sufficient for oneself alone living a solitary life, but something that includes parents, wife and children, friends and fellow-citizens in general; for *man is by nature a social being*."[208] Confucius, whose *Analects* begin with the question, "Is it not delightful to have friends coming from afar?"[209] would agree.

Both Zhu and Thomas, in conceiving of the human being as social, with moral potential that may be developed only in communion with others, grant significance to both the intellect and love that is lacking in interest-based understandings of the self: rather than claiming that people should be free to give rein to their desires without first training them, or alternatively that they should put their own interests wholly aside, Zhu and Thomas counsel that the intellect must be used to identify the real good, and that relationships are important in this process. Their "chastened intellectualism" recognizes that the transformative knowledge necessary to moral self-development will oftentimes come from other people: parents, teachers, friends, or even one's own children.[210]

Believing in the fundamental and universal moral potential of human beings allows both Thomas and Zhu to envision a society in which struggle is a deviation rather than a fundamental characteristic: if all possess this potential, and all need to develop it in the context of loving relationships, whether social or divine, true cooperation rather than competition is an essential quality of the rightful relations between human beings. Such a belief in the innate worth of human beings harmonizes with the needs written into their nature, for, as both Thomas and Zhu would agree, people should strive to become neither self-interested actors, nor selfless comrades, but rather social beings, ideally engaged in the process of mutual support in the pursuit of the good. From their perspective, it is only with and through other people that we can fully become who we are meant to be, and in so doing attain genuine personal happiness. In other words, self-regard can only realize its true ends through solidarity, and vice versa.

On a related note, focusing on the good that is greater than the self, or the social group, as well as the effort needed to achieve it, allows them both to positively engage with the notion of power. In focusing on this good, the person does not ignore his own interests or those of his community, but looks beyond both, to the ways in which they should be shaped, and the limitations thus placed upon them. Since, for them, the good is universal rather than personal, transcending us as individuals and even nations, it makes sense that we would find it in cooperation with the world outside us—which turns out to be precisely the case. It is only by striving to be a co-creator of the universe, or a loving steward of others' cares, that we may fully develop the moral potential that we can intelligently identify in ourselves. In short, focusing on a notion of a universal good that must be striven for by a carefully trained agent, rather than on the wants of the agent prior to such training, allows people to engage with a real notion of authority, properly limited, in a fashion characterized less by struggle than by genuine, loving cooperation. Indeed, it is for us to align ourselves with the good, to the point where such struggles between individuals may be transcended, in favor of a harmony that allows for the flourishing of all. It is the processes through which this may come to pass that we explore in the following chapter.

Chapter 3

Roles, Rituals, and Habits

The Proper Development of the Human Being

> Ideas are important in life, but of themselves they seldom provide starting points. They grow out of facts and experiences and, torn from this soil, lose their life like uprooted trees.
>
> —Huston Smith, *The World's Religions*

As discussed in the previous chapter, both Zhu Xi and Thomas Aquinas believe that human beings, born into a world suffused with moral significance and worth, are themselves of incalculable value. Nonetheless, neither claims that humans come on to the earthly stage completely prepared to play the role assigned to them: much work must be done before their great potential can be realized. We are not born ready, say both thinkers, but we can become ready over time with effort. With the sheer difficulty of this project at the forefront of their minds, they provide neither utopian promises nor apocalyptic threats but rather reasonable hope for human flourishing. In their systems of thought, we find room for neither despair nor delusional optimism concerning the human condition; instead, they tell us that our difficulties, while very real, are nonetheless surmountable. Both thinkers counsel us to learn to fulfill the responsibilities of certain roles—roles that differ quite markedly from those presented by contemporary secular sociologists by being infused with a carefully cultivated and joyfully expressed love for ourselves, our human companions, and the world at large. This love, in turn, informs their theories of authority.

Roles

As Huston Smith notes in the epigraph above, even the most beautiful of abstract ideas needs to become concretely real to people before it can influence their lives for the better. In Confucianism and Christianity, this reality is addressed by the ancient scriptures of each tradition: the idea that we are to develop our moral potential as intelligent agents is given content by way of assigning roles to humanity. In Confucianism, responsibility is laid upon the person to intelligently develop her moral potential in order that she may play a role, alongside Heaven (*Tian*, 天) and Earth (*Di*, 地) in the flourishing of all that is. *The Doctrine of the Mean* (*Zhongyong*, 中庸) proclaims:

> . . . if [people] can fully develop their nature, then they can fully develop the nature of others. If they can fully develop the nature of others, then they can fully develop the nature of things. If they can fully develop the nature of things, then they can assist in the transformation and reproduction of Heaven and Earth. If they can assist in the transformation and reproduction of Heaven and Earth, then they can join Heaven and Earth [as a partner].[1]

Human beings turn out to be co-creators of the cosmos, cooperating with the other great powers within it to nourish and sustain all that is; Wing-tsit Chan goes so far to term the trifold partnership a "trinity."[2]

Christians are not offered such a lofty partnership: their position *under* a triune God is never questioned or challenged. The Biblical account of creation in Genesis first tells us that: "God created man in the image of himself, in the image of God he created him, male and female he created them."[28] After creating the first two human beings, Adam and Eve, "God blessed them, saying to them, 'Be fruitful, multiply, fill the earth and subdue it. Be masters of the fish of the sea, the birds of heaven and all the living creatures that move on earth.'"[3] However, as the text makes clear, Adam and Eve, although masters of all below them, as made in the *image* of God, are not the *equals* of God, and remain subject to his commands: a fact that becomes quite clear when they are banished from paradise after eating the fruit that had been forbidden them. Nonetheless, the role of steward retained by Adam, Eve, and all of their descendants still holds with it a great deal of authority. Some scholars, perhaps most famously Lynn White, Jr., have suggested that the Genesis account is more problematic for the environment than not. According to White, in this account, humans, as the only living beings created in the image of God, are automatically placed in a position superior to the rest of the world, which they are given to control and use as they will; in his reading, their Creator seems to intend the Earth as a present that they will possess, rather than as a reality in which they will share. White argues that the emphasis in Judaism and Christianity on the transcendence of God above nature and the dominion of man over nature has led to a devaluing of the natural world and a subsequent destruction of its resources for utilitarian ends.[4] While a careful examination of this claim is beyond the scope of this chapter, it nonetheless may be claimed in a general sense that in the West, a great deal of re-*interpretation* of fundamental texts such as Genesis may be necessary to living in the world sustainably and well, while in the Confucian tradition, it is more of a question of re-*possession* of certain basic texts and ideas that have, in some cases, been left behind.[5] This book can be of assistance in both projects, by exploring the moral worth assigned to the cosmos by Zhu Xi and Thomas, and investigating the vital cosmic role both assign to members of the human race, one linked to a productive and positive relationship with Heavenly (and, in the case of Confucianism, Earthly) powers. Such a role is inextricably linked with human moral potential, which is developed precisely for the purpose of playing this role lovingly and well.

However, just as the notion of a common good may inspire almost instinctive distrust in people who value self-assertion and the maximization of their individual interests, so too does the notion of an innate human role raise red flags. Such people may well conceive of their own mundane, everyday roles as restrictive or somehow "not them." In fact, this heavy suspicion concerning roles can lead to a situation in which identification with a role becomes suspect in itself. As Adam Seligman explains,

> . . . when we say that we trust in the modern context . . . we are referring not to any particular aspect of [a person's] role incumbency . . . but to the decision making agent herself, an agent that remains irreducible to any decision or set of

> decisions. Indeed, the extent to which I cease to trust her is the extent to which I identify her totally with one or another of her role-incumbencies and see her as subsuming all other commitments to the fulfillment of that one role.[6]

Oftentimes, this suspicion regarding over-identification with one's roles is supported by and manifested in a cultural tendency to separate the self into two parts: the inner, which thinks, feels, and believes, and the outer, which acts and speaks. However, this dichotomy is deceptive in its simplicity. For example, the question of what is left over when all the roles are stripped away turns out to be a complicated one. As Seligman and his co-authors note in *Ritual and Its Consequences: An Essay on the Limits of Sincerity*, the sincere mode, which is set against the socialized, role-determined ritual mode, "is a dynamic that leaves little room for ambiguity, for mixed motives and for the complexity and contradictory character of most human striving."[7] The difficulties presented by the sincere mode are immediately apparent when moral dilemmas involving temptation are considered. For example, I might know that I should not browbeat an undergraduate, or eat the cake left in the common room refrigerator, and very sincerely not want to do either both morally and cognitively. However, if the undergraduate is especially annoying, or the cake especially chocolaty, it is also likely that part of me will want to indulge my less morally defensible instinct, and that this part will be equally sincere in its desire. Which part is the "real" me, my "self"? As Lionel Trilling puts it, having divided our selves into real and ritualized halves, "we are still puzzled to know not only the locus of the self to which we are to be true, but even what it is that we look for."[8]

Various ways of dealing with this problem are to be found, both in the social sciences and without. The following pages will explore the option, found in a great deal of sociological theory,[9] of interpreting social roles as either largely or completely constituting the identity of the individual, before turning to Zhu Xi and Thomas Aquinas for an alternative, more celebratory approach to roles. As will be seen, one of the chief differences between our two thinkers and the social scientists discussed in this chapter is that the former conceive of roles in cosmic terms and loving relationships, while the latter confine themselves to an objective discussion of social concerns. This latter approach is in keeping with the spirit of the scientific method, which aims at achieving empirically defensible hypotheses, generally concerning carefully limited things and events.

Social Roles and the Human Person

The great structural functionalist Talcott Parsons is inclined to see the human being in almost solely role-related terms, defining the human being more or less as a role-taker. In identifying the individual as "a composite *bundle* of statuses and roles,"[10] he explicitly says, "it should be made quite clear that statuses and roles, or the status-role bundle, are not in general attributes of the actor, but are *units* of the social system, though having a given social status may sometimes be treated as an attribute."[11] For Parsons, the roles are hardly even *interpreted* by the social actor, who seems to receive them as set units beyond his or her control to influence, and yet is defined by them nonetheless.

Of course, Parsons is well aware that things do not always go smoothly: as suggested by the term "bundle," everyone has more than one role, and "a compulsive need to excel in an occupational role may cause the actor to encroach on times appropriately allocated to kinship roles, and make him feel that he is exposed to a conflict of expectations as between his boss and his wife."[12] While Parsons admits that this problem might be located within the employee and husband himself, he is quick to add that "the source of the conflict may not be ego-made. It may be imposed upon the actor from the malintegration of the social system itself."[13] This idea of misaligned communal or institutional frameworks becomes a particularly fertile intellectual field for his student, Robert Merton.

Merton had good reasons to develop a theory of "malintegrated" structures. Living and working in the mid-twentieth century, with the horrors of the concentration camps of World War II still a vivid memory, and watching the struggle of black people in the United States to achieve equal human rights, Merton was anxious to trace social problems not to race or ethnicity, but rather to problems in social organization. Thus, for example, when confronted with white unionists who claimed that black workers were somehow intrinsically "un-unionizable," Merton wrote,

> . . . our unionists fail to see, of course, that they have produced the very "facts" which they sometimes observe. For by defining the situation as one in which blacks are held to be incorrigibly at odds with principles of unionism and by excluding them from unions, the unionists then invite a series of consequences which indeed make it difficult if not impossible for many blacks to avoid the role of scab. Out of

> work after World War I, and kept out of unions, thousands of blacks could not resist strikebound employers who invitingly held a door open upon a world of jobs from which they were otherwise excluded.[14]

Given the social conditions of his time, one of the primary aims in Merton's work was to discover how "some social structures exert a definite pressure upon certain persons in the society to engage in non-conformist rather than conformist behavior." Such a project would be of far more than academic interest, Merton claimed, because, "if we can locate groups peculiarly subject to such pressures, we should expect to find fairly high rates of deviant behavior in these groups, not because the human beings comprising them are compounded of distinctive biological tendencies but because they are responding normally to the social situation in which they find themselves."[15]

Moreover, according to Merton, looking at structure rather than the individual leads to new insights about how problems can arise for members of even the most comfortable of social groups in the most placid of eras: "not only is the same pattern sometimes functional for some groups and dysfunctional for others, it can also serve some and defeat other functional requirements of the *same* group. The reason for this resembles the reasons for a pattern having different consequences for different groups. A group has different functional requirements."[16] In short, while social systems are indeed constructed and maintained in order to promote and sustain stability—Parsons's position—they will always promote a certain amount of conflict and volatility as well. As Merton makes clear, this fact is endemic to any social structure in itself, and is not the result of individual human action *per se*. In fact, Merton defines "social disorganization" as the result of various social dysfunctions, which are in turn defined singly as "a specific inadequacy of a particular part of the system for meeting a particular functional requirement."[17] In the Mertonian schema, social frustration is rooted in social structures themselves, and only secondarily (if at all) in individual psyches or souls.

Nor is social frustration the only element to be placed outside of the individual person. The social structure and the roles it provides turn out to have a powerful effect even on personal freedom when personally expressed. One of Merton's most central concepts, the role-set, or "that complement of role-relationships in which persons are involved by virtue of occupying a particular social status,"[18] makes this clear. As Merton notes, "people do not engage in continuous interaction with all those in their role-sets. This is not an incidental fact, to be ignored because familiar, but one integral to the operation of social structure . . . It should be emphasized that we are dealing here with structural arrangements for such insulation, not with the fact that people *happen* to conceal part of their role behavior from others."[19] It is the opacity of the structure that grants the human being a freedom and agency over and against the tyranny of social roles and expectations, to indulge in a bit of self-gratification or even much-desired "free time": thus, for example, Seligman confesses that "I allow my wife to believe that it takes me much longer to grade student papers than it actually does so she does not ask me to take the children to the swimming pool."[20] However, this is a rather shadowy freedom, limited to the dark corners and blind spots of social life: in an odd way, the structure of roles is all-encompassing, deciding even how and in which way people are allowed *not* to play them.

Parsons and Merton posit a self that does something with regard to its roles: juggling them or moving between them. The language they (and Seligman in the quote above) use suggests that there exists an agent hidden under all of these roles, looking for opportunities to exercise personal agency. This common intuition is shared by other sociologists. Although, as Ralf Dahrendorf puts it, "to a sociologist the individual *is* his social roles,"[21] he is aware of the limitations of this perspective. As he admits in the hypothetical case of Herr Schmidt, a middle-class German man, "many of his characteristics cannot conceivably be inferred from his positions: whether he is a good or a bad teacher, a strict or lenient father; whether or not he can control his emotions; whether or not he is satisfied with his life."[22]

In short, Dahrendorf is claiming that what role-centered definitions of the individual cannot illumine is an individual's *style*. This style includes character—a person is often talkative or taciturn, quick-tempered or easy going, upbeat or cynical "across the board," in a way that transcends and/or unites all of the roles without either determining or being determined by them. The person's style may also seem to be reflected in his or her capabilities; someone who is good with details generally remains so regardless of which role he happens to be playing, while someone who is not good at locating things generally remains so whether in the house or out of it. (This does not mean that a stern professor might not be an indulgent father, or that a self-confident hedge-fund manager might not be a shrinking violet on a date with someone she really likes. When personality traits change along with roles, the role focus is relatively unproblematic. However, in the many cases in which they don't, focusing more or less exclusively on roles can leave a great deal of human experience in the dark.) However, according to Dahrendorf, this element of a person's identity is doomed to remain opaque to sociology. While Herr Schmidt is indeed "more than an incumbent of social positions," Dahrendorf throws this aside by immediately adding that "much that his friends know about him neither the casual acquaintance *nor the sociologist knows or wants to know*."[23] Instead, he explicitly draws back from saying anything about the actual person in whom we might theoretically be interested, claiming, "to put the matter paradoxically, at the risk of being misunderstood: even if sociology asks questions about man, it is in substance concerned not with man but with *ways of reducing man's actions to rational terms*. Not only is sociology improperly defined as science of man, but it is *fundamentally indifferent to man as such*."[24] In other words, from Dahrendorf's perspective, sociology proceeds in the reductionist spirit of the scientific method discussed earlier in Chapter 1. As will be seen below, both Erving Goffman and our medieval thinkers diverge sharply from Dahrendorf's way of thinking, although for wholly different reasons.

Goffman has a decidedly more radical view than any of the social theorists discussed thus far, in which the roles one plays wholly constitute who one is. There is no independent agent involved in choosing roles, oppressive or otherwise, for the self "is a *product* of a scene that comes off, and is not a *cause* of it . . . it is a dramatic effect arising diffusely from a scene that is presented, and the characteristic issue, the crucial concern, is whether it will be credited or discredited."[25] Moreover, once this self has been presented to others, "given his attributes and the conventionalized nature of the encounter, he will find a small choice of lines will be open to him and a small choice of faces will be waiting for him. Further, on the basis of a few known attributes, he is given the responsibility of possessing a vast number of others."[26] Hence, not only is the self a product of performance, it is also bound to its continued run: "approved attributes and their relation to face make of every man his own jailer; this is a fundamental social constraint even though each man may like his cell."[27] However, lest the language of people imprisoned within walls of roles lead one to believe that there is a self under all of the roles, Goffman writes, "in analyzing the self then we are drawn from its possessor, from the person who will profit or lose most by it, for he and his body merely provide the peg on which something of collaborative manufacture will be hung for a time. And the means for producing and maintaining selves do not reside within the peg."[28]

The common thread running through these discussions is the sense that roles are something that restrict an individual. Parsons's juggler is forced into tight places by his conflicting roles, while Merton's freedom seeker is limited to lurking in the spaces no one cares to look in. The picture becomes even starker in Goffman, who claims that humans have no freedom at all with regard to established roles, which simultaneously imprison and exhaust the human person. On the subject of personal freedom vis-à-vis new roles, Goffman does admit that "it would seem that an individual can more easily make a choice as to what line of treatment to demand from and extend to the others present at the beginning of an encounter than he can alter the line of treatment that is being pursued once the interaction is underway."[29] However, this is not the case for most kinds of social interaction, as most of us spend most of our time in the company of people who know us and have expectations about our performances, and are trapped within our roles. Anyone who has ever returned to her family a "changed person" will recognize the truth of this insight. After long years away from the place where I grew up, I find myself slipping into old patterns of behavior at home, and losing things—keys especially—that I never lose in Boston. A reductionist focus on roles can lead to insights about just how powerful these roles can be in ordinary life.

This is not to say that such insights will be pleasant. Those who like to think of themselves as autonomous, free to pursue their own interests in their own time and manner, are likely to find the role theories of Parsons, Merton, and Goffman unattractive at best and bleak at the worst, for all three scholars claim that true individual freedom in the face of community or society is either terribly scarce or practically impossible.

However, for those who think of themselves as intelligent agents with moral potential, roles can become more attractive as vehicles through which ethical development, and growth in love, can take place. To such views we now turn.

Cosmic Roles and the Human Person

To begin with, both Thomas and Zhu see the importance of the kind of ordinary, everyday roles that are discussed above. Both come from unabashedly hierarchical cultures (a circumstance discussed at length in the Conclusion to this book, as it can be a stumbling block for those of us living in egalitarian societies today), and pay a great deal of attention to social status and the types of behavior that must be observed with regard to it. Thus, for example, Thomas values social hierarchy so much as to claim in his discussion of the cardinal virtue of justice that "in actions and passions a person's station (*conditio personae*) affects the quantity of a thing: for it is a greater injury to strike a prince than a private person."[30] Moreover, a person's station also constrains him or her to act in certain ways: what is virtuous for one social class is not virtuous for others. In Thomas's discussion of the cardinal virtue of temperance, he writes,

> . . . temperance regards need according to the requirements of life, and this depends not only on the requirements of the body, but also on the requirements of external things, such as riches and station, and more still on the requirements of good conduct. Hence the Philosopher adds (Ethic. iii, 11) that "the temperate man makes use of pleasant things provided that not only they be not prejudicial to health and a sound bodily condition, but also that they be not inconsistent with good," i.e., good conduct, nor "beyond his substance," i.e., his means. And Augustine says (De Morib. Eccl. xxi) that the "temperate man considers the need" not only "of this life" but also "of his station."[31]

Meanwhile, Zhu, as a disciple of Confucius, believes strongly in the rectification of names (*zhengming*, 正名). *The Analects* shows Confucius's concern that titles such as "father," "son," "minister," "ruler," and "friend" be clearly defined, as well his belief that so doing would provide models of behavior that would produce social harmony when properly followed.[32] Likewise, Zhu tells his students, "illuminating virtue means obtaining it in oneself, and, having attained clarity, not concealing it. If fathers and children have affection, ministers and their princes have righteousness, husbands and wives have differentiation, older and younger have order, and friends have loyalty, then to begin with there will be no mistakes."[33] Thus, for example, in Zhu's estimation, men and women are not free to enter into equal partnerships: their roles as husbands and wives are to constrain them into certain hierarchical relationships that in turn will demand certain forms of behavior between them. So far, Zhu and Thomas seem to be going along with the social theorists who claim that roles *restrict* the individual who plays them.

Nonetheless, the references to the virtues of temperance and justice in Thomas, and to virtuous states of relationship in Zhu, tells us that the roles are not value-free concerns: to the contrary, the implication in their work is that the social order and its roles are to be celebrated. Thomas feels that social status is indispensable in the process of identifying the content of the virtue of temperance, and Zhu feels that proper behavior in social relationships is inextricably linked to the time-honored Confucian project of "illuminating virtue (*mingde*, 明德)."[34]

Moreover, both Thomas and Zhu link the social order to their cosmological accounts. Thomas's idea of social inequality fits in very well with his notion of divinely ordained cosmic inequality, which he understands to be a good in itself:

> . . . formal distinction always requires inequality, because as the Philosopher says (Metaph. viii, 10), the forms of things are like numbers in which species vary by addition or subtraction of unity. Hence in natural things species seem to be arranged in degrees; as the mixed things are more perfect than the elements, and plants than minerals, and animals than plants, and men than other animals; and in each of these one species is more perfect than others. Therefore, as the divine wisdom is the cause of the distinction of things for the sake of the perfection of the universe, so it is the cause of inequality. For the universe would not be perfect if only one grade of goodness were found in things.[35]

Given Thomas's understanding of inequality being woven into the nature of the universe as a whole by a loving and good God, it is hardly surprising that he finds such inequality (when properly ordered) to be good and just in the human realm. Thus, he writes,

> . . . if one man surpassed another in knowledge and virtue, this would not have been fitting unless these gifts conduced to the benefit of others, according to 1 Peter 4:10, "As every man hath received grace, ministering the same one to another." Wherefore Augustine says (De Civ. Dei xix, 14): "Just men command not by the love of domineering, but by the service of counsel": and (De Civ. Dei xix, 15): "The natural order of things requires this; and thus did God make man."[36]

Zhu Xi, on the other hand, directly assigns particular manifestations of principle (*li*) itself to the relationships structured around social roles: "a father and a son have the principle of a father and a son, and a ruler and his minister have the principle of a ruler and minister."[37]

Thus, for Zhu, social roles, and their proper performance, are facets of the goodness that permeate and sustain the universe at large.

In placing social roles into a cosmic context that is in itself innately good, Thomas and Zhu go a long way toward giving positive value to social roles. Moreover, this context, far broader than that adopted by the social scientists, allows them to see social roles as modes of participation in this wider, morally charged order. Given this perspective, these roles suddenly become valuable in a way that is overlooked in social scientific theory. Through giving the roles moral value, and connecting them to moral development and cosmic fate, Zhu and Thomas not only assuage the fears of the person who is afraid of disappearing under the roles, but also address the intelligent agent with moral potential who needs to see his or her roles in a positive light—as contributing to the development of him- or herself.

Thus, unlike the social theorists addressed above, who discuss a person's disappearance into or under his roles in a dispassionate and objective way—much as scholars using the scientific method probe natural phenomena (as discussed in Chapter 1) and the political philosophers of the early modern period sought to conduct value-free studies of the human person (as discussed in Chapter 2)—both Zhu Xi and Thomas Aquinas *celebrate* the rediscovery of the essential humanity of the individual who plays his cosmic role to its fullest. According to Zhu, the person who begins to approach the understanding of the Confucian sage (*shengren*, 聖人), the person who may genuinely co-create with Heaven and Earth, through embracing the realities and context of her given nature will experience great joy: "according to the Principle of Heaven and Earth and the ten thousand things, nothing exists in isolation and everything naturally has its opposite. All this is naturally so and is not [so] manipulated. I often think of this in the middle of the night, and [am so happy] that I dance with my hands and feet without realizing it."[38] Meanwhile, in Thomas, a change in focus from the self to the God in whose image we were created and whom we are meant to imitate as well as we can, when accompanied by divine attention to the person, results in the person becoming more and more like God—a qualitative shift beyond the power of the person to achieve on his or her own:[39]

> . . . nothing can act beyond its species, since the cause must always be more powerful than its effect. Now the gift of grace surpasses every capability of created nature, since it is nothing short of a partaking of the Divine Nature, which exceeds

> every other nature. And thus it is impossible that any creature should cause grace. For it is as necessary that God alone should deify, bestowing a partaking of the Divine Nature by a participated likeness, as it is impossible that anything save fire should enkindle.[40]

In short, in reading the roles prescribed in the *Doctrine of the Mean* and *Genesis* as divinely or cosmically given as opposed to merely socially assigned, Thomas and Zhu assuage the kinds of concerns raised by social theorists such as Goffman and Parsons: although the person may well be subsumed by his or her role, or to the end to which the role tends, this happens in order that the self may reach a more joyful and glorified state than is possible otherwise. Moreover, infusing these roles with love (a practice in keeping with their overall comprehensive approach, in which no element of human or natural existence is neglected), makes a significant difference in how they are experienced as well. For the rest of the chapter, we will be discussing the ways in which people may prepare and be prepared to play the cosmic roles, and will close by considering what such a value-laden notion of role has to offer discussions of authority.

Given their understanding of the sacred, non-negotiable nature of the cosmic roles, the question of how best to prepare for and fulfill them is a central concern for both Thomas and Zhu. Their treatments have a great deal in common: as discussed in previous chapters, both focus on the importance of developing the entire person, but with emphasis on the intellect. In addition, both offer safeguards against not only despair but also delusional optimism when surveying this arduous but achievable goal.

However, differences between them exist as well. Briefly, Thomas seems to be more focused on the individual and his or her virtues, while Zhu pays a great deal of attention to the process of socialization in creating the good person. Before we continue, this basic difference must be addressed, lest the discussion below lead to simplistic and inaccurate readings of either or both.

A Methodological Issue

To begin with, it is clearly not the case that Zhu and his fellow Confucians are uninterested in individual virtue: in fact, A. S. Cua identifies Confucianism as an "ethics of virtue," pointing out that "throughout its long history, Confucianism has stressed character formation or personal cultivation of virtues (*te* [*de*]). Thus it seems appropriate to characterize Confucian ethics as an ethics of virtue."[41]

On the other hand, although Thomas is most often categorized as a virtue ethicist, there are those who favor a reading of Thomas based less on personal development of virtue and more on laws and precepts. For example, Kevin Flannery argues that "Aristotle and Thomas both accept moral absolutes, even with respect to particular acts . . . an Aristotelian ethical theory must be understood as having the general structure of an Aristotelian science. The moral analysis of particular acts involves, therefore, recognizing that acts are part of a larger structure, made up of analogues or first principles, theorems, definitions, etc."[42]

The question of whether to frame an exploration in terms of socially acceptable rules or personal virtues thus comes down not to fundamental differences between the two thinkers, but rather questions of emphasis. A virtue-based approach to Thomas is backed up by sheer numbers, as Eleonore Stump points out:

> . . . as Aquinas's treatment in his *Summa theologiae* and other works makes clear, his is a virtue based ethics. He does sometimes discuss moral principles or rules. So, for example, in *ST* he devotes one question each to the precepts of justice and of fortitude. But the precepts of justice turn out to be simply the Ten Commandments, and the precept of fortitude seems to be only the biblical commandment to be afraid of God rather than human beings. On the other hand, in 170 questions in the second part of the second part of *ST* (as well as in various other works), Aquinas lays out his account of the virtues for human beings.[43]

Such questions describe and analyze the virtues in great detail. On the other hand, the Confucian tradition in general does not treat virtues in such a way: Cua notes the "absence of definitions of important terms such as *jen* [*ren*, humaneness], *li* and *yi* [justice]."[44] The difference between Thomas and Zhu on this issue may be seen more clearly through comparing their treatments of their central virtues.

In Thomas's *Summa theologiae*, the central virtue of *caritas* is given twenty-four questions, further subdivided into dozens of articles, analyzing the virtue in terms of what it is in itself, what its subject is, what its object is, what its precepts are, how it is expressed, what is set against it, and what cooperates with it.[45] In Zhu's *Treatise on Humaneness* (*Renshuo*, 仁說), concerning the similar virtue of *ren* or humaneness, by contrast, there is a poetic celebration of its dignity and worth. (A very important note to keep in mind, given the oft-unquestioned tendency to view Confucian philosophy as less rigorous than its Western or Indian counterparts: Zhu's comparative lack of analysis is intended to inspire rigor in creativity of interpretation and practical application. As Wm. Theodore de Bary puts it: "for the Chinese the idea is not so much to analyze and define concepts precisely as to expand them, make them suggestive of the widest range possible of meaning."[46])

Another difference lies in the fact that, when Zhu defines virtue in a general sense, there is a focus on its interpersonal aspect that is missing in Thomas's more self-centered approach. While Thomas says that "virtue is a good quality of the mind, by which we live righteously, of which no one can make bad use,"[47] Zhu claims that,

> "Virtue" means being able to act upon seeing the good and being sure to reform upon hearing of faults; to be able to govern oneself; to be able to govern one's family; to be able to serve father and elder brothers; to be able to instruct sons and younger brothers; to be able to manage servants; to be able to serve superiors; to be friendly with relatives and acquaintances; to be able to choose friends; to be able to maintain integrity; to be able to extend kindness; to be able to fulfill a trust; to be able to relieve distress; to be able to correct faults; to be able to plan things for men; to be able to accomplish things for the people; to be able to resolve conflicts; to be able to decide right and wrong; to be able to promote the beneficial and abolish the harmful; to be able to hold office and reinvigorate offices.[48]

Such emphasis on the interpersonal qualities of virtue is reflected in Zhu's reverence for *LI* (禮).[49] *LI* is variously translated as "rite,"[50] "propriety,"[51] and "decorum,"[52] depending on issues of both translator preference and context. Whether denoting religious and social rituals themselves, their successful performance, or the virtue that enables such successful performance, *LI* is always used by Confucians in connection with appropriate behavior. It is with the third meaning in mind that Zhu links *LI* to his cosmological account: "nature is merely humaneness, righteousness, propriety (*LI*) and wisdom."[53]

While Zhu characteristically follows Mencius in linking the virtue of humaneness to commiseration, that of righteousness to shame and aversion, that of propriety to reverence, and wisdom to knowledge of right and wrong, he does not conceive of the relationship between the virtues and the feelings in exactly the same way as Mencius does. While Mencius says that commiseration and pity is the *sprout (duan,* 端) or beginning of the virtue of humaneness, Zhu says that commiseration is the *feeling*, while the humaneness is the *nature*: "Mencius said, 'The commiserating heart is the sprout of humaneness.' Humaneness is nature, commiseration is emotion . . . nature is substance, and emotions are function."[54] In Zhu's system, as is discussed in this section, the feelings are the *expression* of the nature,[55] while in Mencius's, the feelings are the *beginning* of the virtues.

To begin, Zhu claims, "in human beings, humaneness, righteousness, propriety and wisdom are the nature. Although these four have shape and form, they are also merely the way in which one possesses heavenly principle [which itself has no shape or form]. Having this honorable endowment of the Dao causes a great many things to come forth, enabling commiseration, shame and aversion, respect and reverence, and the knowledge of right and wrong."[56] For Zhu, these virtues are the substance that makes these emotions with which they are paired possible; indeed, the emotions are proof of the virtues: "how can we see that we have the four [virtues]? Because of the feeling of commiseration, we know that we have humaneness; because of the feeling of shame and aversion, we know that we have righteousness."[57]

These virtues are all held to be quite compatible; indeed, they are indispensable to each other. As Zhu says, propriety, righteousness, and wisdom are the expressions of humaneness, or *ren*: "the word '*ren*' has to be seen as combining righteousness, propriety and wisdom; then you will be able see it [fully]. [The virtue of] *ren* is the root of the original substance, [which is] *ren*; propriety is the refinement of *ren*; righteousness is its regulation, and wisdom is the discrimination of *ren*."[58]

Moreover, with more specific reference to *LI*: it is explicitly linked to the sage. According to Zhu, just as everyone else, "at the beginning stages, the sage is likewise only approximating *LI* to attain sincerity for himself; afterwards, he follows it more thoroughly and closely."[59] The valuation of this social virtue is of special importance, not just for reasons of propriety for its own sake (an important consideration), but also because such propriety enables the expression of humaneness. As Tu Weiming points out, "although *jen* [*ren*], especially when used as a comprehensive virtue, gives meaning to *li* [*LI*], *jen* without the manifestation of *li* is also inconceivable."[60] Zhu and others like him place a strong focus on a cooperative balance between these two cardinal virtues, in which *ren* tells one how to feel and *LI* tells one how to act accordingly. The relationship they share is hierarchical, in which neither contradicts the other, but the latter can be set aside in favor of the former in special cases. In a famous conversation in the *Mencius*, "Shun Yu Kuang asked, 'Is it not propriety that men and women may not touch each other when giving and receiving things?' Mencius replied, 'This is propriety.' 'If a man's sister-in-law is drowning, may he pull her out with his hand?' Mencius replied, 'He who does not rescue his drowning sister-in-law is a wolf. That men and women should not touch one another while giving and receiving things is [the general rule of] propriety. But when a sister-in-law is drowning, to rescue her by the hand is a particular exigency."[61]

Nonetheless, such exceptions to the rule notwithstanding, Confucians are generally more concerned with the problems that can arise when social mores are not understood or misapplied. For one thing, as the political scientist Geir Helgesen points out in his article on Confucian education, "if you fail to develop social skills, if you can't get along with your colleagues and friends, professional skills may be useless."[62] For another, the care and concern rooted in *ren* may lead one to wish to comfort a person who is suffering, but such comfort will be ill-expressed by behavior inappropriate to the occasion and relationship. For example, making off-color jokes accompanied by hard slaps on the back may work to cheer up a college football player, but will most likely not work so well with that football player's great-grandmother. One of the great Confucian insights is that, with very few exceptions, all behavior is ritualized: as Adam Seligman and his co-authors note in their *Ritual and Its Consequences: An Essay on the Limits of Sincerity*, "how can we express true sincerity except by filtering it through [social conventions]?"[63] It is clear that Zhu Xi and his tradition recognize the importance of properly behaving in accordance with social custom.

To return to Thomas: he certainly agrees with Zhu about the importance of getting along well with others. As he writes,

> . . . because man is a social animal he owes his fellow-man, in equity, the manifestation of truth without which human society could not last. Now as man could not live in society without truth, so likewise, not without joy, because, as the Philosopher says (Ethic. viii), no one could abide a day with

> the sad nor with the joyless. Therefore, a certain natural equity obliges a man to live agreeably with his fellow-men; unless some reason should oblige him to sadden them for their good.[64]

Moreover, that which enables people to live well and joyfully together is a *virtue*:

> . . . since virtue is directed to good, wherever there is a special kind of good, there must needs be a special kind of virtue. Now good consists in order . . . and it behooves man to be maintained in a becoming order towards other men as regards their mutual relations with one another, in point of both deeds and words, so that they behave towards one another in a becoming manner. Hence the need of a special virtue that maintains the becomingness of this order: and this virtue is called friendliness (*amicitia*).[65]

Nonetheless, this virtue, while connected to one of his cardinal virtues, is not a cardinal virtue itself: unlike Zhu, who identifies *LI* as one of the four most important and fundamental elements of human goodness, Thomas classifies friendliness as one of the "parts" of his core virtue of justice (*iustitia*).[66] Justice is an inherently other-regarding virtue roughly comparable to Zhu's *yi*, or righteousness. Nonetheless, justice in Thomas, while it does recognize social realities such as status (for example, he defines "distributive justice" as the virtue "whereby a ruler or a steward gives to each what his rank deserves"),[67] does not concern itself with matters of social ease *per se*, which Thomas explicitly describes as lacking in comparison with the virtue of justice itself: "[friendliness] *falls short* of the notion of justice, because it lacks the full aspect of debt, whereby one man is bound to another, either by legal debt, which the law binds him to pay, or by some debt arising out of a favor received. For it regards merely a certain debt of equity, namely, that we behave pleasantly to those among whom we dwell, unless at times, for some reason, it be necessary to displease them for some good purpose."[68]

Additionally, Thomas is similar to, but not identical with, Zhu Xi in explicitly recognizing the importance of the family, identifying piety toward one's parents as a virtue.[69] Reaching out to a wider circle, he also observes the important function played by society in the development of the individual and his or her character, especially by way of the laws it promulgates. Thomas believes that the "the proper effect of law is to make those to whom it is given, good:"[70] through acting in accordance with humanly (or divinely) promulgated laws designed to defend the common good, people may be expected to become good themselves. Well aware that not everyone is willing to develop his or her moral potential, he writes,

> . . . a private person cannot lead another to virtue efficaciously: for he can only advise, and if his advice be not taken, it has no coercive power, such as the law should have, in order to prove an efficacious inducement to virtue, as the Philosopher says (*Ethic*. x. 9). But this coercive power is vested in the whole people or in some public personage, to whom it belongs to inflict penalties . . wherefore the framing of laws belongs to him alone.[71]

Given the role played by social law in the development of virtue, the community—and particularly its leadership—is of immense importance to Thomas. Nonetheless, the bulk of his discussion is on the virtues themselves, as previously defined: of the 512 questions in the *Summa theologiae* that Thomas is known to have written himself, 211 concern virtue either directly (as does the bulk of the *Secunda secundae*) or indirectly (discussing matters intimately connected with the virtues, such as habits or vices). On the other hand, various types of law are given only 19 questions (in the *Prima secundae*), and instructions or advice concerning family life is given rarely and then without detail or development (a sample: men should not inflict "irreparable harm" upon their wives and children,[72] and "it is better that you should yourself help your own family, who would be ashamed to beg help from others").[73] In addition, while, as discussed in the Introduction, education was very important to Thomas, the people he was interested in educating were seminary students, and the type of education he was interested in was theological: he certainly did not provide eight-year-olds with tasks to perform or books to read. Unlike Zhu, who compiled a home ritual handbook (discussed further below), Thomas's work on specifically communal ritual was limited to his philosophical and technical discussion of the Seven Sacraments of the Catholic Church, and was meant for a limited and specialized readership of priests; it was certainly not intended to reach as wide an audience as Zhu's *Family Rituals*, which was designed to be useful for the virtuous development and life of ordinary families all over China.

Rather, when discussing the virtues, Thomas focuses on identifying and analyzing them, and on the role of the individual in developing them.

Based on these considerations of emphasis, the remainder of this chapter shall focus on how ritual and ritual education in Zhu, and virtuous habits in Thomas, help to develop intelligent agents with moral potential into people well prepared to play their roles, both social and cosmic, with and in love. Even given this difference, over the course of the discussion, we should keep in mind that the person characterized by virtuous responses to all is the end goal for Zhu's program of education, and that the laws provided to the individual by the community are important for encouraging and defining virtue for Thomas. Moreover, we should also bear in mind that growing in love is important for both philosophers as they seek to provide guidelines for developing in accordance with the roles they perceive as both innate and sacred. Such love will guard against despair during the long and difficult process of growth, as it seeks out and celebrates the good to be found in the self and the world, and also against the kind of delusional optimism that can put that good in danger through carelessness and lack of engagement. Finally, their shared conception of the human person as one who needs to develop his or her moral character has strong implications for the theories of authority to be found in both Thomas and Zhu.

Development of the Self

Zhu Xi and Socialization

> The world of thought is generally regarded as a vast territory. So it is; but it may not be as fantastic as it is touted to be. We have a prejudice that thought is free, untrammeled, infinitely open, unapproachable from outside. And yet—if thought is an internalization of rituals from social life, further developed by decomposition and recombination of its symbolic elements, in the train of impulses to externalize them again—how strange can it be? The private thinking among Chinese villagers in the Han dynasty must surely have been similar to each other because it was related to the rituals that they performed overtly, and thus differed in specifiable ways from the private thoughts, say, of middle-class Americans at

the turn of the twenty-first century.[74]

Perhaps in part due to a recognition of the importance of everyday life and interactions discussed above, Neo-Confucians—and Confucians before them—have always recognized the power of social context. As Randall Collins notes in the passage above, it is rather commonsensical to do so: it only makes sense to think that the communal rituals in which one participates, whether they be NFL-related or more conventionally religious, will have some impact on a person's self and inner life, and notions of propriety and etiquette—whether accepted or rejected—will as well. Nonetheless, as Robert Neville points out, this way of looking at things often raises hackles in contemporary America: "European Enlightenment egalitarianism distrusts manners that have to be learned from others through imitation (Confucius admits that this takes a lifetime). Rather, peasants and poor people are just as excellent as cultivated people if their heart is sincere, according to the typical American."[75]

However, in Confucianism, the rituals of *LI* are not limited to coronation ceremonies or finicky questions about which fork to use at a fancy dinner; rather, in the *Analects* of Confucius, social etiquette is presented as having a truly fundamental role in human society: "Youzi said, 'Among the functions of *LI*, the most valuable is that it establishes harmony.' "[76] This is not an idea solely relevant to the ancient or the medieval worlds; as Neville points out in *Boston Confucianism*, "where ritual propriety is not observed, or where a society lacks the rituals that articulate the diverse positions, needs and merits of its citizens, morality falls back to dependence on the following of moral rules and the happenchance exercise of good will." This state of affairs can be problematic given that, "unlike moral rules and good will, propriety is lodged in the habits of bones and muscles and in the deepest schemes of imagination."[77] In other words, while ritual and its attendant propriety admittedly can be an imposition on human nature, it can also lead to the development and refinement of the same.

In general, the Confucians, with their focus on ongoing process and relationship, are very aware of the transformative power of socialization, be it in the classroom or the temple. While, as Neville notes, "Chinese schools have differed over whether [the pure center of the self] is ever isolable,"[78] it's certainly the case that the Confucian tradition has always argued that the self, whether isolable or not, requires a great deal of training before it can be deemed fully human. Thus, for example, Mencius claims that, "the way of human beings [is that], if they are well fed, warmly clothed, and comfortably lodged but without education, they will become almost like the birds and beasts."[79] People need proper guidance in order to find their true inner nature, and so Mencius counseled kings to "establish seminaries, academies, schools, and institutes to teach the people."'[80]

Zhu followed this charge in his own day,[81] and paid especial attention to early childhood education.[82] Well aware of the limitations of the child's intellect and powers of concentration, he tells his own students, "you cannot teach small children about the Mandate of Heaven [or other such weighty matters]. In teaching small children, you should just get the gist of moral principle across, and only as accompanied by [other] preliminary matters."[83] Such preliminary matters encompass proper social behavior. Thus, Zhu writes, "'clothes are not mussed, feet are not stumbling; before ascending to the main hall, the voice must be raised; when entering a door/household, the eyes must be cast down': all of these rhyming phrases are sayings the ancients used when beginning to teach small children."[84] (Zhu also points out that such short sayings were created by all kinds of people in the ancient era, and for all kinds of purposes. For example, with regard to proper spousal relations and peace in the household, "Mencius' mother added two phrases: 'before walking through the door, ask who is in the room.")[85]

As implied in the discussion above, Zhu's ideal curriculum is based on his understanding of the education offered to people in antiquity: "when people reached the age of eight—from kings and dukes on down to the sons and younger brothers of the common people—they all entered elementary education [or lesser learning, *xiaoxue*, 小學], and were taught the regulations of sprinkling, sweeping, polite conversation and good manners, and the refinements of ritual (*LI*), music, archery, charioteering, calligraphy and mathematics."[86] In Zhu's own time, study of the Four Books he selected out of the Confucian tradition also took on a central role: "in studying, one must first read *The Great Learning*; second, he must read *The Analects*, followed by the *Mencius* and then the *Doctrine of the Mean*. The *Doctrine of the Mean* requires the most intense effort, for its scale is vast [and therefore it should be read last]."[87] Zhu is very insistent about the order in which the Four Books are read, based on his pedagogical theory concerning each one of them: "Require people to first read the *Great Learning*, in order that its scope may be established [in their minds]; then have them read the *Analects*, in order to set up the foundation [for further learning]; then have them read the

Mencius, in order to have them see the ways in which the [themes of the prior readings] are further developed; and then have them read the *Doctrine of the Mean*, in order to seek the minute and exquisite aspects of the teachings of the ancients."[88] His confidence in his curriculum is manifest when he exclaims, "if you can understand these Four Books, there is no book you cannot read, there is no principle you cannot examine, and there is no affair that you cannot handle!"[89]

As the last phrase in this quotation suggests, for Zhu, education was meant not only to develop a child's intellectual skills and train him in basic Confucian philosophy, but also to foster the kind of virtue that should accompany engagement with the affairs of other humans and the world at large: "in elementary education, the ancients cultivated small children's good sprouts of sincerity and reverence so that such might come to be seen."[90] Thus, in addition to performing humble tasks such as sweeping, children are to learn how to behave in a socially acceptable way: "elementary education is about affairs, such as how to serve the prince, serve the father, serve the elder brother, get along with friends, etc.; it is only to teach the student to act according to certain rules."[91] That children need such basic education, in the smallest of tasks, is not at issue. The *Yulei* tells us that "a child moved aside the fire and made a mess as he replenished the coals. The Master said, 'You can put the fire out by brushing it thusly. I do not love people who brush things aside; this is a disrespectful way of lighting a fire. Therefore the sages taught children sprinkling, sweeping and polite conversation, wanting people to be careful with all things.'"[92]

While Zhu recognized that such lessons may be learned without the benefit of a formal education ("certain sons and nephews outside the home, although they have not discussed the lessons of the worthies, when they come and go out of the house they are [still] neat and tidy. This is because their elders and superiors at home taught and admonished them to be like this from the beginning"),[93] ideally speaking, such basic training should prepare the student for greater things. The difference between preliminary and advanced education is less about substance and more about depth: "adult education [or greater learning, *daxue*, 大學] is about bringing forth the principle in all these things [children study]."[94] According to Zhu, once they had matured sufficiently, students in the ancient world were intended to begin adult education: "when they reached the age of fifteen, they would all enter into adult education, which was about penetrating principle and rectifying the mind-and-heart, the Way of self-cultivation [*xiuji*, 修己] and leadership [*zhiren*, 治人]."[95] In Zhu Xi's time, that both periods of education should come together into a cohesive whole is not at question:

> . . . someone asked, "is it not so that adult education and elementary education are not divided into two? Elementary education is about affairs, adult education about penetrating their principle: then how do you set the boundaries between them?" The Master answered, "They are only one affair. Elementary education is about things that are near, like studying how to serve relatives, elders, and moreover about truly understanding these affairs. Adult education is building on this foundation to more minutely investigate their principle, and thus to see what the essence of serving relatives really is, and what the essence of serving elders really is."[96]

Zhu's attention to the preliminary stages of education testifies to his belief that they are necessary to reach the point where the lessons of advanced education may be well-learned.[97]

Confucians realize that not all of this education is formal; they see quite clearly that it begins in the home. Indeed, they recognize that a child is trained in good, bad, and neutral ways by her parents, even at moments in which the parents are unaware of doing any training at all. In fact, to a certain extent, children *become their parents* through imitating them and absorbing their behaviors. As Joel Kupperman notes, "in Confucius' view, the self that a person develops (assuming that things go reasonably well), will be based on a primitive layer of imitation of parents (who had imitated their parents etc.), as well as of behavior that had been encouraged by parents. Are these things merely causes of the person one becomes? It is hard to deny that they become, generally speaking, constitutive."[98] As Kupperman says, "to speak for myself: increasingly I am aware at some moments of patterns of thought and reactive behavior that are uncannily and uncomfortably like one or the other of my parents."[99]

Given the importance of parenting, Zhu takes care to provide advice to mothers and fathers in his work. For example, in a chapter entitled "The Way to Regulate the Family" in his *Jinsilu*, he offers a moral model via Cheng Yi's panegyric to his mother, who did not allow her children to "speak harshly" (*eyan maren*, 惡言罵人) to their social inferiors, the "servant class" (*lingbei*, 令輩).[100] Reflecting on the success of her efforts, Cheng Yi explains, "it is not that we were naturally like this, but that we were taught to be so."[101] It should be noted here that, while this teaching has to do with kindness, such kindness does not mean that social distinctions are obliterated: the difference between inferior and superior social classes remains. As will be discussed more fully in Chapter 4, the hierarchical structure of society is left intact. Nonetheless, in situations where there is injustice between classes or people of different ranks, it should be recognized that, "at bottom, the issue is not the abuse of authority by those above versus the subversion of authority by those below, but the universal violation of the spirit of the [*LI*] on all sides giving free vent to unbridled lust, arbitrariness, caprice, cruelty, ambitions, and greed. The issue is obedience to the [*LI*]."[102] Therefore, such obedience is constitutive of the good life, and associations in accordance with it based upon mutual respect and performance of complementary duties are thus conceived of more as partnerships than as relationships of dominance and submission.

Hence, even after formal education has ended, adults have to act in certain ways. In the Preface to his *Family Rituals* (*JiaLI*, 家禮), Zhu writes, "commonly speaking, there is basic and refined ritual (*LI*). With regard to that which is practiced in the home, basic ritual consists of abiding by the norms of social status and giving concrete [expression] to love and respect. Refined ritual involves the composition and specifications of capping [rituals of reaching adulthood], marriage, funerals, and sacrificial rites."[103] He goes on to explain,

> . . . basic ritual involves the ordinary forms in daily use which [people] must not go even one day without performing. Refined ritual is all that through which one regulates the end and the beginning of the road of people [their lives]. Although the enactment of refined ritual has its seasons and its implementation has its [particular] place, if one does not speak of it clearly and become familiar with it, when these affairs draw near, one will not be able to do what is suitable and fitting. So, one cannot go one day without speaking of these.[104]

Unfortunately, from this point of view, "during the Three Dynasties, the ritual texts were adequate. However, in the texts that exist today, the regulations on homes, utensils and clothing, and the instructions on coming and going, rising and sitting, are no longer appropriate for this era."[105] The pressing need for contemporary guides to proper behavior leads Zhu to "presume to adhere to [the example of] Confucius through promoting ideas which were [once] lost,"[106] and to write his manual on the rituals to be performed in the home.

Of course, merely going through the motions of any of the practices he describes will not be sufficient for his purpose. As Confucius points out, behaving in accordance with *LI* is meaningless without sincere emotion behind it: "Ziyou asked about filial piety. Confucius answered, 'Today when people speak about filial piety, they mean providing nourishment for their parents. But they also can provide nourishment for dogs and horses. If one is not reverent, where is the difference?' "[107] Clearly, the rituals of proper social interaction that we learn in elementary education, study more fully in adult education, and practice throughout our lives are not meant to be a straightjacket within which we chafe and which binds us.[108] Rather, as Neville writes,

> . . . the Confucian point . . . is to modify the unacceptable unconscious feelings themselves by having those feelings participate in rituals of harmonization. The psychodynamic Freudian mechanism for modifying the unacceptable unconscious feelings has been to get them expressed and understood in a controlled environment, such as psychotherapeutic treatment. This mechanism has not always been very successful, and often the goal of treatment is just to learn to live with the unacceptable feelings. The Confucian tradition too has emphasized practices of self-analysis and discernment. Nevertheless it has also emphasized practices of harmonious meditation, movement, and the development of skills such as calligraphy for the purpose of tranquillizing the violent contradictions of the unconscious heart. The ritualized practice of harmonious feeling and movement can bring infantile rage into peaceful repose. Of course, all this must be embedded in larger patterns of harmonious social and personal life, but that too is part of the Confucian project.[109]

Moreover, ritual propriety produces not only peace and harmony, but, as Zhu points out in his discussion of basic ritual (above), it gives concrete expression to love. For Zhu, of the four cardinal virtues, *ren* is often paired with *LI*: "*ren* and *LI* are categorized under *yang* [the active principle], righteousness and wisdom are categorized under *yin* [the passive principle]; *ren* and *LI* are the function, righteousness and wisdom are the substance."[110] Indeed, he writes, "*ren* is the left hand, and *LI* is the right hand."[111] In the end, he believes that "*LI* is the expression of *ren*."[112] Note here that, unlike Thomas, who classifies his virtue of social ease, "friendliness," under the category of justice, Zhu goes out of his way to identify *LI*, a cardinal virtue in its own right, much more closely with *ren* than with *yi* or righteousness (the virtue roughly approximating Thomas's justice), claiming, for example, that "*ren* contains *LI*, and righteousness contains wisdom"[113] and that while *ren* also encompasses wisdom, "righteousness does not have *LI*."[114] Reading Zhu can thus make Christians more aware than they might have been otherwise that expressing the central Christian virtue of *caritas* requires a certain sense of what's appropriate in given situations, and raise the possibility that focusing on ritual propriety can have truly theological and salvific significance as they deepen their relationship with God, and also with their neighbors, in their daily lives.

According to moral philosopher A. S. Cua,

> . . . when we turn to the constitutive rules or the *li* [*LI*] that perform the ennobling function, we are concerned not merely with regulation of conduct, but more fundamentally with the realization of *tao [dao]*, the Confucian vision of human excellence. . . . The special role of *li* lies in their being the constitutive, rather than instrumental, means to the attainment of *jen* [*ren*] . . . for ultimately the good life is also an elegant and beautiful form of life.[115]

Moreover, the Confucian approach also recognizes that "although man has always been conditioned by a given structure beyond his control, the ultimate ground of his self-realization lies within his own nature."[116] In a similar vein, Henry Rosemont notes: "there are many ways to be a good teacher, spouse, sibling, friend, and so forth; if Confucian persons aren't free, autonomous individuals, they aren't dull, faceless automatons, either."[117] Thus, rather than negatively conceiving of the acts of *LI* as things that artificially constrict and suppress one's natural autonomy, it might be wise to recognize that the Confucian valuation of *LI* positively embraces the reality that we are social creatures in social contexts, who need to develop whatever moral potential we have in concert with others, in a spirit of love.

In fact, without this love, it seems that none of the other virtues will come into play: "Someone asked, '*ren* is that which is obtained first of all; is this why we say "*ren yi li zhi*" [in this order]?' The master replied, 'First you have this beginning principle, and the three others are deduced from it."[118] He also says, "*ren* is the first of the four sprouts [of virtue]."[119] Moreover, the other virtues—including *LI*—are seen as expressions of *ren*. "[The virtue of] *ren* is the root of the original substance [which is] *ren*; propriety is the refinement of *ren*; righteousness is its regulation, and wisdom is the discrimination of *ren*."[120] In fact, the other virtues are seen as coming forth out of *ren*: "*ren* includes the other three. Righteousness, propriety and wisdom are all flowing things, so that all are gradually deduced from *ren*."[121] *Ren* is thus seen as integral to the other three cardinal virtues, which are not stolid entities, but rather dynamic and expressive in nature: "*Ren* is in affairs. If you cannot see it in affairs, then how can you see it?"[122] Moreover, as Zhu notes, "doing a suitable thing: this is also *ren*."[123]

The difficulty of the process of learning to do and then actually doing a suitable thing cannot be denied. Indeed, religious faith is necessary in a characteristically practical Confucian way: the student will need it to keep going down the long road that may be traveled before any real understanding or progress is attained. As Zhu warns, the process will teach the participant more about her own limitations than she had ever imagined: "in the beginning you say you can do a hundred things; in the end you're unable to do even one!"[124] As he goes on to explain, "this saying speaks of the evils that befall the person who does not focus on one thing but greedily reads too widely."[125] The presence of *li* (principle) and *ren* in even the smallest of things and affairs means that each must be carefully considered and valued: rushing through the process in order to get to the next step will not suffice. With such statements, Zhu clearly means to dispel any delusional optimism students may have concerning their own abilities for speedy advancement along the moral road: the religious faith of Zhu reminds us that commitment, and over a long period of time, will be necessary for true learning and living in accordance with the deepest truths recognized by his tradition.

However, neither should people despair when they find themselves struggling; when his students face challenges that seem beyond their capacity to meet, Zhu tells them to adjust their expectations in a spirit of moderation and modesty: "one cannot want to do everything at once. In a day, a man can only eat three bowls of rice, [and] cannot eat ten or more days' worth of rice at one sitting: just so, in a day you can read only so much, and your efforts have a limit as well. You cannot want to do everything at once."[126] In paying due attention to the difficulties of moral cultivation while maintaining his belief in the fundamentally good nature of human beings, Zhu offers a reasonable hope for human advancement, both on the individual and communal levels.

This hopefulness is reflected in the mission of his educational project, which is designed to produce a person who acts in love toward all: the co-creator of the cosmos. The proper portrayal of this role will be discussed further below; for the present, we turn to Thomas Aquinas.

Thomas Aquinas and the Virtues

As previously noted, Thomas focuses less on socialization than does Zhu. Thus, the following discussion, concentrated as it is on the formation and matter of the individual person, may indirectly lead one to think of Thomas as an individualist. But he definitely sees the person as a social being: "in order that man may do well, whether in the works of the active life, or in those of the contemplative life, he needs the fellowship of friends."[127] While the importance of other human friends is questionable in the afterlife,[128] it is well to bear in mind through the course of this discussion that, as Torrell puts it,

> Thomas never thinks of man in the individualistic terms that have predominated in Western civilization since the Renaissance and Reformation. He always sees him as engaged with the community of the saved, which he calls ecclesia or populus, a community of Christ's faithful (*congregatio fidelium*), communion of saints (*societas sanctorum*), or Mystical Body of Christ—to be sure, without ever abstracting from the great human family of which it is a member by birth.[129]

To begin: Thomas was no Stoic. In the *Prima Secundae*, he begins his answer to question 24 in seeming agreement with the position of that school on the passions: "[the Stoics] held that every passion of the soul lessens the goodness of an act; since the admixture of evil either destroys good altogether, or makes it to be less good. And this is true indeed, if by passions we understand none but the inordinate movements of the sensitive appetite, considered as disturbances or ailments."[130] However, as he immediately goes on to explain, he does not limit his own definition of passion to these terms: "but if we give the name of passions to all the movements of the sensitive appetite, then it belongs to the perfection of man's good that his passions be moderated by reason. For since man's good is founded on reason as its root, that good will be all the more perfect, according as it extends to more things pertaining to man."[131] As the discussion continues, it becomes less and less Stoic, as he develops his position that *amor*, or love, the passion that responds to any good perceived by the human being, is practically inescapable:

> . . . passion is the effect of the agent on the patient . . . the first change wrought in the appetite by the appetible object is called "love," and is nothing else than complacency in that object; and from this complacency results a movement towards that same object, and this movement is "desire"; and lastly, there is rest which is "joy." Since, therefore, love consists in a change wrought in the appetite by the appetible object, it is evident that love is a passion: properly so called, according as it is in the concupiscible faculty; in a wider and extended sense, according as it is in the will.[132]

Before moving forward, I should note that Thomas's conception of love, here explained narrowly in terms of a positive attitude, turns out to be much broader. As he explains,

> We find four words referring in a way, to the same thing: viz. love [*amor*], dilection [*dilectio*], charity [*caritas*] and friendship [*amicitia*]. They differ, however, in this, that "friendship," according to the Philosopher (Ethic. viii, 5), "is like a habit," whereas "love" and "dilection" are expressed by way of act or passion; and "charity" can be taken either way.

> Moreover these three express act in different ways. For love has a wider signification than the others, since every dilection or charity is love, but not vice versa. Because dilection implies, in addition to love, a choice [*electionem*] made beforehand, as the very word denotes: and therefore dilection is not in the concupiscible power, but only in the will, and only in the rational nature. Charity denotes, in addition to love, a certain perfection of love, in so far as that which is loved is held to be of great price, as the word itself implies [Referring to the Latin "*carus*" (dear)].[133]

This systematic classification promises a careful distinction between similar terms that join together in overarching ways. Nonetheless, Thomas's usage of these terms turns out to be not nearly as precise as one might expect on the basis of this passage. In particular, as Peter Kwasniewski points out in his introduction to a partial translation of Thomas's *Commentary on the Sentences of Peter Lombard*, "the translator's trouble begins with *amor/amare* and *dilectio/diligere* . . . [Thomas] never shows the slightest hesitation in using *amor/amare* for *all* loves, supernatural and natural, intellectual and sensual . . . In actual practice, when speaking of *caritas* he readily uses *dilectio* and *amor* (with their verbs) as synonyms, quite interchangeably."[134] Thus, in the *Summa theologiae*, to take just one example, we find him saying that "charity elicits the act of love (*dilectionis*) not only as regards the object, but also as regards the lover (*diligentis*), as stated above. The result is that the man who is more nearly united to us is more loved (*amatur*)."[135] Given this lack of precision in Thomas himself, this discussion will follow the Dominican fathers in not distinguishing between the love of *amor* and the love of *dilectio*—both of which dispose the lover in a positive way to the beloved. As Thomas points out, "to love (*amare*) a man is to wish him good things, as the Philosopher states (Rhet. ii, 4)."[136] Moreover, as we will see below in our discussion of *caritas*, perfect love of one's neighbor requires not only such a wish, but also its active expression.

The importance Thomas assigns to love is not an exception in his treatment of the passions at large. In fact, the value of good passions is so strong as to require that reason cooperate in producing them: "virtue overcomes inordinate passion [and] produces ordinate passion."[137] As Gilson notes, "for Aquinas, the Christian's beatitude is the beatitude of the whole person:"[138] the passions, the intellect, and the will are all to be included, but under Aristotelian reason. In arguing in this way, Thomas provides a much more realistic ethical system than that of the Stoics; as Walter Farrell points out, the passions will always be with us, even with those of us who do not want them: "no matter how many hours he spends practicing facial immobility before a mirror, no man can tell himself that he does not feel love, desire, fear, hatred and the rest."[139]

One of the challenges that Thomas has to face is that, due to a variety of factors, a moral agent may make mistakes in identifying and desiring the genuine or proper good at any given time. (Partly for this reason Thomas sees the passions as morally neutral in themselves: as Kevin White notes, "Aquinas does argue that some passions, such as compassion and shame, are inherently good, and others, such as envy, inherently evil (Ia IIae, q. 24, a. 4), but the paucity of his examples suggests that most kinds of passions are of themselves morally neutral, allowing the presence or the absence of reason's moderating influence.")[140] One such factor has to do with the state of passions in the moment: "according as we are variously disposed in the matter of concupiscence, anger, fear, and other passions, something will at different times be viewed by us as good or evil."[141] Although we may see it differently depending on how we are disposed to it, the thing itself may stay the same, and in many cases will, all else being equal: the objective value or worth of the thing under consideration is understood to withstand the fluctuations of passions on the part of the human agent. Thomas claims that "all knowledge is perfected by the assimilation of the knower to the thing known; hence, assimilation is said to be the cause of knowledge."[142] This assimilation most assuredly is primarily rooted not in the knower, but in the thing known: "the truth which is caused in the rational soul by things, does not follow the estimation of the rational soul but the existence of the things [themselves], since so far as the thing is or is not, speech is [likewise] true or false."[143] Here, as elsewhere, the possibility for objective or accurate forms of moral and other knowledge remains a key tenet for Thomas.

The dispositions that influence our capacity for true knowledge may be either momentary or long-standing. The latter type Thomas calls habits (*habitus*). Quoting Aristotle, he defines a habit as a "disposition whereby that which is disposed is disposed well or ill, and this, either in regard to itself or in regard to another."[144] While Thomas considers that "some [habits] can be caused by nature, and some not,"[145] those which are "not" are the main focus of his treatment.

Generally speaking, Thomas holds us responsible for our dispositions. He does admit of some cases where the agent is not responsible for her actions, but they are few.[146] In his understanding, it is within our control to develop habits in our powers of reason and will through the choices we make and the things that we do over time: "if the acts be multiplied a certain quality is formed in the power which is passive and moved, which quality is called a habit."[147] Such habits do not necessarily carry with them any moral value. For example, furrowing one's brow while thinking, humming tunelessly when reading, or swinging one's arms while walking are all forms of behavior that, in their individual instances, Thomas would place in the categories of "act of man (*actus hominus*)" as opposed to the morally significant category of "human act (*actus humanus*)."[148] If a person tends to do these things on a regular basis, to the point where they become characteristic of him or her, they may be called habits, for " 'habit' implies a disposition in relation to a thing's nature, and to its operation or end, by reason of which disposition a thing is well or ill disposed thereto."[149]

Nonetheless, as discussed below, the habits that keenly interest

Thomas are those with moral weight: the virtues and the vices. In fact, the vast majority of habits are either morally desirable or reprehensible. In the Thomistic scheme, irrational habits are vices, and habits that are in accord with reason are virtues.[150] In an effort to forestall those who would assign a more static quality to virtue, he explains that sometimes we can be careless with differentiating between the virtue and that toward which it tends: "sometimes we give the name of a virtue to that to which the virtue is directed, namely, either to its object, or to its act: for instance, we give the name Faith, to that which we believe, or to the act of believing, as also to the habit by which we believe. When therefore we say that 'virtue is the limit of power,' virtue is taken for the object of virtue."[151] Further emphasizing the dynamism of such attributes, Thomas defines virtues as *operative habits*.[152]

These virtues are quite comprehensive: in Thomas's understanding, the entire person needs perfection. With an eye to achieving this fully comprehensive happiness, Thomas takes care to differentiate between the rational and irrational souls, the latter containing both the "vegetative" part (which controls digestion, etc., and is not linked to the virtues)[153] and the part which, though irrational in itself, is "in a sense receptive of reason."[154] The irrational soul is the part of the soul most closely linked to the body and its appetites, and needs its own special set of virtues, distinct from those of the rational soul: "virtue, too, is divided into classes in accordance with this differentiation of the soul. Some virtues are called intellectual and others moral; wisdom and understanding and prudence are intellectual; liberality and temperance are moral virtues."[155] Thomas adopts the basic Aristotelian moral anthropology, and also divides the virtues accordingly:

> . . . for a man to do a good deed, it is requisite not only that his reason be well disposed by means of a habit of intellectual virtue; but also that his appetite be well disposed by means of a habit of moral virtue. And so moral differs from intellectual virtue, even as the appetite differs from the reason. Hence just as the appetite is the principle of human acts, in so far as it partakes of reason, so are moral habits to be considered virtues in so far as they are in conformity with reason.[156]

Thomas agrees with Aristotle in giving a fundamental role to reason in the exercise of virtue: in the quote immediately above, moral habits become virtues "in so far as they are in conformity with reason."

Finally, Thomas agrees with Aristotle in ranking the intellectual virtues more highly than the moral. According to Aristotle, "if happiness is an activity in accord with virtue, it is reasonable to assume that it is in accordance with the highest virtue, and this will be the virtue of the best part of us . . . [contemplation] is the highest form of activity (since the intellect is the highest thing in us, and the objects it apprehends are the highest that can be known) . . ."[157] Thomas betrays a similar sensibility when he writes, "the intellectual virtues are about those things whereby a man is made happy; both because the acts of these virtues can be meritorious, as stated above, and because they are a kind of beginning of perfect bliss, which consists in the contemplation of truth."[158]

However more or less important than the intellectual virtues the moral virtues turn out to be, there is no doubt that they, as virtues, are extraordinarily significant for the person who possesses them. As Thomas quotes with approval: "Augustine says (De Moribus Eccl. vi): 'No one can doubt that virtue makes the soul exceeding good': and the Philosopher says (Ethic. ii, 6): 'Virtue is that which makes its possessor good, and his work good likewise.'"[159] Thus, as Zagzebski puts it, "a virtue is a deep quality of a person, closely identified with her selfhood, whereas natural faculties are only the raw materials for the self."[160] Such identity means we associate people with their virtues, and see virtues as constitutive of their very selves, as "characteristics which become natural and enduring through long practice, *thereby making the individual, in one way or another, the person she is*: a brilliant mathematician, a brave soldier, or a faithful wife, and, likewise, negatively, a mathematical moron, a contemptible coward, or a despicable cheat."[161]

Part of the justification for such value-laden terminology may rest in a Thomistic notion of the free will of the agent in creating his own virtues or vices. As Thomas says,

> . . . man acts from judgment, because by his apprehensive power he judges that something should be avoided or sought. But because this judgment, in the case of some particular act, is not from a natural instinct, but from some act of comparison in the reason, therefore he acts from free judgment and retains the power of being inclined to various things. For reason in contingent matters may follow opposite courses, as we see in dialectic syllogisms and rhetorical arguments. Now particular operations are contingent, and therefore in such matters the judgment of reason may follow opposite courses,

> and is not determinate to one. And forasmuch as man is rational is it necessary that man have a free-will.[162]

Thus, a person has freedom to choose to do things that will or will not develop habits. Whichever habits are formed, however, will in time develop a life of their own, influencing not only the will, but also the intellect. As Eleonore Stump explains,

> [with every wrong action] there is a misprogramming of the intellect, and the misprogrammed intellect twists the will, which in turn misprograms the intellect further. These misprogrammings can progress until they reach the point where a man like [Nazi Franz] Stangl, who at first could hardly bear the painless death of the severely disabled, subsequently was able to oversee with a quietened conscience tortures and killings that now sicken even those who read only pale descriptions of them.[163]

As Thomas points out, a bad habit or vice makes us disinclined to perceive the true good, for "to anyone that has a habit, whatever is befitting to him in respect of that habit, has the aspect of something lovable, since it thereby becomes, in a way, connatural (*connaturale*) to him, according as custom and habit are a second nature (*vertitur in naturam*)."[164] In the words of religious studies scholar Judith Kay, with bad habits, "the good becomes obscured from us, and we are unable to discern which of our many longings is truly human. We become mistaken about the overall good that gives truly human shape to our lives. We become repulsed by true goods and attracted by false ones."[165] Hence, as Thomas tells us, "the sweet is pleasant but to some, the sweetness of wine is most pleasant, to others, the sweetness of honey, or of something similar. Yet that sweet is absolutely the best of all pleasant things, in which he who has the best taste takes most pleasure."[166] (In this, Thomas follows the teaching of Aristotle very closely: "the object of wish is the good, but for the individual it is what seems good to him; so for the man of good character it is the true good, but for the bad man it is any chance thing."[167]) The person who is good will desire what is good and the person who is less than proactive about moral development, sadly, will not, and, by failing to do so over time will endanger attainment of his or her true last end.

As discussed in Chapter 2, according to Thomas, we are beings born with original sin who are nonetheless created to see the face of God. This supernatural end, to be fully enjoyed by the blessed after death,[168] requires more than the intellectual and moral virtues he takes from Aristotle, the latter of whom does not think much about life after death, saying simply, "the future is obscure to us."[169] He does go into slightly more detail several lines later, but the still rather vague picture hardly resembles anything like a Thomistic beatific vision: "if any effect of good or evil reaches [the dead] at all, it must be faint and slight, either in itself or to them—or if not that, at any rate not of such force and quality as to make the unhappy happy or to rob the happy of their felicity."[170] Moreover, he sees death itself chiefly in terms of a test of virtue rather than an occasion for its continued exercise: "the more completely a man possesses virtue, and the happier he is, the more he will be distressed at the thought of death. For to such a man life is supremely worth living; and he is losing the greatest blessings, and he knows it: and this is a grievous thing."[171] As a Christian, Thomas not only has a far more robust theory of the afterlife, but also believes that we are born desiring God himself.

The idea that human beings have an innate desire for God may seem odd to contemporary readers, who live in secular societies that socially and legally treat religion as a matter of personal conscience, or even taste. As Torrell tells us, the strangeness of this idea is due to

> . . . the complete change in perspective that intervened between the thirteenth century and the epoch begun by the Renaissance and the Reformation, when the word "nature" . . . began to signify nothing more than "pure" nature, as was said, which means the nature of a man solely defined as a rational animal, without the least supernatural gift, without the least vocation to share the divine condition or to see God. That nature clearly can have no aspiration to share the divine life for which it was not made; it finds itself in that regard in a state of simple non-repugnance, like the marble that certainly can become a statue under the hands of Michelangelo, but that neither asks for not wishes it, and had no "desire" for it.[172]

Saint Thomas's understanding of human nature is quite incompatible with this account. For Thomas, every human being is created with the innate desire for God. As he explains,

> . . . it is impossible for any created good to constitute man's happiness. For happiness is the perfect good, which lulls the appetite altogether; else it would not be the last end, if something yet remained to be desired. Now the object of the will, i.e., of man's appetite, is the universal good; just as the object of the intellect is the universal true. Hence it is evident that naught can lull man's will, save the universal good. This is to be found, not in any creature, but in God alone; because every creature has goodness by participation. Wherefore God alone can satisfy the will of man.[173]

Thus, the simple, even biological inclination toward the good that is experienced through *amor* as a basic passion is developed in the Thomistic system to become the basis for the virtue of *caritas*, which much like the virtue of *ren* is deeply grounded in human nature. *Caritas*, or charity, is principally love (here, *dilectio*) for God: "God ought to be loved [*dilegendo*] chiefly and before all out of charity."[174] This virtue Thomas defines as one of the "theological virtues [*virtutes theologicae*]."[175] Such theological virtues are meant to aid people in attaining their last end, and serve as the earthly foretaste of the eternal happiness that awaits the blessed in the next life.[176]

However, this is not to say that the theological virtues have no bearing on the here and now. For one thing, while *caritas* is primarily directed toward God, it is not solely directed at God. Thomas understands that love of neighbor is intimately linked to love of God: "it is specifically the same act whereby we love God, and whereby we love our neighbor."[177] His reasoning for this claim is as follows:

> . . . habits are not differentiated except their acts be of different species. For every act of the one species belongs to the same habit. Now since the species of an act is derived from its object, considered under its formal aspect, it follows of necessity that it is specifically the same act that tends to an aspect of the object, and that tends to the object under that aspect: thus it is specifically the same visual act whereby we see the light, and whereby we see the color under the aspect of light. Now the aspect under which our neighbor is to be loved, is God, since what we ought to love in our neighbor is that he may be in God . . . Consequently the habit of charity extends not only to the love of God, but also to the love of our neighbor.[178]

Moreover, this is also the same habit through which we love ourselves as partakers of and participants in the goodness that is God.[179]

The this-worldly nature of *caritas* becomes even clearer when it is realized that the love of *caritas* must be expressed in overt action. Thomas says that "charity cannot remain lifeless"[180] and that "charity is essentially a virtue ordained to act."[181] Therefore, people are required to positively exert their *caritas* in neighbor-directed acts of beneficence (*beneficentia*, which Thomas says "simply means doing good to someone,"),[182] almsgiving (*eleemosyna*),[183] and fraternal correction (*correctio fraterna*).[184] In fact, if people do not engage in these activities, they will experience the loss of *caritas* and its attendant joy and peace,[185] for venial sins or lassitude in its exercise will contribute to the diminution of *caritas*.[186] Furthermore, as questions 34–43 warn us, it is dangerous to stop engaging in these activities because doing so might allow or even encourage the development of vices that are opposed to the virtue of *caritas*, whether directly (hatred, 34) or indirectly through opposing its internal acts of joy (sloth [35] and envy [36]) and peace (discord [37], contention [38], schism [39], war [40], strife [41], and sedition [42]), and its more external act of beneficence (scandal [43]).

A great deal of care is hence necessary to maintain and develop *caritas*, which can be completely destroyed by one mortal sin. The theological virtue of charity is different from the acquired virtues in that it can disappear so quickly and completely:

> . . . if indeed charity were an acquired habit dependent on the power of its subject, it would not necessarily be removed by one mortal sin, for act is directly contrary, not to habit but to act. Now the endurance of a habit in its subject does not require the endurance of its act, so that when a contrary act supervenes the acquired habit is not at once done away. But charity, being an infused habit, depends on the action of God Who infuses it, Who stands in relation to the infusion and safekeeping of charity, as the sun does to the diffusion of light in the air . . . Consequently, just as the light would cease at once in the air, were an obstacle placed to its being lit up by the sun, even so charity ceases at once to be in the soul through the placing of an obstacle to the outpouring of charity by God into the soul. Now it is evident that through every mortal sin which is contrary to God's commandments, an obstacle is placed to the outpouring of charity, since from

> the very fact that a man chooses to prefer sin to God's friendship, which requires that we should obey His will, it follows that the habit of charity is lost at once through one mortal sin.[187]

The trouble *caritas* may require, however, is more than worthwhile. While, as discussed in Chapter 2, Thomas disagrees with Augustine's claim that one cannot speak about real virtue outside of a Christian context, he nonetheless shares a sense with the latter about the importance of *caritas*, calling it the mother of all other virtues[188] (the conclusion to this chapter discusses this issue in more detail). Much like Zhu's *ren*, Thomas's *caritas* takes center stage, and is identified as springing out of the deepest and most fundamental places of the human being. Given the predominant place he assigns to the threefold love of God, self, and other, it is hardly surprising that, rather than granting the individual human person complete autonomy or freedom in deciding her own ends, he writes, "a man's will is not right in willing a particular good, unless he refer it to the common good as an end."[189] Hence, the inclination toward the good, whether instinctive (*amor*) or rational (*dilectio*), which causes a desire for the flourishing of the same good, is fully realized in *caritas*, which carries with it a strong focus on helping others.

As the above discussion strongly implies, the project of developing ourselves to play our proper role as stewards is a daunting one. People may begin to despair when they consider the complex demands involved, especially if they have already developed a second nature comprised of rather too many bad habits. Nonetheless, in Thomas's understanding, there is always hope for progress even in the worst sinner, so long as he or she remains committed to the project of living in accordance with the deepest truths of Christianity.

First, while habits are indeed strong, they never completely overcome the moral actor; Thomas understands that free will always remains. As he explains,

> . . . the position of a habit in the soul is not the same as that of a form in a natural thing. For the form of a natural thing produces, of necessity, an operation befitting itself; wherefore a natural form is incompatible with the act of a contrary form: thus heat is incompatible with the act of cooling, and lightness with downward movement (except perhaps violence be used by some extrinsic mover): whereas the habit that

> resides in the soul, does not, of necessity, produce its operation, but is used by man when he wills. Consequently man, while possessing a habit, may either fail to use the habit, or produce a contrary act; and so a man having a virtue may produce an act of sin.[190]

Moreover, for purposes of hope: it is equally possible for a man or a woman possessing a vice to produce an act of virtue. As noted in Chapter 2, Thomas believes that "evil is the privation of good,"[191] and that this evil can never become more fundamental than good: "if the wholly evil could be, it would destroy itself; because all good being destroyed (which it need be for something to be wholly evil), evil itself would be taken away, since its subject is good."[192] If some good always remains even within the most dissipated or malicious character, it is always there to be exerted. With this kind of thinking, Thomas departs from Aristotle, the latter of whom writes

> . . . there was a time when it was open to the [sick man] not to be ill; but when he had thrown away his chance, it was gone; just as when one has once let go of a stone, it is too late to get it back—but the agent was responsible for throwing it, because the origin of the action was in himself. So too it was first open to the unjust and licentious persons not to become such, and therefore they are voluntarily what they are; but now that they have become what they are, it is no longer open to them to be such.[193]

In Thomas, we see no room for such despair; nor for that matter, for what we might term Aristotle's delusional optimism regarding the truly virtuous: people are never fully "safe," nor completely lost, so long as they are alive.

Second, while human virtue can be developed on the basis of human effort over time, Thomas also reminds us that God can work within us at any moment in accordance with His divine plan and will:

> . . . human virtue directed to the good which is defined according to the rule of human reason can be caused by human acts: inasmuch as such acts proceed from reason, by whose power and rule the aforesaid good is established. On the other hand, virtue which directs man to good as defined

> by the Divine Law, and not by human reason, cannot be caused by human acts, the principle of which is reason, but is produced in us by the Divine operation alone.[194]

With this understanding in mind, it is hardly surprising that Thomas explicitly disapproves of both despair and presumption. The former, which Thomas says "consists in a man ceasing to hope for a share of God's goodness,"[195] is set against the latter, defined as twofold: one type in which "a man relies on his own power, when he attempts something beyond his power, as though it were possible to him," and the other involving "inordinate trust in the Divine mercy or power."[196] Thomas considers them both vices: "for just as it is false that God does not pardon the repentant, or that He does not turn sinners to repentance, so is it false that He grants forgiveness to those who persevere in their sins, and that He gives glory to those who cease from good works."[197] On the other hand, despair is particularly "dangerous," says Thomas, because "when hope is given up, men rush headlong into sin, and are drawn away from good works,"[198] while presumption encourages sinful behavior with its characteristic belief that one may obtain "glory without merits, or pardon without repentance."[199] (Particularly gloomy Christians may wish to take note of Thomas's judgment that, while both are sins, presumption is "less grave than despair, since, on account of His infinite goodness, it is more proper to God to have mercy and to spare, than to punish: for the former becomes God in Himself, the latter becomes Him by reason of our sins."[200]) Like Zhu, Thomas counsels reasonable hope for human advancement, based on a cooperative relationship with God in which divine intervention is not viewed as a substitute for human effort, but rather as assisting it. Here, as elsewhere, Thomas takes into account the complexity of human experience, and in so doing, provides lessons as to how we can harmonize its various elements—in this case, as stewards of a genuinely common good.

Fulfilling the Role

The teachings of both Zhu and Thomas on the proper development of the self—becoming more sagelike in the first case, and more like God in the second—have significant results not merely in terms of the kind of person one is to become, but also in the kind of activities in which one is to participate—in short, in terms of the kind of role one is to undertake.

Zhu Xi: Assisting the Universe

In Zhu's case, as Michael Kalton puts it, "nothing about the Confucian framework systematically limits its applicability only to humans."[201] Rather, as Tu Weiming says, in this tradition, it is possible to "see ourselves in terms of a series of concentric circles: self, family, community, nation, world, and cosmos."[202]

The documents of the tradition bear out this reading. One of the most famous essays in the Neo-Confucian tradition, Zhang Zai's (張載, 1020–1077) "*Western Inscription*" (*Ximing*, 西銘), begins:

> I call Heaven, father, and I call Earth, mother. Even such a small creature as I finds a place in their midst./ Therefore that which fills the cosmos I regard as my substance and that which directs the cosmos I consider my nature. / All people are my brothers and sisters, and all things are my companions.[203]

As noted here, and in the discussion of the cosmological account in the *Jinsilu*, "not only are we and the rest of the world inseparably intertwined, not only do we share significant constituents, we have the same fundamental nature."[204] As Zhu says in his cosmological account, "humaneness is wood, righteousness is metal, propriety is fire, wisdom is water, and faithfulness is earth."[205] This understanding of the universe leads to a value system that does not place human desires and ends on a plateau above those of the rest of the world, but includes a reference to all other parts of existence. Such an understanding is intended to imbue people with a respect for the oftentimes mute forces of nature, in all of its forms, great and small. Rodney Taylor claims that "the 'Western Inscription' is not simply a description of the interrelatedness of all things, it is a call to act in a manner that recognizes such interrelatedness."[206]

Of course, if humans do not respond to this call, the Chinese tradition as a whole tells us that disaster may well result. As Livia Kohn explains, "potentially a great source of disharmony in the cosmos, humanity is not only in a position of central importance but also in one of highest responsibility. Earthquakes, floods and tornadoes are thus entirely our own fault, a sign that all is not well in the lives of people and the government of the land."[207] Tu Weiming claims that this intense awareness of the natural environment, and our relationship with it, especially as expressed in the doctrine of the trinity of Heaven,

Earth, and humankind, "transcends secular humanism, a blatant form of anthropocentrism characteristic of the intellectual ethos of the modern West. Indeed, it is in the anthropocosmic spirit that we find communication between self and community, harmony between human species and nature, and mutuality between human beings and Heaven."[208] Cua offers a different reading of this doctrine, one perhaps more in keeping with the Western "secular humanism" censured by Tu: "[The trinity of Heaven, Earth, and man] is unabashedly anthropocentric, for the natural order is always potentially subject to practical causation and thus conformable to moral wishes and desires. Failure in practical causation is assigned to *t'ien-ming*, but this again requires self-examination of where the failure lies."[209] Given the impossibility of wholly controlling the actions of Heaven—or even of predicting them—demonstrated by Confucius, and discussed earlier in Chapter 2, I side with Tu in this case. Zhu Xi's worldview does not place humans at the center of the universe, but rather as sharing center stage with two other key players—Heaven and Earth. Moreover, neither are human interests given center stage. Indeed, in this vision, the human project becomes one that features the essential characteristics and supreme values of "mutuality between self and community, harmony between human species and nature, and continuous communication with Heaven."[210]

Thomas Aquinas: Bringing About the Good of All

While Thomas claims that people act in a God-like manner merely by using the innate human power to rationally decide between different courses of action—"man is said to be made to God's image, in so far as the image implies *an intelligent being endowed with free-will and self-movement*"[211]—it's also the case that he conceives of far greater identification with the divine. As Colman O'Neill puts it, in the case of Thomas, the light of grace is conceived of not as a static, but a dynamic quality: "[grace] raises up the essence and faculties of the creature so that he or she can *act* in a divine fashion."[212] Once a person, with the help of divine grace through theological and divinely infused[213] virtues, becomes like God, he or she will be moved to act in a God-like manner, which will involve the communication of goodness:

> . . . the more perfect something is in its power, and the higher it is in the scale of goodness, the more does it have an appetite for a broader common good, and the more does it

> seek and become involved in the doing of good for beings far removed from itself. Indeed, imperfect beings tend only to the good proper to the individual, while perfect beings tend to the good of the species. But more perfect beings tend to the good of the genus, while God, Who is most perfect in goodness, tends towards the good of being as a whole. Hence it is said by some people, and not inappropriately, that the good, as such, is diffusive, because the better a thing is, the more does it diffuse its goodness to remote beings . . . God, Who is most perfect in goodness and Who diffuses His goodness in the broadest way, must be in His diffusion the archetype for all diffusers of goodness.[214]

Of course, no human being can ever achieve the perfection of God as archetype. As Gilson notes,

> . . . each one of us *is*, but in an incomplete and deficient manner . . . A sort of margin keeps us a little short of what we are defined to be. We do not fully achieve the human essence nor even the complete notion of our own individuality. Hence, it is not merely a question of being, but of a permanent effort to maintain ourselves in being, to conserve ourselves, to realize ourselves. It is just the same with all other sensible beings around us.[215]

This humbling realization will be explored further in Chapter 5.

For the present, suffice to note that while human beings can never become completely like God, they are required as his stewards to devote themselves to increasing the good of others, in a broad and far-reaching manner. As political philosopher Richard J. Regan explains, in the Thomistic understanding, "reason itself can discern an order in nature that makes *moral* demands on human behavior. Because these demands do derive from an order of nature, their observance rewards humans with the contentment of self-fulfillment, and their non-observance punishes humans with the discontent of a failed nature."[216] Moreover, he adds, "so too, the society that disregards communal moral goods reaps natural sanctions of self-deformity and communal dissatisfaction. Organized society exists precisely to enable its members to perfect themselves both physically and morally. To the extent that an organized society works to disorder and frustrate its members morally, it disorders and frustrates itself."[217] Working communally to perfect ourselves and the world, in accordance with our role as God's stewards, will thus enable us to become far greater than the role-takers described in the beginning of this chapter.

Thus, the cosmic and social roles of Confucianism and Christianity are very different from the social roles of Parsons, Merton, and Goffman. Fulfilling one's role through internalizing the lessons of the sages, or through focusing more specifically on individual virtue, means growing in love. Such growth, in turn, means sharing ever deeper and more meaningful relationships with one's family and friends, and the ability to play the social roles that these relationships entail lovingly and well. Rather than forlornly looking for a self that is not dictated by social interaction, or deciding that such a self does not exist, Zhu's co-creator and Thomas's steward develops his or her humanity to heights hitherto impossible and unimagined. Their religious sense of roles, which allows them to look beyond their empirical practice or social function, enables them to see these roles as realities to be celebrated.

Conclusion

For both Thomas and Zhu, we are simultaneously called to develop our power and to do so as to cause the good to prevail for all, to the extent that we can by nature, whether supernaturally assisted or otherwise. While perfect Christians and perfect Confucians are hard to come by—if not theoretically impossible, in the former case—the human race as a whole, and individuals in particular, are called to try to play a role in which goodness is communicated and flourishing is the result, in both a cosmic and a mundane sense. Both Thomas and Zhu believe that real progress toward these goals is possible: their descriptions of the intricacies of the process on the one hand, and of the resources available to human beings as they attempt it on the other, make a case for reasonable hope as opposed to despair or delusional optimism about humanity's prospects for achieving a common good.

Of course, there are differences in their accounts of how to achieve this. Again, as should be clear from this chapter, Zhu does not appeal to supernatural powers to help in the project of realizing one's *ren* in communion with others, past and present; rather, he concentrates his efforts on improving human education and socialization. The fundamental quality of love, or *ren*, is there for people to grasp, if only they will make the effort to do so. Rather than appealing to divine powers or Heavenly mercy, Zhu, like Confucius, Mencius, and Xunzi, teaches his students about the value of ordinary perseverance and dedication, in accordance with one of his Four Books, which famously says, "if another person succeeds by one effort, you will use a hundred efforts. If another person succeeds by ten efforts, you will use a thousand efforts. If one can go this way, even if he is stupid, he must become intelligent, and even if he is weak, he must become strong."[218] Not everyone will become a sage, a true co-creator of the universe, but all may grow in the natural and fundamental virtue of *ren*.

On the other hand, in Thomas's thought, humans cannot themselves acquire or develop the virtue of charity, which must be gratuitously bestowed on the individual by God.[219] While, as discussed in this chapter and in Chapter 2, the acquired virtues are real virtues for Thomas (as they are not for Augustine), it cannot be denied that he feels that all these are deficient without *caritas*, or charity: "[if] we take virtue as being ordered to some particular end, then we speak of virtue being where there is no charity, in so far as it is directed to some particular good . . . [if] this particular good be a true good, for instance the welfare of the state, or the like, it will indeed be a true virtue, *imperfect, however, unless it be referred to the final and perfect good*."[220] The question of which resources are available to and necessary for the project of full self-development hence continues to divide Zhu and Thomas.

However, they agree that people should fall prey neither to despair nor delusional optimism as they travel the road to actualize their moral potential, but should rather remain committed to the process of moral development in accordance with the truths recognized by their respective traditions. While the road will be long and often twisting, and there is never certainty that we will reach the desired end, there is always hope that the next turn or corner will provide us with a new lesson from our teacher or a new insight from God that allows us to go on our way a little wiser and with more to sustain us on the journey.

In addition, both Zhu and Thomas counsel that it is necessary to grow in love, so that one's proper human role may be realized in a performance that enriches the self, the human community, and the world. To positively playing this role, and in so doing exercising true authority, we turn in the next chapter.

Chapter 4

Exercising Authority

With great power comes great responsibility.

—Uncle Ben, *The Amazing Spider-Man*

The Government and the Common Good

As discussed in Chapter 2, a powerful and influential position in contemporary politics is firmly grounded in the belief that the role of the government should be limited to ensuring the freedom of individuals to express themselves as they wish, both economically and socially. As Richard Regan points out, "libertarians tend to deny that [a consensus on basic rational principles of moral good to govern the activities of organized society, and public policies] is necessary, desirable, or even possible in a free society. For them, the only absolute moral principle in a free society is commitment to freedom itself. Citizens, in a word, need agree only on the right to disagree."[1] Indeed, "libertarians fear that even assent in principle to an objective order or moral goods with social dimensions will entail broadscale restriction of citizens' freedom."[2]

Of course, not only libertarians eschew consideration of the role government may play in shaping and maintaining a common consensus regarding questions of meaning and morality. As Liu Wei (刘蔚) demonstrates, it is entirely possible to embrace a broad and proactive role for government in the realm of culture without directly engaging with such questions. In an article published in 2008, Liu makes a series of proposals concerning the part the central government of the People's Republic of China should play in the development of the culture *industry*, proceeding on the premise that "the culture industry as a newly emerging industry plays an increasingly large role in economic advancement."[3] It is very clear that Liu considers this role to be primarily economic in character: "the culture industry's cluster policy is categorized as a part of industrial policy; it is a type of method to advance economic development and regulate structures, [and] it is also a means by which to exploit areas and cities with flourishing cultural economies."[4] Proceeding on this basis, Liu sets aside the question of exactly what is to be produced; instead, he focuses on assigning the government a role in economic and logistical facilitation:

> . . . government should facilitate the clusters' formation through the areas of specialized training, basic infrastructure, and other improvements in the commercial environment. In upgrading industry clusters, the aim of the government is to encourage competition, not to work against competition. The heart of government investment should be in improving the industrial environment within the industrial clusters, and in encouraging the public goods—or the development of standards for public goods—that influence industrial cluster development.[5]

Liu's ideal government is similar to that of the libertarians' in its laissez-faire attitude toward the content or moral worth of those cultural products or goods that are to contribute to the flourishing of the Chinese economy. However, such silence—studied or otherwise—is not universal, and broader approaches to the exercise of government authority, which include but are not limited to economic concerns, are certainly available.

For example, both the Christian and the Confucian traditions see the importance of government support when it comes to the material well-being of citizens. Such support, however, is not in the mold of modern socialist states. According to an article in the *Atlantic*, in Sweden,

> . . . because of the 40 percent tax rate on her husband's job, a new mother may be forced to take that second, highly taxed job to supplement the family's finances; in other words, she leaves her toddlers behind from eight to five (in that convenient universal day care) so she can go take care of other

people's toddlers or empty the bedpans of elderly strangers. (As Alan Wolfe has pointed out, "the Scandinavian welfare states which express so well a sense of obligation to distant strangers, are beginning to make it more difficult to express a sense of obligation to those with whom one shares family ties.")[6]

Confucian and Catholic theories of welfare are designed to prevent this sort of problem. According to Joseph Chan, "the Confucian emphasis on securing material welfare for the people does not imply a nanny state that takes care of every aspect of people's lives from the cradle to the grave. The government's job is rather to provide the conditions in which people can make a living so that they can help their families and relatives if they are in need."[7] Likewise, from the Catholic point of view, Charles Curran tells us that the ideal "government does not usurp the role of the family or more basic groups but helps them to achieve their purposes,"[8] giving as an example government assistance with the cost of higher education. According to both traditions, the government should be responsible for those matters that individuals or small groups do not have the power to successfully address. As Rosemont notes, in Confucianism, "a central government is [important] to the good society, because there are necessary ingredients of human flourishing—especially economic—that the family (and local community) cannot secure on their own; repairing dikes, ditches and roads, distributing grain from bumper harvest to famine areas, establishing academies, etc."[9] Such material concerns are also addressed in the Catholic Christian tradition; as Curran points out, one issue for which a state may be responsible is the clean air that benefits all.[10]

As paradigmatic representatives of these two traditions, neither Zhu Xi nor Thomas Aquinas disdains the mundane concerns addressed by Liu Wei in his article. Thomas was of the opinion that "a man in hunger is to be fed rather than instructed, and as the Philosopher observes (Topic. iii, 2), for a needy man 'money is better than philosophy.'"[11] (Not surprisingly, as regards the quote from Aristotle about the comparative value of money and philosophy, while granting that contingencies may arise in particular situations that temporarily increase the relative value of the former, "the latter is better simply.") Zhu, meanwhile, as a government official in Fujian Province from 1151–1158, had neither the leisure nor the inclination to set aside pecuniary affairs. In later years, he told his students, "When I was assistant magistrate in T'ung-an [Tong'an], I kept close account of the taxes and custom duties. Every day I checked the items and signed my name to avoid any corruption by officials."[12]

However, their concerns do not stop at the level of economics. The Confucian and Catholic conceptions of a common good include not only material but also ethical concerns: neither Zhu nor Thomas believes that the morality of the goods produced can be removed from the public equation. While neither approves of the kind of moral tyranny feared by libertarians—a topic further discussed in Chapter 5—both Thomas and Zhu argue that the government has the authority to intervene in moral matters: in fact, they argue that such intervention is partially constitutive of proper governmental authority itself.

An important point to keep in mind here is that such intervention is understood to be in the interests of the individual. In the Confucian and Catholic conceptions, the common good is compatible with the individual good: the former is understood to enable the good of individual members of society. As Charles Curran points out,

> . . . in the Catholic tradition, the purpose of the state has been to work for the common good, which differs in theory from both individual goods and the collective good . . . In theory, the common good by definition flows back to the good of individuals and does not contradict or limit the proper good of individuals [nor of individual groups] . . . The state can and should intervene to help a particular group such as workers, but this ultimately contributes to the common good and the good of other members of society.[13]

Confucian theory likewise provides a system in which people, through playing their own part to the fullest, simultaneously enrich their own lives and the life of the community at large: "ideally, a harmonious social order will allow for individual self-realization . . . Rather than all voices singing the same note, each distinct voice sings a different note that taken collectively comprise a chord."[14] This society does impose certain restrictions as, after all, in order for harmony to emerge, "everyone must still sing from the same songbook." Nonetheless, it also enables individuals to "maintain a degree of autonomy and uniqueness," as "the goal is not oneness in the sense of identity of the parts."

The primarily cooperative starting point of both Zhu and Thomas leads both to conceive of political and personal forms of authority as fundamentally harmonious. Others view this latter relationship to be far more tenuous. For example, John Kekes writes that "discussions of authority tend to go wrong from the beginning. They start with considering authority, and then usually without notice or excuse, switch to the consideration of political authority."[15] He concludes, "the right question to ask therefore is how to tell real from spurious authorities, rather than the politically inspired one of why reasonable people would subject themselves to authorities."[16] As the remainder of the chapter shall show, neither Thomas nor Zhu would impose such a marked boundary between personal and political authority: rather, both believe that the kind of personal authority described by Kekes should be constructively operative in political contexts, and that answering his first question goes a long way toward answering the second.

The comprehensive approach to the common good taken by Zhu and Thomas as representatives of their respective traditions neither cuts government off from all involvement with public morality nor places a hard and fast boundary between the economic and moral spheres. As Cua points out, such boundaries cannot exist in the Confucian tradition, for the world in which our economic activities take place is "seen as a setting for moral striving."[17] If the world is primarily moral in character, then the government that orders and maintains it has to take a moral role, by providing guidelines and models for good personal development.[18] As Richard Madsen explains, "[in the Confucian context] civility does not simply mean tolerance for rivals in a world of competitive coexistence—as in the context of the liberal-egalitarian vision of civil society. It means the eventual achievement of a kind of social consensus."[19] The common good, then, includes moral as well as economic concerns.

Such a social consensus is also seen as necessary in the Catholic tradition. As Richard Regan points out, from a Catholic perspective, "the freedom of individuals and society to make decisions should not be confused with the substance of the decisions made . . . a public consensus on moral good should inform the whole political process of decision making and the exercise of political freedoms."[20] This is particularly important, according to Regan, "because the human person is more than an economic producer, human society has other and higher purposes than economic production . . . Organized society, therefore, exists to provide the human person not only with conditions of material well-being but also and especially with conditions conducive to the communication of truth, beauty, and goodness."[21]

Exactly what these conditions are, or what the common good will look like, is difficult to say. One response to this complicated problem is to simplify the notion of the good at which a society aims. Unfortunately, this approach often leads to a lowest common denominator style of thinking. As Mary Keys argues, "in reducing the meaning of 'good' to one univocal measure of happiness, measuring 'welfare' in units of pleasure or utility, and weighing all aspirations, aims, and ends according to this unitary criterion, utilitarianism taken for teleological, good-based theory is reasonably accused of irrational reductivism."[22] Another complication presents itself when we realize that various schools of thought—not to mention different individuals—will conceive of the common good in highly diverse ways. This renders the concept suspect among many people. Again, Mary Keys: "with regard to the 'common' claim [in the common good], some realists might argue that the term is and indeed can be no more than a mask for hypocrisy and the will to power, or for acquiring or protecting greater wealth or freedom or other benefits that one has no intention of sharing."[23] She attributes suspicion of the common good in the West to a currently popular framework for conceiving of the common good:

> . . . utilitarian theory in particular has given the common good a bad name by aiming at a maximized "public welfare" that necessarily privileges what brings happiness qua utility or pleasure to some over what similarly benefits others, only fewer of them or less intensely. Orienting ethical and political life toward the (in)famous "greatest good for the greatest number," utilitarianism too easily ends by employing some members of society, or at least their labor and public contributions, as mere means to the happiness of others. However ruefully, utilitarianism thus regards the well-being of these unfortunate persons, groups, or classes, and in the most extreme instances or radical theories their very lives and selves, as expendable.[24]

Noting a similar problem in the East, the Confucian scholar Sor-hoon Tan writes that "the problem in authoritarian or totalitarian polities is not one of 'the whole' oppressing individual members, but one of some groups or individuals oppressing other groups and individuals in the name of the whole."[25]

Regardless of the very real harm that can be and has been done in the name of the common good, the concept may still be rescued and positively utilized. As regards the reductionist problems of the utilitarian approach: the Catholic Christian approach to the common good, which includes the recognition that "humans have the capacity and the desire to inquire after truth, to appreciate beauty, and to love other humans," and that "this spiritual dimension is at the core of human personality and can only be achieved in concert with others,"[26] avoids the problems of focusing too intently on the maximization of happiness or pleasure narrowly defined. Meanwhile, according to Tan, "Confucian 'organic relations' among individuals forming communities do not subordinate individuals to some mystical 'whole' and its purpose;"[27] rather, all are understood to be striving toward the flourishing of both the self and the community, together. Such conceptions of the human person and community pave the way for government to justifiably take a proactive role in the realm of morality. (The character of the relationship between the self and society also circumscribes the power to be rightfully held by any government or individual leader—a topic to be discussed more fully in Chapter 5.)

Both the Confucian and Catholic traditions believe that the government should take such a role. In Confucianism, as Tu Weiming explains, "the strong belief in the inseparability of morality and politics and in the correlation between the self-cultivation of the rule and the governability of the people makes it difficult to conceive of politics as a mechanism of control independent of personal ethics. Indeed, the etymology of the word *cheng* [*zheng*] 政 (politics) is 'rectification' (*cheng* [*zheng*] 正) with a distinctive moral overtone."[28] On a similar note, Regan writes that, in the Catholic analysis, "the purpose of the state is to promote the common goal of developing human personality both materially and spiritually."[29] More particularly, the ideal Confucian or Catholic approach to governance involves virtuous individuals who lead other individuals to fulfillment and virtue in community.

Before moving forward: I am aware that many problems still remain with a focus on the common good, howsoever defined, which its proponents are often loath to admit. As Curran points out, whatever its gains in recent years, such a focus on the part of the Catholic tradition meant that "Catholic social teaching arrived on the human rights bandwagon somewhat late and out of breath."[30] Meanwhile, on the Confucian side, some are skeptical that such a thing as a truly common good in which all aspects of each individual may flourish even exists: "the problem with Confucianism has not lain in its claim that a life shared and lived in relation with others is a morally flourishing life. The problem has lain in its assumption that the different aspects of a person's social identity, which correspond to the different goods that go into the common good, can all somehow be subsumed and ordered under some grand harmonizing principle."[31] I will deal with these issues in more detail in the Conclusion to this book. For the present, I note that the difficulty of attaining a proper balance between the individual and society, or of harmonizing one's complex self with a complex community, must always be addressed and attended to—a statement with which Thomas and Zhu would certainly agree.

While neither Thomas nor Zhu singled out the ability to rule effectively as a virtue in and of itself, they both believed that superiority in virtue leads to stronger claims for exercising authority. In particular, they argued that proper rule must be exercised with care and concern, in a spirit of *ren* and *caritas*. Their conception of a cosmic moral order, in which humans are rooted and in accordance with whose objective and enduring moral demands they are expected to intelligently and communally develop their innate moral potential, provides the context within which we are called to proactively and positively exercise authority over the world around us—but never in an absolute way. As will be discussed more fully in Chapter 5, human beings are outranked, as it were, by angels in Thomas's hierarchy of being. As for Zhu, it is well to note here once more that he does not conceive of human beings as being completely separate from the rest of creation in their virtuous character; it is rather merely that things (animals, plants, and inorganic elements) are unable to fully develop the good that is within them: "concerning *qi*, in [possessing] consciousness and [the ability to] move, people and animals are the same; concerning *li*—the endowment of humaneness, righteousness, propriety, and wisdom—the abilities of animals in this sense cannot be *complete*."[32] In their systems of thought, the lack of senior status on the one hand, and of a sharp difference in kind between the ruler and the ruled on the other, correlate with teachings encouraging governments of cooperative stewardship rather than tyrannical control or exploitation.

As the sections below will explain, a universal common good is meant to be sustained and nurtured by human beings, who are called to keep things in proper order. Moreover, this order is meant to be reflected in the human race itself, with a hierarchy based on moral development: those who develop themselves in communion with the sacred, non-negotiable demands of the cosmos and the obligations of their human nature, and who lovingly engage with their environments, are those who have a rightful claim to exercise true authority on behalf of the flourishing of all.

Sacred Calling for Human Beings in General to Exercise Authority

Zhu Xi: The Human Endowment

As previously noted, according to the *Doctrine of the Mean*, one of the Four Books enshrined by Zhu as the foundation of Confucian orthodoxy, human beings are called to participate in the ongoing transformation of the cosmos:

> . . . if [people] can fully develop their nature, then they can fully develop the nature of others. If they can fully develop the nature of others, then they can fully develop the nature of things. If they can fully develop the nature of things, then they can assist in the transformation and reproduction of Heaven and Earth. If they can assist in the transformation and reproduction of Heaven and Earth, then they can join Heaven and Earth [as a partner].[33]

As A. S. Cua explains, "what the theme of the central harmony of man and the world points to is precisely the ceaseless, creative, and transformative character of the *tao* of Heaven and Earth in relation to the *tao* of man. The relation is intrinsic to the nature of each. Man, Heaven and Earth form a unity—a dynamic creative unity that admits of no special description nor categorization."[34] As he goes on to note, this text is not intended as discussion of an "academic question," but is meant to generate practical results: although this text "is a main source of Chinese metaphysical speculation, by itself the text does not appear to be a metaphysical treatise in any systematic sense . . . Thus we meet with no description or classification of the types of entities in the world, nor do we encounter the notion of the world as a name, referring, or descriptive expression. Instead, we are given a sort of *theme*, a vision that can be developed in a number of ways."[35] (See "A Methodological Issue" in Chapter 3 for Wm. Theodore de Bary's similar insight regarding the open-endedness of Confucian philosophical concepts.)

That it is human beings as opposed to birds, beasts, or trees that are to form this unity with Heaven and Earth is, according to Zhu, not only inferred but also *seen*. The special endowment received by human beings is immanent in the very shape and structure of their bodies: "the heads of people are round, like Heaven, and their feet are square, like Earth. They are impartial and upright, and all this is through receiving the upright *qi* of Heaven and Earth, so they know the Principle of Heaven (*daoli*), and have knowledge. Things receive the biased *qi* of Heaven and Earth, so that the birds and the beasts are born wild, and the heads of the grasses and the trees grow facing downwards, while their tails are above."[36] As peculiarly accurate scaled-down models of the cosmos, with round heads on top and square feet on the bottom, Zhu believes that people participate in the great power of Heaven and Earth: "there is nothing that human beings cannot know, and nothing they cannot do."[37] As we can see here, Zhu—in good company with Thomas, who also subscribes to a positive view of human intelligence (in Chapter 3, see "Thomas Aquinas and the Virtues")—is largely silent on the possibility that human knowledge, as opposed to the knowledge that may be gathered by specific individuals, may be faulty by nature. As Yung-sik Kim points out, "Chu Hsi [Zhu Xi] did not engage in discussions of how one can obtain knowledge or how one can be sure that what one knows is sound, the key questions in Western epistemology."[38] Schwartz ventures that "the notion that these patterns of the good human order are all, as it were, 'close at hand' may account for what may seem to be both the epistemological and moral optimism of Confucian ethics."[39]

Confucians are aware that people can—and do—use their power in inappropriate ways that damage the world around them. Even aside from direct material abuse (such as industrial pollution, over-fishing, or destroying woodlands or jungles), Chinese philosophy and religion in general warn that lapses in personal and communal virtue can lead to disaster: "Potentially a great source of disharmony in the cosmos, humanity is not only in a position of central importance but also in one of highest responsibility. Earthquakes, floods and tornadoes are thus entirely our own fault, a sign that all is not well in the lives of people and the government of the land."[40] Rather than causing such problems, the rightful purpose of the human endowment is to aid in the flourishing of all that is, and in a uniquely special way. It is an ancient Confucian idea that not only is it possible but also necessary for people to do this, for the great Way or *Dao* (道) of Heaven and Earth will not become manifest on its own. *The Analects* tells us, "Confucius said, 'it is humankind that makes the Way great; the Way cannot make humankind great."[41] In Zhu's words, we must make the benevolent feelings of Heaven and Earth visible: "someone asked, 'how may the emotions of Heaven and Earth be seen?' [Zhu] answered, 'When people are upright and honest (*zhengda*), then it is possible to see the upright and honest feelings of Heaven and Earth. Heaven and Earth are purely upright and honest; in them there are no evil or petty places.' "[42]

Thus, it is our job as a race to make manifest the uprightness and honesty of Heaven and Earth, to overcome all that is evil, petty, or otherwise against the true character of reality, and in so doing bring ourselves and our neighbors—whether human or otherwise—into vibrant and prosperous cooperation with the elements of the cosmos. As Michael Nylan notes, "[not surprisingly] the character for 'king' (three parallel horizontal lines joined by a vertical) shows the king to be one who joins, symbolizes, and stabilizes the parallel moral realms of Heaven, Earth, and Man."[43]

As is evidenced by Zhu's repeated references to "knowledge," a clear perception and judgment of reality is requisite to carry out the tasks of forming the unity, making the Way great, and manifesting the *zhengda* of Heaven and Earth. Zhu tells us that the rightful individual ruler "will not allow sensual desires to fatigue his mind-and-heart, the small to injure the great, or the secondary to destroy the fundamental."[44] Rather, his or her virtue will be as large and deep as Earth, and as high and brilliant as Heaven.[45] Even more strongly, in a belief that harmonizes with his convictions about the necessity of people manifesting the goodness of Heaven and Earth, Zhu tells us that the sage not only "is of the same *substance* of Heaven and Earth,"[46] but that he is also "of the same *function* as Heaven and Earth."[47] Of course, as discussed in previous chapters, we have to develop our moral potential in order to be and act as do Heaven and Earth. Experience tells us that different people achieve this development at different times, at different rates, and to different degrees: a topic further discussed below (see "The Exercise of Authority by Particular Individuals Within the Human Community").

Thomas Aquinas: The Power of Reason and Intellect

For the present, we should consider that, in Thomas's tradition, the story is told that, at the very beginning of human history, God set men and women above the rest of His creation. After bringing Adam and Eve to life, "God blessed them, and God said unto them, Be fruitful, and multiply, and replenish the earth, and subdue it: and have dominion over the fish of the sea, and over the fowl of the air, and over every living thing that moveth upon the earth."[48] However, as will be demonstrated below, this authority over the earth was seen as attendant on certain responsibilities. Thomas holds a sensibility similar to Zhu's concerning a potential within the world that needs to be brought to fruition. Moreover, like Zhu, he does not conceive of this potential as value-free in character. As Nichols notes, for Thomas,

> . . . there is only one universe, a single, integrated and unified cosmos of which all are citizens, albeit with differing roles. The total good of the universe consist in the interrelationship of things, *ordo rerum ad invicem*, "the ordering of things to one another." Ultimately this is not just an aesthetic question—a matter of the *pattern* of the world, the "rich and complex" tapestry God has made. More than this, it is a question of the *purpose* of the universe, and the way in which all the beings which constitute the world in their inter-relation conspire, whether consciously or not, to serve the final purpose of God, his saving plan.[49]

Thomas sees that human beings have a very important role as "co-conspirators" in God's plan for creation. To begin with, he sees that "two things pertain to the care of providence—namely, the 'reason of order,' which is called providence and disposition; and the execution of order, which is termed government. Of these, the first is eternal, and the second is temporal."[50] While "God has immediate providence over everything," as regards this temporal government, Thomas says, "there are certain intermediaries of God's providence; for He governs things inferior by superior, not on account of any defect in His power, but by reason of the abundance of His goodness; so that the dignity of causality is imparted even to creatures."[51] Indeed, as it puts it even more strongly in the *Summa contra gentiles*, "the perfection of divine providence demands that the execution of the divine rule be accomplished by those that participate more fully in divine goodness."[52] (A tricky proposition for egalitarians: the lack of equality between individuals, or, more broadly, between humans and the rest of the world, both with respect to each other and to God, is seen as a reflection of divine love and gratuitous generosity. Thomas writes: "perfect goodness would not be found in created things unless there were an order of goodness in them, in the sense that some of them are better than others. Otherwise, all possible grades of goodness would not be realized, *nor would any creature be like God by holding a higher place than another*."[53])

Further, it is built into things not only to participate in God's goodness, but also to share it with others. In a system where "everything is on account of its operation,"[54] and "every created thing attains its ultimate perfection through its proper operation,"[55] intellectual creatures such as humans have an unquestionably authoritative calling:

> . . . the intellectual power by itself is capable of ordering and ruling; hence, we see that the operative power follows the direction of the intellective power, when they are combined in the same subject. In man, for instance, we observe that the bodily members are moved at the command of the will. The same is evident even if they are in different subjects . . . Therefore, the rational plan of divine governance demands that other creatures be ruled by intellectual creatures.[56]

Indeed, as he points out in the *Summa theologiae*, "in virtue of the divinely established natural order the lower natural things need to be subject to the movement of the higher."[57]

Thus, Thomas, like Zhu, believes that the human being as intellectual creature is uniquely positioned in the material world to take on a superior and ordering role. However, such a power comes with a responsibility to "participate more fully in divine goodness," for, as Thomas tells us, "the governance of every provident ruler is ordered either to the attainment, or the increase, or the preservation of the perfection of the things governed. Therefore, whatever pertains to perfection is to be preserved by providence rather than what pertains to imperfection and deficiency."[58] Clearly, humans are not intended to move through the world as a shopper moves through Wal-Mart, simply taking what they want without regard for any but personal concerns: rather, human beings are meant to facilitate the perfection of all around them. (As I noted in Chapter 1, I do not mean to sentimentalize Thomas's account, in which some things are undeniably there for the use and convenience of others; from Thomas's point of view, animals exist in part so that we can eat them. Nonetheless, we are not to be excessively cruel to them, implicitly because of their value as parts of God's creation, and explicitly because of the impact such cruelty may be expected to have on our interactions with other human beings.[59])

This moral charge, like all moral charges, is difficult. As Regan points out, "moral reasoning is a complicated business, and . . . careful reflection on the relation of contingent events to first moral principles is essential to the correct understanding and formulation of secondary precepts of the natural law."[60] While noting, "ordinary citizens, of course, do not typically engage in such reflection and reasoning," Regan also recognizes that "for that matter, professionals may also fail to do so, or at least to do so adequately." Thomas held a similarly realistic respect for the spiritually and morally elite.[61] As a member of a religious order himself, Thomas is quite aware that those living in the "state of perfection" are not always "perfect" themselves.[62] With such caveats in mind, Thomas, like Zhu, is willing to confront the fact that the ability to successfully conduct moral reasoning varies in different people, and may increase or decrease at different times in an individual's life. It is this topic that is treated in the section below.

The Exercise of Authority by Particular Individuals Within the Human Community

Zhu Xi and the Need for Social Hierarchy

As Confucius says in the *Doctrine of the Mean*, "although Heaven and Earth are vast, people still find something with which to be dissatisfied."[63] As this is a reality true of all human times and places, and as human beings tend to have different, not to say mutually contradictory ideas about how to deal with it, there must be some way to adjudicate between different views and opinions, and this way must be readily available to people within their communities. In the Confucian tradition, this way involves setting some people in positions higher than those of others.

The *Doctrine of the Mean* tells us: "the person in a lowly position, although good, [does not gain] respect, and not respected, does not gain the confidence [of others]. If the person has not such confidence, the people will not follow him or her."[64] That such a person might be very good is noted by Zhu, who says in his commentary on this chapter that, " 'the one in the lowly position' refers to a sage in a lowly position, like Confucius, who, although good in the ways of *LI*, was [still] not in a respected position."[65] As every student of Confucius knows, whatever his successes after his death, he was forced throughout his lifetime to repeatedly confront political failure: a particularly jarring failure, as he never attained a position from which he could realistically hope to implement his social vision. As Wenshan Jia notes,

> . . . in the history of Chinese politics, *wei* [position or positioning in the primary onto-cosmology] determines who has or who does not have the right to think, articulate and theorize (*ming*). This is evidenced by the two age-old Chinese sayings that go like, "Words do not flow from those without rectified names" (*ming bu zheng yan bu shun*) and "words from the persons of low positions are futile" (*ren bei yan qin*). It is also confirmed by the classical Chinese adage: "Do not conduct the political affairs unless you are in the position to do so."[66]

As the *Doctrine of the Mean* proclaims, "he who is not the son of Heaven [emperor] cannot decide the rituals, cannot regulate the standards, and cannot make lawful the written characters."[67] Many things need to be decided, and, according to the Confucian tradition, only those in authority will be able to decide them.

Of course, people other than the emperor can be involved in such decisions, and ideally other people are. As Jiang points out, "the ideal Confucian political norm, the rule of ritual [*LI*], is built upon a model of intimate political authority, exercised by the sage-king and a group of learned scholar/officials whose shared experience of moral and ritual cultivation gives them the ability to govern . . . [The] ruling literati class became an intimate group with intricate relationships among themselves, governing the empire on behalf of the emperor."[68] As this passage argues, both the emperor and the men who surrounded him were ideally trained in the ritual that promoted virtue, and it is from such self-development that they were able to govern other people. The virtuous qualifications requisite to filling inherently necessary positions of authority are discussed further in the section below.

Thomas Aquinas and the Need for a Ruler

Thomas has similar ideas about authority and how it works. First of all, he says, "man is naturally a social being."[69] As he explains in his essay *On Kingship* (*De regno*),

> . . . nature has prepared food, hair as covering, teeth, horns and claws for the purpose of [self-] defense, or at least swiftness

> in flight, for animals other than the human being. The human being, however, is made with no natural provisions given to him for these things. Instead of all these, the human is given reason, by use of which he might arrange all these things for himself by the work of his hands. One person is not able to arrange all of these things for himself, for one person may not sufficiently provide for life by himself. It is therefore natural that human being[s] should live in the society of many.[70]

As the last phrase of the passage above implies, his ideal society will extend beyond the confines of the home. As discussed in the beginning of this chapter, Thomas, along with Zhu, believes that "despite its fundamental role in human existence and its primordial naturalness, a lone family unity or household is incapable of complete self-sufficiency."[71] Hence, in his commentary on Aristotle's *Politics*,[72] his most detailed treatment of the community as such, he explains that Aristotle divides his discussion of the city (*communitate civitatis*) into three parts:

> First, he shows what a city's components are. For, just as a village is made up of several households, so a city is made up of several villages. Secondly, he says that the city is a perfect community [*communitas*], which he proves from the fact that, since every association [*communicatio*] among all human beings is ordered to something necessary for life, that community will be perfect which is ordered to this, that human beings have sufficiently whatever is necessary for life: and such is the city. For it is of the nature of the city that in it should be found all things that suffice for human life; and so it happens to be. And for this reason it is made up of several villages, in one of which the art of the smith is practiced, in another the art of the weaver, and so of the others. Wherefore it is evident that the city is a perfect community. Thirdly, he shows to what the city is ordered. It is first made for the sake of living, namely, that human beings might find sufficiently that from which they might be able to live; but from its existence it comes about that human beings not only live but that they live well, in so far as by the laws of the city the life of human beings is ordered to the virtues.[73]

Having conceived of society in such a fashion, he writes in the *Summa theologiae*: "now a social life cannot exist among a number of people unless under the presidency of one to look after the common good; for many, as such, seek many things, whereas one attends only to one. Wherefore the Philosopher says, in the beginning of the *Politics*, that wherever many things are directed to one, we shall always find one at the head directing them."[74] As Thomas puts it in a different context, "Just as in virtue of the divinely established natural order the lower natural things need to be subject to the movement of the higher, so too in human affairs, in virtue of the order of natural and divine law, inferiors are bound to obey their superiors."[75] Evidence of such hierarchical thinking is everywhere in his thought. For example, when discussing the demonic world of all things, he claims that "since action follows the nature of a thing, where natures are subordinate, actions also must be subordinate to each other;"[76] see also Curran's remarks on the angelic hierarchy.[77]

The reference here to immortal angels reminds us that the need for leadership endures not only through space but also time: as Regan points out, from a Thomistic perspective, the Marxist-Leninist dream of a stateless society is both unrealistic and undesirable: "what workers 'need' depends to some extent on what they think they need, and it is unlikely that all will have the same view on the subject . . . Collective decisions will have to be made about what is produced, how much of each item will be produced, and conditions of work . . . One may choose not to call the machinery of authoritative decision-making 'the state,' but that is what it really is."[78] Arguably not only from a Thomistic but also a commonsensical perspective, political ordering, and hence authority, is necessary so that people's material and virtuous well-being may be fully developed.

The importance of the virtuous development of people provides the beginnings of an answer to the question of: whose authority? Not surprisingly, Thomas sees those who are advanced in virtue as most capable of leading others:

> . . . if one man surpassed another in knowledge and virtue, this would not have been fitting unless these gifts conduced to the benefit of others, according to 1 Peter 4:10, "As every man hath received grace, ministering the same one to another." Wherefore Augustine says (De Civ. Dei xix, 14): "Just men command not by the love of domineering, but by the service of counsel": and (De Civ. Dei xix, 15): "The natural order of things requires this; and thus did God make man."[79]

As always, Thomas views this state of affairs in a positive light, refusing to characterize it as a punishment meted out to those who live in a state of sin. While he recognizes that power may be abused, he does not hence draw the conclusion, automatic to so many people today, that inequality should be at the least whittled away at and ideally abolished. Rather, he takes care to differentiate between good and bad exercises of authority: "subjection is twofold. One is servile, by virtue of which a superior makes use of a subject for his own benefit; and this kind of subjection began after sin. There is another kind of subjection which is called economic or civil, whereby the superior makes use of his subjects for their own benefit and good; and this kind of subjection existed even before sin."[80] Thomas, like Zhu, is confident in claiming that there is such a thing as a rightful ruler, and that he or she will be both morally virtuous and intellectually knowledgeable—a topic further discussed below.

Qualifications for Leadership

Zhu Xi: The Moral Model

The importance of having the right people in office in Confucianism cannot be overestimated. In this tradition, the ruler's personal moral goodness (or lack thereof) is seen to affect and influence all within the realm. As Confucius told a king, "if you desire what is good, the people will be good. The virtue of the ruler [*junzi*, 君子] is like the wind, and that of inferior persons is like grass. The grass must bend under the wind above it."[81] Not only was the Confucian king deemed capable of manifesting a natural/divine order, he was also understood to be able to effect the moral transformation of others through this manifestation. This reliance on people—not institutions or laws—to bring about peace and prosperity pervades the tradition from its earliest inception. Zhu is thus sounding a very Confucian theme when he writes, "if you have the ruler, and you have the minister, then you have government."[82] He continues, "the administration of government lies in human beings. In the *Jiayu* it is written, 'the administration of government lies in getting human beings'; this really says it all. [Here] 'human beings' means 'worthies and ministers.' This is to say that the superior person administers government by obtaining [good] men, and that such obtaining is achieved through his own self-cultivation."[83] As always, it is well to note that such self-cultivation is conceived of in extraordinarily stringent terms: "'extending sincerity to all under Heaven' refers to the substance of the sage's virtue: it may be augmented by nothing under Heaven. He who fully develops his nature: there is no virtue he does not realize; therefore there is in him no selfish desire. He investigates and follows the law of heaven within himself. Thus, of the great and the minute, the refined and the coarse, there is not a hair's breadth [of potential] that is not developed."[84]

The personal morality of the ruler is a key and characteristic Confucian concern. As Tu notes:

> . . . the moral integrity of the ruler, far from being his private affair, is thought to be a defining characteristic of his leadership. He must realize that what he does in private is not only symbolically significant but has a direct bearing on his ability to lead, for the kind of people he can attract to take responsible positions in the government depends, in large measure, upon his personal character. Without the participation of qualified personnel, the conduct of government, unlike the growth of plants, will be slow and stagnant. The ruler's moral integrity is therefore an indispensable condition for good government.[85]

Nor is the importance of the leader's character limited to his ability to make effective personnel appointments. The Confucian tradition envisions the ruler's morality as not only attracting other good people, but also using the power of his virtue to set things right within his society. In fact, it is only such good rulers with such power who will be able to do so. Zhu writes,

> . . . amongst the people born of Heaven, there must arise brilliant people who rise to become leaders to rule the others. The rulers will govern the people so that quarrels will stop, lead them so that the sustenance and support of life will follow, and teach them so that the principles of human relations are clear. Then the way of human beings will be established, the way of Heaven will flourish, and the way of Earth will be at peace.[86]

Of course, the wise person may not have been born that way. As noted in previous chapters, there are occasionally those who are born with *qi* "bright and clear, pure and unadulterated, and who do not have a hair's worth [of] cloudy and turbid [endowment],' and these "do not have to study but already can [know the truth], like [sage kings] Yao or Shun."[87] Nonetheless, most of us fall into a second category, in which the individual "has to study and then knows, has to act and then extends."[88] In the end, such distinctions matter little: whether her knowledge is innate or earned, she who has knowledge is fit to rule. As Jiang points out, "for the Confucians, those who have mastered the ritual skills after the vigorous training and praxis would find at their disposal power of wisdom that is inaccessible to ordinary people. In other words, such power is the result of the ritual praxis that provides the basic framework for the subsequent rational thinking and political action."[89]

On a practical level, these same Confucians were not stupid, and had no difficulty realizing that such ideal conditions did not often come to pass. As Tu Weiming puts it, they "certainly did not see their emperors as sage-kings. They also noticed that, historically, sages did not necessarily become kings. . . . The implication of honouring Confucius as 'the uncrowned king' is obvious."[90] Nonetheless, the Confucian tradition was powerful enough to create the widespread impression in the Han and other dynasties that "emperors who failed to demonstrate sagely qualities were, at most, probationary kings . . . This [perception] is a far cry from the unquestioned loyalty toward one's ruler-father found in late imperial China."[91] Like Thomas, Zhu and his tradition promoted the accountability of the ruling class rather than democracy, in part by demanding a great deal of those on top.

In the words of Zhu, "the one who is able to *fully develop* his nature, there is nothing his knowledge cannot clarify, and no place he cannot be."[92] (As will be discussed further in Chapter 5, while there is theoretically no one thing that the sage cannot know, this does not mean that the sage does in fact know everything.) Such a person will also have the moral power necessary to govern others. According to Zhu,

> . . . the sage can make insincere people dare not give full rein to their empty and absurd words. When one's luminous virtue becomes bright, he or she will naturally have the mind-and-heart and will to serve the people in awe [of the responsibility]. Therefore [because of the sage's moral power], no lawsuits will be raised or heard: they will go away of themselves. Concerning yourself with this, you can know the root and the branches, and what is first and what is last.[93]

As we can see from the passage above, the Confucian tradition has always been wary of lawsuits, which are certain signals that all is not well in communal relationships, and have aimed at a society where such proceedings would be unnecessary. Nonetheless, in their typically practical way, they adjudicate cases when the need arises. Confucius sums up the position very well: "With regard to hearing lawsuits, I am the same as other people. But what we need is to have no lawsuits."[94]

Even before that day arrives in a perfectly ordered, sage-ruled society, Zhu sees the virtuous leader as playing a very important role shaping the characters and subsequent social interaction of the people under his or her command. This may seem to strip the people under command of autonomy, but this is not the Confucian understanding. As Chong points out,

> . . . autonomy as self-directedness is not necessarily equivalent to liberation from institutional arrangements. The liberal conception of autonomy as absence from constraint and noninterference from part of others is insufficient to guarantee self-directedness. For self-directedness to obtain, strength of character and effort are required to maintain an integral sense of self together with ideals which form an important part of this self. In this sense, autonomy is an achievement concept.[95]

Such an achievement, open to all, is of critical communal value. As Chaihark points out, even in the liberal West, "the success of a constitutionalist government depends on the disposition of its citizens. One might call this the 'political culture'; it might also be described as the civic virtue of citizens."[96] Such virtue, so communal in impact, can have a great influence for the good, and Confucians warn that its absence will have the opposite effect. The *Great Learning* says, "[when] one home is humane [*ren*], the entire country flourishes in humaneness; through the propriety of one home, the nation becomes proper. Through one person's perversity, a nation can fall into chaos . . . This is to say that one sentence can ruin affairs, and one man can order the nation."[97] In his commentary on this passage, Zhu writes: "this talks about the effectiveness of education in the nation."[98] Such education, to be led by the "one man," the *junzi* (君子),[99] is to be moral in scope. According to Zhu:

> . . . when [those in] superior positions do these three things [treating the old as the old should be treated, treating their elders as they should be treated, and treating the helpless with compassion] there will be effective results [in those] below: such influence will be successful, so it is said that regulating the family [well] leads to governing the nation [successfully]. It may also be seen that the hearts-and-minds of human beings are similar, and that there cannot be one single person who is an exception [to this rule]. It is the *junzi* who must find that which makes them similar, extend the organization of things, and help each person and his or her neighbors to obtain all that they desire. Then above and below, and all throughout the four directions [north, south, east and west], will be governed in uprightness, and all under Heaven will be at peace.[100]

Thus, in his analysis, the wise person is to order. It should be noted here that a person who does not do these things is not the rightful ruler, a topic more fully discussed in Chapter 5. For the present, it is well to keep in mind that this central message can be used in ways both reactionary and revolutionary:

> . . . there is no mistaking the ability of Confucian traditions to transmit core texts and concepts relatively intact across generations, but that does not imply that their influence has been uniformly conservative on the political level. Though one of the primary concerns of the texts of the Confucian canon is the theoretical task of defining legitimate authority, contesting that definition was a preoccupation of entrenched political powers, as well as reformers and peasant revolutionaries. Far from being solely reactionary or progressive, Confucian texts were read as providing a vision of a normative social order, one that was invoked both in defense of and as a challenge to the status quo.[101]

Moreover, Zhu's rightful ruler will not only be wise, but also filled with *ren*, for wisdom is but one manifestation of *ren*: "[The virtue of] *ren* is the root of the original substance [which is] *ren*; propriety is the refinement of *ren*; righteousness is its regulation, and wisdom is the discrimination of *ren*."[102] True authority, then, requires a person capable of identifying the good and lovingly moving toward it, with and on behalf of those led.

Thomas Aquinas: Prudent Lawmaker

While the *Summa theologiae* approaches the topic of authority (*praelationis*) from a variety of angles (for example, it explains that only those in positions of rightful authority may lawfully pass judgment on others[103] or punish wrongdoers,[104] and also that such persons have been "entrusted with" the common good[105]), it does not discuss the nature of authority in itself. Hence, in this section, we will turn back to Thomas's earlier writing, in which he addresses the topic more directly and systematically.

In his *Scriptum super sententiis* (*Commentary on the Sentences of Peter Lombard*), Thomas notes, "[with regard to] mode or form, authority is good in all cases, consisting indeed in an order in which some are rulers, and others are subjects . . . speaking simply, all authority is from God."[106] Authority is a gift from God, and, from this perspective, it is always a gift, both to the one who holds it and the one who submits to it.

As previously discussed, this does not mean that authority is a wholly unproblematic concept. As Thomas puts it, in actual concrete practice, "some authority is not from God, namely because its abuses are not of God, or because the unjust actions by which the authority is attained are likewise not from God."[107] Clearly, there is some role for virtue to play here in order that the good gift of authority from God is not abused or wasted by the individuals who receive it.

As any student of Thomas knows, he, like Zhu, views sensual desires with a certain amount of suspicion. He does not view desires as evil in and of themselves; in fact, although he gives comparatively little space to lust's opposing vice, as it "is not found in many, since men are more inclined to pleasure," he does identify a deficiency of natural sexual passion as problematic: "the contrary vice is comprised under insensibility."[108] Nonetheless, the strength and impetuosity of the desires, whether sexual or otherwise, can cause grave disorder and confusion within the human person due to original sin, after the loss of original justice:

> . . . now the whole order of original justice consists in man's will being subject to God: which subjection, first and chiefly, was in the will, whose function it is to move all the other parts to the end . . . so that the will being turned away from God, all the other powers of the soul become inordinate.

> Accordingly the privation of original justice, whereby the will was made subject to God, is the formal element in original sin; while every other disorder of the soul's powers, is a kind of material element in respect of original sin.[109]

Such disorder in the soul leads to problems with the intellect. As should be obvious to anyone who's ever spent time with others, or, for that matter, himself, even when people know what they *should* do, they oftentimes do not do it. Thomas blames this situation on the original sin that rendered our passions disordinate:

> . . . sometimes man fails to consider actually what he knows habitually, on account of some hindrance supervening, e.g. some external occupation, or some bodily infirmity; and, in this way, a man who is in a state of passion, fails to consider in particular what he knows in general, in so far as the passions hinder him from considering it. Now it hinders him in three ways. First, by way of distraction . . . Secondly, by way of opposition, because a passion often inclines to something contrary to what man knows in general. Thirdly, by way of bodily transmutation, the result of which is that the reason is somehow fettered so as not to exercise its act freely; even as sleep or drunkenness, on account of some change wrought on the body, fetters the use of reason. That this takes place in the passions is evident from the fact that sometimes, when the passions are very intense, man loses the use of reason altogether: for many have gone out of their minds through excess of love or anger. It is in this way that passion draws the reason to judge in particular, against the knowledge which it has in general.[110]

When pondering the diminished intellectual capacity of humankind as a race, Thomas does not draw the conclusion that individual persons are incapable of enlightenment sufficient to legitimate their power over others. He does not avoid such a conclusion by subscribing to a simplistic or deontological view of morality, in which rules are there to be unthinkingly grasped and unquestioningly followed. Rather, his emphasis on the cardinal virtue of prudence, which he defines as "the right reason about things to be done"[111] means that the moral agent has a great deal of responsibility in determining what the law is in particular situations:

> . . . since choice is about things in reference to the end, rectitude of choice requires two things: namely, the due end, and something suitably ordained to that due end. Now man is suitably directed to his due end by a virtue which perfects the soul in the appetitive part, the object of which is the good and the end. And to that which is suitably ordained to the due end man needs to be rightly disposed by a habit in his reason, because counsel and choice, which are about things ordained to the end, are acts of the reason. Consequently an intellectual virtue is needed in the reason, to perfect the reason, and make it suitably affected towards things ordained to the end; and this virtue is prudence. Consequently prudence is a virtue necessary to lead a good life.[112]

Moreover, there are different kinds of prudence, depending on the different kinds of ends that it serves: "the individual good, the good of the family, and the good of the city and kingdom are different ends. Wherefore there must needs be different species of prudence corresponding to these different ends, so that one is 'prudence' simply so called, which is directed to one's own good; another, 'domestic prudence' which is directed to the common good of the home; and a third, 'political prudence,' which is directed to the common good of the state or kingdom."[113] Such prudence is to be exercised by the rightful ruler—and, crucially, by the ruled. No proponent of mindless obedience, he also conceives of a related kind of political prudence to be exercised by those ruled: "it is manifest that prudence is in the ruler 'after the manner of a mastercraft' (Ethic. vi, 8), but in the subjects, 'after the manner of a handicraft.'"[114] His teachings on the importance of personal conscience[115] and tyranny[116] are also relevant in this context.

Nonetheless, that people with more highly developed prudence and other virtues have a natural superiority over those who do not is clear. In his sustained discussion of wisdom and government in the *Summa contra gentiles*, Thomas writes: "now, since man possesses intellect, sense, and bodily power, these are interrelated within him by a mutual order, according to the disposition of divine providence, in a likeness to the order which is found in the universe. In fact, corporeal power is subject to sense and intellectual power, as carrying out their command, and the sensitive power is subject to the intellectual and is included under its command."[117] More pertinent to our purposes, he adds:

> . . . on the same basis, there is also found an order among men themselves. Indeed, those who excel in understanding naturally gain control [*naturaliter dominantur*], whereas those who have defective understanding, but a strong body, seem to be naturally fitted [*a natura videntur institute*] for service, as Aristotle says in his *Politics* (I, 5, (1254 b 25). The view of Solomon is also in accord with this, for he says: 'The fool shall serve the wise' (Prov. 11:29); and again: 'Provide out of all the people wise men such as fear God . . . who may judge the people at all times (Exod. 18:21–22).[118]

According to Mark Murphy, in passages like these,

> Aquinas affirms that those who excel in intellect are naturally rulers. But the sense in which those who excel in intellect are naturally rulers is the same sense in which, for example, those who excel physically are naturally Olympic champions. Their physical prowess is such that it makes them particularly apt to excel in athletic activities, but more than physical prowess is required for one to be an Olympic champion: 'just as Olympic prizes are not for the finest and the strongest, but for contestants, since it is only these who win' (*Nicomachean Ethics*, 1099a3–5), it is not the intelligent who hold political authority, but those who attain to political authority in the proper way.[119]

Thus, he continues, "the possession of political authority results from receiving it by a lawful method"[120] and "unlike the other defect in the origin of authority, in which authority is obtained improperly, the unfitness of the ruler does not release the subject from his obligation to obey."[121]

In response, I argue that the personal character of the ruler is important as being that out of which his dictates flow, and that such dictates will be influenced by his personal character. Murphy's example shows the importance of natural aptitudes, properly developed: while he is certainly correct in pointing out that only those who are properly registered with the Olympic Committee can be Olympic champions, it is also the case that such champions had to have and develop natural potential before registering at all—a point that Murphy slights in this context. Moreover, as will be discussed further in Chapter 5, Thomas makes the argument that "unfitness in the ruler" can in fact release the subject from his obligation to obey—or, even more strongly, bind the subject to moral disobedience.

It is unquestionably the case that Thomas agrees with the Confucians regarding the importance of having a wise leader in charge. As he writes, "the usage of the multitude, which according to the Philosopher is to be followed in giving names to things, has commonly held that they are to be called *wise* who order things rightly and govern them well. Hence, among other things that men have conceived about the wise man, the Philosopher includes the notion that it belongs to the wise man to order."[122] Moreover, *none but* the wise man should order:

> . . . now, just as in the activities of one man disorder arises from the fact that understanding follows the lead of sensual power, while the sensual power is dragged down to the movement of the body by virtue of some disorder of the body, as is evident in the case of men who limp, so also does disorder arise in a human government as a result of man getting control, not because of the eminence of his understanding, but either because he usurps dominion for himself by bodily strength or because someone is set up as a ruler on the basis of sensual affection.[123]

In a markedly optimistic development of this train of thought, Thomas posits that, even when the wise men are not themselves the rulers, such an order can still continue to assert itself to a certain extent, so long as the clever do not join the ranks of the wicked: "nor is the natural order entirely perverted by such disorder, for the dominion of fools is weak unless strengthened by the counsel of the wise."[124] Nonetheless, negatively speaking, it is not wise to trust to either the natural strength of the order or the disinclination of the clever to associate themselves with the foolish. On the more positive side, it's also not wise to forego all that the competent person has to offer when occupying a position of leadership. As Dan Daly points out, precisely as demonstrated in Thomas's treatment of prudence, "virtue delivers, dialectically, knowledge and a way to the end, which the natural law only heuristically points to. Thus, virtue too has an informative and illuminative role."[125] It follows that only the virtuous person should make laws—a conception familiar to scholars of Thomas.

This is an important thesis both on its own and in its relation to the common good. First, we should remember that Thomas takes the common good very seriously indeed: "According to the Philosopher (Ethic. i, 2) the common good of the nation is a divine thing, wherefore in olden times the rulers of a commonwealth were called divines, as being the ministers of divine providence, according to Wisdom 6:5, 'Being ministers of His kingdom, you have not judged rightly.' "[126] Hence, if "every law is ordained to the common good,"[127] we can be sure that Thomas takes law seriously as well, if only by association. Moreover, law is necessary to human society in addition to the virtuous ruler, for "no man is so wise as to be able to take account of every single case; wherefore he is not able sufficiently to express in words all those things that are suitable for the end he has in view. And even if a lawgiver were able to take all the cases into consideration, he ought not to mention them all, in order to avoid confusion: but should frame the law according to that which is of most common occurrence."[128]

Such framing will be carefully circumscribed. The scope of true law is not infinite, nor its content limitlessly malleable:

> . . . as Augustine says (De Lib. Arb. i, 5) "that which is not just seems to be no law at all": wherefore the force of a law depends on the extent of its justice. Now in human affairs a thing is said to be just, from being right, according to the rule of reason. But the first rule of reason is the law of nature, as is clear from what has been stated above (91, 2, ad 2). Consequently every human law has just so much of the nature of law, as it is derived from the law of nature. But if in any point it deflects from the law of nature, it is no longer a law but a perversion of law.[129]

(For a discussion of the process by which rightful human laws are determined, see Ia IIae, q. 95, a. 2, resp.). Given such a state of affairs, when it comes to legislation and jurisprudence in particular cases, as Mary Keys puts it, "the bad man's perspective will not suffice."[130] It is necessary to have good people in high places in order that genuine laws, aimed at a genuine common good, may be promulgated and enforced.

Sounding a note that harmonizes with Confucian ideas about the relationship between government and self-cultivation, all rightful laws in the Thomistic system are intended to lead to human flourishing. Thomas quotes Aristotle with approval: "the Philosopher says (Ethic. ii, 1) that the "intention of every lawgiver is to make good citizens."[131] As Thomas explains,

> . . . a law is nothing else than a dictate of reason in the ruler by whom his subjects are governed. Now the virtue of any subordinate thing consists in its being well subordinated to that by which it is regulated: thus we see that the virtue of the irascible and concupiscible faculties consists in their being obedient to reason; and accordingly "the virtue of every subject consists in his being well subjected to his ruler," as the Philosopher says (Polit. i). But every law aims at being obeyed by those who are subject to it. Consequently it is evident that the proper effect of law is to lead its subjects to their proper virtue: and since virtue is "that which makes its subject good," it follows that the proper effect of law is to make those to whom it is given, good.[132]

This engagement by the government is necessary, for, as Keys points out,

> While [those with fundamentally good hearts and wills], in adopting at least some of the evils characteristic of their times, may perhaps plead invincible ignorance, still their lives will not attain the rich human fulfillment they might otherwise have achieved. In such circumstances, clear, authoritative law may be the voice of foundational reason, a spur to moral reflection and advancement. Imagine youths growing up in a community where recreational use of narcotics is the norm. With all the good will in the world, they may not see the problem with this practice. But laws on the books, which criminalize the practice and further mandate educational explanation of the harm it entails for persons and societies, may be the needed pedagogue to help them "fulfill [the good] they desire to do."[133]

In this conception, the state has a very positive role to play in bringing about the common good of society. Indeed, as Curran points out, "in the Catholic understanding, the state is primarily directive and not coercive. If citizens feel that their government is primarily coercive, such a government will be very insecure."[134] Thomas's ruler, while willing to engage in violent forms of behavior in order to protect the common good against disturbances either internal or external,[135] will not be primarily coercive if she is truly wise, as evidenced by his treatment of wisdom in the *Summa theologiae*. In the section on the theological virtues, he directly links the deepest wisdom of all to *caritas*: "it belongs to wisdom as a gift of the Holy Ghost to judge aright about [Divine things] on account of connaturality with them . . . Now this sympathy or connaturality for Divine things is the result of charity, which unites us to God, according to 1 Corinthians 6:17: 'He who is joined to the Lord, is one spirit.' "[136] Thus, the ordering of his wise person, with her genuine, loving concern for the common good, based in part on her self-understanding as a social being whose moral potential must be developed in and on behalf of a community, will be directive rather than coercive, and lead to the improvement—from the ground up, and from the inside out—of all that are under her care.

Conclusion

A great deal is made of the question of immanence and transcendence in the Confucian tradition. As noted in Chapters 1 and 2, Zhu Xi neither conceives of nor depends on a transcendent God standing outside of the rest of existence. As Mary Evelyn Tucker points out, "the art of Confucian spirituality might be described as discovering one's cosmological being amidst daily affairs. For the Confucian the ordinary is the locus of the extraordinary; the secular is the sacred; the transcendent is in the immanent."[137]

Nonetheless, it may be argued that there is something in the universe that is not immanent *yet*. As noted above, Zhu Xi believes that human beings put the good feelings and character of Heaven and Earth into concrete play. It is virtue, expressed on a small scale, which makes the great goodness of the cosmos manifest: "the lesser virtues are manifestations of the entire substance [of virtue]; great virtue is the root of the ten thousand manifestations. . . . This speaks of the Way of Heaven and Earth."[138] In fact, once human individuals have begun to manifest their own virtue, Zhu tells us that their impact will be cosmic in scope: "then the way of human beings will be established, the way of Heaven will flourish, and the way of Earth will be at peace."[139] The goodness of Heaven and Earth, previously not immanent, becomes immanent.

Meanwhile, for Thomas, it is rather more immediately clear that there are both immanent and transcendent elements at work in the universe. God's transcendent will is seen in the immanent good of the proper ordering of all that is:

> . . . things participate in the divine goodness to the extent that they are good, by way of likeness. Now, that which is the greatest good in caused things is the good of the order of the universe, for it is most perfect, as the Philosopher says (Metaphysics, XI, 10, 10 (1075a 12). With this, divine Scripture is also in agreement, for it is said in Genesis (1:31): "God saw all the things He had made, and they were very good," which He simply said of the individual works, that "they were good." So the good of the *order* of things caused by God is what is chiefly willed and caused by God.[140]

In Thomas's formulation, "to govern things is nothing but to impose order on them."[141] Thus the immanentization of the good order, which serves the good of the part and the whole, is also reflective of the transcendent good of God.

Therefore, with or without God, the end result is very similar for both philosophers: humanity in general is to assume a position of authority in the world at large, and individuals in particular are to assume positions of authority within the human race, so that the potential flourishing of all may be realized in a comprehensive common good that touches on all aspects of existence, including—and in a special way—the moral. Thus, authority, conceived of as completely separate from its abuse, is welcomed and engaged with in an extremely positive way by both thinkers, as a channel through which loving concern and assistance may be provided to those who need it.

Of course, rightfully exercising this authority is a very complex project requiring a very comprehensive view of the world. As discussed in previous chapters, Zhu and Thomas do not simplify matters by leaving important considerations out of their doctrines regarding the universe, human nature as it is, or human nature as it should be. Rather, in embracing as much of reality as they can, they provide models in which opposing urges and diverse concerns can be balanced and made complementary to each other. In fact, far from viewing human beings as either unable or unfit to put concentrated power to just and fair use, both

Zhu and Thomas enthusiastically welcome the challenges of authority, and think that it can indeed be exercised on behalf of the good of all.

In addition to the perennial merits of its comprehensiveness, the optimism of their approach is perhaps particularly timely in our own age. In an article entitled "The Case for Moral Education," Geir Helgesen invites us to contemplate

> . . . the present world situation with that of an airplane high up in the sky, in which the passengers, after having traveled for hours, suddenly discover that there are no pilots in the cockpit. This easy-to-imagine (and for frequent flyers frightening!) illustration might be an exaggeration of the feelings of the ordinary citizen, but nevertheless it touches on a question in the contemporary world which is basic, existential, and difficult to answer: "Where are we heading?" It goes without saying that this question is decisive in the field of political socialization.[142]

This question is decisive everywhere, in all fields and for all people. As Regan points out, "[whether or not] territorially limited self-sufficiency was possible even in premodern times, it can be strongly argued that in the modern world national bodies politic are incapable of the self-sufficiency envisioned [in the past]."[143] Globalization means that we are all flying together on the same flight.[144]

Of course, we cannot all fit in the cockpit at once, and those of us left in the back may fume over our inability to direct the course. Nonetheless, that someone needs to be flying the plane, and that we can't all do it at once, is clear to anyone who thinks twice. That someone, however, in taking the controls of the plane is also accepting responsibility for its course and, to a certain extent, its fate.

According to Zhu and Thomas, this state of affairs is not necessarily a problem, and, certainly, if they are right—and the most readily available common sense seems to say that they are—it is wise to have good, intelligent people who truly care for the common good in charge of making the decisions that affect us all, including those that impact upon our own personal freedoms.

Unfortunately, that such people are not often those who are in charge is apparent to nearly anyone with any experience of human authority. In a characteristically crotchety letter to his son, J. R. R. Tolkien wrote: "the most improper job of any man, even saints (who at any rate were at least unwilling to take it on), is bossing other men. Not one in a million is fit for it, and least of all those who seek the opportunity . . . The mediaevals were only too right in taking *nolo episcopari* [I do not wish to be a bishop] as the best reason a man could give to others for making him a bishop."[145] As Tolkien points out, humility is a desirable quality for those in power to have. Indeed, even given a strongly positive view of authority, a certain amount of humility remains requisite in its proper exercise—a topic discussed in the next chapter.

Chapter 5

Limiting Authority

> Conceal from the patient the true end of Humility. Let him think of it not as self-forgetfulness but as a certain kind of opinion (namely, a low opinion) of his own talents and character. Some talents, I gather, he really has. Fix in his mind the idea that humility consists in trying to believe those talents to be less valuable than he believes them to be. No doubt they are in fact less valuable than he believes, but that is not the point. The great thing is to make him value an opinion for some quality other than truth, thus introducing an element of dishonesty and make-believe into the heart of what otherwise threatens to become a virtue. By this method thousands of humans have been brought to think that humility means pretty women trying to believe they are ugly and clever men trying to think they are fools. And since what they are trying to believe may, in some cases, be manifest nonsense, they cannot succeed in believing it and we have the chance of keeping their minds endlessly revolving on themselves in an effort to achieve the impossible.
>
> —C. S. Lewis, *The Screwtape Letters*

The Contemporary Distaste for Humility

Humility is not a particularly trendy virtue. Attacks are launched upon it from all directions. In the literature of the secularist Ayn Rand, currently popular with political conservatives in the United States, we find the climactic speech of John Galt, who declaims, "discard the protective rags of that vice which you call a virtue: humility—learn to value yourself, which means: to fight for your happiness—and when you learn that *pride* is the sum of all virtues, you will learn to live like a man."[1] The almost commonsensical appeal of her perspective has a great deal to do with how many of us conceive of the self. As Adam Seligman points out, in the contemporary world we often "seek the core of the self in the image of the self-actualizing agent who realizes his or her autonomous will. The more this will is realized, the more the self does, as it were, exist."[2] When fulfillment of the will is linked so strongly to the very existence of the self, virtues like humility, which takes such concerns as less than paramount, are bound to be viewed with a great deal of suspicion and dislike.

Moreover, when we consider that this assertion-centered way of conceiving of the human person rules out neither the advisability nor the practice of sacrifice on behalf of others—a practice arguably necessary at some point in any functioning society—we can begin to wonder why humility is either requisite or commendable. For example, following the sociologist Charles Horton Cooley, it is possible to come to the conclusion that "the group self or 'we' is simply an 'I' which includes other persons."[3] If one adopts this view, evidently altruistic behavior—like giving up one's life for one's brother—starts to seem more like the behavior of an interested actor with a particularly large and inclusive sense of self. At the same time, humility, in addition to bearing the weight of general unattractiveness, starts to seem less and less relevant to or important for the human community.

Given this context, it is hardly a shock to find that discussions within and about the Christian and Confucian communities continue to struggle with the difficulty of embracing and enthusiastically practicing humility. As Brian Daley points out, it is unfortunately often the case that, "in the Christian tradition, we identify humility with a perversely cultivated lack of self-esteem, and the tradition that has identified it as a virtue we regard as simply expressing neurotic negativity, unfounded guilt, or a piously cloaked ideology of male domination."[4] Similar charges have been leveled against the humility espoused by the Confucian tradition. He Zhen (何震, late nineteenth–early twentieth century), a proponent of radical social and political reform in early twentieth-century China, bitterly castigates the ancient Chinese historian and philosopher Ban Zhao (班昭, fl. first century CE), whose *Admonitions for Women* (*Nüjie*, 女誡) "shows that first of all she emphasizes the ignoble and weak nature of women. She says women are inferiors and should be humble and yielding as well as respectful and deferential. They should place others before themselves and must accept all insults and hardships, as if ever kneeling in fear."[5] Worse than accepting insults, following the Confucian tradition can even mean death, as we see in a famous passage from Zhu's *Jinsilu:* "Someone asked, 'sometimes there are lonely widows, who are poor with no one to look after them. Are they permitted to marry again?' The Master [Cheng Yi] replied, 'People of recent times are afraid of starving to death, and for this reason it is said [that widows can remarry]. However, starving to death is an extremely insignificant affair, [while] failing in matters [such as maintaining chastity] is extremely significant.' "[6] Such statements as this one by Cheng Yi, were, not surprisingly, often read in ways injurious to women.

Nonetheless, a close reading of this exhortation suggests that the idea that widows should die rather than remarry is more of a recognition of the dignity of women, in this case to be expressed through their chastity, than a misogynistic disregard for female life—a reading supported by Cheng Yi's report that his own father arranged for the remarriage of a female cousin, due to the compassionate concern that she would remain unhappy without a life partner.[7] In other words, Cheng Yi and his colleagues understood that both principle and context play a great role in making moral decisions—a point unfortunately often lost in the generations that followed them. Given that He Zhen was a member of one of those later generations, one can sympathize with her angry proclamation that "we can see that the Confucian insistence on ritual decorum is nothing more than a tool for murdering women."[8]

All these critiques have merit. Scholar of humility Lisa Fullam concurs with Ayn Rand's argument that the word "humility" often implies pointless or false self-abasement, pointing out that those who deny or otherwise misrepresent their talents and virtues in the name of modesty or humility are engaging in dishonest behavior, if not toward others then toward themselves: "at best, such [statements connote] a failure of my intellect to gauge my ability with any accuracy at all."[9] Regarding the idea that humility is in essence a vice urged upon the weak by the strong, Fullam notes, "we have to be aware of humility's capacity to serve as a weapon, a virtue urged on the vulnerable to maintain their vulnerability, in the way that some voices opposing civil rights for minorities and women declared that they should know their place instead of being 'uppity.' "[10] It is indubitably the case that perversions of truth and human dignity in the name of humility are dismayingly profuse.

But being aware of these problems does not stop Fullam herself from embarking on an intellectual exploration of humility. Indeed, declining to positively engage with the concept can lead to problems like those above: if humility is understood to be a disposition that belongs and applies only to the weak, stupid, and/or dishonest, then it cannot serve as a virtue for the powerful or the truthful. However, in Fullam's estimation, humility is indeed a virtue that applies to the strong,[11] the intelligent,[12] and the honest.[13]

Such an estimation is also apparent in the lives and work of Zhu Xi and Thomas Aquinas. In his study of Zhu Xi, Chen Lai tells us, "when Zhu was eight or nine years old, he read [in] the *Mencius*: 'the sage is of the same kind as I am.' The hope of becoming a sage moved him to an 'unspeakable joy.' "[14] Likewise, in his popular biography of Thomas, Chesterton tells us of the anecdotal tradition that Thomas "was a large and heavy and quiet boy, and phenomenally silent, scarcely opening his mouth except to say suddenly to his schoolmaster in an explosive manner, 'What is God?' "[15] Zhu thought he could become a sage; Thomas thought that he could learn the answer to his question. Both childhood stories, whether historical or apocryphal, are important because they imply a certain amount of humility in the children involved: Zhu did not think that he was a sage, but that he could *become* one, and Thomas did not think he knew God, but that God was *knowable*. This sense of humility in the face of possibility was to infuse their entire adult careers, and their doctrines concerning authority, or legitimate power understood as fairly exercised or justly wielded,[16] in particular. This chapter will consider both thinkers in a discussion about how humility is necessary to any true exercise of authority. That Thomas Aquinas, a friar who took vows of poverty and obedience, considers humility a virtue is perhaps not a surprise. However, the question of how Zhu Xi views this disposition is a bit more complex. The next section first delves into what Zhu has to say on the topic before considering Thomas's more straightforward treatment.

Zhu Xi and Thomas Aquinas on Humility

Zhu Xi: A Virtue or Not?

To begin, Chinese has several words that may be rendered as "humility" in English—throughout this discussion, I provide the original Mandarin for each term I so translate on the basis of both common usage and dictionary definitions—none of which appear in the two lists of the virtues most often provided by Zhu. Humility is not included in the four virtues of Mencius, which Zhu utilizes in his definition of human nature: "nature is merely humaneness, righteousness, propriety and wisdom."[17] Nor is humility included in the slightly expanded list of virtues that corresponds to the five material elements of his cosmological account: "humaneness is wood, righteousness is metal, propriety is fire, wisdom is water, and faithfulness is earth."[18] (Perhaps characteristically, Zhu dodges the systematic question of why there are two sets of virtues, explaining instead the role the fifth virtue plays in relation to the other four: "Someone asked, 'Humaneness, righteousness, propriety and wisdom are the four virtues of the nature, but there to these is also added the character of 'faithfulness,' [to create] the so-called 'five natures.' How can this be?' [Zhu] answered, 'Faithfulness is that which gives integrity and substance to the other four.'"[19]) But this is not to say that there is no such thing as humility in Zhu's thought, nor that it is a disposition of which he disapproves. For one thing, these two lists are not conceived of as providing an exhaustive register of all virtue. For example, elsewhere he also discusses sincerity (*cheng*, 誠), loyalty (*zhong*, 忠), and trustworthiness (*fu*, 孚).[20] Notably, this series of virtues involves fidelity to others and to a high standard of conduct that encourage a certain kind of self-forgetfulness in their attainment, as does his treatment of filial piety and fraternal respect (discussed below). For another, the figure of the sage provides reasons for humble self-assessment.

First of all, the near impossibility of attaining sagehood is inherently humbling to the would-be *shengren*. The most revered figure in Zhu's tradition warns that sages are few and far between: "Confucius said, 'Perfect indeed is the mean! Rare indeed is the one who can practice it!'"[21] Nor are the clever and well-behaved necessarily any closer to the achievement of sagehood: "Confucius said, 'I know why the Way is not practiced: those who are intelligent surpass it, and those who are stupid do not measure up to it. I know why the Way is not illuminated: worthies surpass it, and the unworthy do not attain it.'"[22] Moreover, neither of these two outcomes is to be desired as better than the other: "Zigong asked, 'Shi or Shang: which is the worthier [person]?' The Master said, 'Shi goes too far, and Shang does not go far enough.' [Zigong] replied, "Then the superiority is with Shi?' The Master said, 'To go too far is the same as falling short.'"[23]

Attaining the proper mean is therefore extraordinarily difficult, a process that involves stumbling and unceasing, humbling effort, even for those who are naturally intelligent and innately inclined to virtue.

(Again, as noted above, although it is theoretically possible that a wise man may have been born that way, the vast majority of us fall into a second category, in which the individual "has to study and then knows, has to act and then extends."[24]) Zhu himself believed that

> . . . self-cultivation begins with an awareness that learning to be fully human involves pain and suffering. The vigorous exercise that is required for realising the great joy of inner peace ('knowing that one is sincere upon self-examination') is strenuous. The four words that Chu Hsi [Zhu Xi] . . . employed to encourage his students shortly before he died, *chien-k'u kung-fu* [*jianku gongfu*] 艱苦功夫 (the hard and painful effort) capture well the spirit of a lifelong commitment to and a continuous process of self-education.[25]

Therefore it makes a great deal of sense that Confucianism in general says that the truly good person is humble: "Confucius said, 'The superior person has righteousness as substance, puts it into practice by way of propriety, *expresses it by way of humility (sun,* 孫*)*, and accomplishes it in faithfulness. This is the superior person!' "[26] Confucius himself, who was famously critical of his own performance as a son, a government minister, a younger brother, and a friend, provides a model of humility.[27] Confucius's willingness to so criticize himself is hardly surprising given his social context, for, as Jane Geaney points out, "Classical Confucian texts depict a society that is convinced of the importance of shame as a distinctively human experience."[28] She continues, "in the Confucian texts, and presumably in the Confucian view, the boundaries between inside and outside the person are relatively flexible. It seems that impurity can derive from inside as well as outside the person."[29] Such a recognition—which may be viewed as possibly pathological in what Philip Rieff terms a "therapeutic culture" like our own—is bound to increase humility in those still struggling with various forms of impurity.

Moreover, even when one has reached the pinnacle of human achievement, humility will still be a necessary disposition. According to Confucius, whether sage, worthy, or *junzi*, when the good person "is in a superior position he is not proud."[30] In fact, as Joseph Chan points out, "Confucius puts demanding standards of moral behavior on the rulers and gentlemen, not the common people."[31] In a similar way, according to Yü Ying-shih, Zhu never intended for his teachings to reach a wide audience:

> . . . the Master Zhu said, "Hold on to a share of the Principle of Heaven, and eliminate a share of human desire." This saying is directed at the scholar-officials, not at the ordinary person. *Because the scholar-officials were to be the political and social leaders in the future, they had to understand the difference between profit and righteousness.* This saying of Master Zhu's is certainly not directing the common people to cease desiring "profit," or to cease wanting to eat, but rather is aimed at the scholar-officials.[32]

More humility is required of the ruler than of the common people, then, on the grounds that their standards are higher and more difficult to reach, given their greater responsibilities. As Pei-Yi Wu points out, in the Confucian tradition, "those who were most prone to self-examination were precisely those who were expected to be paragons of virtue, exemplars for the masses."[33] Zhu himself says that it is the *sage* who is never satisfied:

> Zheng asked about [the passage in the *Analects* in which Confucius says] "Which of these [have I been able to do]?" The Master answered: "This saying is hard to explain. The sage is humbling [*qian*, 謙] himself, saying 'I have not [attained] these [qualities].' The sage is often dissatisfied [with himself]. Although ordinary people see that he extends his humaneness to the utmost warmth, and his righteousness to the utmost refinement, the sage only cares for the deficient places he sees [in himself]."[34]

This is not to say that the sage does not perceive his own virtue; it is rather that the sage is *chiefly conscious* of his or her shortcomings. The Confucian tradition does not prize dishonesty! As Cua points out, humility "is not incompatible with just pride in moral achievement as it is exemplified in the attainment of jen [*ren*] (humanity) and i [*yi*] (righteousness)."[35] Humility does not cause stupidity in the sage that would prevent him from grasping the mean, but rather causes him to focus on that which requires improvement in himself.[36]

That even the sage will have some shortcomings is highly probable. Indeed, from a metaphysical point of view, Zhu knows that "the heart of fire has blackness, and at the heart of *yang* is *yin* . . . *Yin* is the substance of *yang*, and *yang* is the substance of *yin*. Water that is bright on the inside is dark on the outside, and fire that is dark on the inside is bright on the outside."[37] In most if not all things a little of the opposite is to be found: even in the sage, who might be successfully tempted to do or say the wrong thing—or even something that he does not mean. In such a case, the erring sage is not to be harshly punished or judged, but rather to be viewed with compassion and even amusement. When discussing a chapter in the *Analects* that features Confucius boldly claiming that Heaven would protect him from the enemies closing in around him, one of Zhu's students said, "it may be seen that the Master typically would not speak like this, he is always of such a humble appearance, and this statement is dissimilar to [his general personality]." The *Yulei* reports Zhu's response as being one of amusement: "Laughing, [Zhu] replied, 'But this was really an emergency situation; Confucius said this aloud without meaning to.' "[38]

Hence, humility and its attendant gentleness are viewed as playing an indispensable role in virtuous behavior for all. In Zhu's understanding, "there is nothing under Heaven which does not have [its own] nature," and the virtues are included in this assessment. He goes on: "humaneness is categorized under affection; righteousness belongs to firmness; propriety belongs to humility (*qianxun*, 謙遜); and wisdom belongs to clarifying distinctions."[39] That such humility is to be encouraged from an early age is apparent not only in his emphasis on the importance of the ritual education that promotes propriety, discussed in Chapter 3, but also in his professed belief that the humility learned at home through the development of piety toward one's parents and respect for one's elder siblings is inseparable from the cultivation of *ren*. In the following passage, Zhu Xi analyzes the relationship between the domestic and the universal virtues:

> . . . a student asked, "someone [once] asked Yichuan [Cheng Yi], 'does the saying, "filial piety and fraternal respect are the foundation of *ren*" mean that it is through filial piety and fraternal respect that we arrive at *ren*?' Yichuan replied, 'No.' I do not understand how this is so." [Zhu Xi] replied, "You cannot speak of 'arriving at' *ren*. In speaking of *ren* and moral principle, you cannot use the language of place, and it is places that you can speak of arriving at. Similarly, it is not that filial piety and fraternal respect are over here, and *ren* is over there; thus, there is no reason in saying that one arrives at *ren* through filial piety and fraternal respect . . . Master

> Cheng was merely saying, 'attaining ren to the utmost is thus obtaining filial piety and fraternal respect to the utmost; attaining filial piety and fraternal respect to the utmost, is then *ren*.'" [Zhu Xi] also said, "filial piety and fraternal respect are affairs of *ren*."[40]

Above all, Zhu shows his high estimation of humility in his commentary on Chapter 33 of the *Doctrine of the Mean*:

> . . . in [many texts] it is written: "over her embroidered robe she puts on a plain garment . . ." The ancients studied for themselves [not to impress others]. Therefore their hearts were like this [quotation]. The embroidered robe is therefore realized in daily life. Simple, unadorned, and modest are the clothes [the superior person] wears on the outside—he is patient, refined and reasonable—and the beauty of the brocade robe is [underneath], at his center. The petty person is the opposite; he exposes [much] on the outside with nothing at his core to follow it up.[41]

In other words, the good Confucian quietly gets down to the business of doing the right thing at the right time. Rather than loudly proclaiming her own moral worth, she prefers to let her actions speak for themselves, and for her virtue to show itself over time.[42] An alternative reading of the superior person is that she is simply bland. In an article, reproduced in English as "The Chinese Notion of 'Blandness' as a Virtue: A Preliminary Outline," French scholar François Jullien writes,

> It may appear paradoxical—going against ordinary judgment as it does—to say that blandness (*la fadeur*) could be evaluated positively. However, it is a basic intuition where the most diverse currents of Chinese thought flow together, whether Daoist or Confucian, and which goes back to antiquity. Moreover, this virtue of blandness itself extends to the most diverse domains of literate culture: from the 'metaphysical' intuition of the great process of the cosmos to the moral and psychological valuation of the sage, and, finally, to aesthetic judgment.[43]

However, given the decidedly unbland character of Mencius, who advocated the execution of unlawful rulers (to be discussed further below), as well as the generations of Confucians who followed him in publicly demanding high standards of conduct from their rulers and proclaiming, in the words of Tu Weiming, "the right of the people to rebel against a tyrannical dynasty, the right of the aristocracy to remove an unjust imperial household, the right of the imperial clansmen to replace an unsuitable king, and the right of the bureaucrats to remonstrate with a negligent ruler,"[44] Jullien's is a difficult position to maintain. Rather, the Confucian tradition shows us that humility need not be bland at all.

To close, humility is important for Zhu, even though he seems to view it more as a pleasant outcome of genuine virtue, or a suitable accompaniment thereto, than as a virtue in and of itself.[45] A humble attitude, moreover, is not only to be esteemed for its own merits, but also for the way in which it accurately reflects the finitude of the human intellect: a topic with relevance for the proper limitation of authority, as discussed further below.

Thomas Aquinas: Definitely a Virtue

In contrast to Zhu, Thomas devotes a great deal of time to showing how humility is a virtue, and, moreover, against some who would say that it is not. As James Keenan pointed out to me in a personal communication, making a case for the virtuousness of one of his virtues is not exceptional to his treatment of humility: Thomas does the same with regard to Christian virtues such as religion,[46] chastity,[47] and mercy.[48] In all of these discussions, when conflicts arise between Christian and Aristotelian ethics, Thomas does not hesitate to place himself firmly in the camp of the former.[49]

Nonetheless, the fact that Aristotle did not call humility a virtue is somewhat of an issue for the Aristotelian Thomas. Thus, in his discussion of virtue, he considers the objection that "every moral virtue is about actions and passions, according to Ethic. ii, 3. But humility is not reckoned by the Philosopher among the virtues that are about passions, nor is it comprised under justice which is about actions. Therefore it would seem not to be a virtue."[50] In his response, Thomas says, "the Philosopher intended to treat of virtues as directed to civic life, wherein the subjection of one man to another is defined according to the ordinance of the law, and consequently is a matter of legal justice. But humility, considered as a special virtue, regards chiefly the subjection of man to God, for Whose sake he humbles himself by subjecting himself to others."[51] It is in passages like these that I find reason to disagree with Lisa Fullam's different reading of Thomas's treatment of humility. She claims that "Thomas missed the communal resonance of humility entirely."[52] Arguing that he is not alone in doing so, she prefers Benedict's treatment: "by construing humility as an essential virtue for communal living, Benedict has introduced a new emphasis on the ramifications of humility for relationships between people, while the desert ascetics, Augustine, and Thomas all tend to downplay this aspect of the virtue."[53] On the other hand, I argue that, while Thomas introduces a personal God unknown to Aristotle into his discussion, it is clear that, for him, humility is not only a religious virtue, but also a social and political one: the voluntary subjection to others counseled in Thomas's treatment of humility has a great deal of communal resonance.

This virtue enables one to take a balanced look at oneself and one's gifts: "there is in man something great which he possesses through the gift of God; and something defective which accrues to him through the weakness of nature."[54] While the virtue of magnanimity involves the gifts one has from God, humility involves an awareness of the latter: "humility makes a man think little of himself in consideration of his own deficiency;" such awareness then leads to good opinions of others: "humility makes us honor others and esteem them better than ourselves, in so far as we see some of God's gifts in them."[55] In interpreting this passage, I find myself again differing with Fullam. Responding to the dynamic character of Thomas's thought, she writes that "if humility is a continual interplay of the appetite for self-aggrandizement and the intellect's self-assessment . . . then moral truth becomes intrinsically a process, not a static target. And if virtues are a reflection of human nature, rather than an externally-imposed code, we do not create virtues out of whole cloth; rather, we discover them in the process of our moral development. In sum, moral truth with a 'hermeneutic of humility' is a personal, communal process of discovery."[56] While she notes that "moral norms are not empty or meaningless, by any means," she advises that we approach "morals not just as humble persons, but as persons who conceive moral norms humbly"[57] in order that we may develop true discernment and moral creativity.

While this is an intriguing argument, I do not believe that it is one with which Thomas would be entirely comfortable. While different places might have equally valid interpretations of what is and is not appropriate in given situations, the basic fundamentals never change. Reason must work within the confines of the natural law, which eternally remains, regardless of whether we care to notice it or not: "we must say that the natural law, as to general principles, is the same for all, both as to rectitude and as to knowledge."[58] Of course, as a member of a society meeting another great civilization (the ancient Greek) via a third great civilization (the Muslim),[59] Thomas was well aware that not all cultures share the same values. But, in this, it is the cultures that are failing, and not the law:

> . . . as to certain matters of detail, which are conclusions, as it were, of those general principles, it is the same for all in the majority of cases, both as to rectitude and as to knowledge; and yet in some few cases it may fail, both as to rectitude, by reason of certain obstacles (just as natures subject to generation and corruption fail in some few cases on account of some obstacle), and as to knowledge, since in some the reason is perverted by passion, or evil habit, or an evil disposition of nature; thus formerly, theft, although it is expressly contrary to the natural law, was not considered wrong among the Germans, as Julius Caesar relates (De Bello Gall. vi).[60]

Thus, with his conception of a universal objective standard, Thomas explicitly raises the possibility that entire societies might be evil in some respect. The same, of course, is true for individuals, who might be led astray by their will, their intellect, or both. In defining moral truth as "a personal, communal process of discovery," Fullam's approach errs on the side of slighting objective moral reality.

In any case, while these two virtues may not seem to be particularly complementary, Thomas is insistent that "magnanimity and humility are not contrary to one another, although they seem to tend in contrary directions, because they proceed according to different considerations."[61] These considerations, while different, are alike in their foundation: "humility restrains the appetite from aiming at great things against right reason: while magnanimity urges the mind to great things in accord with right reason. Hence it is clear that magnanimity is not opposed to humility: indeed they concur in this, that each is according to right reason."[62] In fact, even aside from conceiving of humility as *complementary* to magnanimity, Thomas views the former as *necessary* to the latter. As he points out, no one can be solely great in and of himself:

> . . . it surpasses man to need nothing at all. For every man needs, first, the Divine assistance, secondly, even human assis-

> tance, since man is naturally a social animal, for he is not sufficient by himself to provide for his own life. Accordingly, in so far as he needs others, it belongs to a magnanimous man to have confidence in others, for it is also a point of excellence in a man that he should have at hand those who are able to be of service to him.[63]

The magnanimous person must be humble enough to admit her dependence on and need for others lest her confidence in her own abilities become unreasonable. Thomas recognizes that even virtuous magnanimity unchecked can lead to serious problems: "as to the hope whereby a man relies on his own power, there is presumption if he tends to a good as though it were possible to him, whereas it surpasses his powers, according to Judith 6:15: 'Thou humblest them that presume of themselves.' This presumption is contrary to the virtue of magnanimity which holds to the mean in this kind of hope."[64] Moreover, to look at things from the opposite end, in Thomas's understanding, a properly humble person need not eschew attempts at accomplishing great things. As Mary Keys puts it, "Classical 'elitism,' for lack of a better term, is effectively undercut in Aquinas's account, but (contra Nietzsche et al.) without rendering universal mediocrity and pusillanimity the only viable alternatives."[65]

In short, the problem posed by Screwtape in the epigraph to this chapter is thus avoided: one need not convince oneself that one is worse than one is. According to Thomas, humility does not mean lack of truthfulness when it comes to human greatness. In fact, if he claimed otherwise, he would be guilty of inconsistency, for he says that honesty is a virtue.[66] In Fullam's turn of phrase, "for Thomas, knowing the truth about ourselves is knowing the truth about ourselves."[67] In fact, "humility in its epistemological dimension is exactly the pursuit of a morally accurate self-understanding."[68] Such a self-understanding will involve recognition of the limitations imposed on our intellects by our finite nature, which in turn will influence the amount of authority we can rightfully exercise—a topic discussed more fully in the section below.

Humility Grounded in Finite Nature and Knowledge

One robust finding in social-psychological research on accuracy and bias in self-evaluation is that people perceive themselves to be better than others.[69] Oftentimes, as may be imagined, this perception is fundamentally flawed—as are other judgments that we habitually make. This section surveys the ways in which Zhu Xi and Thomas Aquinas approach the limitations of the human intellect.

Zhu Xi and the Way

As discussed in Chapter 4, the ideal Confucian state of affairs involves wise people in charge. This, however, does not mean that the wise have all the answers and thus know exactly what to do at every given moment.

To begin with, in Confucianism, there is something that even the sage does not know. The *Doctrine of the Mean* not only exhorts people to exercise morally grounded authority, but also assigns limitations to that use. In particular, it provides the explicit acknowledgment that no one fully comprehends the pattern and meaning of existence: "In the utmost reaches [of the Way of the superior person], there is something which even the sage does not know."[70] As is often the case in Confucian philosophy, this theoretical premise flows very smoothly into more prosaic observations. From Zhu Xi's perspective, given that everything in the universe is comprised of morally charged *li* and *qi*, if there is that which the sage does not know in the furthest reaches of the universe, he does not have all of the moral answers. Naturally, if the sage does not have all of the answers, the rest of us should be prepared to acknowledge that we do not, either.

As the sage's will is always contingent on an incomplete understanding of events, we should not be surprised to find that his job is not to impose his will on the people and things around him. Rather, he is called to cooperate with Heaven and Earth as a partner, not as a replacement; in Zhu's words, "the sage is of the same substance as Heaven and Earth,"[71] and "the sage is of the same function as Heaven and Earth."[72] People on the path to sagehood are not encouraged to narrowly focus on themselves and their own personal interests or desires as though these were the center or the apex of the universe, but rather to bring themselves into alignment with forces far greater than they are. The humility urged by the Classics, and by Zhu Xi himself, is necessary to focusing on the elements that we can, over time, more fully *share* with others.

As always, this process of self-cultivation in human and cosmic community will be a humbling one. In speaking of the sage king Wen, the *Great Learning* says, "in the Book of Poetry, it is said, 'Profound was King Wen! With how fine and splendid a feeling of reverence did he regard his resting places!' As a sovereign, he rested in humaneness. As a minister, he rested in reverence. As a son, he rested in filial piety. As a father, he rested in kindness. In communication with his subjects, he rested in good faith."[73] Zhu's commentary on this passage reads:

> . . . this is to show where the sage rests: simply that he rests in the good. These five [resting places] are the places in which he attains his greatness every day. Concerning these [five], the student must study carefully their pure and profound store [of wisdom], and then extend them out to exhaust their abundance. Then, in all affairs under Heaven, he will know where to rest, and there will be nothing for him to doubt.[74]

As Confucius's remarks above on his own shortcomings attest, achieving such restfulness is a difficult task. Moreover, it is a lifelong one. In what Irene Bloom calls "the world's briefest autobiography," Confucius said to his disciples, "At fifteen, I set my mind-and-heart on learning. At thirty, I stood firm. At forty, I had no doubts. At fifty, I knew the law of Heaven. At sixty, I obeyed it effortlessly. At seventy, I could follow the desires of my heart, without crossing the line."[75] Thus, the superior person is one who humbly submits to a lifelong process of development and cultivation, that he or she may be increasingly able to set her own desires aside in favor of the concerns of Heaven and Earth, in hopes that she may finally find rest in a place where there will be nothing left to doubt.

Nonetheless, even the sage who has nothing left to doubt will still be unaware of certain things. As noted earlier, the humility that the disciple needs in order to persevere at the long and often painful task of self-cultivation, with all its stumbling blocks and moments of failure, is not to be discarded when he attains his goal of sagehood. While the virtues attendant on sagehood or its near achievement definitely qualify him to lead—as discussed in Chapter 4—the finite character of his wisdom means that he will never have all of the answers, and will thus have to place limitations on his authority accordingly. Moreover, as discussed further below, the sage or the worthy must also recognize rightful limitations on his authority by paying close attention to claims of others, and to the insights that may be available from the unlikeliest of people. It is in recognizing his own limitations, and refusing to allow his own interests or preconceptions to take exclusively center stage, that the sage or the worthy exercises humility, perhaps most importantly when he occupies a position of power.

Thomas Aquinas and God

Like Zhu Xi, Thomas Aquinas believes that the wise should exercise authority over the-not-so-wise, and that wisdom is a prerequisite to good rule. Nonetheless, also like Zhu, Thomas neither presumes that it is possible for human beings to know all that there is to know nor that it is virtuous for them to believe that they can. In fact, says Thomas, "man's first sin was pride."[76] This pride involved, among other things, the desire "that by his own natural power he might decide what was good, and what was evil for him to do."[77] In Thomas's estimation, the "natural power" of human beings is simply not up to such a task, for they are created for an end and a purpose wholly beyond their power to imagine. In his concise formulation: "matters of faith surpass natural reason."[78] As Pinckaers notes, "these words of Scripture usually play a leading role because they possess a status of their own; they are sparks of a higher light coming from the intellect (*intellectus*) which is superior to discursive reason . . . For Thomas, the words of Scripture, even when very simple in their formulation, can open up more direct access—far more than the most elaborate scholastic reasoning—to the reality theology addresses."[79]

Indeed, in responding to the question, "Whether any created good constitutes man's happiness," Thomas replies that even attaining an angelic state does not represent the fullness of all that God has in store for those who love Him: "the summit of man does indeed touch the base of the angelic nature, by a kind of likeness; but man does not rest there as in his last end, but reaches out to the universal fount itself of good, which is the common object of happiness of all the blessed, as being the infinite and perfect good."[80] A point crucial to any Thomistic discussion of authority is that, even though the blessed will enjoy this supernatural end after death,[81] they will never know God as He is: "the happiness of God, Who, in understanding his Essence, comprehends It, is higher than that of a man or angel who sees It indeed, but comprehends It not."[82]

If this is true of the blessed, it is even more so for those of us still on earth. From this perspective, people in a mortal state of existence should be very careful about claims to understand God's will.

Thus, it is quite fitting that Thomas not only identifies pride as a vice, but also sets humility against it as a virtue,[83] one that he defines in the following terms: "it belongs properly to humility, that a man restrain himself from being borne towards that which is above him. For this purpose he must know his disproportion to that which surpasses his capacity. Hence knowledge of one's own deficiency belongs to humility."[84] Here as elsewhere in Thomas, a deep sense of hierarchy pervades: humans are capable of only so much in the cosmic order, and must be cognizant of their place in any actions they undertake, lest they exceed the bounds assigned to them. Certainly, knowledge of ultimate meaning, rightness, and ends is possible due to a Divine Revelation that far exceeds anything humans could rightfully ascertain on their own.[85] Nonetheless, even in the face of such Revelation, everyone—the wise most of all—must acknowledge that not all answers have been provided, and the virtue of humility will certainly aid in this venture. Nor is the incompleteness of our knowledge limited to our understanding of the nature and goodness of God: it also includes the fact that we often do not know the entire story with regard to temporal affairs, a topic discussed further in the following section.

Humility in Community

As discussed in Chapters 2 and 3, Zhu Xi and Thomas Aquinas conceived of the person as an intelligent agent called to develop her moral potential in communion with others. This section focuses on the role played by humility in this communal process of cultivation.

Zhu Xi and Social Inferiors

Confucius says, "Walking with three people, there is sure to be my teacher. I find what is good in them and follow it, and find what is not good in them and change it [in myself]."[86] While this passage certainly opens up the prospect that we can learn what *not* to do from those whom we perceive to be our social or moral inferiors, this is not the only possibility that arises. It is possible—and nothing in the passage says otherwise—that the people with whom Confucius was walking were his students; indeed, this must often have been the case. Nonetheless he speaks of finding good to emulate in his companions—a useful reminder to those who might not be particularly attentive to the lessons younger, less articulate, or poorly educated people might have to impart.

It is a truism that our inability to know everything often includes an ignorance as to where it is that moral insight is to be found. It is with this kind of failing in mind that Zhu Xi counsels humility to his students with statements such as: "many people think they are mature and accomplished, and thus are not willing to ask questions of their [social] inferiors. As a result they are ignorant their entire lives."[87] (Such people might also be ignorant in the moment: as Stephen Angle puts it, "we are all prone to lapses if we do not focus our attention, so asking questions is a way [of exhorting oneself] to focus."[88]) Such proclamations concerning the virtue of exercising humility before the humble are, of course, buttressed by the constant reminders, discussed in Chapter 2, of all the problems and pain most students will encounter in their endeavors to improve themselves.

Clearly, this advice does not attack the concept of social inferiority *per se*. This system is not offering an early version of Marxism, nor even liberal egalitarianism: in passages like these, Zhu eschews the rhetoric of individual "empowerment" or self-assertion. Hierarchy, with all of its implications regarding the authority of some over others, indubitably remains.

Nonetheless, such authority is never absolute. As Tu points out, "in the realm of political culture, [the Confucian] universalist claim that all must regard self-cultivation as the root led to the obvious conclusion that politics was inseparable from morality and that morality must take precedence over politics."[89] Such morality is always deeply rooted in communal activities and relationships, all of which are reciprocal in nature. In fact, reciprocity is one of the central concerns of the tradition, as evidenced by the following passage from the *Analects*: "Confucius said: 'Shen! There is one thread that runs through my Way.' Zengzi replied, 'Yes.' Confucius went out. The other disciples asked, 'What did he mean?' Zengzi answered: 'The master's way is loyalty and reciprocity, and that is all.' "[90] As Zhu writes,

> . . . if I do not wish those above me to be without propriety in their dealings with me, then my attitude toward those below [must be affected], and I cannot dare to treat [my inferiors] without propriety. If I do not wish my inferiors to treat me disrespectfully, then my attitude toward my superiors [must be affected], and I cannot dare to treat them disrespectfully. Extending to before and after, left and right, there is nothing that is not like this. Then the location of my self, up and down, the four directions; long and short; wide and narrow, that and this: all are one [in this way], and all without exception correspond to this.[91]

As is clear in the passage above, Zhu conceives of relationships between people, although hierarchical, as reciprocal arrangements in which each party owes something to the other. In Confucianism in general, despite the abuses that may occur in the name of proper role performance, systematically unequal relationships "are in reality reciprocal. If the son honors the father, the father has to care for the son . . . Reciprocity in conjugal relationships is characterized by respect. Reciprocity, therefore, not power, governs these relationships. Reciprocity assumes the integrity of the other party."[92] Such associations, based upon mutual respect and performance of complementary duties, are thus conceived of more as partnerships than as relationships of dominance and submission. Each party retains his or her dignity in the face of the other, and force or cruelty on the part of the partner with superior status is not accepted. As Terry Woo puts it, the Confucian "conception of authority does not condone cruelty and inhumaneness in the senior partner. The senior partner in fact would have clear responsibilities and blind authority would be contrary to the spirit of *jen*."[93] Proud self-assertion without reference to the needs and feelings of the other party is not acceptable: Confucian authority figures are expected, at the least, to be humble enough to realize that those over whom they have power may have valuable insights into their character and actions.

That such insights may be held by one's inferiors is only to be expected in a tradition fully aware that moral insight is not the sole province of any one individual or even social class. Zhu understands that meaningful participation in the Confucian trinity of Heaven, Earth, and Humankind does not require an expert understanding of obscure scriptures or even a rigorous meditation practice; rather, he believes that it can be achieved by the most uneducated of people. In fact, simply by engaging in the creation of new life, men and women both exercise and gain insight into the universal process of production and reproduction.[94] This insight is no less true for being partial: Zhu believes that people can gain significant knowledge of the very nature of reality by participating in the ordinary round of life. (This, of course, does not mean that people cannot or do not make mistakes in their assumptions or understandings. See "Intelligent Agents with Moral Potential" in Chapter 2 for discussion of Zhu Xi's and Thomas Aquinas's doctrines of human evil and ignorance.) To quote the *Doctrine of the Mean* once more: "Common men and women, however ignorant, may possess [knowledge] of [the Way] . . . Common men and women, however ordinary, can carry it into practice."[95] Moreover, given that *everyone's* knowledge is partial, even that of the sage, Zhu raises the distinct possibility that someone who has never learned the specifically Confucian art of investigating things may yet know a great many things that the professionals will never have the time to explore or question. This realization, like the doctrine of the investigation of things, counsels a certain humble openness to finding moral and other insight in the unlikeliest of places, and from the unlikeliest of people. As Tu Weiming points out, "the belief that a humble person can become the exemplar of humanity and thus assume a godlike status in the pantheon of the virtuous is widely held among modern as well as traditional Chinese."[96] A good Confucian, like Zhu, must realize his own limitations, and limit his exercise of authority accordingly, perhaps most especially in being humble enough to admit that today's dishwasher may be tomorrow's great statesman. Moreover, even if the dishwasher is destined never to reach any heights higher than kitchen manager, the Confucian tradition still insists that this person may have something important to say that his superiors would do well to notice, and which will have a limiting impact on their exercise of authority. Finally, the conscious realization of the moral potential within all other human beings, while requiring humility, also promotes love of those people and the goodness within them: a topic discussed further below.

Thomas Aquinas and Revelation

As a devout follower of Jesus of Nazareth, deeply conversant with Christian scripture, Thomas was certainly familiar with the passage in Luke's gospel that reports Jesus as exclaiming: "I thank thee, O Father, Lord of heaven and earth, that thou hast hid these things from the wise and prudent, and hast revealed them unto babes."[97] Given Christ's esteem for the simple and the childlike, it is hardly surprising that Thomas, as Chesterton puts it, "takes the view that the souls of all the ordinary hard-working and simple-minded people are quite as important as the souls of thinkers and truth-seekers."[98] In Thomas's understanding, God has made the words of scripture available to everyone, and its saving truths open to all:

> [One disadvantage if truth were left solely to the inquiry of reason] is that few men would have knowledge of God: because very many are hindered from gathering the fruit of diligent inquiry, which is the discovery of truth . . . some indeed on account of an indisposition of temperament, by

> reason of which many are naturally indisposed to knowledge: so that no efforts of theirs would enable them to reach to the attainment of the highest degree of human knowledge, which consists in knowing God, [while others] are hindered by the needs of household affairs . . . Accordingly the divine clemency has made this salutary commandment, that even some things which reason is able to investigate must be held by faith: so that all may share in the knowledge of God easily.[99]

Knowledge of God is, in Thomas's opinion, the most important and valuable knowledge one can have; its universal availability through the Scriptures and the Church thus has certain practical effects that the wise will bear in mind. As Aidan Nichols puts it, "according to Aquinas, exclusion from the free and happy life is the result of sin, both original and personal, and the light of faith, by making possible for all and sundry without exception that supernatural knowledge of God which embraces the natural knowledge of God, also opened the door to the practice of the virtues for everyone."[100] (As Nichols explains, Thomas here differs markedly from Aristotle, who "considered that those engaged in manual labor would always lack the basic human cultivation—the *paideia*, the education—necessary for acquiring the moral virtues and so would not be able to get underway in this whole project."[101]) The possibility of growth in virtue renders every person in the Christian communion both valuable and lovable.

Outside of the Christian communion, Thomas's respect and admiration for the pagan philosopher Aristotle shows his belief that the very wise need not be Christian. Moreover, his high estimation of non-Christian people is not limited to the wise, but is also granted to the simple. On purely naturalistic grounds, he notes that people may be quite virtuous without being particularly bright: "man may be virtuous without having full use of reason as to everything, provided he have it with regard to those things which have to be done virtuously. In this way all virtuous men have full use of reason. Hence those who seem to be simple, through lack of worldly cunning, may possibly be prudent, according to Matthew 10:16: 'Be ye therefore prudent [Douay: 'wise'] as serpents, and simple as doves.' "[102]

Given such considerations, as well as awareness of his own limitations, Thomas is open to assigning his neighbors value that might not result from immediate experience or knowledge:

> . . . if we set what our neighbor has of God's above that which we have of our own, we cannot incur falsehood. Wherefore a gloss [St. Augustine, QQ. lxxxiii, qu. 71 on Philippians 2:3, "Esteem others better than themselves,"] says: "We must not esteem by pretending to esteem; but we should in truth think it possible for another person to have something that is hidden to us and whereby he is better than we are, although our own good whereby we are apparently better than he, be not hidden."[103]

As Keys puts it, in a way with which Confucians would agree: "even the wisest human sage cannot correctly discern the full mystery of each human soul, the Creator's relationship to it and designs for it, and its intimate response to divine promptings. These things God alone, who 'sees in secret' (see Mt 6:1–16) and knows what is in the hearts of humans, can perceive and judge."[104]

On a related note, the limitations of our knowledge are not limited to either the inner state of our neighbors or the supernatural realities discussed above: for example, Thomas never takes it upon himself to define the common good. Josef Pieper argues that this is perhaps because the common good is beyond our power to exhaustively define: "it appears impossible to give a truly exhaustive, definitive definition of the *bonum commune*; for no one can state with complete finality what the potentialities of the human community are, what the human community 'fundamentally' is."[105] Hence, Thomas, while expressing a strong preference for monarchical government,[106] never assumes, as Zhu Xi does, that this is the only type that can or does work.

Given all these factors, the wise and learned must be humble even in the face of those who appear to be otherwise, for fear of missing something that they might not have seen in their studies or contemplations. As Lisa Fullam observes, "humility's second-level, indirect function is to eliminate the kind of pride that keeps me from seeing that there could possibly be anything for me to learn from others, whether bee-keepers, or mentors of any kind."[107] Further, the value assigned to others, both in terms of what we can learn from them and of who they are in themselves, can lead to practical results as well: taking people seriously flows very smoothly into taking their needs seriously, and into an ethic of service in society.

Moreover, even aside from the value humility can lead one to place on the sometimes hidden gifts of others, and its subsequent supporting role in questions of social justice, it plays another important role in those who have both the opportunity and the aptitude for developing their intellects, and who end up in positions of authority. For such people, humility is also advisable because, as Keys points out,

> . . . those reasoners, theoretical and practical, who, through believing in things unseen yet attested to by divine authority, accustom themselves to self-doubt and humility, are more capable of wonder at the otherness of beings; more apt to proceed with due caution and care in their study; and more cognizant of the possibilities for error in their conclusions and unethical misuse of their results (cf. SCG I.5.4; ST II-II 130, 2, ad 3; 133, 1, ad 4).[108]

To put it another way, humility is a vital virtue in inspiring the love for others that makes us take them and their concerns seriously, even when they are not particularly successful at pursuing their own interests. As Fullam puts it, "humility opens the door to solidarity with humanity. Because we tend to favor the rich and powerful by social instinct, we are called particularly to ensure that our attention rests on the despised and the outcast. If we are Christians, that focus becomes primary as well because it was Jesus' primary focus."[109]

Thus it is that, for Thomas as well as for Zhu, authority may never be absolute: the rightful exercise of authority must include the humility to admit that one does not have all of the answers, and to listen to those around one, however humble themselves, for insight. Such humility in turn will open its possessor up to the possibility for true love and respect for those who are being governed, and remind her of her own limitations, lest pride blind her and lead her to do more or other than she ought when she is in a position of power. Quite clearly, for Thomas Aquinas, a properly humble attitude is very important for acting within the bounds set for authority. In his school of thought, authority should be lovingly exercised on behalf of the common good, in the interests of which the leader is expected to humbly submit his own personal will and desires when necessary: a topic discussed more fully in the section below.

Humility and Authority

As noted in the first section of this chapter, humility is often viewed as a weak, sometimes even craven, disposition, and is hence associated with the powerless. Nonetheless, both Zhu Xi and Thomas Aquinas make a compelling case for it as a virtue inherently fitting for the strong. This section considers what each had to say about leaders who allow selfish pride to infuse their exercise of power.

Zhu Xi and the "Mere Fellow"

Service to the people, as discussed above, is a necessary activity for any rightful ruler. If a ruler does not benefit the people, the Confucian tradition says flatly that he is no longer a ruler. In one of the most famous and influential passages in all of Confucian history, when asked about the assassination of an ancient king, Mencius replied: "he who injures humanity is a thief. He who injures righteousness is a brute. Someone who is a thief and a brute is called a mere fellow. I have heard of the execution of the mere fellow Zhou, but I have not heard of the killing of a ruler." [110] To be a king, one must be a king, so to speak, and the people are justified in removing those from the throne who do not truly belong there. As Csikszentmihalyi points out, Mencius was hardly jumping on a popular bandwagon with this teaching; for example, "both Mozi and Han Feizi accept the sovereign authority of a monarch" and neither "accepts a strong version of the Confucian doctrine of *ming*, which introduces both a degree of uncertainty about the effectiveness of even the best potential ruler and a position from which to question the authority of the monarch."[111] Mencius' iconoclastic teaching was not only remarkable for its pugnacity, but also for the way it endured throughout the Confucian centuries.

Zhu Xi proceeds in accordance with such Mencian theories in his own work. In commenting on the passage in the *Great Learning* which says, "to have the people in accordance with the Way is to have the nation, and to lose the people is to lose the nation,"[112] Zhu writes, "having all under Heaven is being able to keep the mind-and-heart [of the people] and not lose it, and thus to desire what the people desire."[113] Of course, in the vast majority of cases, this means desiring the flourishing of the community for, according to Zhu, for "to love (*hao*, 好) the good and to hate evil, this is human nature."[114]

Unfortunately, as any student of history knows, the failures of East Asian rulers throughout the centuries to hold themselves accountable to and on behalf of their people are legion. Nonetheless, a persuasive argument may be made that such failures occurred only to the extent that

Confucian ideals and rituals were set aside.[115] For example, as Virginia Suddath points out,

> . . . although for over twenty-two centuries the Chinese emperor was reverently considered the Son of Heaven, he was compelled not only to uphold the institutions established by the founder of the dynasty, but also, ideally, to observe the customs, felt as commands, of his long list of ancestors. These practices are what would evolve into the Confucian *li*, established in the Confucian tradition by the sages of antiquity, those wise enough and virtuous enough to comprehend the requirements of heaven. The emperor would have been instructed in this tradition from earliest childhood by teachers specially appointed to educate future rulers. As well, he would have internalized the understanding as to how his actions would be noted and evaluated by historians, as the writing of history was a long-established state institution. And in addition to these powerful, but relatively amorphous controls, there were explicit instructions that were established to meet the same ends. There was the system of remonstrance (*taijian*), by which officials were charged with the solemn duty of closely observing the Emperor's behavior and decisions and advising him of his faults. As well, there was the Censorate (*yushitai*) that performed similar duties with regard to officials.[116]

Clearly, an immense amount of *flexibility* is expected of those in charge in this kind of system: the ruler is called to respond to circumstances as they arise with an open mind and heart.[117] From the perspective of Confucians like Zhu Xi, someone who lacks the humility to consider diverse points of view and to let go of plans or policies that stand between his people and their flourishing is not qualified to lead.

This kind of thinking is not of merely academic significance. As noted above, it gives rise to "the right of the people to rebel against a tyrannical dynasty, the right of the aristocracy to remove an unjust imperial household, the right of the imperial clansmen to replace an unsuitable king, and the right of the bureaucrats to remonstrate with a negligent ruler."[118] The ruler who is proud, and takes notice only of his or her own selfish desires, and who, moreover, does not love the people and what they love, will be removable. In the end, the need for humility is manifold: it is necessary in order to truly consider the advice and insights of those around one, and for accepting the moral demands inherent in the role of government. In a more negative formulation, humility is necessary for tempering the kind of pride that leads the unwary to transgress the rightful bounds of authority in favor of personal gratification or selfish design, or that hardens the heart-and-mind against developing affection for others.

Thomas Aquinas and the Tyrant

In Thomas's understanding, any just use of human power requires that it be in accordance with the natural law. As Richard Regan points out, "the state in Thomistic theory, though hierarchically supreme in organized society, is not an absolute arbiter of morality:"[119] "unlike Aristotle, Aquinas relates human law to a natural law implicit in God's creative plan, and this natural law places moral limits on human law."[120] (This natural law, incidentally, is not meant solely for the benefit of humans, for, as Thomas writes: "to take away their proper action from things is to disparage the divine goodness."[121]) According to Thomas, a law that transgresses the divinely given natural order is simply not a law: "a tyrannical law, through not being according to reason, is not a law, absolutely speaking, but rather a perversion of law."[122] Therefore, so-called "unjust laws" "do not bind in conscience."[123] Thomas does see—and immediately provides—exceptions to this rule: "except perhaps in order to avoid scandal or disturbance, for which cause a man should even yield his right, according to Matthew 5:40–41: 'If a man . . . take away thy coat, let go thy cloak also unto him; and whosoever will force thee one mile, go with him other [*sic*] two.' " However, there are limits even to this: "laws may be unjust through being opposed to the Divine good: such are the laws of tyrants inducing to idolatry, or to anything else contrary to the Divine law: and laws of this kind must nowise be observed, because, as stated in Acts 5:29, 'we ought to obey God rather than man.' "

In fact, attempts by tyrants to spurn the natural order—either through unjust usurpation of power or unjust exercise of it—are punished in Thomas's system. As regards the first, Thomas says in the *Scriptum super sententiis* that one in whom is found a "defect in the mode by which the [authority] was acquired, namely through violence or through simony, or other illicit mode of acquiring"[124] has no claim to authority, and none are bound to obey him: "he who steals (*surripit*) dominion through violence is not really the prelate or ruler; and therefore when opportunity knocks, anyone may repel such kind of rule."[125]

Furthermore, as regards the misuse of authority that was originally properly assigned, Thomas writes in the *Summa theologiae*: "the power granted to a king is so great, it easily degenerates into tyranny, unless he to whom this power is given be a very virtuous man: for it is only the virtuous man that conducts himself well in the midst of prosperity, as the Philosopher observes (Ethic. iv, 3)."[126] As Thomas knows full well, "perfect virtue is to be found in few."[127] Therefore, in Thomas's understanding, God Himself laid down guiding principles for leaders lest their lack of perfect virtue lead them astray, dictating in the Hebrew Bible "how rulers should behave towards their subjects: namely, that they should not proudly despise them, or ill-treat them, and that they should not depart from the paths of justice."[128]

While Thomas is quite clearly in favor of a fairly powerful ruling class—see his definition of sedition as a sin,[129] and his statements regarding the rectitude of the wise ruling the not-so-wise[130]—he also understands that there are cases in which rising up against one's sovereign is wholly justifiable. In his essay "On Kingship," he explores the legitimate options open to people subjugated by those who have departed from the paths of justice:

> . . . if a king chosen by the masses tyrannically abuses the royal power, it is not unjust that the same king be deposed or have his power curbed by the masses. It must not be reckoned that the masses are acting unfaithfully in deposing the tyrant, even if they had previously subjected themselves to him in perpetuity, because he himself has deserved that the covenant with his subjects should not be kept, since, in ruling them, he did not act faithfully as the office of a king demands.[131]

Although Thomas is silent on the matter of regicide, it may be imagined that deposing the king from his throne may involve violence.

In any case, just as in Zhu Xi's Confucianism, in Thomas's Christianity a tyrant, or a person who does not act in wisdom and love, may be removed from the throne. In addition to being crucial with regard to recognition of one's own limitations and the gifts of others, the virtue of humility turns out to be essential to good government in its opposition to the pride that can lead one to ignore his or her lawful obligations and the requirements of government, and/or to exceed the rightful bounds set for office.

Conclusion

Both Thomas and Zhu, despite their belief in the efficacy of assigning more power to some people than to others, can also see where such a practice may become problematic. Quite clearly, neither supports the kind of tyranny that transpires when one person proudly decides all the rules for himself. Here, as always, embracing their comprehensive understanding of the universe precludes narrowness and superficiality in our own perspectives today: just as we must strive to hold opposing urges in productive harmony within ourselves, so too must we be open to the fact that other people's opposing opinions may in fact have merit. To put the point more keenly, we must be humble enough to admit that we may be wrong at any given moment in time, and about any given issue.

As the moral philosopher Ralph McInerny notes in a poignant turn of phrase, "each of us is limited in seemingly unlimited ways."[132] Even the most virtuous of us cannot be wholly insured against harming others, the wisest of us cannot be certain that he or she will never make a mistake, and the most powerful members of our race know that there are many things beyond their control. While they do so in different ways, both Zhu and Thomas recognize these inescapable facts of the human condition, and counsel a genuine humility before them.

Nonetheless, such humility is not intended to excuse one from making an effort. As Wing-tsit Chan notes, while Zhu may be best known for his polemics against Buddhism, he also finds a great deal to censure in Daoism when the topic of humility comes up:

> . . . to [Zhu], Lao Tzu's [Laozi's] teaching of humility, emptiness, and frugality was merely intended to conserve energy, and his idea of keeping the spirit and concentrating the vital force was merely to conserve and not to spend them . . . Just as the Buddhists were afraid to die, so the Taoists were anxious to live. This is utter selfishness. Being selfish, Lao Tzu was irresponsible. 'The tactics of Lao Tzu,' Chu Hsi [Zhu Xi] said, 'is to be willing to do a thing only if it is perfectly safe and convenient. If there is the slightest inconvenience, he would not do it.' . . . In Chu Hsi's words, "Lao Tzu is one

> who takes advantage of others and is not willing to take responsibility. He simply maintains himself and does not care if the universe is overthrown."[133]

For Zhu the Confucian, humility means not dodging responsibility by meekly refusing to do anything, but rather taking responsibility for all actions and emotions that have turned out badly, or, in circumstances that have turned out well, striving to do even better next time.

On a similar note, as discussed above, Thomas pairs the virtue of humility with that of magnanimity, which "makes a man deem himself worthy of great things in consideration of the gifts he holds from God: thus if his soul is endowed with great virtue, magnanimity makes him tend to perfect works of virtue; and the same is to be said of the use of any other good, such as science or external fortune."[134] The good person, in Thomas's estimation, aims high.

In fact, both Zhu and Thomas encourage the development of humility especially in the politically, economically or socially dominant. While their references to kings and rulers may make them seem outdated in the contemporary democratic age, they have a great deal of resonance in a world where technology has made production faster, places closer, and social monitoring more efficient than ever before. While not having the titles granted to the powerful in the past, today's leaders often find themselves with more power than they know what to do with. In this context, Thomas and Zhu seem particularly prescient with their intuition that humility is not only helpful but *necessary* in the strong.

More generally, as Lisa Fullam has observed, regardless of historical context, those without humility are not fit to be in power, for the "[vicious extremes of the virtue of humility] are, on the one side, a moral narcissism that fails to acknowledge the other, and on the opposite side, a self-nihilating other-centeredness that fails to value oneself at all."[135] Neither of these vices is desirable in people with authority, for the one encourages pushing the reach of authority too far, and the other not far enough. Neither situation is to be desired, for the human community both needs people to act authoritatively, and to know when to stop. Humility can certainly help with the latter project, and can do so without impairing the former. Indeed, in helping us to see where and how and why power should be limited, humility can assist with the effective exercise of authority: those with humility, in realizing what they cannot or should not be doing, will be all the better able to focus their efforts correctly and efficiently on behalf of the common good.[136]

Humanity's dual ability to foster one end of the project of authority without fettering the other is perhaps most apparent in the role it plays in supporting and cooperating with a genuine love for others. As Keys notes, "equality alone does not lead to an ethos of service, to placing oneself—even physically—*below* another person to attend directly to his or her needs, including their basic physical welfare. Such service, if sincere, requires a humility and a love (*charity* in its original meaning)."[137] If we have the kind of humility that accompanies genuine love, we will then be able to exercise whatever authority is given us in the proper way: humbly and authoritatively all at once, in a way that will lead to mutual flourishing and fulfillment.

Conclusion

The Virtue of Humble Authority

> [The thoughts of Plato, Spinoza, Kant, Schelling, Hegel and Schopenhauer] seemed to him fruitful when he read, or was himself devising refutations of other teachings. . . . But he had only to forget that artificial line of thought, and to return direct from real life to what had appeared satisfactory so long as he kept to the given line of thought—and suddenly the whole artificial edifice tumbled down like a house of cards.
>
> —Leo Tolstoy, *Anna Karenina*

> This is an interesting planet. It deserves all the attention you can give it.
>
> —Marilynne Robinson, *Gilead*

Dealing with Reality

Our lives move beyond one sphere of endeavor on a day-to-day basis. While the world admittedly does contain scholars like the dry and pedantic Mr. Casaubon in *Middlemarch*, who is essentially consumed by his research, as well as single-minded athletes, stockbrokers, and doctors, most of us who have the luxury of doing so habitually—and willingly—leave off our work to devote time to other concerns. We want to see our family and friends, pay the bills, go shopping, read a book, or run at the end of the day for pleasure.[1] Daily existence invites us to exercise all of our human faculties—mental, emotional, and physical—

and often in a communal setting. (One of the great tragedies, in fact, of the current era, at least in the United States, is the inability of people to do just this. Whether overworked at a company that's downsized, or between three different part-time jobs, or, for that matter, unable to find employment at all, people are suffering the effects of not being able to work, play, and think.)

Moreover, one need not be a professional student of philosophy or Russian literature in order to believe that this invitation speaks to what makes us fully human. Recently, several books have appeared on best-seller lists in the United States that reflect on the poverty of lives too narrowly lived. For example, the Harvard ethicist Michael Sandel has questioned the fairness and worth of a narrowly market-oriented, utilitarian cultural framework that denies the intrinsic value of any person, practice, material good, or life goal.[2] Meanwhile, other writers concerned by what they perceive to be increasing social fragmentation are turning to religious traditions for possible counter-influences. Atheists such as the evolutionary biologist E. O. Wilson and the moral psychologist Jonathan Haidt have found themselves in company with the Roman Catholic *New York Times* columnist Ross Douthat in investigating the positive role that religion can and does play in bringing people together into morally, socially, and politically effective communities.[3]

Religion, as understood by these authors, is not neatly contained within the holy texts of a given tradition. In fact, writers like Alain de Botton are explicitly grappling with the fact that, if ideas are to be effective, they must move beyond the page: "writing a book can't be enough if one wishes to change things."[4] Although an atheist himself, de Botton is intrigued by the tendency of religious doctrines to *live* outside the scriptures in which they are set forth:

> . . . [religions] have managed to combine theories about ethics and metaphysics with a practical involvement in education, fashion, politics, travel, hostelry, initiation ceremonies, publishing, art and architecture—a range of interests which puts to shame the scope of achievements of even the greatest and most influential secular movements and individuals in history. For those interested in the spread and impact of ideas, it is hard not to be mesmerized by examples of the most successful educational and intellectual movements the planet has ever witnessed.[5]

Having reached this conclusion about the social usefulness of religion, de Botton's project is an optimistic one: he hopes and believes that he and his colleagues can learn from the religious in order to build secular traditions that play a similarly broad and deep role in the lives of the unchurched. However, it's not precisely obvious that this goal is possible, chiefly because the bonds that hold a religious community together—namely, explicitly institutionalized dogma and practice—can often seem at odds with a secular culture that highly prizes individual empowerment and choice, and looks askance in principle at any factors that could constrain either.[6]

Nonetheless, as Chesterton puts it, "there are only two kinds of people, those who accept dogmas and know it, and those who accept dogmas and don't know it."[7] People who reject openly institutional dogmas often hold personally authoritative beliefs that are just as strong; for example, that skepticism is the highest virtue, or that the chain of events that led to the existence of human beings was both purposeless and morally meaningless. As I argued in the Introduction to this book, those who acknowledge their dogmas as such—in this case, broadly speaking, the religious—are able to band together in communities that are not only powerful, but also potentially aware of the kinds of self-generated problems that might arise in the pursuit of their way of life and the goals they wish to achieve.

The careful reader may have noted my use of the word "potentially." It is empirically quite possible to live one's entire life within a religious community without ever learning to question one's own moral standing or that of the group at large; the institutions of religion do not always provide safeguards against either the extravagant pride or the excessive timidity that can prevent the exploration of such issues, nor against the kind of rigid hierarchies that can encourage the former in the powerful and the latter in the rank and file. Nonetheless, in the cases of Christianity and Confucianism, we find clear clues about the nature of genuine authority deeply embedded in the persons and teachings of their founding figures.

During his lifetime, Jesus provided Christians with a model of humble behavior, eschewing the pursuit of political power and material riches in favor of preaching amongst and serving the poor. Furthermore, the stories he tells promote humility by challenging those of his listeners who feel morally or religiously comfortable. Especially in the parable of Lazarus and the rich man, in which the latter is being punished in the afterlife for having ignored the former's suffering on Earth,[8] the message that human beings are not good at assessing their own moral performance comes through loud and clear. As James Keenan puts it, "In the Gospel stories, people are surprised to find out how sinful they are . . . they do not recognize their sinfulness. So why do we think we recognize our sinfulness?"[9] Not only the moral but also the intellectual implications of such passages should, when taken seriously, give Christians pause.

However, in Jesus' teaching, humility is not an excuse to hide in the shadows. The apostle Peter, bristling with what turns out to be empty bravado during much of the Gospel narrative, provides the clearest illustration of this message. Peter, whom Jesus correctly predicts will abandon him in his time of need,[10] is nonetheless entrusted with the leadership of the early church after Jesus' ascension into Heaven.[11] In other words, the Christian Gospels tell us that we must be prepared to take on great responsibilities that, if we know ourselves honestly and well, we are not naturally equipped at the outset to fulfill.

Meanwhile, on the Confucian side, Michael Nylan and Thomas Wilson remind us that Confucius became great precisely when he developed a sense of humility. In *Lives of Confucius*, they do a great deal to dispel pious myths about Confucius's angelic temperament by discussing the ancient historian Sima Qian's (司馬遷,135–86 BCE) thesis that, "until he was in his mid-sixties, Kongzi [Confucius] was a sanctimonious and arrogant know-it-all."[12] In Sima's account, we find a Confucius who is all too human, and who has to be humbled through adversity before he can become a sage, or a "man whose eagerness to learn exceeded his eagerness to teach."[13]

Moreover, Confucius, like Jesus, not only encourages humility in his followers, but also prepares them for positions of authority. For example, while he certainly does not hesitate to put the rather overly confident Zigong down when he overestimates his own competence,[14] Confucius also considers this same disciple fit to occupy government office.[15]

The balance between the humility necessary to face one's own limitations on the one hand, and the authority to put power and influence to good use on the other, is not easy to strike—and fortuitously so. In the very difficulty of such a project lies its effectiveness, even its charm: steadily working toward perfection rather than expecting or demanding it fosters both humility and confidence, both of which are necessary to act justly in a world that we cannot wholly control but can deeply influence. As members of the traditions founded by Jesus and Confucius, Thomas Aquinas and Zhu Xi share their challenging understanding of the nature of rightful power, and provide us with a valuable perspective on how to engage with the world in which and the people with whom we live.

Engaging with Diversity, Engaging with Paradox: The Virtue of Humble Authority

It is a fundamental premise of this book that one of the greatest tasks of contemporary life is to work toward harmonizing as much diversity within and between people as possible. The project may also be instructively formulated in more negative terms: to circumvent situations in which certain concerns are brought forward to the harmful exclusion of others.[16]

As undertaking this sort of task involves confronting issues of power and its rightful use and limitation, there is no question but that religious traditions will be involved in this task. Indeed, as religious studies scholar William Scott Green points out, they have to be:

> . . . because religion is comprehensive, it is fundamentally about power; it therefore cannot avoid politics. Religion has the ability to ground the use of force in a cosmic and moral order; therefore, religion constitutes the ultimate legitimation of any political system. Overtly and covertly, religion influences political structures and activity by encouraging and enforcing some attitudes and behaviors and by discouraging and disparaging others. It articulates frameworks of values and truth that ground and inform a society's sense of destiny, leadership, community, and individuality.[17]

Engaging with religion on a political level first and foremost hence has a very practical benefit, namely, that a significant element in many power relations will be addressed.

Moreover, the comprehensiveness that Green identifies as characteristic of religious traditions provides us with a basis for harmonizing ideas rather than trying to forcefully replace one with the other. Rather than striving toward, or even merely idealizing pure or undefiled conditions—in which, for example, all Americans are Democrats, Republicans, or members of the Green Party—and regarding the continued existence of elements that don't perfectly balance with these ideal conditions as problems or necessary evils, it might be better *from the outset* to look for fruitful ways of cooperation between concepts that are more or less oppositional. One pertinent example might involve finding harmonious ways of resolving the tension between ideas like "democracy" and "hierarchy." Rather than setting them against each other, we might look for ways of combining them. Confucius's willingness to take students from all social classes, and Jesus' choice of poor fishermen and tax collectors to be the leaders of his movement after his passing, show us a fundamentally harmonious way of thinking about hierarchy and democracy: not destroying the former to make room for the latter, but making hierarchy more dynamic and responsive to the ever-surprising turns that reality inevitably ends up taking. In a democratic hierarchy, while true authority is possible with reference to ontological order and human development and achievement, it is explicitly feasible that the most unexpected of people may have insights as yet unseen by the wise. Moreover, such insights may be not only into the order of existence, but also into the character of authority figures.

This kind of context both grants more value to individuals and makes more demands of them than does a great deal of secular social theory. As Adam Seligman has noted in *Modernity's Wager*, given a narrowly conceived empowerment, focusing solely on the ability of a person to express his or her autonomous will,[18] "one is left with nothing but a set of instrumental relations with the surrounding world, the calculus of wills that defines markets or contracts."[19] From Seligman's point of view, the rise of this "rational actor" is a tragic development, for this kind of self is crippled, or at the very least incomplete as a human being:

> . . . what type of self exists without either shame or that authority toward which one feels shame? The calculations of the private conscience as "sole arbiter of moral behavior" leaves one, in Agnes Heller's terms, defined by a narcissistic project and deaf to the calls of love, empathy, charity and sympathy. For it is through the external authority that the communal self, that very sense of shame, enters, to define us in terms of desiderata beyond those of any calculative reason.[20]

Thomas Aquinas and Zhu Xi provide a much fuller and more robust anthropology of the individual, one that includes reference to ontological authority and ways in which human beings can cooperate with it. As they are fundamentally interested not in the fulfillment of atomic individuals, nor in the fate of a mysterious "collective" that is somehow bereft of individual persons and their desires, but rather in human flourishing in community, by way of intelligent development of human moral potential, each human person is incredibly important to them as someone with moral potential that is unique, who can help in building the common good in a distinctive and irreplaceable way. This person is far more important than the cog in the collectivist machine, and simultaneously more and less than the self-interested rational actor: more, because more is possible and valued in him, and less, because his desires can never take center stage in an exclusive way.

From their perspective, then, the contemporary individual is not wholly free to use her human rights in any way she sees fit, but rather is called to develop virtues that will assist her in exercising and limiting her own power: in particular, one I call "humble authority." This virtue, properly grounded in the recognition of an objectively moral order, as well as of the parameters of human nature and the responsibilities attendant upon the human role, enables its possessor to both properly exercise and limit his or her use of power. Insofar as it upholds and even enhances the dignity of the individual person, by (a) referring to objective standards of value that must be continuously re-interpreted, (b) requiring his or her loving engagement with society and the world at large, and (c) providing neither utopian promises nor apocalyptic threats but rather reasonable hope for human flourishing, humble authority is a particularly vital contribution to contemporary discussions of individual rights and empowerment.

I do not call this a "new virtue." As Lisa Fullam points out,

> a genuinely new virtue would require a new human capacity that can be perfected. New virtues on a small scale are easily imagined: to be a courteous driver requires the development of roads and vehicles, for example. But the basic act of being considerate, a fundamental virtue of communities, is as old as those communities themselves. Where new cardinal virtues are posited they represent a different moral anthropology—as it were, a different slicing of the cake of human capacity, rather than a claim that a wholly new human capacity was discovered.[21]

In much the same way, the virtue of humble authority, never explicitly identified or defined by Zhu and Thomas, slices their cake into different pieces rather than attempting to bake a whole new one. My project is thus one of emendation, as defined by Lee Yearley: "emendation utilizes modern theoretical analyses and formulations to clarify, test and reformulate the ideas the texts present. It involves complex decisions about what is and is not fundamental to the tradition."[22] As Yearley warns, "the actual process of emendation is a complicated and, at time, dangerous, activity. Emendation, that is, might so change the original that a disinterested observer could well wonder what role the traditional text played."[23] I hope that the role the traditional texts have played in this argument is clear: through exploring Confucian and Catholic cosmologies, anthropologies, and theories of power, I have attempted to demonstrate that, while neither Zhu Xi nor Thomas Aquinas ever explicitly addressed nor defined the virtue of humble authority, both proceeded on the fundamental premise that humility in the ruler or leader was necessary. I have simply sliced the cake in a way that did not occur to either to do. As Alasdair MacIntyre has argued, such development is necessary for the continued vibrancy of any tradition.

Certainly, both Confucianism and Catholicism have undergone such development, and continue to do so in new and unexpected ways. As Wm. Theodore de Bary notes,

> . . . for any help that Confucianism may give us today, we must look at these questions from a Neo-Confucian perspective. Just as the latter found in their classical legacy no exact models to be followed in their own present situation but had to develop new forms in which to deal with changed historical circumstances, what can be learned today from the Confucian and Neo-Confucian past can only suggest new possibilities, not provide precise models.[24]

Likewise, the Catholic tradition, "especially in an era with its remarkable advances in technology and human power," does well to realize that "a rediscovery of a viable humility may prove a necessary precondition for achieving wonder and reinvigorating philosophy and political philosophy as Aristotle understood them."[25] This project has been an attempt to develop the traditions in response to contemporary realities.

The question may be raised whether enough emendation has taken place in this very regard. For example, as I noted in Chapter 4, neither Zhu Xi nor Thomas Aquinas favored democracy: arguably the most revered form of government in the world today, with its tenets given lip service even by dictators. Although Thomas admits the viability of several different forms of government, he explicitly claims that "a kingdom is the best of all governments."[26] Meanwhile, Zhu Xi assumes the standard Confucian stance that good kings and emperors are requisite for true social peace and prosperity. Hence, "Catholic social teaching arrived on the human rights bandwagon somewhat late and out of breath,"[27] while Confucian dominated societies had to wait for Western influences before developing democratic systems of government.

Nonetheless, even given these caveats, the teachings of Thomas and Zhu concerning government and authority are of useful application in democratic society: given that such societies feature some people in positions of power over many others, decisions must still be made concerning how they should exercise their electorally granted authority in positive ways—decisions that should arguably be made with consideration of questions of objective morality, human moral potential, and the cultivation of morality.

Both Zhu and Thomas also strike a healthy balance between the extremes of a legalistic position that slights the role played by human beings in implementing and interpreting laws and a more personalistic outlook that gives a charismatic or otherwise powerful tyrant *carte blanche* to do as he or she pleases. The person with humble authority is rooted in a community both cosmic and human, and trained in accordance with objective points of reference, those of the *LI* for Zhu, and those of the natural law and revelation for Thomas. In other words, a strong regulatory system is a constitutive element of the virtue. The rules that function as a precondition for humble authority can also serve other purposes—for example, reining in those who would abuse their power. On the other hand, as has been discussed throughout this book, the rules on their own are not enough: the virtue of humble authority also entails continuous reinterpretation of laws in the service of the flourishing of the common good.

All of this is complicated, perhaps depressingly so: it's easier and more pleasant to think that laws can run society, or that just handing the reins over to a good person, howsoever defined, will solve all the world's problems. Nonetheless, neither is true. Perhaps, in the end, one of the most valuable lessons Thomas and Zhu have to teach us is one of the most obvious, and hence one of the easiest to ignore or forget: it's a difficult business to be good, and an even more difficult business to be good in a complex society.

In the end, although it is important to promote greater egalitarianism (as does much scholarship and cultural practice), we also need to think about how to exercise whatever power most of us will end up having over some others (parents over children, teachers over students, bosses over employees, etc.). In drawing our attention to this fact, both Zhu and Thomas have something to offer to us today, not despite their archaic ideas about social organization, but precisely because of them. And this something is due in part to their comprehensively religious outlook.

For the purposes of this book, a religious person is one committed to a tradition that (a) holds that the deepest truths about existence are not reductively materialist in character, and (b) provides methods and personal models for better aligning ourselves with these truths. As I have argued throughout, commitments to such a tradition also opens one's eyes to the complexity of life, and encourages certain attitudes, both intellectual and emotional, before it. The remainder of this book will explore these aspects of their thinking, before turning to the wider implications of the comparison undertaken here in order to claim that it (a) calls attention to the positive role that religious traditions can play in contemporary society, (b) provides a case study of how common ground may be found between religious cultures, and, in doing the latter, (c) presents two constructive ways of dealing with religious difference, before concluding with some thoughts about the viability and value of the virtue of humble authority today.

The Complexities of Life

Our world, according to Christianity, Confucianism, and many other religious traditions, is bewilderingly complex, each and every part of it demanding certain responses from human beings. For example, chapters of the Jewish Talmud range freely between discussions of human dignity ("[all human beings] share one inestimable privilege, viz. of having been created in the divine likeness")[28] and more commonplace concerns ("some vegetables are recommended as more beneficial than others").[29] When reading from the Talmud several years ago—in particular, the sections concerning black cumin and the dryer aspects of tort law—I could not help but think of Chesterton's remark that "there is no such thing on earth as an uninteresting subject; the only thing that can exist is an uninterested person. Nothing is more keenly required than a defence [*sic*] of bores."[30] This statement approaches the deep sensibility of the Talmud, which is grounded in the premise that there is no such thing as an unimportant subject or action, as the smallest or most profane act is imbued with the presence of God. There is something almost unbearably affirmative about a religious tradition that includes prayers of gratitude to be said after answering the call of nature.[31]

There is also something almost unbearably arduous about this view, which carries with its invitation to joy a heavy responsibility. If every moment in life is a precious gift from God, even the smallest sin becomes a grave offense: the Talmud warns that "when standing his trial [in the World to Come], man will have brought up against him many misdeeds which he at the time thought too trivial to worry about."[32] Imbuing all of life with dignity has both its rewards and its costs.

Thomas and Zhu, like the deeply religious sages who contributed to the complexly layered and often paradoxical Talmud, were not specialists of the kind that dominate the academy today. Rather than focusing on one topic or subject to the practical exclusion of all or most others, they were open to all facets of existence—intellectual and emotional, material and spiritual, objective and subjective, practical and theoretical, musical, artistic, scientific, philosophical, and religious. They wrote about the nature of the universe and the ways of its operation; they wrote about the nature of human beings, as encompassing intelligence, passion, and sociality; they wrote about personal morality and political order; and they wrote about how finite beings must recognize their own finitude, not only so that they may accept it, but also that they may develop themselves to their fullest capacity. Moreover, they saw all these concerns as being woven together in the woof and warp of a web unimaginably textured, in which each thread crosses countless others in more ways than humans can conceive.

The pattern they perceived gave both meaning and existence to all that they said and did, and weighted every thought, word, and action with responsibility—and value. Such value carries with it the strong implication that tension between two parties or interests in this world should not be solved by oppressing one or the other, but by somehow struggling to a fruitful new harmony between them: an exceptionally delicate project in practice, and one, moreover, that they knew could be disrupted at any moment by yet another new idea or new impulse. Nonetheless, they persevered in meeting the world in all its complexity, adopting certain guiding principles—for example, that human beings are born with the moral imperative to develop their talents in, through, and for serving each other—and accepting the apparently infinite ways in which people might live in accordance with them. Whether as teachers or stockbrokers, sports fans or players, unemployed persons or employed persons, parents or cousins or friends, Thomas and Zhu would tell us in the contemporary world that each of us has an irreplaceable value and a unique responsibility to our communities.

The Desire for Simplicity

It is in this embrace of complexity, perhaps, that Zhu Xi and Thomas Aquinas crash up most spectacularly—and helpfully—against a purely scientific outlook. As discussed most fully in Chapter 1, the contemporary sciences are often explicitly reductionist, grounded in a paradigm with the explicit goal of stripping away all superfluous hypotheses and concerns in order to get at the fundamental truth of matters. As the scientific method has been a very productive mode of engaging with both the natural and the human worlds, we often wish to replicate its values and principles in more humanistic areas of study—or, more precisely, unconsciously assume that doing so is the only intelligent way to proceed, and that the simplest answer is the best one.[33] The preeminence of the scientific method is often enhanced by the fact that there is a certain elegance about it that is aesthetically pleasing, a rigor and accountability that is morally pleasing, and a demonstrability that is intellectually pleasing.

All of these pleasant factors are especially attractive in the world of today. As I noted in the Introduction to this book, life in the contemporary era is often quite exhausting. We know that we want different things, often at the same time, and we know that we are surrounded by individuals with similarly complex lives and personalities, in a global community that keeps on generating new and conflicting points of view without having bothered to first resolve the tensions between the old ones. It is natural under these circumstances to gravitate toward methods and narratives that offer hard cold facts, narrowly measurable results, and, especially, the relief of simplicity and certainty. Everyone can agree that a rock will fall more quickly than a sheet of paper, and that adding certain kinds of fertilizer to certain kinds of soil will increase crop yields. The promise of a world in which similarly simple and unquestionable statements can be made about human thought and behavior can be very attractive in the midst of too many options to count.[34]

Lessons for the Contemporary World

Facing the Truth(s)

Whether fortunately or unfortunately, notwithstanding the power and potential of the scientific method, it is not sufficient for all forms of human enquiry. As Dennis Wrong noted decades ago, reductionist abstractions such as "economic man" and "sociological man" can eventually blind the person who trades in them to other facets of human existence that are immediately apparent to anyone paying attention outside of the classroom.[35] In real life, we are very complex creatures who listen to music; do the laundry, whether willingly or unwillingly; like some people better than others; are known for our personal idiosyncratic gestures, expressions, and turns of phrase; and rationalize our way into unethical decisions at some points and morally surpass ourselves at others. Indeed, when we meet someone who attempts to completely identify herself with her job, or his relationship with his spouse, or her character in Dungeons and Dragons, we tend to think of that person as somehow stunted or limited. We intuitively know that there is more to human life than one narrowly defined interest, characteristic, focus, or goal,[36] however much we may forget this basic fact during political elections in general or health care debates in particular. In perhaps wearying and wearisome fact, oftentimes the only way forward, in politics or elsewhere, is realizing that the other person is more than the slogans he or she happens to be saying at this point in time—in other words, by allowing people to be as complicated as they are.

This process also requires us to recognize the complexity of even individual human activities, and to admit that perhaps one group has more than one reason for pushing to keep taxes low, while another has more than one for wanting to raise them. Our own everyday lives provide us with ample lessons in this regard. A networking meeting, for example, is an occasion to make useful contacts, but can also provide an opportunity to get out of work early and eat some nice canapés, or even an excuse not to do household chores later in the evening. When we invite friends over for dinner, we are certainly interested in enjoying their companionship, but the meal will also provide us with the calories we need to live, and allow us to send status signals via the kind of food we put on the menu and the way in which we serve it. If we are hosting the dinner with a partner, preparation will often involve negotiations between the hosts as to the division of labor, which in turn are parts of an ongoing relationship. Finally, sex between a husband and a wife who want to have a baby is certainly about reproduction, but it can also be an expression of love, a satisfaction of desire, a fulfillment of marital duties, a way to make up after a fight, and/or an excuse not to clean up the kitchen for the present. In all of these cases, we not only find that different motivations can sit alongside each other quite comfortably, but also that we have multiple reasons for acting as we do: very few human activities are about one thing and one thing only.

In short, as the best-selling authors mentioned at the beginning of this chapter have recognized, the human experience remains irreducibly composite. It is when the inescapability of complexity becomes clear that a religious tradition may be especially well positioned to help us.[37]

As I noted in the Introduction, religious traditions have had thousands of years to develop their ideas about existence in general, and human nature in particular. Rather than giving us reified and narrow abstractions about life developed in isolation from other disciplines or intellectual traditions, what they can offer us are great intellectual symphonies that have intricate parts for every instrument.[38] Thus, for example, when Thomas addresses the nature of God in exhaustively scholastic detail, and Zhu approaches principle from a variety of angles, this painstaking work is explicitly placed within a broad and fertile context that includes places for poetry, scientific observation, and drinking wine. Moreover, they both know that the answers to even seemingly simple questions are often not so simple, and that the process itself of addressing them will frequently turn out to be complex, unpredictable, and destabilizing. In a world where we arguably confront more radical difference more often and intimately than they did, and are daily assaulted by more information than any other generation in human history, looking to Thomas, Zhu, and other great religious thinkers can show us the kinds of integrating and harmonizing moves we need to make in order to at least attempt to do justice to the multiple aspects of the human experience, and to the many different groups of people on the planet, without falling into unproductive extremes of rigidity or relativism, self-regard or solidarity, or despair or delusional optimism. The virtue of humble authority, woven together from strands of the teachings of Thomas and Zhu, is one means to constructively address both the exercise and limitation of power.

Defending Cultural Comparison

Throughout this project, I have also attempted to show that there are similarities between Zhu and Thomas, as removed as they are from one another culturally and geographically. According to Virginia Suddath, this is a rather embarrassingly pointless endeavor: "the earlier claim and project of comparative philosophy—the attempt to determine overarching commonalities between the Western and non-Western traditions—has been debunked."[39] This book demonstrates that I question such "debunking." Looking at Zhu and Thomas shows us that people with completely different theologies can share common ground, and, moreover, that finding such common ground is of extraordinary practical and moral importance.

The escalating levels of communication and interdependence between all countries of the globe demonstrate that finding common—not identical—ground between cultures and civilizations is not a project that can be easily set aside. As Henry Rosemont writes, "there is nothing wrong with seeking a worldwide consensus on a proper ordering of basic human values; indeed, that search must go forward if we are to see an end to the ethnic, racial, religious and sexual violence that have so thoroughly splattered the pages of human history with blood and gore since the Enlightenment."[40] To be clear, I understand this worldwide consensus to be a goal perhaps never to be fully achieved. Nonetheless, as this book demonstrates, I also consider such consensus worthwhile—carefully, and with caveats—to pursue. My comparison of Thomas Aquinas and Zhu Xi herein is submitted as evidence that the project of finding points of contact between traditions is both feasible and fruitful; in particular, I offer the "Methodology" section of the book's Introduction and my section called "A Methodological Issue" in Chapter 3, both of which provide detailed discussion of methodological concerns pertinent to my comparative work, as well as the conclusions to Chapters 1 through 5, all of which put Thomas and Zhu into conversation with each other, to demonstrate that common ground exists between them despite, or even through, their differences—the latter possibility discussed in the section below.

Message for a Pluralistic Society

If Thomas had in fact developed a theory of the virtue of humble authority, he would have done so on the basis of different premises and reasoning from Zhu's. His universe, created by God and suffused by a conscious divine presence, has a distinctive character that is, to put it mildly, not shared by Zhu's. Nonetheless, Zhu and Thomas arrive at practical and moral conclusions that are compatible and mutually supportive.[41]

Hence this book provides a model for genuine religious expression that *harmonizes* with other beliefs and worldviews. Rather than prescribing a dilution, weakening, or ghettoization of religious beliefs and values, it suggests that it is possible to exercise and even develop our religious conviction in a secular world, and in the cooperative company of others who disagree with us on salient points of doctrine or philosophy. The virtue of humble authority itself draws our attention to this fact, as it calls on people both to be humble and to act—something we'd do well to keep in mind in the blur of religious and secular options currently available.

As we begin this process, it's a good idea to reflect on the experience of people who have achieved success in comparable circumstances. While a lengthy biographical exploration of either Thomas Aquinas or Zhu Xi is outside of the scope of this project, a brief look at each man demonstrates that he was both humble and authoritative enough to ask questions and answer them to the best of his ability.

With regard to Thomas Aquinas: his great work, the *Summa theologiae*, was formatted as a conversation, in which he raised questions, considered a wide range of options for answering them, and then presented his own arguments—sometimes agreeing with his dialogue partners, sometimes not, but always trying to work his way closer to the truth by engaging with the best thought of his time. It is as well to reiterate here that he had a very liberal idea of what the "best thought" might be, and certainly did not confine himself to Christian interlocutors; not only did he engage deeply with Aristotle, but also with the work of Muslim philosophers such as Avicenna (c. 980–1037),[42] and Averroes (1126–1198),[43] the latter of whom is often referred to simply as "The Commentator": a significant mark of respect by a scholar who refers to Aristotle himself as simply "The Philosopher." In other words, Thomas was humble enough to ask questions, and authoritative enough to move beyond the bounds of his own tradition in search of new insights and information.

Zhu Xi, meanwhile, as we have seen, asked his students to doubt, and to develop new perspectives and insights of their own, but always with the understanding that anything they discerned was part of a whole unimaginably greater than they were. In his own words: "moral principle is infinite. What our predecessors said does not necessarily exhaust it."[44] Moreover, he practiced what he preached: rather than being vain enough to throw the Buddhists aside without a second glance, or too intellectually humble to respond to the very real challenges they raised for his own way of thinking, Zhu not only read widely in Buddhism but also went on to develop a truly Confucian metaphysics in response, without which his tradition would have been immeasurably poorer.

Moreover, both Thomas and Zhu displayed this intellectual courage in circumstances that were often less than comfortable or congenial. We can learn from their basic example today as we respond to far more complex destabilization and uncertainty, noting that they embraced neither relativism or rigidity; they neither fell to unhealthy degrees of either self-regard or excessive solidarity; and, perhaps most significantly, they kept going in their work with a sense of hope, not presuming to either despair or delusional optimism with regard to the future. As we know, both went on to profoundly influence their traditions and the lives of countless millions. Even more broadly, they contributed to a sense of universal human dignity that, among other things, helped to inspire the human rights movements of the twentieth century and beyond.

This last consideration should show us that although Thomas and Zhu are undoubtedly rooted in their historical and social environments, they transcend these circumstances to have something to say to those of us in the present day who aren't Catholic Christians, Neo-Confucians, teachers, or scholars. Taking their comprehensive approach seriously can help us to be committed and *hopeful* as we realize the complexities of life in the contemporary world but still push forward, step by step, on a daily basis, to do what we can, both singly and as members of our communities, to work toward a better world, in which more of us are able to exercise and limit our power on behalf of a truly common good.

Humble Authority in Action

Justice, Love, and Wonder

If we do indeed follow them, and attempt to develop the virtue of humble authority in our own lives, we will soon reach the conclusion that some of us cannot cheerfully ignore the rest, as often is the case. In one of his sermons, the Dominican friar and priest Herbert McCabe draws our attention to the injustice of what often passes for social and economic advancement in the contemporary era: "by progress [is meant] people (some people) getting richer. But this turns out to be accompanied by a vast number of people being hungry and poor; it is accompanied by regimes of oppression and torture; it is accompanied by wars in which 20 million people have died since 1945."[45]

Aiding and abetting the physical violence and oppression practiced in many parts of the world is the kind of intellectual violence that seeks to cripple, overwhelm, or destroy different points of view or values. Despite their depressingly many contributions to both kinds of violence, it is nonetheless the case that religious traditions are very well-poised to harmonize the various tensions of individual and social life today, having developed intellectual, artistic, moral, spiritual, and scientific ways of looking at people that mutually inform each other.[46] Perhaps their most fruitful contribution to our understanding of human existence is their invitation to forego reductionist thinking in favor of embracing our complexity.

Moreover, as has been discussed throughout this book, this kind of multi-faceted approach can inspire a sense of love, as we see in Thomas Aquinas and Zhu Xi: both saw reasons for care and concern in every direction they looked. Thomas and Zhu believed that there was more to the story than just personal interests or just material realities, and—in a perhaps stunningly unhumble way—attempted to describe all of it. Zhu, in addition to being a scholar-official who established a highly successful school of philosophy, was a poet who drank until he got drunk, and Thomas, the rational philosopher who logically deduced his way through hundreds of questions in the *Summa theologiae*, was also a man who lost himself in prayer and composed sacred music. They both saw all elements of life as being important, and did their best to honor every facet that they could feel and imagine, as well as those they could see, deduce, or infer.

Moreover, their sense of wonder in all of this is striking: they did not "throw up their hands in horror at the over-awesome incomprehensibility of creation,"[47] but, rather, rejoiced that there was so much to see. Perhaps the universe can be horrific if one thinks of oneself as an atomic individual, adrift in a meaningless void, or as at the complete mercy of forces far beyond one's control. However, if one thinks of oneself as an intelligent agent with moral potential to be developed in communion with one's family, community, race, world, and cosmos, the universe may instead come to be seen as the setting for shared moral striving. In realizing oneself as a part of all that is, one may come to care very much for the flourishing of everything that is, and to seek to do everything one can to make it better—and to avoid as much as possible doing anything that would make it otherwise. This inclusive approach, in which everything one can think of—and many things one can't—has a value in and of itself, leads to a connected sense of self and world, one in which one's own personal difficulties are not viewed in a vacuum, but rather as an infinitesimal part of the process in which "the whole creation has been groaning as in the pains of childbirth right up to the present time."[48]

Do We Really Need Religious Belief?

In closing, the question arises: Can the virtue of humble authority be useful, or workable, without the religious belief of Thomas or Zhu? The answer to this question is neither yes or no, but *to a certain extent*. A sense of the sacred is not necessary for one to recognize that all is not within her power, nor that insights may come from unexpected places. Nor does an understanding that some individuals are more morally and intellectually fit than others to inhabit places of power require a religiously charged cosmology.[49]

Thomas of course would argue that such an approach is unsatisfactory, as Christians have long argued that only service that leads to God can fulfill us, and Zhu would also find it odd and dangerous to separate humanity from the sacred order, from a teleological sense of what it is that we are supposed to do and be: the Confucians have always believed that taking the first small step in the wrong direction is the beginning of a very unfortuitous journey. Their sense that there is a higher purpose to human life is certainly not uniquely or exclusively medieval; as Charles Taylor notes, in the contemporary era, "the sense that there is something more presses in. Great numbers of people feel it: in moments of reflection about their life; in moments of relaxation in nature; in moments of bereavement and loss; and quite wildly and unpredictably. Our age is very far from settling in to a comfortable unbelief."[50]

In the end, aside from such predilections, past and present, I believe that a truncated version of the virtue works to a certain extent, but only to that certain extent. While it is possible for secular humanists to accept a stripped-down version of this virtue for successful use, its complete development and subsequent full efficacy require a reverence and love for all of existence that those with a wholly materialist view may find hard to attain. As this book has attempted to show, while modernist secular tropes can be quite convincing and insightful in a variety of ways, they do not address the entire person, or all that might well be significant to the person, as does the religious thought of Thomas and Zhu. While the scientific method of engaging with the world encourages the setting aside of love, and the secular view of the human person as self-interested actor makes love an optional concern, and social science leaves out considerations of love when considering social organization and its roles, the work of Thomas and Zhu is wholly suffused by *caritas* and *ren*. The love of the realities they see—the moral order of the cosmos, the moral potential of the human race—infuses all of their teachings about self-development and social organization, both of which are structured in accordance with the understanding that people should *want* what is best for each other and for the world. For both these thinkers, people should be authoritative enough to do what needs to be done in order to accomplish this best, and humble enough to pause or stop when the best is not being served: the religious love of Thomas and Zhu serves to inspirit and strengthen the virtue of humble authority in moments of doubt or temptation.

Today, we need to face more fully the multifold tasks of harmonizing tensions within ourselves and between each other on behalf of the common good, in concert with people who agree with us and people who do not. Love for our neighbors, and faith that our efforts, even when most thwarted, are somehow significant, can help us to persevere as we confront the oftentimes deafening cacophony before, around, and behind us.

Moreover, even aside from such functional concerns, being open to the sacred character of the universe means being open to the joys of elements of reality hitherto untouched, and perhaps forever indiscernible, by pure science or unadulterated logic. In the end, perhaps only those lovingly open to such joys are both willing and able to exercise rightful authority to its genuine fullest, and no further.

Notes

Introduction

1. See Adam Seligman, *Modernity's Wager: Authority, the Self, and Transcendence* (Princeton, NJ: Princeton University Press, 2000), p. 4. Philip Rieff provides a succinct formulation of the same principle: "power may come out of the barrel of a gun; but authority comes out of the projection—and introjection—of ideals" (Philip Rieff, "The Impossible Culture: Wilde as a Modern Prophet," in *The Feeling Intellect: Selected Writings*, ed. Jonathan Imber [Chicago: University of Chicago Press, 1990], p. 278).

2. A note concerning spellings: with regard to Chinese characters, this book will rely primarily on *pinyin* Romanization. When Wade Giles spellings arise in quoted texts, conversion to *pinyin* will be provided.

3. Aaron Stalnaker, *Overcoming Our Evil: Human Nature and Spiritual Exercises in Xunzi and Augustine* (Washington, DC: Georgetown University Press, 2006), p. 23. Such a dichotomy is reductionist, and not even particularly representative of reality past or present. As Jeffrey Stout puts it, "the categories that most obviously require scrutiny in this context are the matched pair, *tradition* and *modernity*. Traditionalism needs to define these concepts dichotomously; otherwise, it cannot impose the sharp and simple partition it uses to justify rejection of 'modern politics itself.' The half-conscious thought at work in this dichotomy is that genuine modernity, being in essence anti-traditional, does not have traditions. Modernity, specifically, modern democracy, is something that brings about the demise of tradition, and leaves us *after virtue* . . . [Ethical traditions rendered invisible by such an approach] are both the strand of Romantic traditionalism to which the new traditionalists owe their basic tropes and the strand of Emersonian thinking carried forward in the work of Whitman and Dewey" (Jeffrey Stout, *Democracy and Tradition* [Princeton, NJ: Princeton University Press, 2004], p. 119). Moreover, as Thomas Metzger points out, to the extent that "modernity" does in fact exist as a phenomenon or condition qualitatively new and different in human history, it is often perceived as a good thing: "modernization is an extremely popular phenomenon around the world, which would hardly be the case if it worsened the quality of life" (Thomas

Metzger, *A Cloud Across the Pacific: Essays on the Clash Between Chinese and Western Political Theories Today* (Hong Kong: Chinese University Press, 2005), p. 40. I wish to note here that, in choosing to make Thomas Aquinas and Zhu Xi partners in conversation, I wish neither to over-reify nor demonize "modernity," howsoever defined.

4. 在中國歷史上, 前固有孔子, 近古有朱子, 皆在中國學術思想史及中國文化史上發出莫大聲光, 留下莫大影響。Ch'ien Mu (錢穆), *Chu tzu hsin hsueh-an* (朱子新學案) (Taipei: San min (台北: 三民), 1971), p. 1.

5. 孔子集前古學術思想之大成, 開創儒學, 成爲中國文化傳統中一主要骨幹。 Ibid., pp. 1–2.

6. Wm. Theodore de Bary, "Some Common Tendencies in Neo-Confucianism," in *Confucianism in Action*, ed. David S. Nivison and Arthur Wright (Stanford, CA: Stanford University Press, 1959), p. 27. For a more detailed history of the term, see John H. Berthrong, "Boston Confucianism: The Third Wave of Global Confucianism," in *Confucianism in Dialogue Today: West, Christianity and Judaism*, ed. Liu Shu-Hsien, John Berthrong, and Leonard Swidler (Philadelphia: Ecumenical Press, 2004), especially pp. 26–27.

7. 朱子崛起, 不僅能集北宋以來理學之大成, 亦可謂其乃集孔子一下學術思想之大成。Ch'ien, 2.

8. See Wing-tsit Chan, ed., trans., *A Source Book in Chinese Philosophy* (Princeton, NJ: Princeton University Press, 1963), p. 588.

9. Wing-tsit Chan, "Introduction," in *Chu Hsi and Neo-Confucianism*, ed. Wing-tsit Chan (Honolulu: University of Hawaii Press, 1986), p. 3.

10. Julia Ching, *The Religious Thought of Chu Hsi [Zhu Xi]* (New York: Oxford University Press, 2000), p. 209.

11. John Paul II, *Fides et Ratio: The Relationship Between Faith and Reason (Encyclical Letter)* (Washington, D.C.: United States Catholic Conference, 1998), Section 49, p. 75.

12. Brian Davies, *The Thought of Thomas Aquinas* (Oxford: Clarendon Press, 1992), p. vii; italics added.

13. For more on this crisis, see James T. C. Liu, *China Turning Inward: Intellectual-Political Changes in the Early Twelfth Century* (Cambridge, MA: Council on East Asian Studies, Harvard University, 1988), p. 18.

14. As Wm. Theodore de Bary points out, "if today Chinese civilization seems almost synonymous with Confucian culture, we need to be reminded of the long centuries during which Buddhism and Daoism exerted a powerful and formative influence. For nearly eight centuries, from the fall of the Han (220 CE) to the rise of the Song (960), Chinese culture was so closely identified with Buddhism that neighbors like the Japanese and the Koreans embraced the one with the other and thought of great Tang China, the cynosure of the civilized world, as perhaps more of a 'Buddha-land' than the 'land of Confucius'" (Wm. Theodore de Bary and Irene Bloom, ed., *Sources of Chinese Tradition, Volume One: From Earliest Times to 1600*, 2nd ed. (New York: Columbia University Press, 1999), p. 540.

15. Nor were the Buddhists their only perceived enemy. As the distinguished scholar Wing-tsit Chan points out, Neo-Confucians vigorously attacked not only Buddhism but also Daoism as "heterodox traditions" (see Chan, *Chu Hsi: New Studies* [Honolulu: University of Hawaii Press, 1989], p. 486).

16. See ibid., p. 509, for a brief discussion of Zhu's treatment of Buddhism.

17. Carsun Chang, *The Development of Neo-Confucian Thought* (New York: Bookman Associates, 1957), p. 129.

18. Wm. Theodore de Bary, *Neo-Confucian Orthodoxy and the Learning of the Mind-and-Heart* (New York: Columbia University Press, 1981), p. 1. His followers internalized this kind of rejection in a profound way. See Peter Bol, *This Culture of Ours: Intellectual Transitions in T'ang and Sung China* (Stanford, CA: Stanford University Press, 1992), pp. 339–340, for a discussion of their self-understanding as an "embattled minority struggling with a self-interested mainstream."

19. According to Hoyt Tillman, it is possible that the early reversals suffered by the Tao-hsueh [*Daoxue*, Zhu's Confucian "School of the Way"] actually contributed to the school's long-term success: "efforts by intolerant chief councilors to suppress the fellowship and exclude its members from the examinations and official posts inadvertently promoted unity within the fellowship itself" (*Confucian Discourse and Chu Hsi's Ascendancy* [Honolulu: University of Hawaii Press, 1992], p. 252).

20. M. D. Chenu, O. P., *Toward Understanding Saint Thomas*, trans. A.-M. Landry, O. P., and D. Hughes, O.P. (Chicago: Henry Regnery Company, 1964), p. 15.

21. See Chapter 2 for discussions of Thomas's differences with Augustine concerning the moral status of non-Christians.

22. Jean-Pierre Torrell, O. P., *Saint Thomas Aquinas: Volume 1. The Person and His Work*, Robert Royal, trans. (Washington, D.C.: The Catholic University of America Press, 1996), p. 129.

23. Bonnie Kent, "Habits and Virtues (Ia IIae, qq. 49–70)" in *The Ethics of Aquinas*, ed. Stephen J. Pope (Washington, D.C.: Georgetown University Press, 2002), p. 116.

24. See McInerny, *Aquinas* (2004), p. 21.

25. Davies, p. vii.

26. Alasdair MacIntyre, *Whose Justice? Which Rationality?* (Notre Dame, IN: University of Notre Dame Press, 1989), p. 366.

27. For more on this topic, see Andrew J. Dell'Olio, "Zhu Xi and Thomas Aquinas on the Foundations of Moral Self-Cultivation," *Proceedings of the American Catholic Philosophical Association*, 77 (2003): 235–246.

28. I put this term in caps to distinguish it from the *li* (理) discussed in the first chapter. Although the characters and their meanings are very different, their pronunciation—down to the tone (3rd) in Mandarin Chinese—is the same.

29. As Fergus Kerr points out, "anachronism is always a risk when one calls on earlier thinkers to refute current arguments" (*After Aquinas: Versions of*

Thomism [Malden, MA: Blackwell Publishing, 2002], p. 208). To be clear, I do not argue that either Zhu or Thomas ever explicitly or consciously formulated the virtue I derive from their work. See the section below on Methodology for further discussion of this issue.

30. Thomas Aquinas, *Summa Theologica,* trans. Fathers of the English Dominican Province, ed. Kevin Knight (http://www.newadvent.org/summa/), 2003: IIae IIae, q. 64, a. 6, resp.

31. 世人多慎於擇婿，而忽於擇婦。。。所系甚重，豈可忽哉！ (*Jinsilu* 6:9, in *Zhuzi quanshu,* vol. 13, p. 228).

32. L. Carrington Goodrich and Chaoying Fang, trans., eds., *Dictionary of Ming Biography 1368–1644: Volume II* (New York: Columbia University Press, 1976), p. 1024.

33. Ibid., p. 1026.

34. MacIntyre, p. 366.

35. James F. Keenan, SJ, "Proposing Cardinal Virtues," *Theological Ethics* 56 (1995): 715. Outside the field of virtue ethics, Xinzhong Yao uses a similar approach in his work comparing Christianity and Confucianism: "Confucian *jen* and Christian *agape* can be contrasted in their particular aspects, but share a great deal in their universal aspects" (Xinzhong Yao, *Confucianism and Christianity: A Comparative Study of Jen and Agape* (Brighton, UK: Sussex Academic Press, 1996), p. 68.

36. Keenan, "Proposing Cardinal Values," p. 714.

37. Ibid., p. 715.

38. Robert Cummings Neville and Wesley J. Wildman, "On Comparing Religious Ideas," in *The Human Condition,* ed. Robert Cummings Neville (Albany: State University of New York Press, 2000), pp. 14–16.

39. Aaron Stalnaker, "Comparative Religious Ethics and the Problem of Human Nature," *Journal of Religious Ethics,* 33, no. 2 (June 2005): 191.

40. At the outset, I should note that using this translation does create one linguistic problem: the title given to the work by the Dominican Fathers is "*Summa theologica.*" However, this title is grammatically inaccurate: as a summary of theology, as opposed to a theological summary, what Thomas actually wrote was a *Summa theologiae.* While I use the more accurate title in the main text, in my footnotes, I use the title given it by my translation for purposes of citation.

41. Wing-tsit Chan, *Reflections on Things at Hand: the Neo-Confucian Anthology Compiled by Chu Hsi and Lü Tsu-chien* (New York: Columbia University Press, 1967), pp. vii–viii.

42. Lee Yearley, "Two Strands of Confucianism" in *Confucian Political Ethics,* ed. Daniel A. Bell (Princeton, NJ: Princeton University Press, 2007), p. 139.

43. Metzger, *A Cloud Across the Pacific,* p. 108.

44. Ibid., p. 140.

45. Lee H. Yearley, *Mencius and Aquinas: Theories of Virtue and Conceptions of Courage* (Albany: State University of New York Press, 1990), p. 200.

46. John H. Berthrong, *All Under Heaven: Transforming Paradigms in Confucian-Christian Dialogue* (Albany: State University of New York Press, 1994), p. 7. In his work, Berthrong addresses this issue by looking at "texts in terms of form, the dynamic interaction of form and the world, and the necessary unification of these two traits into the why, how, and what of any entity or event among the other things of the world" (ibid., p. 9).

47. May Sim, *Remastering Morals with Aristotle and Confucius* (New York: Cambridge University Press, 2007), p. 67. Stephen Prothero has a similar comparative approach, identifying not shared goals or practices, but rather "family resemblances" across the religious spectrum. See *God Is Not One: The Eight Rival Religions That Run the World—and Why Their Differences Matter* (New York: HarperCollins, 2010), esp. pp. 12–13.

48. Stalnaker, *Overcoming Our Evil*, p. 24.

49. See Charles Taylor, *A Secular Age* (Cambridge, MA: The Belknap Press of Harvard University Press, 2007), esp. pp. 4–13, for an extended discussion of these stances, which Taylor names "belief" and "unbelief," respectively. I have changed the terminology to make it more applicable to Confucian perspective and practice, not to foreground the contemporary tendency to replace adherence to "religion" with personal focus on "spirituality" (see below for a brief discussion of this trend).

50. Taylor, *A Secular Age*, p. 531. Philip Rieff makes a similar argument: "contemporary culture is in such a turmoil of new ways that none of them can show to advantage. The field is too crowded" (Philip Rieff, "The Impossible Culture," p. 288).

51. Richard Dawkins, *The God Delusion* (New York: Houghton Mifflin), 2006, p. 308. While Dawkins's hostility toward the religious enterprise is perhaps to be expected, it was rather more surprising and dismaying to see Sir Anthony Kenny, who specializes in using the tools of analytical philosophy to study the work of Thomas Aquinas, conflate faith with mindless fanaticism: "the idea that faith is an irrevocable commitment, which goes far beyond any evidence that could be offered in its support, is explicitly stated by Christian thinkers as different from each other as Aquinas, Kierkegaard and Newman. It is the degree of commitment involved in faith, rather than its religious object, that is really objectionable. Not all fanaticism is religious fanaticism, as the history of Nazism and Stalinism makes abundantly clear" ("The Irrevocability of Faith," October 22, 2007, http://entertainment.timesonline.co.uk/tol/arts_and_entertainment/the_tls/article2717498.ece, retrieved June 30, 2010). That this understanding of religious belief appears to be defensible to men from such widely different intellectual backgrounds signals a serious problem that must be addressed by the explicitly religious.

52. See Terry Eagleton, *Reason, Faith & Revolution: Reflections on the God Debate* (New Haven: Yale University Press, 2009), esp. p. 37, for a similar discussion.

53. For a more detailed discussion of this thesis, see John Milbank's *Theology and Social Theory: Beyond Secular Reason*, 2nd ed. (Malden, MA: Blackwell Publishing, 2006), esp. pp. 1–3. Throughout this highly complex work, Milbank's basic argument is that Christianity has a uniquely peaceful metaphysics, which he contrasts with various secular perspectives that, in his reading, are always based on supposing the ontological primacy of struggle and violence. As will become clear throughout the course of this book, I would only disagree with his claims for Christian uniqueness in this regard: Confucianism, which does not have a creation story *per se*, but rather a narrative that begins *in media res* with the discovery of certain arts by sages that conduce to human peace and prosperity, also points in this general direction (see James Legge, ed., trans. *The Shoo King, Or The Book of Historical Documents*, 2nd ed. (Taipei: Chin-hsüeh shu-chu [1893–1895], 1969), esp. the Books of T'ang and Yu.

54. See Taylor, *A Secular Age*, p. 331.

55. See William C. Spohn, *Go and Do Likewise: Jesus and Ethics* (New York: The Continuum Publishing Company, 2000), pp. 33–34, for his comparison of the two terms.

56. Catherine M. Bell, *Ritual: Perspectives and Dimensions* (New York: Oxford University Press, 1997), p. 182.

57. See Milbank, esp. pp. 401–402, for a presentation of a similar methodology.

58. See Thomas Aquinas and Fra Rainaldo da Piperno, *Supplement to the Third Part of the Summa Theologica*, trans. Fathers of the English Dominican Province, ed. Kevin Knight (http://newadvent.org/summa/), 2003: q. 92, a. 1, ad. 14, http://newadvent.org/summa/5092.htm).

59. See *Yulei* (語類), chap. 1, in *Zhuzi quanshu* (朱子全書) (Shanghai: Shanghai guji chubanshe; Hefei shi: Anhui guji chubanshe (上海: 上海古籍出版社: 合肥市: 安徽 教育出版社), 2002), vol. 14, p. 117, and *Jinsilu* (近思錄) 2.91, in *Zhuzi quanshu*, vol. 13, p. 189.

60. 學者先要會疑。*Jinsilu* 3.15, in *Zhuzi Quanshu*, vol. 13, p. 195.

61. David L. Hall and Roger T. Ames, "Sexism, With Chinese Characteristics," in *The Sage and the Second Sex: Confucianism, Ethics and Gender*, ed. Chenyang Li (Chicago: Open Court, 2000), p. 91.

62. I do not mean to claim that this will always be the case. As Prothero reports, there are "friendly" atheists looking for ways in which "believers and non-believers [may] coexist in a spirit of mutual toleration" (see Prothero, p. 328). Such efforts may well lead to the development of more comprehensive narratives or life "packages" over time.

63. Note my use of the word "fairly": we should be careful about drawing too pronounced a line between academia and the rest of the world: a study recently published in *Sociology of Religion* reports that, despite the secular status of most institutions of higher education, nearly 75 percent of professors report some belief in God, or a "higher power." Only 10 percent of professors are atheists, and another 13 percent are agnostic. These findings suggest that

while college professors are more inclined to disbelief (as measured by "theism") they actually compare more closely to the general population than to the usual stereotype of the modern liberal elite in academia. See Neil Gross and Solon Simmons, "The Religiosity of American College and University Professors," in *Sociology of Religion* 70, No. 2, Summer 2009: 101–129.

64. See his TED talk, entitled "The Lost Art of Democratic Debate," available at http://www.ted.com/talks/lang/eng/michael_sandel_the_lost_art_of_democratic_debate.html (retrieved June 29, 2010). See also the article entitled "How Facts Backfire" by Joe Koehane, published in the *Boston Globe* on July 11, 2010, retrieved July 13, 2010 (http://www.boston.com/bostonglobe/ideas/articles/2010/07/11/how_facts_backfire/), in which the author summarizes research demonstrating that people of all backgrounds fail to truly or fairly consider facts that challenge their personal beliefs.

65. Barry Schwartz, *The Paradox of Choice: Why More is Less* (New York. HarperCollins Publishers, 2005), p. 20.

66. This muted approach may have its moral ramifications as well. Andrew Flescher argues that people in relatively wealthy secular societies often do as much as or even less than what is ethically expected of them (see *Heroes, Saints and Ordinary Morality* (Washington, D.C.: Georgetown University Press, 2003), p. 1. Moreover, expectations are arguably often low to begin with: according to David Norton, modern ethics "is typically minimalist (a) with respect to the kinds of situations and choices that count as moral, and (b) in its conception of moral character" (David L. Norton, "Moral Minimalism and the Development of Moral Character" in *Midwest Studies in Philosophy* XIII (1988), p. 80.

67. I am indebted to Adam Seligman for this insight.

68. J. R. R. Tolkien, *The Fellowship of the Ring: Being the First Part of THE LORD OF THE RINGS* (New York: Houghton Mifflin, 1994), p. 254.

Chapter 1. An Objectively Moral Universe

1. Kathleen Norris, *Amazing Grace: A Vocabulary of Faith* (New York: Penguin Riverhead Books, 1998), p. 239. Norris herself has personal experience with such perspectives: "one of my writer friends, on hearing that I had joined a church, said, 'What's the matter? Did you have a lobotomy?'" (ibid., p. 105).

2. As Michael Lipka reports, in a 2013 Pew Research Center study, 70 percent of Americans reported attending religious services on either a monthly or a yearly basis, while 37 percent reported attending once a week or more (http://www.pewresearch.org/fact-tank/2013/09/13/what-surveys-say-about-worship-attendance-and-why-some-stay-home/).

3. Martin Luther, *The Table Talk of Martin Luther*, trans. William Hazlitt (1872; books.google.com, Google Books: 2008, 164 http://books.google.com/books?id=ZUAuAAAAYAAJ&client=firefox-a)

4. Ibid., p. 144.

5. Isaac Newton, *Newton's Philosophy of Nature: Selections from His Writings* (Whitefish, MT: Kessinger Publishing, 2003), p. 3.

6. Newton, p. 10.

7. "It is good to remember from time to time that our Western science—and there seems to be no other—did not start with collecting observations of oranges, but with bold theories about the world" (Karl Popper, "Back to the Pre-Socratics: The Presidential Address," *Proceedings of the Aristotelian Society* (New Series) 59 (1958–1959), pp. 2–3). See Joseph Needham, Ling Wang, and Peter J. Golas, *Science and Civilisation in China* (Cambridge, UK: Cambridge University Press, 1954) for a book-length argument against the West-centric element of his claim.

8. Newton, p. 3. What is true of the scientific method is true of the disciplines that found themselves on its principles. As analytic philosopher Steven Toulmin explains, "in course of time (we may guess) current ideas about the explanatory goals at which the major disciplines of science should be aiming will be reformulated yet again, as they have been in the past. With these further changes, there will come also changes in the criteria for appraising proposed conceptual variants; with them, changes in the actual bodies of established scientific concepts and explanatory procedures; and, with these in turn, changes in the sets of propositions which it is 'open'—i.e. meaningful in that scientific context—to consider as *either* true *or* false. Yet we can no more anticipate such strategic change than Bach could write Beethoven's Choral Symphony. At no point can we therefore demonstrate, as Kant hoped, that the basic rational forms of our scientific understanding are final and immutable" (Stephen Toulmin, "Rationality and Scientific Discovery" in *Philosophy of Science Association: Proceedings of the Biennial Meeting of the Philosophy of Science Association 1972* (1972), p. 405. See also Karl Popper, *Conjectures and Refutations: The Growth of Scientific Knowledge* (New York: Routledge, 2002), esp. pp. xi–xii.

9. Richard Harvey Brown and Elizabeth L. Malone, "Reason, Politics, and the Politics of Truth: How Science is Both Autonomous and Independent," in *Sociological Theory* 22, no. 1 (Mar. 2004): 112.

10. http://edinburghcreationgroup.org/

11. Toulmin, p. 391. Metzger makes a similar point with his definition of discourse: "a discourse consists not only of premises shared by people who regard them as true or uncontroversial and platitudinous. It consists also of the questions that are implied by these necessarily vague premises, and that these people agree are the significant questions worth arguing about" (see Metzger, *A Cloud Across the Pacific*, p. 90).

12. This phenomenon may be an effect as well as a cause of trends in Western culture. The ethical philosophers Martha Nussbaum and Servais-Theodore Pinckaers have charted a Western resistance to feelings back to Plato and the rise of nominalism, respectively. See Martha C. Nussbaum, *The Fragility of Goodness: Luck and Ethics in Greek Tragedy and Philosophy* (New York: Cambridge University Press, 1986), esp. p. 15, and Servais-Theodore Pinckaers,

O. P., "The Sources of the Ethics of Thomas Aquinas," Mary Thomas Noble, O. P., trans., in Pope, Stephen J., ed. *The Ethics of Aquinas* (Washington, D.C.: Georgetown University Press, 2002), esp. p. 26.

13. Colin Jerolmack and Douglas Porpora, "Religion, Rationality, and Experience: A Response to the New Rational Choice Theory of Religion," in *Sociological Theory* 22, no. 1 (Mar. 2004): 141.

14. Ibid., p. 156.

15. Metzger, *A Cloud Over the* Pacific, p. 8.

16. See Antonio Damasio, *Descartes' Error: Emotion, Reason, and the Human Brain* (New York: Penguin, 2005), and Antonio Damasio, *The Feeling of What Happens: Body and Emotion in the Making of Consciousness* (Fort Washington, PA: Harvest Books, 2000).

17. This is not to say that our leanings are deterministic: events, persons, or things in the world can break through our habits and dispositions, alerting a person to new perspectives hitherto unimagined or unconsidered by him or her. See as well note 2 of Chapter 2 for further discussion of how none of the elements discussed in this project is considered to be deterministic.

18. Nussbaum, p. 13.

19. See Humphrey Carpenter, ed., *The Letters of J. R. R. Tolkien* (New York: Houghton Mifflin, 2000), p. 15.

20. John Paul II, Section 3, p. 6.

21. Ibid., Section 28, p. 45.

22. Harold Blumer, *Symbolic Interactionism: Perspective and Method* (Englewood Cliffs, NJ: Prentice Hall, 1969), p. 2.

23. Ibid., pp. 3, 6–7.

24. Linda Zagzebski, *Virtues of the Mind: An Inquiry into the Nature of Virtue and the Ethical Foundations of Knowledge* (Cambridge Studies in Philosophy. Cambridge, UK: Cambridge University Press, 1996), p. 50. Calling this ability "wisdom," Zagzebski writes, "the nature of wisdom may be elusive, but it is clear that whatever it is, wisdom is an epistemic value qualitatively different from the piling up of beliefs that have the property of justification, warrant, or certainty. Wisdom is neither a matter of the properties of propositional beliefs, not is it a matter of the relations among such beliefs; it is a matter of grasping the whole of reality" (ibid., p. 50). As will be discussed further in the Conclusion, not even the most fundamental of the natural sciences—physics—can grasp the whole of reality.

25. Ibid., p. 226.

26. See Karyn Lai, "Confucian Moral Self-Cultivation: Some Parallels with Musical Training" in *The Moral Circle and the Self: Chinese and Western Approaches*, ed. Kim-chong Chong, Sor-hoon Tan, and C. L. Ten (Chicago: Open Court, 2003), esp. p. 131.

27. As the rest of my discussion focuses on religion, I take a moment here to note that such a full-bodied approach is also available outside the field or realm of religion, and may in fact be important to the advancement of the

natural sciences. Jonah Lehrer notes that "the paradox of neuroscience is that its astonishing progress has exposed the limitations of its paradigm . . . Much of our experiences remain outside its range" (Jonah Lehrer, "The Future of Science is . . . Art?" http://seedmagazine.com/news/2008/01/the_future_of_scienceis_art.php). As he goes on to explain, the insights expressed in art and literature can be of enormous benefit to scientists, pointing out that great novels have endured "because they *feel* true. And they feel true because they capture a layer of reality that reductionism cannot . . . By taking these artistic explorations seriously, neuroscientists can better understand the holistic properties they are trying to parse. Before you break something apart, it helps to know how it hangs together. In this sense, the arts are an incredibly rich data set, providing science with a glimpse into its blind spots. If neuroscience is ever going to discover the neural correlates of consciousness, or find the source of the self, or locate the cells of subjectivity—if it's ever going to get beyond a glossary of our cortical parts—then it has to develop an intimate understanding of these higher-order mental events. This is where the current methods of science reach their limit" (ibid.). Moreover, he argues, such an approach may well be profitable across a wide range of the sciences: "maybe a simile will help unlock the secret of dark matter" (ibid.).

28. For similar discussions, see David Burrell's *Aquinas, God and Action* (Notre Dame, IN: University of Notre Dame Press, 1979) for his exploration of the mutually sustaining relationship between logic and empirical observation in Thomas, as well as Jean Porter's work on the continuing importance of the natural law tradition for Christian ethics, a trend that Thomas himself did a great deal to popularize (Jean Porter, *Nature as Reason: A Thomistic Theory of the Natural Law* [Grand Rapids, MI: Wm. B. Eerdmans Publishing, 2005]; Jean Porter, *Natural and Divine Law: Reclaiming the Tradition for Christian Ethics* [Grand Rapids, MI: Wm. B. Eerdmans Publishing, 1999]).

29. James A. Weishipl, *Friar Thomas D'Aquino: His Life, Thought, and Work* (Garden City, NY: Doubleday, 1974), p. 3.

30. Frederick Copleston, *History of Philosophy, Volume II: Medieval Philosophy from Augustine to Duns Scotus* (New York: Random House, 1993), p. 8. This did not prevent different thinkers from reaching different theoretical conclusions: as he somewhat laconically notes, people's "philosophical ideas were by no means the same on all points" (ibid., p. 7).

31. Maurice de Wulf, *History of Mediaeval Philosophy*, trans. Ernest C. Messenger (London, New York: Nelson, 1952), p. 20. Given modern skepticism concerning the mixture of religious and philosophical thought, de Wulf is particularly concerned to defend the claims the medieval era has to possessing a genuine philosophy in scholasticism, asserting that "the religious character of scholasticism is not enough to define it" (p. 18) and that scholastic philosophy, "apart altogether from the dogma that it had in view, offered a rational explanation of the universal order of things," and "quite a number of doctrines have no direct connection with Catholicism" (ibid., p. 19).

32. See Pinckaers, especially p. 17.

33. Jacques Maritain, *St. Thomas Aquinas* (1958; Nd.edu, Jacques Maritain Center, University of Notre Dame: 2009), chap. 1, http://www2.nd.edu/Departments//Maritain/etext/thomas.htm

34. Davies, p. 14.

35. Thomas Aquinas, *Summa Contra Gentiles*, Anton C. Pegis, James F. Anderson, Vernon J. Bourke, and Charles J. O'Neil, trans. (Notre Dame, IN: University of Notre Dame Press, 1992), bk. I, chap. 7, sec. 1, p. 74.

36. *Summa theologica*, IIa IIae, q. 9, a. 1, ad. 2. See also *Summa contra gentiles*, bk. I, chap. 7, sec. 2, p. 74: "the knowledge of the principles that are known to us naturally has been implanted in us by God; for God is the author of our nature." As the author of our nature is a God who "so loved the world, that He gave His only begotten Son, that whosoever believeth in him shall not perish, but have everlasting life" (Jn 3:16) and, moreover, who created all things in the most excellent way (see Thomas Aquinas, *Compendium theologiae*, I:100, http://www.corpusthomisticum.org, Fundación Tomás de Aquino, 2008–2009), "whatever arguments are brought forward against the doctrines of faith are conclusions incorrectly derived from the first and self-evident principles embedded in nature" (*Summa contra gentiles*, bk. I, chap. 7, sec. 7, p. 75).

37. Ibid., Ia, q. 1, a. 8, ad. 2.

38. See Ibid., IIa IIae, q. 2, a. 10, ad. 2.

39. "The consideration of creatures is necessary not only for instruction in the truth, but also for the elimination of errors (est etiam necessaria creaturarum consideratio non solum ad veritatis instructionem, sed etiam ad errores excludendos)" (*Summa contra gentiles*, bk. II, chap. 3, sec. 1, p. 32).

40. *Summa theologica*, IIa IIae, q. 2, a. 4, ad. 1.

41. Davies, p. 280. Davies lists John Hick, Alvin Plantinga, and Terence Penelhum as proponents of such a view. Kerr has a complementary reading: "the God who is present in the world as source and goal of all things is so much more mysterious than those who see signs of divinity everywhere that argument is required. *The point of insisting that argument for God's existence is required is, then, not to convince hypothetical open-minded atheists*, or even to persuade 'fools', so much as to deepen and enhance the mystery of the hidden God. From the start, the 'theistic proofs' are the first lesson in Thomas' negative theology. *Far from being an exercise in rational apologetics, the purpose of arguing for God's existence is to protect God's transcendence*" (Kerr, p. 58; italics added).

42. *Summa contra gentiles*, bk. I, chap. 9, sec. 2, pp. 77–78.

43. See Nichols, p. 41, for further discussion of this theme.

44. *Summa theologica*, IIa IIae, q. 4, a. 1; quoting Hebrews 11:1.

45. Ibid., Ia, q. 12, a. 13, ad. 3.

46. Ibid., IIa IIae, q. 2, a. 3, ad. 1.

47. Ibid., ad. 3.

48. Ibid., q. 50, a. 4, resp.

49. Ibid., q. 4, a. 2, resp.

50. Kerr, 158. Cf. also *Summa theologica*, Ia IIae, q. 3, a. 7, ad. 2. This focus on the will and desires also transforms what we might think of as intellectual positions (an atheist stance, for example) into sins, and those who hold them into sinners who may or may not be qualified to exercise authority over Christian believers (see IIa IIae, q. 10, a. 1, resp.). I mention this chiefly to bring attention to the fact that, regardless of his respect for people outside of the Christian communion, there are elements in Thomas's thought that can render him problematic in interreligious dialogue.

51. Nor does he disparage the human body; see the discussion of his understanding of the human person in Chapter 2.

52. *Summa Theologica*, IIa IIae, q. 1, a. 4, ad. 3.

53. Ibid., q. 6, a. 1, resp.

54. Ibid., Ia IIae, q. 113, a. 8, resp.

55. Ibid., Ia, q. 8, a. 8, ad. 2.

56. Kerr, 159.

57. *Summa theologica*, Ia IIae, q. 4, a. 4, resp. See also the *Supplement* to the *Summa theologica*, most likely prepared by his assistant, Fra Rainaldo da Piperno, who compiled the work from selections from Thomas's commentary on the Fourth Book of Peter Lombard's *Sentences* after Thomas' death: Thomas Aquinas and Fra Rainaldo da Piperno, *Supplement to the Third Part of the Summa Theologica*, trans. Fathers of the English Domincan Province, ed. Kevin Knight (http://newadvent.org/summa/), 2003: q. 92, a. 1, ad. 14. N.B.: *The Sentences of Peter Lombard* (Petrus Lombardus, c. 1100--1160), a bishop and scholastic theologian, served as the standard textbook of theology in medieval universities. Thomas's commentary on this work, the *Scriptum super sententiis*, written between 1252 and 1255, is generally viewed as his first great theological synthesis (see Eleonore Stump, *Aquinas* [London: Routledge, 2003, pp. 3–5]). For more information on Lombard and his influence, see Philipp W. Rosemann, *The Story of a Great Medieval Book: Peter Lombard's "Sentences"* (Peterborough, Ontario: Broadview Press, 2007).

58. Nichols, p. 197.

59. Ibid., p. viii.

60. Julia Ching, *Confucianism and Christianity: A Comparative Study* (New York: Kodansha International, 1977), p. 15. In passing: a fact often overlooked in discussions of Confucianism today, which often focus on the impact that the West has had on the tradition, is that Confucianism played a significant role in the development of modern Western philosophy: "introduced to Europe by Jesuit missionaries in the seventeenth and eighteenth centuries, Chinese philosophy—mostly in the form of Confucianism—made a real impact upon European intellectual circles, especially in the Age of Enlightenment, the cultural legacy of which we are all heirs" (Ibid., p. xxiii).

61. 子不語: 怪,力,亂,神。 *Analects* 7:20, in *Xin yi sishu fuben* (*新譯四書讀本*), ed. Xie Bingying (謝冰瑩) (Taibei: San min shu ju (臺北: 三民書局), 1967), p. 140.

62. 子曰, 「素隐, 行怪, 後世有述焉: 吾弗为之矣」。Chapter 11, *The Doctrine of the Mean*, in Xie, p. 100.

63. Ching, *Confucianism and Christianity*, p. 145.

64. Ibid., p. 178.

65. Yao, p. 38. Tucker has a similar idea: "the [West Asian religious traditions] can be described as prophetic and historically based religions; the [South Asian religious traditions] can be seen as mystical religions and religions of liberation; [Confucianism and Daoism] can be understood as religious worldviews of cosmic and social harmony" (Mary Evelyn Tucker, "Introduction," in Tu Weiming and Mary Evelyn Tucker, eds. *Confucian Spirituality: Volume One. Volume 11A of World Spirituality: An Encyclopedia of the Religious Quest* (New York: The Crossroad Publishing Company, 2003), p. 3.

66. Ren Jiyu, "Chu Hsi and Religion," in Wing-tsit Chan, ed., *Chu Hsi and Neo-Confucianism* (Honolulu: University of Hawaii Press, 1986), p. 357.

67. Benjamin I. Schwartz, *The World of Thought in Ancient China* (Cambridge, MA: Bellknap Press, 1985), p. 125.

68. Wm. Theodore de Bary, "Some Common Tendencies in Neo-Confucianism," in *Confucianism in Action*, ed. David S. Nivison and Arthur Wright (Stanford, CA: Stanford University Press, 1959), p. 39.

69. Wm. Theodore de Bary, "Zhu Xi's Neo-Confucian Spirituality," in *Confucian Spirituality: Volume Two* (Volume 11B of *World Spirituality: An Encyclopedia of the Religious Quest)*, ed. Tu Weiming and Mary Evelyn Tucker (New York: The Crossroad Publishing Company, 2004), p. 74.

70. Yao, p. 213. Thus it is, for example, that Julia Ching can make the general statement that "Christianity is constituted by belief in the God of Jesus Christ, whereas ethical values—rather than belief in God—determine who is Confucian" (Ching, *Confucianism and Christianity*, p. xxii).

71. Ching, *Confucianism and Christianity*, p. 69. This lack of central focus on God is accompanied by lack of interest in how the world came to be. Part of the reason behind this state of affairs is no doubt linguistic: "although there are words in Chinese that can be used to render the English word 'create', they do not occupy nearly so central a place in the system of thought and are relatively lacking in emotive power. Far more vital in the Chinese tradition are the twin concepts *sheng* (give birth or be born, produce) and *ch'eng* (become, fulfill, complete), along with *hua* (transform). In all these cases there is hardly any notion of an agent; the controlling metaphor is that of growth and development within the actual process of nature" (Alison Harley Black, *Man and Nature in the Philosophical Thought of Wang Fu-chih* [Seattle: University of Washington Press, 1989], p. 4). Certainly, the Chinese-speaking Zhu Xi "does not appear to have been interested in the beginnings of Heaven and Earth" (Ch'ien Mu, "Historical Perspectives on Chu Hsi's Learning," in *Chu Hsi and Neo-Confucianism*, p. 39).

72. Julia Ching, *The Religious Thought of Chu Hsi* (New York: Oxford University Press, 2000), p. 52; see also Ching, *Confucianism and Christianity*, p. 143.

73. Ching, *Confucianism and Christianity*, p. 105.

74. He says, "From the fourteenth to the nineteenth centuries, 'humanism' by and large implies the following few elements: (1) a kind of educational program grounded in classical [Greek, Roman] studies; (2) a belief that humankind's perspective and interest have a central place in the cosmos; (3) a belief that reason and autonomy are the foundation for the existence of humankind; (4) a belief that reason, a spirit of skepticism, and the scientific method are the only suitable tools for discovering truth and constructing human society; (5) a belief that the foundation of ethics and society must be gained in the midst of autonomy and moral equality (从14 世纪到19 世纪以来, "humanism"大本包含以下几个层面的涵义: (1) 一种基于古典学习的教育程序 (program); (2) 相信人类的视角 (perspective) 、利益和在整个于民宇宙中的中心地利; (3) 相信理性 (reason) 和自律 (autonomy), 将其作为人类存在的基础; (4) 相信理性、怀疑精神和科学方法是发现真理和建构人类社群的确一恰当的工具; (5) 相信伦理和社会的基础要在自律和道德平等中获得)" (Peng Guoxiang (彭国翔), *Rujia chuantong: zongjiao yu renwenzhuyi zhi jian* (儒家传统: 宗教与人文主义之间) [Beijing: Beijing daxue chuban she (北京: 北京大学出版社), 2007], pp. 3–4). Concerning religion and the Abrahamic traditions, he says, "these three major religious traditions all come out of Western Asia, [and] they possess three shared fundamental characteristics: (1) they all believe in an external, personal God; this external personal God transcends the world of humanity, and sets the law and order for the human world; (2) they all have an organized institution of specialists (church) and personnel specializing in theological knowledge; (3) they all have a sole scripture that constitutes the written medium of the objects of their faith. These three characteristics constitute the three traditional fundamental conditions of 'religion' [in the] West (这三大宗教传统都起源于西亚, 具有三个共同的基本特征: (1) 都信仰一个外在的人格神, 这个外在的人格神超越于人类世界, 决定人类世界的秩序; (2) 都具有专门的组织机构 (教会) 和专门的神织人员; (3) 都有一部唯一的经典构成其信仰对象的语言载体。这三个特征, 构成西方传统 "religion" 的三项基本条件)" (ibid, 7).

75. 首先, 如果我们以 "人文" 和 "宗教" 这两个词历史上在中文语境中本来的涵义为准, 那么, 我们就不妨既可以说儒学是一种 "人文主义," 是 "人文精神"的集中体现, 也可以说是一种"宗教," 就像它曾经好毫无疑问地在历史上和佛教, 道教一道被作为一种 "宗教" 那样。其次, 即便我们在使用 "人文主义" 和 "宗教" 这两个词时是对应于西方的 "humanism" 和 "religion," 只要我们的理解不局限与近代以来主流的 "世俗人文主义" 和仅以西亚一神教为模式的 "宗教," 那么, 我们同样可以既将其儒家传统视为一种人文主义, 又将其视为一种宗教。第三, 即便在严格对应于西方近代以来主流的 "secular humanism" 和仅以西亚一种一神教的 "religion" 的情况下使用 "人文主义" 和 "宗教" 范畴的其中之一, 那么, 我们仍然可以看到儒家传统之中同时具有 "人文主义" 和 "宗教" 的成分。" Ibid., p. 10.

76. Tu Weiming, "The Unity of Knowing and Acting: From A Neo-Confucian Perspective," in *Humanity and Self-Cultivation: Essays in Confucian Thought* (Berkeley: Asian Humanities Press, 1979), p. 86.

77. 「予欲無言! 」子貢曰: 「子如不言, 則小子何述焉? 」子曰: 「天何言哉! 四時行焉, 百物生焉; 天何言哉? 」*Analects* 17.19, in Xie, p. 275.

78. 天地以生物为心者也。*Renshuo*, in *Zhuzi quanshu*, vol. 23, p. 3279.

79. Chung Tsai-chun, *The Development of the Concepts of Heaven and of Man in the Philosophy of Chu Hsi* (Taiwan: Institute of Chinese Literature and Philosophy, Academia Sinica, 1993), p. 114.

80. 問: 「天地之心亦靈否? 還只是漠然無為? 」曰: 「天地之心不可道是不靈, 但不如人恁地思慮。 伊川曰: 『天地無心而成化,聖人有心而無為。 』」*Yulei*, chap. 1, in *Zhuzi quanshu*, vol. 14, pp. 116–117; italics added.

81. Yü, Ying-shih, "Between the Heavenly and the Human," in *Confucian Spirituality: Volume One* (Volume 11A of *World Spirituality: An Encyclopedia of the Religious Quest)*, ed. Tu Weiming and Mary Evelyn Tucker (New York: The Crossroad Publishing Company, 2003), p. 76.

82. Roger T. Ames, "*Li* and the A-theistic Religiousness of Classical Confucianism," in *Confucian Spirituality: Volume One* (Volume 11A of *World Spirituality: An Encyclopedia of the Religious Quest*), ed. Tu Weiming and Mary Evelyn Tucker (New York: The Crossroad Publishing Company, 2003), p. 165.

83. See Ching, *Confucianism and Christianity*, p. 176, for her reading of early Confucianism as expressing faith in a "supreme, personal deity."

84. See Deborah Sommer, "Ritual and Sacrifice in Early Confucianism: Contacts with the Spirit World" in *Confucian Spirituality: Volume One*. (Volume 11A of *World Spirituality: An Encyclopedia of the Religious Quest*), ed. Tu Weiming and Mary Evelyn Tucker (New York: The Crossroad Publishing Company, 2003), p. 217, for her discussion of how even such relatively anthropocentric ancient Confucians as Xunzi never questioned the existence of Heaven.

85. 子曰 : 「未能事人, 焉能事鬼! 未知生, 焉知死! 」此說盡了 。*Yulei*, chap. 3, in *Zhuzi quanshu*, vol. 14, p. 153.

86. 今且須去理會跟前事, 那箇鬼神事, 無形無影, 莫要枉費心力 。Ibid.

87. 鬼神只是氣 。Ibid., p. 154. I use Wing-tsit Chan's translation in order to convey both the energy and the matter encompassed by this term. See Chapter 2 for a discussion of how *li* and *qi* are not wholly compatible with Western conceptions of form and matter.

88. Patricia Buckley Ebrey, trans., intro. *Chu Hsi's Family Rituals: A Twelfth Century Chinese Manual for the Performance of Cappings, Weddings, Funerals and Ancestral Rites* (Princeton, NJ: Princeton University Press, 1991), p. xxvi. This quotidian air is increased by the fact that homely and matter-of-fact advice is offered alongside ritual instructions in Zhu's handbook. In Ebrey's translation: "All servants are expected to get along harmoniously. The master and mistress should scold any who quarrel as soon as they hear of it. If the quarreling does not stop, they should beat them with a staff, the one in the wrong being beaten more severely. If one is willing to end the quarrel and the other refuses, only the one who refuses should be beaten" (ibid., p. 34).

89. See ibid., p. 109.

90. See ibid., pp. 176–177.

91. 雖聖人不作 [窮得這道理], 這天理自在天地間 。 *Yulei*, chap. 9, in *Quanshu*, vol. 14, p. 307.

92. See Rodney Taylor, "The Religious Character of the Confucian Tradition," in *Philosophy East & West* 48, no. 3 (1998): 84.

93. Wm. Theodore de Bary, *The Liberal Tradition in China* (New York: Columbia University Press, 1983), p. 59. According to some, the type of book learning valued and practiced by the Confucians had its limitations. Merle Goldman argues that "the most serious failing of Confucianism was its exclusive concern with human affairs conceived in a rather restrictive fashion. Confucius defined knowledge as 'knowing man' in the political, moral and social sense. When Zhu Xi affirmed study as humanity's noblest pursuit, he meant its object to be practical only in the sense of serving correct action. Lack of analytical interest in the physical sciences and aversion to law characterized much of Confucian thinking. Neither did Confucianism ever overcome the primary agrarian values and antimercantile prejudice which so hamstrung the Chinese imagination" (René Goldman, "Moral Leadership in Society: Some Parallels between the Confucian 'Noble Man' and the Jewish 'Zaddik'" in *Philosophy East and West* 45, no. 3 (1995): 358.

94. 讀書以觀聖賢之意; 因聖賢之意, 以觀自然之理。*Yulei*, chap. 10, in *Zhuzi quanshu*, vol. 14, p. 314. Such study of the Classics is a necessary—but not sufficient—cause of full-self development. Even though Zhu never used the rhetoric familiar to Christians about the importance of being like unspoiled little children, which might have opened the doors of Confucian enlightenment to the uneducated, he nonetheless expanded the ranks of those who might achieve it: "In Chu Hsi's [Zhu Xi's] hands, the entire orientation of the *Ta-hsueh* [*Daxue*] text had changed; a sort of 'democratization' of the work had taken place. A guidebook for the political elite had now become a guidebook for anyone and everyone hoping to become part of the moral elite. That anyone might follow the program proposed by the *Ta-hsueh* according to Chu's [Zhu's] reading and thereby join the moral elite rested on the philosophical premise, laid out in the opening lines according to Chu's [Zhu's] reading, that each and every individual is born good—with an inborn luminous virtue—but must struggle throughout life to keep from falling away from that good" (Daniel K Gardner, trans, ed. *Chu Hsi and the Ta-hsueh: Neo-Confucian Reflection on the Confucian Canon* [Cambridge, MA: Harvard University Press, 1986], p. 58). Also see my Chapter 5 for discussion of the differences in moral expectations for various social classes.

95. 於不疑處有疑, 方是進矣。*Jinsilu* 3.75, in *Quanshu*, vol. 13, p. 206.

96. 義理儘無窮, 前人恁地說, 亦未必盡。 須是自把來橫看堅看, 儘入深, 儘有在。*Yulei*, chap. 9, in *Zhuzi quanshu*, vol. 14, p. 309.

97. Sim, p. 67.

98. 是氣清明純粹, 而無一毫昏濁。。。不待學而能, 如堯舜是也。 *Yulei*, Chapter 4, in *Zhuzi quanshu*, vol. 14, 194.

99. See Chapters 2 and 3 for detailed discussions concerning the role God plays in human life.

100. 橫渠先生謂范巽之曰: 吾輩不及古人, 病源何在? 巽之請問, 先生曰: 此非難悟。設此語者, 蓋欲學者存意之不忘, 庶遊心浸熟, 有一日脫然如大寐之得醒耳。 *Jinsilu* 2.91, in *Zhuzi quanshu*, vol. 13, p. 189.

101. Stalnaker, *Overcoming Our Evil*, p. 280.

102. 學者須是務實。*Jinsilu* 2.62, in *Zhuzi quanshu*, vol. 13, p. 185.

103. See Okada Takehiko, "Chu Hsi and Wisdom as Hidden and Stored," in *Chu Hsi and Neo-Confucianism*, ed. Wing-tsit Chan (Honolulu: University of Hawaii Press, 1986), p. 203, for a discussion of how early Chinese scholars applied principles deduced from natural phenomena to human affairs.

104. 地間只是這箇道理流行周遍。 不應說道聖人不言, 這道理便不在。 這道理自是長在天地間。*Yulei*, chap. 9, in *Zhuzi quanshu*, vol. 14, p. 308.

105. 太極動而生陽, 動極而靜, 靜而生陰, 靜極復動。一動一靜, 互為其根, 分陰分陽, 兩儀立焉。陽變陰合, 而生水、火、木、金、土。五氣順布, 四時行焉。五行, 一陽一陰也; 陰陽, 以太極也; 太極, 本無極也。*Jinsilu* 1.1, in *Zhuzi quanshu*, vol. 13, p. 167.

106. 無極之真, 二五之精, 妙合而凝。乾道成男, 坤道成年女。而氣交感, 化生萬物。萬物生生, 而變化無窮焉。Ibid.

107. 極只是天地萬物之理。 *Yulei*, chap. 1, in *Zhuzi quanshu*, vol. 14, p. 113.

108. Livia Kohn, "Chinese Religion," in *The Human Condition: A Volume in the Comparative Religious Ideas Project*, ed. Robert Cummings Neville (Albany: State University of New York Press, 2000a), p. 23.

109. 才有物, 便有理。 天不曾生箇筆, 人把兔毫來做筆。 才有筆, 便有理。*Yulei*, chap. 4, in *Zhuzi quanshu*, vol. 14, p. 189.

110. Chung-ying Cheng, "Chu Hsi's Methodology and Theory of Understanding" in *Chu Hsi and Neo-Confucianism*, ed. Wing-tsit Chan (Honolulu: University of Hawaii Press, 1986), p. 170. See also Berthrong, *All Under Heaven*, p. 88.

111. Chen Chun (1159–1223), in Wing-tsit Chan, trans., comp., *Neo-Confucian Terms Explained: The Pei-hsi Tzu-i* (New York: Columbia University Press, 1986a), p. 107; italics added.

112. 竹椅便有竹椅之理。*Yulei*, Chapter 4, in *Zhuzi quanshu*, vol. 14, p. 189.

113. Galia Patt-Shamir, "Moral World, Ethical Terminology: The Moral Significance of Metaphysical Terms in Zhou Dunyi and Zhu Xi" in *Journal of Chinese Philosophy* 31, no. 3 (Sept. 2004): 355.

114. Chung, p. 260. As A. S. Cua notes, "Chinese thinkers, in general, do not pay attention to the distinction between normative and descriptive statements. This feature of Confucian ethics may be considered a defect or a virtue, depending on a philosopher's viewpoint. The defect lies in the Confucian neglect of the importance of conceptual clarification; the virtue, in its unwavering moral concern with man as inherently capable of harmonizing his

actions and intentions with things and events in the world. The theme of central harmony thus deeply imbues the lives and thought of the Confucian thinkers and agents" (A. S. Cua, "Confucian Vision and Experience of the World," in *Moral Vision and Tradition: Essays in Chinese Ethics* [Studies in Philosophy and the History of Philosophy, Volume 31], ed. A. S. Cua [Washington, D.C.: The Catholic University Press, 1998], p. 35).

115. 理無形體。*Yulei*, chap. 1, in *Zhuzi quanshu*, vol. 14, p. 117.

116. 這箇道理, 各自有地頭, 不可只就一面說。在這裏時是恁地說, 在那裏時又如彼說, 其賓主彼此之勢各自不同。Ibid., chap. 8, in *Zhuzi quanshu*, vol. 14, p. 276.

117. 只是見不透, 所以千言萬語, 費盡心力, 終不得聖人之意。 大學說格物, 都只是要人見得透。 *Yulei*, chap. 9, in *Zhuzi quanshu*, vol. 14, p. 311.

118. 皆有怵惕惻隱之心; 非所以內交於孺子之父母也, 非所以要譽於鄉黨朋友也, 非惡其聲而然也。*Mencius*, 3A6, in Xie, p. 377; translation in Chan, *Source Book*, p. 65.

119. Robert Cummings Neville, *Boston Confucianism: Portable Tradition in the Late-Modern World* (Albany: State University of New York Press, 2000), p. 176.

120. Ibid., pp. 176–177.

121. 道何嘗息, 只是人不由。*Jinsilu* 14.4, in *Zhuzi quanshu*, vol. 13, p. 282.

122. 只有兩件事: 理會, 踐行 。*Yulei*, chap. 9, in *Zhuzi quanshu*, vol. 14, p. 299.

123. 學者大要立志。Ibid., chap. 8, in *Zhuzi quanshu*, vol. 14, p. 280.

124. 為學在立志。Ibid.

125. 天下之物某不有理。 Zhu's comment on chap. 6 of "*The Great Learning*," in *Zhuzi quanshu*, vol. 6, p. 20.

126. 聖賢千言萬語, 只要人不失其本心。 *Yulei*, chap. 12, in *Zhuzi quanshu*, vol. 14, p. 358. The topic of the original goodness of human nature will be explored further in Chapter 2.

127. de Bary and Bloom, p. 669.

128. 天地以生物为心者也。*Renshuo*, in *Zhuzi quanshu*, vol. 23, p. 3279; italics added.

129. James Legge, ed., trans. *Confucius: Confucian Analects, The Great Learning, & The Doctrine of the Mean*. New York: Dover Publications (1895)/1970; he also says that it is "perfect virtue" (see Glossary, p. 452).

130. Chen Chun, in Wing-tsit Chan, trans., ed., *Neo-Confucian Terms Explained: The Pei-hsi Tzu-i* (New York: Columbia University Press, 1986a), p. 59.

131. de Bary and Bloom, p. 43.

132. 天地以生物为心者也, 而人物之生, 又各得夫天地之心以爲心者也。故語心之德, 雖其總攝貫通無所不交備, 然一言一蔽之, 則曰仁而已也。*Renshuo*, in *Zhuzi quanshu*, vol. 23, p. 3279.

133. 仁則為慈愛之類。*Yulei*, chap. 20, in *Zhuzi quanshu*, vol. 14, p. 705.

134. 說仁,便有慈愛底意思。Ibid., chap. 6, in *Zhuzi quanshu*, vol. 14, p. 245.

135. 仁發出來便做那慈愛底事。Ibid., chap. 20, in *Zhuzi quanshu*, vol. 14, p. 704.

136. In Tokugawa Japan (1602–1868), followers of Zhu Xi's Neo-Confucianism made efforts to "find common ground for integration with Shinto . . . Neo-Confucianism could be naturalized by its integration with Shinto mythology, ethics, and practices . . . the naturalistic cosmology of Neo-Confucianism was compatible with the emphasis on nature and seasonal cycles in Shinto (Tucker, "Introduction," p. 253). Moreover, efforts to nativize Confucianism and Neo-Confucianism had an impact on the native traditions themselves: "[Confucianism] has served . . . to transform as well as be transformed by its encounter with Japanese thought, traditions, and institutions" (ibid., p. 266). Meanwhile, "Neo-Confucian philosophy remained alive and well" throughout centuries of Korean discourse: "despite an ever-broadening range of scholarly interest, philosophy was not forgotten . . . The collected writings of the scholars of [the Choson dynasty after 1649] almost always include essays and letters dealing with philosophical and ethical issues . . . And, as before, the [Zhu Xi] formulation of Neo-Confucianism continued to supply the parameters within which most Korean debates over how best to answer [such] questions took place" (Peter H. Lee, and Wm. Theodore de Bary, eds. *Sources of Korean Tradition, Volume One: From Earliest Times to the Sixteenth Century* [New York: Columbia University Press, 1996], p. 194). Finally, it should also be borne in mind that many Westerners also found—and continue to find—his ideas appealing.

137. Johannes Adrianus Aertsen, *Nature and Creatures: Thomas Aquinas' Way of Thought* (Brill Academic Publishers, 1997), p. 237.

138. Immanuel Kant, *Critique of Pure Reason*, Bxxxi, in *Classics of Western Philosophy*, p. 885; italics added.

139. *Summa theologica*, Ia, q. 47, a. 1, resp. See also *Compendium theologiae*, I.100: "things were produced by God in a supremely excellent way; for the most excellent Being does everything in the most excellent way (Productio rerum a Deo optime facta est: optimi enim est optime facere unumquodque)."

140. See Metzger, *A Cloud Across the Pacific*, p. 116, for his discussion of this issue with regard to political theories and human suffering.

141. *Summa theologica*, IIa IIae, q. 64, a. 1, ad. 1. See also ibid., Ia, q. 65, a. 2, resp.

142. Kerr, p. 139. The widespread beliefs to which Kerr is referring to are Manichean in tenor: "again and again, he resists views which he suspects of Catharist dualism. His insistence that the aptitude for receiving divine grace is a good on the part of a creature with a human nature, which sin can never totally destroy, is another illustration of his determination to head off any temptation to succumb to Manichean dualism (ST 1.48.4; 1–2.85.2)" (ibid.).

143. Videmus enim res quasdam infimi gradus participare divinam similitudinem quantum ad esse tantum, velut inanimata; quaedam autem quantum

ad esse et vivere, ut plantae; quaedam autem quantum ad sentire, ut animalia; supremus autem modus est per intellectum, et maxime Deo conveniens. *Compendium theologiae*, I:75. Note on the *Compendium:* according to Eleonore Stump, Thomas most likely began this, the fourth of his theological syntheses, immediately after completing the *Summa contra gentiles*, from 1265–1267 (Stump, *Aquinas*, p. 5). She notes, "among Aquinas' four theological syntheses, the *Compendium theologiae* is unique in the brevity of its discussions and in having been organized around the theological virtues of faith, hope and charity . . . Had it been completed, it might have provided a novel reorientation of the vast subject matter of medieval theology, but Aquinas wrote only ten short chapters of the second section, on Hope, and none at all of the third section on Charity . . . since most of the 246 chapters in the section [on Faith] simply provide much briefer treatments of almost all of the theological topics Aquinas had already dealt with in the *Summa contra gentiles*, the *Compendium* as he left it seems important mainly as a précis of material that is developed more fully in the other work and in [the] *Summa theologiae*" (ibid., p. 8).

144. Nichols, pp. 85–86.

145. *Summa Theologica*, IIa IIae, q. 64, a. 6, resp.

146. Etienne Gilson, *Thomism: The Philosophy of Thomas Aquinas*, trans. Laurence K. Shook and Armand Maurer, 6th ed. (Toronto: Pontifical Institute of Medieval Studies, 2002), p. 318.

147. Ibid.

148. *Summa theologica*, IIIa, q. 23, a. 1, ad. 2.

149. *Summa contra gentiles*, bk. II, chap. 3, sec. 1, p. 32.

150. *Summa theologica*, Ia IIae, q. 93, a. 1, resp.

151. Kerr, pp. 31–32. As Kerr notes, "Again and again we return to the doctrine of creation. The creation of the world is explained by the immense bounty of the God who wills to share his goodness. We can participate in God's beatitude by knowledge and love, anticipating here and now what will only be fulfilled eschatologically. Indeed, it is in view of their participation in divine bliss that reasoning creatures were created in the first place" (p. 131).

152. Ibid., p. 114.

153. *Summa theologica*, Ia, q. 8, a. 1, resp. See also *Compendium theologiae*, I:130: "God is necessarily present to all things insofar as they have existence. But existence is that which is the most intimately present in all things. Therefore God must be in all things (Deum adesse omnibus rebus inquantum esse habent. Esse autem est id quod rebus omnibus intimius adest. Igitur oportet Deum in omnibus esse)."

154. See Davies, p. 15, for further discussion of this claim.

155. See Kerr, p. 33, and Robert Pasnau, *Thomas Aquinas on Human Nature: A Philosophical Study of Summa theologiae Ia 75–89* (Cambridge: Cambridge University, 2002), p. 19, for discussions of how all else is subordinate to God in Thomas's scholarship.

156. *Summa theologica*, IIa IIae, q. 161, a. 3, resp.

157. Ibid., ad. 1.

158. Nichols, p. 158. Kerr makes a similar point: "It is precisely as we perform acts of knowing and loving, particularly acts of knowing and loving God, that we are imaging God as Trinity" (Kerr, p. 127).

159. "Since the principles of acts are the habits and powers, and everything exists virtually in its principle, therefore, secondarily and consequently, the image of the Trinity may be considered as existing in the powers, and still more in the habits, forasmuch as the acts virtually exist therein" (*Summa theologica*, Ia, q. 93, a. 7, resp.).

160. Ibid.; italics added.

161. Georg Wieland, "Happiness (Ia IIae, qq. 1–5)," in *The Ethics of Aquinas*, ed. Stephen J. Pope (Washington, D.C.: Georgetown University Press, 2002), p. 58.

162. *Nicomachean Ethics*, 1106b.21–23, p. 41. With so many elements to balance and consider, it is no wonder that Aristotle says flatly, "it is a difficult business to be good" (*Nicomachean Ethics*, 1109a.24, p. 48).

163. *Summa theologica*, Ia IIae, q. 93, a. 4, resp.

164. Ibid.

165. Ibid., q. 18, a. 1. He goes on to explain, "and thus it may happen that an action which is good in its species or in its circumstances is ordained to an evil end, or vice versa. However, an action is not good simply, unless it is good in all those ways: since 'evil results from any single defect, but good from the complete cause,' as Dionysius says (Div. Nom. iv)."

166. Ibid., a. 10, ad. 2.

167. Daniel Westberg, "Good and Evil in Human Acts (Ia IIae, qq.18–21)" in *The Ethics of Aquinas*, ed. Stephen J. Pope (Washington, D.C.: Georgetown University Press, 2002), p. 92.

168. *Summa theologica*, IIIa, q. 1, a. 1, resp. Thomas uses this reasoning to prove that it is fitting that God should become incarnate in the person of Jesus of Nazareth: "hence it belongs to the essence of the highest good to communicate itself in the highest manner to the creature, and this is brought about chiefly by 'His so joining created nature to Himself that one Person is made up of these three—the Word, a soul and flesh,' as Augustine says (De Trin. xiii). Hence it is manifest that it was fitting that God should become incarnate." His point about the *rightness* of the incarnation of beauty and truth is congruent with a strand of thought in Catholic tradition supportive of literary creativity, from Dante's famous assertion that "art is the grandchild of God" to J. R. R. Tolkien's doctrine of "sub-creation." Tolkien believed he was approaching divinity in writing his works; he writes bluntly, "Fantasy remains a basic human right; we make in our measure and our derivative mode, because we are made: and not only made, *but made in the image and likeness of a Maker*" (J. R. R. Tolkien, *The Tolkien Reader* [New York: Ballantine Books, 1966], p. 75). In fact, he says, "so great is the bounty with which [the Christian] has been treated that he may now, perhaps, fairly dare to guess that in fantasy he may actually assist in the effoliation and multiple enrichment of creation" (ibid., pp. 89–90).

169. Davies, p. 207.

170. *Summa theologica,* Ia IIae, q. 99, a. 1, ad. 2.

171. Ibid., IIa IIae, q. 27, a. 1, resp.

172. Ibid., q. 23, a. 6, resp.

173. 文王猶勤, 而況寡德乎! *Yulei*, Chapter 11, in *Zhuzi quanshu*, vol. 14, p. 348.

174. 今日看了, 明日又看; 早上看了, 晚間又看; 飯前看了, 飯後又看。Ibid., Chapter 10, in *Zhuzi quanshu*, vol. 14, p. 321. Sheer repetition, while certainly helpful in the learning process, is nonetheless not to be engaged in for its own sake: "in reading books, you should not count the number of times you read; when the number is sufficient [for understanding], then stop (讀書不可記數, 數足止也)" (ibid., p. 322).

175. 讀書之道, 用力愈多, 收功愈遠。 先難而後獲, 先事而後得, 皆是此理。」Ibid., chap. 10, in *Zhuzi quanshu*, vol. 14, p. 320. The passage goes on to emphasize this point by way of concrete example: "He also said, 'concerning the method of reading books: it is necessary to use effort in reading. With a book you will first need a great deal of effort, and then afterwards not quite as much. In the beginning, you will need to spend 100% of your effort [to understand] a book, but afterward you will need to spend 80 or 90% of your effort on a book; then afterward you will need 60 or 70% of your effort, and then finally you will need to spend 40 or 50% (又云：「讀書之法; 須是用工去看。 先一書費許多工夫, 後則無許多矣。 始初一書費十分工夫, 後一書費八九分, 後則費六七分, 又後則費四五分矣。」)'" (ibid., chap. 10, in *Zhuzi quanshu*, vol. 14, pp. 320–321).

176. [君子之道]及其至也, 雖聖人亦有所不知焉。*The Doctrine of the Mean*, Chapter 12, in Xie, p. 30.

177. *Summa theologica*, Ia IIae, q. 68, a. 1, ad. 2.

178. Ibid., IIa IIae, q. 45, a. 6, resp. See also *Summa contra gentiles*, bk. I, chap. 2, sec. 1, p. 61: "[the pursuit of wisdom] is more sublime because it is through this pursuit that the human being especially approaches to a likeness to God Who made all things in wisdom." In addition, Thomas describes wisdom as "more perfect [than other virtues] because, in so far as a man gives himself to the pursuit of wisdom, so far does he even now have some share in true beatitude" (ibid.).

179. Some argue that a limited form of deification takes place when the human person turns toward God. According to Brian Davies and Fergus Kerr, in the Thomistic system, the likeness to God resulting from contemplation and understanding goes far beyond the likeness of imitation. Kerr writes, "the divine reality occupies the minds of the blessed in such a way as to be the condition as well as the object of knowledge . . . When the blessed human mind sees God in himself, 'that very divine essence becomes the form through which the mind knows.' Seeing God face-to-face is so immediate—unmediated—that the human mind may even be said to become 'deiform' (ST 12.5)" (Kerr, p. 79). Davies concurs on similar grounds; he says, "knowledge of God's essence is, for

Aquinas, a special form of God's presence. In this sense, it is deification of the knower" (Davies, p. 251).

180. *Summa theologica,* Ia IIae, q. 3, a. 8, ad. 2.

181. Kerr, p. 160.

182. *Summa theologica,* Ia IIae, q. 5, a. 2., resp; italics added.

183. For example, see Steven Pinker, "The Moral Instinct," in *The Times Magazine,* January 13, 2008, http://www.nytimes.com/2008/01/13/magazine/13Psychology-t.html?pagewanted=4&_r=1) for his argument that our morality is genetically programmed into us, susceptible to damage to the brain's frontal lobes.

184. Ralph McInerny, Ethica Thomistica: *The Moral Philosophy of Thomas Aquinas,* revised edition (Washington, D.C.: The Catholic University of America Press, 1997), p. 10.

185. Charles Taylor, *Sources of the Self* (2nd ed.) (Cambridge, MA: Harvard University Press, 1992), p. 107.

Chapter 2. Intelligent Agents with Moral Potential

1. Pinker is aware that the very term raises hackles in many contemporary academics. In *The Blank Slate,* he discusses the appeal of denying such a thing as human nature: "if the slate of a newborn is not blank, different babies could have different things inscribed on their slates. Individuals, sexes, classes, and races might differ innately in their talents, abilities, interests, and inclinations" (Steven Pinker, *The Blank Slate: The Modern Denial of Human Nature* [New York: Penguin Books, 2002], p. 141). Thus it is that "to acknowledge human nature, many think, is to endorse racism, sexism, war, greed, genocide, nihilism, reactionary politics, and neglect of children and the disadvantaged. Any claim that the mind has an innate organization strikes people not as a hypothesis that might be incorrect but as a thought that it is immoral to think" (ibid., p. viii). However, the Blank Slate is not inherently any kinder or gentler: "we come across the metaphor of the blank slate in the writings of a man who may have been responsible for sixty-five millions deaths: 'A blank sheet of paper has no blotches, and so the newest and most beautiful words can be written on it, the newest and most beautiful pictures can be painted on it.' Mao Zedong" (ibid., p. 156). Moreover, on a more positive note, "far from being conducive to discrimination, a conception of human nature is the reason we oppose it . . . Regardless of IQ or physical strength or any other trait that can vary, all humans can be assumed to have certain traits in common. No one likes being enslaved. No one likes being humiliated. No one likes being treated unfairly, that is, according to traits that the person cannot control. The revulsion we feel towards discrimination and slavery comes from a conviction that however much people vary on some traits, they do not vary on these. This

conviction contrasts, by the way, with the supposedly progressive doctrine that people have no inherent concerns, which implies they could be conditioned to enjoy servitude or degradation" (ibid., p. 145).

2. To clarify: I am not arguing that conceptions of moral duty inevitably disappear in such a value-free universe. To the contrary, Michael Puett has claimed that it is precisely a perceived lack of natural morality that led ancient Chinese moral philosophers to establish codes of conduct: "the discussion one finds in early Chinese texts [*Nature Emerges from the Decree* (Xing zi ming chu); the *Laozi*] about continuity arose not out of a worldview of immanence but rather out of a concern that the world was too fractured, too fragmented, and that order had to somehow be built out of this" (Michael Puett, "Innovation as Ritualization: The Fractured Cosmology of Early China," in *Cardozo Law Review* 28, no. 1 [2006]: 27). I mention this to point out that no worldview is capable of dictating behavior or attitude: people are always free to react to the reality they perceive in the manner they choose, and some kind of faith commitment is always necessary to consistently propel them in positive directions.

3. For example, the autonomous will may not always be directly or solely focused on questions of interest in dictating the forms of behavior and courses of actions to be pursued by the agent. In Peter Blau's example, otherwise self-interested actors can engage in "behavior resulting from the irrational push of emotional forces *without being goal-oriented*, for instance, a girl's irrational conduct on dates that is motivated by her unconscious conflicts with her father" (Peter Blau, *Exchange and Power in Social Life* [New York: J. Wiley, 1964], p. 5).

4. Tom Shippey, *The Road to Middle-Earth: How J.R.R. Tolkien Created a New Mythology* (New York: Houghton Mifflin, 2003), p. 135.

5. *Nicomachean Ethics*, 1130a1–2, p. 115.

6. Pierre Manent, *An Intellectual History of Liberalism*, Rebecca Balinski, trans. (Princeton, NJ: Princeton University Press, 1995), p. 22.

7. Ibid.

8. Hirschman, Albert O. *The Passions and the Interests: Political Arguments for Capitalism before Its Triumph* (Princeton, NJ: Princeton University Press, 1977), pp. 13–14.

9. Ibid., pp. 23–24.

10. Ibid., p. 48. Although this discussion of the modern West focuses primarily on the effects of linking interest to morality, it should be noted that there were other sources for modern, anti-authoritarian conceptions of virtue. For example, Benjamin Nelson finds grounds for such developments in the Protestant Reformation; see "*Conscience* and the Making of Early Modern Cultures: Beyond Max Weber," in *On the Roads to Modernity: Conscience, Science and Civilizations*, ed. Toby E. Huff (Totowa, NJ: Rowman and Littlefield, 1981), esp. pp. 74–75, for his analysis of Luther's doctrine of the "absoluteness of the freedom of the individual conscience in the deepest recesses of the now distinctively religious sphere."

11. Allan Bloom, *The Closing of the American Mind* (Simon & Schuster: New York, 1988), p. 175.

12. David Hume, "A Treatise of Human Nature," in Alasdair MacIntrye, ed. *Hume's Ethical Writings: Selections from David Hume* (Notre Dame, IN: University of Notre Dame Press, 1980), p. 225.

13. MacIntyre, *Whose Justice?* p. 304.

14. Hume, pp. 230–231.

15. Ibid., p. 231.

16. Taylor, *Sources of the Self*, pp. 344–345.

17. Manent, p. 53.

18. Bernard de Mandeville, The Grumbling Hive (1705; http://andromeda.rutgers.edu/~jlynch/, Jack Lynch: 2009), lines 409–414, http://andromeda.rutgers.edu/~jlynch/Texts/hive.html)

19. Hirschman, pp. 18–19.

20. Louis Dumont, *From Mandeville to Marx: The Genesis and Triumph of Economic Ideology* (Chicago: University of Chicago Press, 1977), pp. 61–62.

21. John H. Berthrong, *The Divine Deli: Religious Identity in the North American Cultural Mosaic* (Maryknoll, NY: Orbis Books, 1999), pp. xx–xxi; italics added.

22. Rieff, "For the Last Time Psychology!" in *The Feeling Intellect* (1990), p. 36.

23. James Samuel Coleman, "Individual Interests and Collective Action," in *Individual Interests and Collective Action: Selected Essays*, ed. James Samuel Coleman (New York: Cambridge University Press, 1986), p. 312. Coleman, who most assuredly subscribes to the "rational choice" school of social theory ("a major aspect of socialization is not the 'internalization of norms', but rather coming to see the long-term consequences to oneself of particular strategies of action, thus becoming more completely a rational, calculating person" (Coleman, "Collective Decisions," in ibid., p. 31)), feels that "indeed, if they did not do so, the basis for society would hardly exist."

24. Manent, p. 33. With the disappearance of such inscribed ends so also disappeared the notion that there are some things which it is better for human beings not to know: an idea very familiar to Thomas Aquinas, who wrote, "it is better for us not to know low and vile things, because by them we are impeded in our knowledge of what is better and higher; for we cannot understand many things simultaneously; because the thought of evil sometimes perverts the will towards evil" (*Summa theologica*, Ia, q. 22, a. 3, ad. 3). A similar idea is found in the fiction of J. R. R. Tolkien, a medievalist by profession: Elrond, one of the wisest characters in the *Lord of the Rings*, observes, "It is perilous to study too deeply the arts of the Enemy, for good or ill" (J. R. R. Tolkien, *The Fellowship of the Ring: Being the First Part of* THE LORD OF THE RINGS [New York: Houghton Mifflin, 1994], p. 254).

25. Hirschman, p. 13.

26. Robert Neville suggests conceiving of social obligation in a different way: "where social contract theory says that no one is responsible for anything unless assigned the responsibility by civil society, I say everyone is responsible for everything unless civil society channels it elsewhere" (Robert C. Neville, *Ritual and Deference: Extending Chinese Philosophy in a Comparative Context* [New York: State University of New York Press, 2008], p. 12).

27. Emile Durkheim, *The Division of Labor in Society*, trans. George Simpson (Glencoe, IL: Free Press, 1933), p. 204.

28. Hirschman, p. 126.

29. As Kam Louie points out in his study of twentieth-century China, "while in the late Ch'ing [Qing] period, progressive thinkers had looked to Chinese tradition as a means of strengthening China, by the second decade of the twentieth century this was no longer the case. A series of national catastrophes culminating in the Twenty-One Demands made by Japan in 1915 had caused many young intellectuals to become disillusioned with the whole notion of the superiority of Chinese civilization and with the belief that a policy of 'Chinese learning for substance and Western learning for use' was sufficient to save China from further humiliation. By this time, many intellectuals had begun to return from studies abroad, with newly acquired knowledge of 'Mr. Science' and 'Mr. Democracy' . . . Armed with some of the more avant-garde Western theories of the time, the May Fourth Thinkers proceeded to bombard Chinese tradition, choosing Confucianism as their main target" (Kam Louie, *Critiques of Confucius in Contemporary* China [New York: St. Martin's Press, 1980], p. 3).

30. The first session of the National Congress of the Communist Party of China in Shanghai was convened in July 1921.

31. 它是一种腐蚀剂, 使团结涣散, 关系松懈, 工作消极, 意见分歧。Mao Zedong (毛泽东), "Combat Liberalism 《反对自由主义》," speech delivered September 7, 1937, http://www.marxists.org/chinese/17/marxist.org-chinese-mao-19370907.htm. N.B.: I have transcribed the Communist texts cited in this chapter in simplified Chinese characters, as used in the original source documents.

32. 自由主义的来源, 在于小资产阶级的自私自利性, 以个人利益放在第一位。Ibid.

33. However, as de Bary points out, "Despite its name, the 'Great Proletariat Cultural Revolution' emerged not from the 'proletariat' but from a power struggle at the top in which certain leaders, including Mao, sought to enlist the 'masses' (especially students) in a campaign against moderate leaders then in control of the Party and state administration" (Wm. Theodore de Bary and Richard Lufrano, ed., *Sources of Chinese Tradition: Volume Two: From 1600 to the Twentieth Century*, 2nd ed. [New York: Columbia University Press, 2001], p. 474).

34. 资产阶级虽然已被推翻, 但是, 他们企图用剥削阶级的旧思想, 旧文化, 旧风俗, 旧习惯, 来腐蚀群众, 征服人心, 力求达到他们 复辟的目的。无产阶级恰恰相反, 必须迎头痛击资产阶级在意识形态领域里的一切挑战。。。

在当前，我们的目的是斗跨走资本主义道路的当权派，批判资产阶级的反动学术"权威，"批判资产阶级和一切剥削阶级的意识形态。Central Committee of the Chinese Communist Party (中国共产党中央委员会), "Decision Concerning the Great Proletarian Cultural Revolution (The Sixteen Points) (《关于无产阶级文化大革命的决定［即"十六条"］》)," public document promulgated August 8, 1966, http://www.wyzxsx.com/Article/Class10/200803/34610.html

35. de Bary and Lufrano, p. 474.

36. 触及人们灵魂, 是我国社会主义革命发展的一个更深入。Ibid.

37. Jung Chang, *Wild Swans: Three Daughters of China* (New York: Doubleday, 1991), p. 294.

38. Ibid., p. 295.

39. 对立的统一是有条件的、暂时的、过渡的，因而是相对的，对立的斗争则是绝对的。Mao Zedong (毛泽东), "On the Correct Handling of Contradictions Among the People (《关于正确处理人民内部矛盾的问题》)," speech delivered February 27, 1957, http://www.marxists.org/chinese/17/marxist.org-chinese-mao-19570227.htm

40. Manent, p. 13.

41. Martha Nussbaum suggests that true objectivity is impossible, if only because the methods used to arrive at any conclusion will color the result: "We can inquire either in the hard 'philosophical' style or in a mode of writing that lies closer to poetry and makes its appeal to more than one 'part' of the person; or we can use different styles in different parts of the inquiry. But no way is neutral, and it looks as if any choice will prejudice the inquiry in its own favor" (Nussbaum, p. 17). Earlier discussion in my Chapter 1 suggests at least the difficulty of achieving a wholly neutral stance.

42. See Augustine, *Handbook on Faith, Hope and Love*, trans. J. F. Shaw, ed. and rev. Kevin Knight (1887; newadvent.org, *The Fathers of the Church*, 2008), chap. 11 (http://www.newadvent.org/fathers/1302.htm)

43. *Summa theologica*, Ia, q. 48, a. 5, ad. 1. See also *Summa contra gentiles*, bk. III, chap. 7, sec. 2: "evil is nothing but a privation of something which a subject, by its nature, should have . . . Now, privation is not an essence; it is, rather, a negation in substance."

44. Ibid., Ia, q. 49, a. 3, resp. See also *Summa contra gentiles*, bk. III, chap. 12, sec. 1–2: "no matter how much evil be multiplied, it can never destroy the good wholly. In fact, there must always continue to be a subject for evil, if evil is to endure. Of course, the subject of evil is the good, and so the good will always endure."

45. 性譬之水, 本皆清也。以淨器盛之, 則清; 以不淨之器盛之, 則臭; 以汙泥之器盛之, 則濁。本然之清, 未嘗不在。但既臭濁, 猝難得便清。*Yulei*, chap. 4, in *Zhuzi quanshu*, vol. 14, p. 202.

46. 大学之道, 在明明德, 在亲民, 在止于至善。*Text of Great Learning*, in Xie, p. 1. N.B.: *The Great Learning*, originally a chapter in the ancient *Record of Ritual* (*Liji*, 禮記; traditionally believed to have been composed by Confucius

himself), consists of a three paragraph meditation on the cosmos and human politics followed by ten chapters of commentary (traditionally believed to have been written by Confucius's disciple Zengzi [曾子, 505–436 BCE]). Confucians through the ages—especially after Zhu Xi enshrined this chapter as one of his Four Books—have commented on both the text and its original accompanying chapters of commentary.

47. 此三者，大學之綱領也。*Commentary on Great Learning*, in *Zhuzi quanshu*, vol. 6, p. 16.

48. *Summa theologica*, Ia IIae, q. 99, a. 1, ad. 2.

49. Julia Ching, "Chu Hsi on Personal Cultivation," in *Chu Hsi and Neo-Confucianism*, ed. Wing-tsit Chan (Honolulu: University of Hawaii Press, 1986), p. 273.

50. See Mencius 3A6, in Xie, p. 401.

51. 人之有道也; 飽食煖衣, 逸居而無教, 則近於禽獸。 (Mencius 3A4, in Xie, p. 423).

52. 設為庠序學校以教之。 (Ibid.)

53. 直木不待檃栝而直者, 其性直也; 枸木必將待檃栝、烝、矯然後直, 以其性不直也。 (*Xunzi* (荀子), *Xunzi* (荀子) (Sangle.web.wesleyan.edu/etext/, Chinese Philosophical E-Text Archive—Pre-Qin Texts, 1996), chap. 23, http://sangle.web.wesleyan.edu/etext/pre-qin/xunzi.html)

54. 是非之形不明, 則雖守法之吏, 誦數之儒, 亦皆亂。 Ibid., chap. 22.

55. 塗之人可以為禹。Ibid., chap. 23.

56. 承认人性有善及恶的两面。 心性是义理之性, 是有超越性, 即异于禽兽之性。 气之性则是人与万物同有的性。(Yü Ying-shih [余英时], *Xiandai ruxue de huigu yu zhanwang* [现代儒学的回顾与展望] [Beijing: Sanlian shudian (北京: 三联书店)], 2004).

57. 天下未有無理之氣, 亦未有無氣之理。*Yulei*, chap. 1, in *Zhuzi quanshu*, vol. 14, p. 113.

58. 有是理而後有是氣, 有是氣則必有是理。 但稟氣之清者, 為聖為賢, 如寶珠在清冷水中; 稟氣之濁者, 為愚為不肖, 如珠在濁水中。 (Ibid., chap. 4, in *Zhuzi quanshu*, vol. 14, p. 203).

59. 年月日時無有非五行之氣, 甲乙丙丁又屬陰屬陽, 只是二五之氣。人之生, 適遇其氣, 有得清者, 有得濁者, 貴賤壽夭皆然。(*Yulei*, chap. 1, in *Zhuzi quanshu*, vol. 14, p. 122).

60. 有生下來善底, 有生下來便惡底, 此是氣稟不同。日月清明氣候和正之時, 人生而稟此氣, 則為清明之氣, 須做箇好人; 若是日月昏暗, 寒暑反常, 皆是天地之戾氣, 人若稟此氣, 則為不好底人, 何疑！Ibid., chap. 4, in *Zhuzi quanshu*, vol. 14, p. 198.

61. 如得木氣多者, 仁較多; 金氣多者, 義較多 。Ibid., chap. 4, in *Zhuzi quanshu*, vol. 14, p. 205. Note: the Shanghai edition of the Zhuzi quanshu that I am using has water (*shui*, 水) in place of wood (*mu*, 木). Nonetheless, as the text links wood with *ren* in other contexts (see note 62 below), and moreover, identifies wood as the source of the other elements in the same way that *ren* is the source of the other cardinal virtues ("wood [*qi*] is the *qi* that gives birth;

once you have this *qi*, then things may come forth; without this first *qi*, then fire, metal, water cannot come forth of themselves, therefore [it may be said that] wood envelops the other three (木是生氣。有生氣, 然後物可得而生; 若無生氣, 則火金水皆無自而能生矣, 故木能包此三者) (ibid., chap. 6, in *Zhuzi quanshu*, vol. 14, p. 247), I have replaced the reference to water with a reference to wood. (The online version of Chapters 1 through 6 of the *Yulei* at http://sangle.web.wesleyan.edu/etext/song-qing/z1-6.html also has *mu*, or wood, in this passage.)

62. 仁木, 義金, 禮火, 智水, 信土 。Ibid., chap. 6, in *Zhuzi quanshu*, vol. 14, p. 243.

63. 程先生言: 『仁者, 天地生物之心。』Ibid., chap. 5, in *Zhuzi quanshu*, vol. 14, p. 219. (N.B.: in many cases, the *Yulei* does not distinguish between the Neo-Confucian scholars Cheng Hao [1032–1085] and Cheng Yi [1033–1107], simply referring to "Master Cheng.")

64. 天有春夏秋冬, 地有金木水火, 人有仁義禮智。 Ibid., chap. 1, in *Zhuzi quanshu*, vol. 14, p. 125.

65. 天命之謂性。Ibid., chap. 4, in *Zhuzi quanshu*, vol. 14, p. 192.

66. 性只是理。 Ibid., chap. 4, in *Zhuzi quanshu*, vol. 14, p. 195.

67. 邵堯夫說: 『性者, 道之形體; 心者, 性之郛郭。 』此說甚好。Ibid., chap. 4, in *Zhuzi quanshu*, vol. 14, p. 192.

68. 性只是仁義禮智。 Ibid., chap. 4, in *Zhuzi quanshu*, vol. 14, p. 192; italics added.

69. 惟人也得其秀而最靈。*Jinsilu* 1.1, in *Zhuzi quanshu*, vol. 13, p. 167.

70. Chung, p. 231.

71. 『雖愚必明, 雖柔必強』, 也煞用氣力, 然後能至。*Yulei*, chap. 4, in *Zhuzi quanshu*, vol. 14, p. 202. He is quoting *The Doctrine of the Mean*; see *The Doctrine of the Mean*, chap. 20, in Xie, p. 43.

72. 讀書以觀聖賢之意; 因聖賢之意, 以觀自然之理。*Yulei*, chap. 10, in *Zhuzi quanshu*, vol. 14, p. 314. The sages and worthies themselves do not conceive of their project in such terms; see my Chapter 1 for Zhu Xi's handling of this issue.

73. 開卷便有與聖賢不相似處, 豈可不自鞭策! Ibid., chap. 10, in *Zhuzi quanshu*, vol. 14, p. 315.

74. 讀書乃學者第二事。Ibid., chap. 10, in *Zhuzi quanshu*, vol. 14, p. 313.

75. 之為學, 卻是要變化氣稟, 然極難變化。Ibid. Further on this note: Zhu and his colleagues were no ivory tower idealists. According to Yü, "of course they emphasized the transcendent aspect of human nature, but they were also profoundly aware that the *qi* nature is not easy to change (他们当然强调超越的人性, 但也深知气之性不易改变)" (Yü, *Xiandai ruxue*, p. 68).

76. 不可求欲速之功。Ibid., chap. 8, in *Zhuzi quanshu*, vol. 14, p. 284.

77. Ching, *The Religious Thought of Chu Hsi*, p. 24.

78. 方其知之而行未及之, 則 知 尚淺。 既親歷其域, 則知之益明, 非前日之意味。*Yulei*, chap. 9, in *Zhuzi quanshu*, vol. 14, p. 398.

79. 知、行常相須。Ibid.

80. 致知、力行，用功不可偏。 偏過一邊，則 一邊受病。分明自作兩腳說，但只要分先後輕重。 論先後，當以致知為先；論輕重，當以力行為重。Ibid., chap. 9, in *Zhuzi quanshu*, vol. 14, p. 299.

81. de Bary, "Zhu Xi's Neo-Confucian Spirituality," p. 80.

82. Thomas Berry, "Affectivity in Classical Chinese Tradition," in *Confucian Spirituality: Volume One* (Volume 11A of *World Spirituality: An Encyclopedia of the Religious Quest*), ed. Tu Weiming and Mary Evelyn Tucker (New York: The Crossroad Publishing Company, 2003), p. 97.

83. David B. Wong, "Reasons and Analogical Reasoning in Mengzi," in Xiusheng Liu and Philip J. Ivanhoe eds. *Essays on the Moral Philosophy of Mengzi* (Indianapolis, IN: Hackett Publishing Co., 2002), p. 193.

84. Cheng, "Chu Hsi's Methodology and Theory of Understanding," p. 31. See also Antonio Damasio's work on the neurological connections between reason and the emotions, referenced in the Bibliography.

85. 讀書，須是要身心都入在這一段裏面。 *Yulei*, chap. 11, in *Zhuzi quanshu*, vol. 14, p. 333.

86. 學者讀書，須要斂身正坐，緩視微吟。 Ibid., chap. 11, in *Zhuzi quanshu*, vol. 14, p. 334.

87. 聖賢之言，須常將來眼頭過，口頭轉，心頭運。Ibid., chap. 10, in *Zhuzi quanshu*, vol. 14, p. 314.

88. Chan, *Chu Hsi, New Studies*, p. 49.

89. Daniel K. Gardner, "Attentiveness and Meditative Reading in Cheng-Zhu Neo-Confucianism," in *Confucian Spirituality: Volume Two* (Volume 11B of *World Spirituality: An Encyclopedia of the Religious Quest*), ed. Tu Weiming and Mary Evelyn Tucker (New York: The Crossroad Publishing Company, 2004), p. 105.

90. 讀書窮理，當*體之於身*。*Yulei*, chap. 11, in *Zhuzi quanshu*, vol. 14, p. 331; italics added.

91. Ching, "Chu Hsi on Personal Cultivation," p. 274.

92. Tu, *Humanity and Self-Cultivation*, p. 67. None of this, of course, is intended to downplay the importance of rational thinking, as should be clear from the discussion of literary learning above. See A. S. Cua, "Competence, Concern, and the Role of Paradigmatic Individuals," in *Moral Vision and Tradition: Essays in Chinese Ethics* (Studies in Philosophy and the History of Philosophy, vol. 31), ed. A. S. Cua (Washington, D.C.: The Catholic University Press, 1998), esp. p. 147, for further discussion of the "intellectual component" of moral virtue.

93. 為學在立志。*Yulei*, chap. 11, in *Zhuzi quanshu*, vol. 14, p. 381.

94. See *Analects* 6:30, in Xie, p. 132.

95. 能克去已私，复乎天理，則此心之體無不在，而此心之用無不行也。*Renshuo*, in *Zhuzi quanshu*, vol. 23, p. 3280.

96. 仁在事。 若不於事上看，如何見仁? Ibid., chap. 6, in *Zhuzi quanshu*, vol. 14, p. 257.

97. 做一方便事, 也是仁。Ibid., chap. 6, in *Zhuzi quanshu*, vol. 14, 257.

98. 今且須去理會跟前事,那箇鬼神事,無形無影,莫要枉費心力。Ibid., chap. 3, in *Zhuzi quanshu*, vol. 14, p. 153.

99. 子見南子, 子路不說。夫子矢之曰: 「予所否者, 天厭之! 天厭之! 」*Analects* 6:26, in Xie, p. 131.

100. 獲罪於天, 無所禱也。 Ibid., 3:13, in Xie, p. 90.

101. 子疾病, 子路請禱。。。子曰: 「丘之禱久矣。」Ibid., 7:34, in Xie, p. 146.

102. 顏淵死, 子曰: 「噫! 天喪予! 天喪予!」Ibid., 11:9, in Xie, p. 184.

103. 子不語: 怪, 力, 亂, 神。Ibid., 7:20, in Xie, p. 140.

104. [君子之道] 及其至也, 雖聖人亦有所不知焉。*The Doctrine of the Mean*, chap. 12, in Xie, p. 30.

105. Chan, *Chu Hsi, New Studies*, p. 118.

106. Donald J. Munro, *The Concept of Man in Early China* (Stanford, CA. Stanford University Press, 1969), p. 85.

107. 道之不行也, 我知之矣: 知者過之; 愚者不及也。*The Doctrine of the Mean*, chap. 4, in Xie, p. 25.

108. 人一能之, 己百之。人十能之, 己千之。果能此道矣, 雖愚必明, 雖柔必強。Quoted in *The Doctrine of the Mean*, chap. 20, in Xie, p. 43.

109. 人若讀十遍不會, 則讀二十遍; 又不會, 則讀三十遍至五十遍, 必有見到處。 五十遍暝然不曉, 便是氣質不好。*Yulei*, chap. 10, in *Zhuzi quanshu*, vol. 14, p. 323.

110. Ching, *Confucianism and Christianity*, 78.

111. On a related note, Michael Ing's *The Dysfunction of Ritual in Early Confucianism* (Oxford: Oxford University Press, 2013) focuses on the vulnerability not only of humans, but also of the rituals they engage in. Ing thus draws our attention to yet another instance in which Confucians neither expect nor rely on supernatural assistance in succeeding at their various goals.

112. Thomas A. Metzger, *Escape from Predicament: Neo-Confucianism and China's Evolving Political Culture* (New York: Columbia University Press), p. 52.

113. Ibid, p. 17.

114. See Mencius 2A:2, in Xie, p. 377. I render 禮 in capital letters (*LI*) in order to distinguish it from the *li* or principle discussed in the first chapter. See my Chapter 3 for a discussion of the difference between Mencius's and Zhu's understanding of the role played by core virtues.

115. On this note, Bryan Van Norden suggests that "it is probably significant that Mengzi typically (with the exception of 6A7) used a word that means 'sprout,' as opposed to one that means 'seed' (*zhông*). One important difference between a seed and a sprout is that a seed does not require any sustaining nurturance, while a sprout is much more fragile. Indeed, Mengzi used a sprout metaphor to illustrate that, because of the fragility of the human ethical potential, it is possible to fail to recognize what something 'genuinely is' (*qíng*) because one is misled by appearances of instance of that kind raised in very

injurious environments" (Bryan W. Van Norden, "Mengzi and Virtue Ethics," in *Confucianism in Dialogue Today: West, Christianity and Judaism* [Philadelphia: Ecumenical Press, 2004], pp. 120–121).

116. According to A. C. Graham, in Mencius's time, "the *hsing* [nature] of a living thing was commonly understood to be the way in which it develops and declines from birth to death when uninjured and adequately nourished, for example its condition in full health and its term of life. Mencius accepts this usage without question or qualification, and his case is only intelligible when we recognise that he conceives the nurture of the moral inclinations in order to become a sage as exactly parallel to the nurture of the vital energies in order to live out one's term" (A. C. Graham, "The Background in the Mencian Theory of Human Nature," in *Studies in Chinese Philosophy and Philosophical Literature* [In SUNY Series in Chinese Philosophy and Culture] [New York: State University of New York Press, 1986], p. 28). He adds that Mencius "does not suppose like Hsün-tzû [Xunzi] that to follow one's nature is to indulge all spontaneous desires, but in this it is [Mencius] and not Hsün-tzû who is faithful to current usage."

117. See Bol, p. 302.

118. 天運循環，無往不復。宋德隆盛，治教休明。於是河南程氏兩夫子出, 而有以按乎孟氏之傳, 實始尊信此篇而章之, 既又為之次其簡編, 發其歸趣, 然後古者大學教人之法, 聖經賢傳之機指, 粲然復明於世。"Preface to *The Great Learning*," in *Zhuzi quanshu*, vol. 6, p. 14.

119. 雖以熹之不敏, 亦幸私淑而與有聞焉。Ibid.

120. See *Summa theologica*, Ia, q. 85, a. 5, resp.

121. Ibid., q. 3, a. 2, resp.

122. See ibid., q. 50, a. 2.

123. Ibid., q. 3, a. 2, resp.

124. See q. 3, a. 2.

125. Ibid., q. 75, a. 4, resp.

126. Ibid., a. 5, resp.

127. Gilson, p. 222. In a similar vein, he points out, "we must not regard a living being as a machine, inert in itself, but with a soul as its mover . . . For Thomas Aquinas, as for Aristotle, the soul does not just make a body move; it first makes a body" (ibid., 218).

128. *Summa theologica*, IIa IIae, q. 25, a. 5, ad. 2.

129. Pasnau, p. 22.

130. *Summa theologica*, IIa IIae, q. 25, a. 5, ad. 2.

131. See ibid., q. 26, a. 4, ad. 2.

132. See Jane Barter Moulaison, "'Our Bodies, Our Selves?' The Body as Source in Feminist Theology," *Scottish Journal of Theology* 60, no. 3 (2007): 341–359, for a review of second- and third-wave feminist discourse on the body.

133. See *Summa theologica*, Ia IIae, q. 22, a. 1.

134. I am indebted to James Keenan for this insight.

135. See *Summa theologica*, Ia IIae, q. 75, a. 5.

136. Gilson's definition; see p. 252.

137. *Summa theologica*, Ia, q. 84, a. 6.

138. Eleonore Stump, "Wisdom: Will, Belief, and Moral Goodness," in *Aquinas's Moral Theory: Essays in Honor of Norman Kretzmann*, ed. Scott MacDonald and Eleonore Stump (Ithaca, NY: Cornell University Press, 1999), p. 29.

139. *Summa contra gentiles*, bk. III, chap. 2, sec. 6, p. 35. See also *Summa theologica*, Ia IIae, q. 1, a. 2, resp.: "those things that are possessed of reason, move themselves to an end; because they have dominion over their actions through their free-will, which is the 'faculty of will and reason.'"

140. *Summa theologica*, Ia IIae, q. 1, a. 2, resp. See also *Summa contra gentiles*: "if an agent did not incline toward some definite effect, all results would be a matter of indifference for him. Now, he who looks upon a manifold number of things with indifference no more succeeds in doing one of them than another. Hence, from an agent contingently indifferent to alternatives no effect follows, unless he be determined to one effect by something. So, it would be impossible for him to act. Therefore every agent tends toward some determinate effect, and this is called his end. This is true even for seemingly pointless forms of human behavior: "Of course, there seem to be some actions that do not seem to be for an end. Actions done without intention do not stem from the intellect but from some sudden act of the imagination or from a natural source. Thus, a disorder of the humors produces an itch and is the cause of rubbing the beard, and this is done without intellectual attention. So, these actions do tend to some end, though quite apart from the intellect" (*Summa contra gentiles*, bk. III, chap. 2, sec. 9, pp. 37–38).

141. *Nicomachean Ethics*, 1094a.18–23, p. 4. Aristotle considered an infinite regress to be a ridiculous and irrational impossibility, and many philosophers through the ages, in both East and West, have agreed with him. This is not to say that his position is universally accepted. Stephen Hawking tells us that "a well-known scientist (some say it was Bertrand Russell) once gave a public lecture on astronomy. He described how the Earth orbits around the sun and how the sun, in turn, orbits around the center of a vast collection of stars called our galaxy. At the end of the lecture, a little old lady at the back of the room got up and said: 'What you have told us is rubbish. The world is really a flat plate supported on the back of a giant tortoise.' The scientist gave a superior smile before replying, 'What is the tortoise standing on?' 'You're very clever, young man, very clever,' said the old lady. 'But it's turtles all the way down!'" (Stephen Hawking, *A Brief History of Time* [New York: Bantam Books, 1988], p. 1).

142. See ibid., 1097b.21–1098a.21, pp. 15–16.

143. Ibid., 1094a.28–1094b.11, p. 4.

144. McInerny, *Aquinas*, p. 107.

145. Kerr, p. 131.

146. *Summa theologica*, Ia, q. 63, obj. 4. See also *Summa contra gentiles*, bk. I, chap. 36, sec. 3, p. 151: "something is desired in two ways: either because it is good or because it appears to be good." See my Chapter 3 for further discussion of this issue.

147. Ibid., Ia IIae, q. 90, a. 3, resp.

148. Ibid., ad. 2. See my Chapter 3 for further discussion of Thomas's belief in the importance of communal structures.

149. Ibid., q. 21, a. 4, ad. 3.

150. Ibid., q. 5, a. 1, resp.

151. Ibid., q. 1, a. 8, resp.

152. Kent, p. 118.

153. F. C. Copleston, *Aquinas* (Baltimore: Penguin Books, 1967), p. 205.

154. *Summa theologica*, Ia, q. 8, a. 8, ad. 2.

155. John P. Langan, "Augustine on the Unity and the Interconnection of the Virtues" in *The Harvard Theological Review* 72, No. 1/2 (Jan.–Apr. 1979): 93.

156. Augustine, *The City of God*, trans. Marcus Dods, intro. Robert Merton (New York: The Modern Library, Random House, 1950), XXI.16, p. 787.

157. *Summa theologica*, Ia IIae, q. 63, a. 2, resp.

158. Stalnaker, *Overcoming Our Evil*, p. 257.

159. Kent, p. 125.

160. Gilson, p. 405. This continuance is quite robust, and, moreover, ubiquitous in his work: "in every order, in all degrees, Thomism views nature as willed by God for its supernatural end. Here as elsewhere, the end is the cause of causes, and the world has but one end, namely, God . . . occasions for calling upon this view will not be rare. Avoiding it would have to be deliberate" (Ibid., p. 37).

161. Aristotle, *Nicomachean Ethics*, trans. J. A. K. Thomson, ed. Hugh Tredennick, intro. Jonathan Barnes (New York: Penguin Classics, 2004), 1106b21–22, p. 41.

162. Ibid., 1107a1, p. 42. Aristotle adds, "and by that which a prudent man would use to determine it," introducing a decidedly un-deontological tinge to this thought.

163. Ibid., 1114a4–7, pp. 62–63; italics added.

164. Ibid., 1100b35–1101a8, p. 24.

165. See ibid., 1114a.12–22, p. 63.

166. *Summa theologica*, Ia IIae, q. 55, a. 4, obj. 1. The definition given also includes "which God works in us, without us." But this part of the definition he says only applies to the "infused" virtues (in the respondio).

167. Ibid.

168. Ibid., Ia, q. 81, a. 3, ad. 2.

169. Ibid., Ia IIae, q. 71, a. 6, resp.

170. Ibid.

171. Eileen Sweeney, "Vice and Sin (Ia IIae, qq. 71–89)," in *The Ethics of Aquinas*, ed. Stephen J. Pope (Washington, D.C.: Georgetown University Press, 2002), p. 152.

172. *Summa theologica*, Ia IIae, q. 80.

173. Ibid., q. 81, a. 5.

174. Ibid., q. 82, a. 4, resp.

175. Davies, p. 256.

176. James Keenan, "The Problem with Thomas Aquinas's Concept of Sin," in *The Heythrop Journal* 35, no. 4 (1994): 416.

177. Ibid., pp. 415–416.

178. Ibid., p. 415.

179. *Summa theologica*, IIa IIae, q. 144, a. 1, resp.

180. Ibid., ad. 3.

181. See ibid, q. 20, a. 1.

182. Ibid., q. 17, a. 1, resp.

183. G. K. Chesterton, *Saint Francis of Assisi* (New York: Doubleday, 2001), p. 20.

184. Jean-Pierre Torrell, O. P., *Saint Thomas Aquinas: Volume 2. Spiritual Master*, trans. Robert Royal (Washington, D.C.: The Catholic University of America Press, 2003), p. 106.

185. *Summa theologica*, Ia IIae, q. 113, a. 8, resp.

186. Ibid., q. 111, a. 3, resp.

187. Ibid., *Supplement*, q. 1, a. 1, ad. 2. See note 57 in Chapter 1 above about the authorship of the supplement.

188. Ibid., Ia IIae, q. 81, a. 3, ad. 1.

189. Nichols, p. 101.

190. *Summa theologica*, *Supplement*, q. 1, a. 2, ad. 4.

191. Ibid., Ia IIae, q. 63, a. 3, ad. 3.

192. Ibid., q. 68, a. 1, resp. In addition there are also beatitudes (see ibid., q. 69, a. 1, resp.,) and fruits (ibid., q. 70, a. 2, resp.).

193. Ibid., q. 23, a. 6, resp.

194. Ibid., q. 25, a. 6, sed contra.

195. Ibid., resp.

196. Dell'Olio, p. 238. Yearley draws a similar, if more general, comparison: "Confucianism manifests, then, in its own fashion the ontological principle that guides the analysis of this topic in Aristotelian Christianity: the sacred does not destroy but presupposes and perfects the normal. The ordinary is not, that is, obliterated by the religious and replaced by something fundamentally different. Rather, the ordinary provides the basis that is developed into a more actualized form" (Lee Yearley, "Virtues and Religious Virtues in the Confucian Tradition," in *Confucian Spirituality: Volume One* [Volume 11A of *World Spirituality: An Encyclopedia of the Religious Quest*], ed. Tu Weiming and Mary Evelyn Tucker [New York: The Crossroad Publishing Company, 2003], p. 150).

197. Tu, "The Creative Tension Between *Jen* [Ren] and *Li*," in *Humanity and Self-Cultivation*, p. 8.

198. Tu, "The Neo-Confucian Concept of Man," in ibid., p. 79.

199. Kohn, p. 21.

200. Ching, *Confucianism and Christianity*, p. 103.

201. Ching, *The Religious Thought of Chu Hsi*, p. 92.

202. 夫婦之愚, 可以與之焉。。。 夫婦之不肖, 可以能行焉。*The Doctrine of the Mean*, chap. 12, in Xie, p. 30.

203. See Rick Warren, *The Purpose Driven Life: What On Earth Am I Here For?* (Grand Rapids, MI: Zondervan, 2002), pp. 27–30. His solution to these problems: "knowing God's purposes for your life" (ibid., 30).

204. Ibid., pp. 54–55.

205. Max Weber, *The Religion of China*, trans., ed. Hans H. Gerth (Glencoe, IL: The Free Press of America, 1951), pp. 228–229.

206. Alasdair MacIntyre, *After Virtue: A Study in Moral Theory* (Notre Dame, IN: University of Notre Dame Press, 1981), p. 140.

207. Ibid., pp. 139–140. Taylor makes a similar point with regard to the Judeo-Christian tradition: "loving, worshipping God is the ultimate end. Of course, in this tradition God is seen as willing human flourishing, but devotion to God is not seen as contingent on this. The injunction 'Thy will be done' isn't equivalent to 'Let humans flourish,' even though we know that God wills human flourishing" (Taylor, *A Secular Age*, p. 17).

208. *Nicomachean Ethics*, 1097b.8–11, p. 14.

209. 有朋自遠方來, 不亦樂乎? *Analects* 1:1, in Xie, p. 65.

210. As Tu Weiming points out, "despite the uncertainty of one's public image, one frequently learns about oneself through the 'eyes' and 'ears' of other people. Self-knowledge, to a large measure, depends upon an appreciation of the responses of others to one's varied modes of existence" (Tu Weiming, *Centrality and Commonality: An Essay on Confucian Religiousness* [Albany: State University of New York Press, 1989], p. 25).

Chapter 3. Roles, Rituals, and Habits: The Proper Development of the Human Being

1. 能盡其性, 則能盡人之性。 能盡人之性, 則能盡物之性。 能盡物之性, 則可以贊天地之化育。可以贊天地之化育, 則可以與天地參矣。 *Doctrine of the Mean*, Chapter 22, in Xie, p. 48.

2. See *Source Book in Chinese Philosophy*, p. 108.

3. Gen 1:28.

4. Lynn White, Jr., "The Historical Roots of Our Ecologic Crisis," *Science* 155 (March 1967): pp. 1203–1207.

5. See Huey-li Li, "Some Thoughts on Confucianism and Eco-Feminism," in *Confucianism and Ecology: The Interrelation of Heaven, Earth and Humans*, ed. Mary Evelyn Tucker and John Berthrong (Cambridge: Harvard University Press, 1998), pp. 293–312 for a critique of environmental degradation in Confucian countries such as Taiwan, and Philip J. Ivanhoe, "Early Confucianism and Environmental Ethics," in ibid., 59–76, for a discussion of what the ancient tradition has to offer to contemporary ecological discourse.

6. Adam Seligman, "Role Complexity, Risk, and the Emergence of Trust," in *Boston University Law Review* 81, no. 3 (June 2001): 629.

7. Adam B. Seligman, Robert P. Weller, Michael J. Puett, and Bennett Simon, *Ritual and its Consequences: An Essay on the Limits of Sincerity* (New York: Oxford University Press, 2008), p. 7.

8. Lionel Trilling, *Sincerity and Authenticity* (Cambridge, MA: Harvard University Press, 1997), p. 5.

9. Lest the following be taken as "the" social scientist view, I should note here that social scientists can be among those who are uncomfortable with giving roles too exalted a position in the making of the self. As Michael Hechter explains, "at the other extreme, methodological individualists argue that the dynamic force for the genesis of social structures lies in the action of agents pursuing independent interests. In this tradition, structures can emerge either as unintended or as purposeful solutions to the common demands that these individuals face" (Michael Hechter, "From Exchange to Structure" in *Macro-micro Linkages in Sociology*, ed. Joan Huber [Newbury Park, CA: Sage Publications, 1991], p. 46). An example of this trend is Ralph Turner, who does not believe in the power of "the system" to develop or regress on its own; see Ralph H. Turner, *Collective Behavior* (Englewood Cliffs, NJ: Prentice-Hall, 1972), esp. p. 40. For Turner, people interacting and making choices defines society as opposed to structural roles. Meanwhile, in the realm of social psychology, scholars like Theodore Newcomb and his colleagues focus on the more private and internal elements of the process of relationship building: "the first time you interact in any direct way with your professor . . . you are likely to spend a fair amount of your time trying to judge from what he says and does (or what he fails to do) what he is 'really' thinking about: how hurried he is, perhaps, or—more especially—how he sizes you up. It is likely, furthermore, that at the same time he is making some guesses of his own as to what you are thinking. The way in which the both of you act toward one another is, as you can see, vitally affected by what your respective guesses are" (Theodore Newcomb, Ralph H. Turner, and Philip E. Converse, ed. *Social Psychology: The Study of Human Interaction* (New York: Holt, Rinehart and Winston, Inc., 1965), 17–18).

10. Talcott Parsons, *The Social System* (Glencoe, IL: Free Press, 1951), pp. 25–26.

11. Ibid., p. 25.

12. Ibid., p. 281.

13. Ibid.

14. Robert King Merton, "The Self-Fulfilling Prophecy," in On Social Structure and Science, ed. Piotr Sztompka (Chicago: University of Chicago Press, 1996), p. 187.

15. Robert King Merton, "Social Structure and Anomie," in ibid., p. 132.

16. Robert King Merton, "Social Dysfunctions," in ibid., p. 98.

17. Ibid., p. 96.

18. Robert King Merton, "The Role-Set," in ibid., p. 113.

19. Ibid., pp. 117–118. Merton goes on to claim that "if all the facts of one's conduct and beliefs were freely available to anyone, social structures could not operate."

20. Seligman, "Role Complexity, Risk, and the Emergence of Trust," p. 626.

21. Ralf Dahrendorf, "Homo Sociologicus," in *Essays in the Theory of Society*, comp. Ralf Dahrendorf (London: Routledge and Kegan Paul, 1968), p. 76.

22. Ibid., p. 34.

23. Ibid., p. 34; italics added.

24. Ralf Dahrendorf, "Sociology and Human Nature," in *Essays in the Theory of Society, Ralf Dahrendorf* (London: Routledge and Kegan Paul, 1968), p. 95; italics added.

25. Erving Goffman, *The Presentation of Self In Everyday Life* (Garden City, NY: Doubleday, 1973), pp. 252–253.

26. Erving Goffman, "On Face Work," in Erving Goffman, *Interaction Ritual: Essays in Face-to-Face Behavior*, intro. Joel Best (New Brunswick, NJ: Transaction Publishers, 2005), p. 7.

27. Ibid., p. 10. This last possibility—that people may like their cells—comes through very strongly in Charles Horton Cooley's work. It is no deep insight that people generally like receiving the approbation of others and are more or less anxious to receive it. Cooley brings attention to this part of life with his metaphor of the "looking glass self," in which a person constantly imagines how he or she must look to other people. However, as Cooley admits, the metaphor is incomplete and imperfect: "the comparison with a looking glass hardly suggests . . . the imagined judgment, which is quite essential. The thing that moves us to pride or shame is not the mere mechanical reflection of ourselves, but an imputed sentiment, the imagined effect of this reflection upon another's mind" (Charles Horton Cooley, *Human Nature and the Social Order* [New York: Schocken Books, 1964], p. 184). In Cooley's thought, roles may be construed to be heavily dependent upon the perceived opinions of others—a pleasant dependence, when the others are perceived to have positive reactions to a performance—and therefore not wholly up to the individual to construct.

28. Goffman, "Where the Action Is," in *Interaction Ritual*, p. 253.

29. Goffman, "On Face Work," p. 11.

30. *Summa theologica*, IIa IIae, q. 61, a. 2, ad. 3.

31. Ibid., q. 141, a. 6, ad. 3.

32. See *Analects* 13.3, in Xie, p. 208.

33. 明德, 謂得之於己, 至明而不昧者也。 如父子則有親, 君臣則有義, 夫婦則有別, 長幼則有序, 朋友則有信, 初未嘗差也。*Yulei*, chap. 14, in *Zhuzi quanshu*, vol. 14, p. 434.

34. *The Great Learning*, one of the Four Books enshrined by Zhu as the heart of the Confucian curriculum, says that the true way of learning involves "illuminating luminous virtue 明明德"; see my Chapter 2 for discussion of the comprehensiveness of Confucian education, as well as later in this chapter.

35. *Summa theologica*, Ia, q. 47, a. 2, resp.

36. Ibid., Ia, q. 96, a. 4.

37. 父子有父子之理，君臣有君臣之理。*Yulei*, chap. 5, in *Zhuzi quanshu*, vol. 14, p. 216.

38. 天地萬物之理無獨，必有對，皆自然而然，非有安排也。每中夜以思，不知手之舞之足之蹈之也。*Jinsilu* 1:25, in *Zhuzi quanshu*, vol. 13, p. 171.

39. Thomas himself exhibits a certain amount of self-forgetfulness in his quest to become more like the God who governs the universe. For example, as Robert Pasnau notes, the *Summa theologiae* "builds an account of human beings from the ground up. It begins in Ia with the essence of human beings (QQ75–76), works out the capacities (QQ77–83) and operations (QQ84–89), and then throughout 2a develops in careful detail the most essential features. But Aquinas can begin at the ground level only because he has the whole plan in mind. He sees the end at which human beings are aimed, and only with that in mind can he proceed to lay out the fundamentals of human nature" (Pasnau, p. 21). In fact, the very exploration of human beings in this work is undertaken in an effort not to understand them, but rather to understand their first source and cause: "the discussion of human beings in [ST] Ia QQ75–102 is part of a larger project to understand God via creation. The theologian looks to the created world to understand God in just the sense that the art historian looks to the Sistine Chapel to understand Michelangelo" (ibid., p. 19). In other words, the most important element in his thinking is God, and not humankind. In this way, he can be compared to Parsons, Merton and Dahrendorf, in whose work the role is the essential unit of study, not the person; of course, Thomas considers the focus on God to be much more fulfilling than the social theorists imagine their focus on roles to be.

40. *Summa theologica*, Ia IIae, q. 112, a. 1.

41. Cua, "Basic Concepts of Confucian Ethics," in *Moral Vision and Tradition*, p. 269. Of course, there are those who disagree with this assessment. See Li Yuli, *The Unity of Rule and Virtue: A Critique of a Supposed Parallel Between Confucian Ethics and Virtue* Ethics (Singapore: Eastern Universities Press, 2004) for the argument that Confucianism transcends such labels.

42. Kevin L. Flannery, *Acts Amid Precepts: The Aristotelian Logical Structure of Thomas Aquinas' Moral Theory* (Washington, D.C.: Catholic University of America Press, 2001), p. xiv.

43. Stump, *Aquinas*, p. 61.

44. Cua, "Basic Concepts of Confucian Ethics," *Moral Vision and Tradition*, p. 267.

45. See *Summa theologica*, IIa IIae, qq. 23–46.

46. Quoted in Cua, "Basic Concepts of Confucian Ethics," p. 267.

47. *Summa theologica*, Ia IIae, q. 55, a. 4, obj. 1. The definition given also includes "which God works in us, without us." But this part of the definition he says only applies to the "infused" virtues (in the respondio) to be discussed further below.

48. 德謂見善必行, 聞過必改。能治其身, 能治其家; 能事父兄, 能教子弟; 能御童僕, 能肅政教; 能事長上, 能睦親故; 能擇交遊, 能守兼介; 能廣施惠, 能受寄託; 能救患難, 能導人爲善; 能規人過失, 能為人謀事, 能為衆集事, 能借鬥爭; 能興利除害, 能居官舉職。Amended and Emended Lü Family Compact 增补吕氏乡约, in *Zhuzi quanshu*, vol. 24, p. 3595. The English translation is the one published in de Bary and Bloom; see 752. Regarding the text itself: as Emerson Niou explains, "in 1076, the Lu Family Community Compact was [originally] drafted by Lu Dajun in Lantian, Shanxi province, as a means of perfecting oneself and improving community harmony through 'mutual encouragement of virtue and meritorious deeds, mutual correction of faults, mutual association in rites and customs, and mutual sympathy in calamities and hard times (德業相勸, 過失相規, 禮俗相交, 患難相卹).' This compact embodied Confucian idealism, concretizing in social practice the abstract Confucian concept of benevolence. Later, the Lu Family Community Compact was strongly advocated by Zhu Xi and his Confucian companions" (Emerson Niou, "Local Self-Governance with Chinese Characteristics," http://74.125.95.132/search?q=cache:ME7qat1d6AAJ:140.109.171.199/1010meeting/1-2.pdf+%22lu+family+compact%22&hl=en&ct=clnk&cd=1&gl=us&client=firefox-a).

49. I put this term in caps to distinguish it from the *li* (理) discussed in the first chapter. Although the characters and their meanings are very different, the pronunciation—down to the tone (3rd) in Mandarin Chinese—is the same.

50. For example, the title of the 禮記 (*Liji*) is usually translated as the Record of Rites (see de Bary and Bloom) or the *Book of Rites* (Gardner, *Chu Hsi and the Ta-hsueh*).

51. Chan, *A Sourcebook in Chinese Philosophy*.

52. de Bary and Bloom; Legge.

53. 性只是仁義禮智。*Yulei*, chap. 4, in *Zhuzi quanshu*, vol. 14, p. 192.

54. 孟子言: 「惻隱之心, 仁之端也。」仁,性也; 惻隱, 情也。。。性是體, 情是用。*Yulei*, chap. 5, in *Zhuzi quanshu*, vol. 14, p. 226.

55. 情是性之發。Ibid., chap. 4, in *Zhuzi quanshu*, vol. 14, p. 192.

56. 在人, 仁義禮智, 性也。然四者有何形狀, 亦只是有如此道理。有如此道理, 便做得許多事出來, 所以能惻隱、羞惡、辭遜、是非也。*Yulei*, chap. 4, in *Zhuzi quanshu*, vol. 14, p. 191.

57. 何以見得有此四者? 因其惻隱, 知其有仁; 因其羞惡, 知其有義。Ibid., chap. 4, in *Zhuzi quanshu*, vol. 14, p. 249.

58. 「仁」字須兼義禮智看, 方看得出。仁者, 仁之本體; 禮者, 仁之節文; 義者, 仁之斷制; 知者, 仁之分別。*Yulei*, chap. 6, in *Zhuzi quanshu*, vol. 14, p. 249.

59. 初間聖人亦只是略為禮以達吾之誠意, 後來遂加詳密。』 *Yulei*, chap. 3, in *Zhuzi quanshu*, vol. 14, p. 170.

60. Tu 1979, p. 188. Karyn Lai makes a similar point: "to say that ren and li are necessary and sufficient for each other is to make the point that each li-act should be imbued with ren." (Lai, pp. 116–117) See also Joseph Chan,

"Confucian Attitudes Toward Ethical Pluralism," in *Confucian Political Ethics*, ed. Daniel A. Bell (Princeton, NJ: Princeton University Press, 2008), especially pp. 117–118, for a similar argument.

61. (淳于髡曰:「男女授受不親, 禮與?」孟子曰:「禮也。」曰:「嫂溺則援之以手乎?」曰:「嫂溺不援, 是豺狼也。男女授受不親, 禮也; 嫂溺援之以手者, 權也」)" (Mencius 4A17, in Xie, p. 480).

62. Geir Helgesen, "The Case for Moral Education" in *Confucianism for the Modern World*, ed. Daniel A. Bell and Hahm Chaibong (Cambridge, UK: University of Cambridge Press, 2003), p. 161.

63. Seligman et al, p. 106. Regardless of their understanding of sincerity as requiring ritual ("even our own private thoughts can only work through language, and thus can never fully reveal our innermost sincerity [or lack of it]"), the authors still present ritual and sincerity as occupying opposite poles of a continuum: "ritual [in which we submit ourselves to externally given categories of order] and sincerity [which seeks to replace the 'mere convention' of ritual with a genuine and thoughtful state of internal conviction] offer alternative modes of framing social thought, action, and interaction" (ibid., p. 103). The Confucians offer up a wholly different reading of sincerity and ritual: as Fingarette puts it, Confucians have from the beginning believed that "man is transformed by participation with others in ceremony which is communal. Until he is so transformed he is not truly man but only potentially so—the new-born infant, the wolf-boy of the forests or the 'barbarian'" (Herbert Fingarette, *Confucius: The Secular as Sacred* [New York: Harper and Row, 1972], p. 77). In other words, there is no self to be sincere until it has been ritualized.

64. *Summa theologica*, IIa IIae, q. 114, a. 2, ad. 1.

65. Ibid., a. 1, resp.

66. See ibid., a. 2, resp.

67. Ibid., Ia, q. 21, a. 1, resp.

68. Ibid., IIa IIae, q. 114, a. 1, resp.; italics added.

69. Ibid., q. 101, a. 1, 2.

70. Ibid., q. 92, a. 2, resp.

71. Ibid., q. 90, a. 3, ad. 2.

72. Ibid., q. 65, a. 2, ad. 2.

73. Ibid., q. 32, a. 9, ad. 2.

74. Randall Collins, *Interaction Ritual Chains* (Princeton Studies in Cultural Sociology, Princeton, NJ: Princeton University Press, 2004), p. 220.

75. Neville, *Boston Confucianism*, p. 9.

76. 有子曰:「禮之用, 和為貴。」*Analects* 1:12, in Xie, p. 70.

77. Neville, *Boston Confucianism*, p. 10.

78. Neville, *Ritual and Deference*, p. 95.

79. 人之有道也, 饱食、暖衣、逸居而无教, 則近於禽獸。 Mencius 5A4, in Xie, p. 423.

80. 設為庠序學校以教之。 Ibid.

81. See my Chapter 1 for a translation of Zhu's preface to *The Great Learning*, in which he assigns himself a place in the transmission of the Way of Mencius.

82. While, in Neo-Confucian practice, schooling was often denied to girls, Zhu Xi himself had no problem with basic female education: "Someone said, 'Girls should also have education. Aside from the *Classic of Filiality*, is it permitted to teach them to grasp a preliminary understanding of texts such as, for example, the Analects?' Zhu answered, 'This is fine' (問: 「女子亦當有教。自孝經之外, 如論語, 只取其面前明白者教之, 何如？ 」曰: 「亦可」)" (*Yulei*, chap. 7, in *Zhuzi quanshu*, vol. 14, p. 271).

83. 天命, 非所以教小兒。 教小兒, 只說箇義理大概, 只跟前事。*Yulei*, chap. 7, in *Zhuzi quanshu*, vol. 14, p. 271.

84. 「衣毋撥, 足毋蹶; 將上堂, 聲必揚; 將入戶, 視必下」 等嗶韻處, 皆是古人初教小兒語。Ibid., chap. 7, in *Zhuzi quanshu*, vol. 14, p. 271.

85. 母又添兩句曰: 「將入門, 問孰存。 」Ibid.

86. 人生八歲,則自王公以下, 至於庶人之子弟, 皆入小學, 而教之以灑掃應對進退之節, 禮樂射禦書數之文。Commentary on *The Great Learning*, in *Zhuzi quanshu*, vol. 6, p. 13.

87. 學問須以大學為先, 次論語, 次孟子, 次中庸。 中庸工夫密, 規模大。*Yulei*, chap. 11, in *Zhuzi quanshu*, vol. 14, p. 333.

88. 某要人先讀大學, 以定其規模: 次讀論語, 以立其根本: 次讀孟子, 以觀其發越; 次讀中庸, 以求古人之微妙處。 Ibid.

89.若理會得此四書, 何書不可讀; 何理不可究; 何事不可處! Ibid., chap. 11, in *Zhuzi quanshu*, vol. 14, p. 333.

90. 古人小學養得小兒子誠敬善端發見了。 Ibid., chap. 7, in *Zhuzi quanshu*, vol. 14, p. 269.

91. 小學是事, 如事君, 事父, 事兄, 處友等事, 只是教他依此規矩做去。*Yulei*, chap. 7, in *Zhuzi quanshu*, vol. 14, p. 269.

92. 小童添炭, 撥開火散亂。 先生曰: 「可拂殺了, 我不愛人恁地, 此便是燒火不敬。 所以聖人教小兒灑掃應對, 件件要謹。」Ibid., chap. 7, in *Zhuzi quanshu*, vol. 14, p. 271.

93. 某外家子姪, 未論其賢否如何, 一出來便齊整, 緣是他家長上元初教誨得如此。。。」Ibid.

94. 大學是發明此事之理。 Ibid., chap. 7, in *Zhuzi quanshu*, vol. 14, p. 269.

95. [其十有五年] 皆入大學, 而教之以窮理正心, 修己治人之道。 Preface to *The Great Learning*, in *Zhuzi quanshu*, vol. 6, p. 13.

96. 問: 「大學與小學, 不是截然為二。 小學是學其事, 大學是窮其理, 以盡其事否？ 」曰: 「只是一箇事。 小學是學事親, 學事長, 且直理會那事。 大學是就上面委曲詳究那理, 其所以事親是如何, 所以事長是如何。*Yulei*, chap. 7, in *Zhuzi quanshu*, vol. 14, p. 270.

97. See de Bary and Bloom, pp. 767–768, for a discussion and translation of Zhu's commentary on the *Elementary Education* (小學). For the *Xiaoxue* and Zhu's commentary thereon, see *Zhuzi quanshu*, vol. 13, pp. 377–499.

98. Joel Kupperman, "Tradition and Community in the Formation of Character and Self," in *Confucian Ethics: A Comparative Study of Self, Autonomy and Community*, ed. Kwong-loi Shun and David B. Wong (Cambridge, UK: Cambridge University Press, 2004), p. 116.

99. Ibid., p. 118. In keeping with the Confucian emphasis on the importance of socialization, Kupperman goes on to list other social "constitutive factors" in his personal identity: "at other moments I find myself thinking and acting in ways that can be identified with middle-class groups in the place where I grew up, Chicago, and with that time . . . No doubt there are many other elements in the collage. To mention one: it is often observed that one of the results of long and reasonably successful marriages is increased similarity in responses, so that two people can come to have much the same outward look."

100. See *Jinsilu* 6:17, in *Zhuzi quanshu*, vol. 13, p. 230.

101. 非性然也, 教之使然也。*Jinsilu* 6:17, in *Zhuzi quanshu*, vol. 13, p. 230.

102. de Bary, *The Liberal Tradition in China*, pp. 36–37.

103. 自其施於家者言之, 則名分之守, 愛敬之實, 其本也; 冠、婚、喪、擊儀章度數者, 其文也。Preface to the *Family Rituals*, in *Zhuzi quanshu*, vol. 21, p. 3626.

104. 其本者有家日用之常體, 固不可以 一日而不修, 其文有皆所以紀綱人道之終始, 雖其行之有時, 施之有所, 然非講之索明、皆之索熟, 則其臨事之際, 亦無合宜而應節, 是不可以一日不講宜皆焉也。Ibid.

105. 三代之際, 禮經備矣, 然其存於今者, 宮廬器服之製, 出人起居之節, 皆已不宜於世。Ibid., 3626–3627.

106. 以竊自附於孔子從先進之遺意。Ibid., p. 3627.

107. 子游問孝。子曰: 「今之孝者, 是謂能養。至於犬馬, 皆能有養; 不敬, 何以別乎。」Analects 2:7, in Xie, p. 76.

108. In a similar vein: the *LI* are not deterministic. As Neville points out, one "cosmological theme important to Confucianism (and Daoism) is spontaneity . . . Confucianism has never held to a strict determinism of the sort that intrigued Western scientists for the last several centuries" (Neville, *Ritual and Deference*, p. 6). Thus, for example, as discussed above, Mencius explicitly recognized that there are cases in which the *LI* must be set aside.

109. Neville, *Ritual and Deference*, p. 107.

110. 仁禮屬陽,義智屬陰, 仁禮是用, 義智是體. *Yulei*, chap. 6, in *Zhuzi quanshu*, vol. 14, p. 245.

111. 仁是左手, 禮是右手。Ibid., p. 249.

112. 禮者, 仁之發。Ibid.

113. 仁包禮, 義包智。 Ibid., chap. 6, in *Zhuzi quanshu*, vol. 14, p. 249.

114.仁與智包得, 義與禮包不得。Ibid., chap. 6, in *Zhuzi quanshu*, vol. 14, p. 249.

115. Cua, "Basic Concepts of Confucian Ethics," in *Moral Vision and Tradition*, p. 298.

116. Tu, "Li as Process of Humanization," in *Humanity and Self-Cultivation*, p. 20.

117. Henry Rosemont, Jr., "Whose Democracy? Which Rights? A Confucian Critique of Modern Western Liberalism," in *Confucian Ethics: A Comparative Study of Self, Autonomy and Community*, ed. Kwong-loi Shun and David B. Wong (Cambridge, UK: Cambridge University Press, 2004), p. 64.

118. 問:「仁得之最先, 蓋言仁具義禮智。」曰:「先有是生理, 三者由此推之。」*Yulei*, chap. 6, in *Zhuzi quanshu*, vol. 14, p. 246.

119. 仁 為 四 端 之 首。Ibid., chap. 6, in *Zhuzi quanshu*, vol. 14, p. 249.

120. 仁者, 仁之本體; 禮者, 仁之節文; 義者, 仁之斷制; 知者, 仁之分別。Ibid., chap. 6, in *Zhuzi quanshu*, vol. 14, p. 249.

121. 仁所以包三者, 蓋義禮智皆是流動底物, 所以皆從仁上漸漸推出。Ibid., chap. 9, in *Zhuzi quanshu*, vol. 14, p. 247.

122. 仁在事。若不於事上看, 如何見仁。Ibid., chap. 6, in *Zhuzi quanshu*, vol. 14, p. 257.

123. 做一方便事, 也是仁? Ibid.

124. 其始也, 自謂百事能; 其終也, 一事不能! Ibid., chap. 10, in *Zhuzi quanshu*, vol. 14, p. 321.

125. 言人讀書不專一, 而貪多廣閱之弊。Ibid.

126. 不可都要滚去, 如人一日只喫得三碗飯, 不可將十數日飯都一齊喫了。一日只看得幾段, 做得多少工夫, 亦有限, 不可滚去都要了。Ibid., chap. 10, in *Zhuzi quanshu*, vol. 14, p. 319.

127. *Summa theologica*, Ia IIae, q. 4, a. 8.

128. See ibid.

129. Torrell, *Saint Thomas Aquinas: Volume 2*, p. 277.

130. *Summa theologica*, Ia IIae, q. 24, a. 3.

131. Ibid.

132. Ibid., q. 26, a. 1.

133. Ibid., a. 3, resp.

134. Peter A. Kwasniewski, Introduction to *On Love and Charity: Readings from the Commentary on the Sentences of Peter Lombard, by Thomas Aquinas*, trans. Peter A. Kwasniewski, Thomas Bolin O. S. B., and Joseph Bolin (Washington, D.C.: The Catholic University of America, 2008), p. xxiii.

135. *Summa theologica*, IIa IIae, q. 26, a. 7, ad. 3.

136. Ibid., a. 6, obj. 3. In another example of the interchangeable usage of *amor* and *dilectio*, the rest of the objection states, "Now to all our neighbors we wish an equal good, viz. everlasting life. Therefore we ought to love (*diligere*) all our neighbors equally." While Thomas disagrees with this reasoning (see ad. 3), he does not disagree with Aristotle's claim.

137. Ibid.

138. Gilson, p. 405.

139. Walter Farrell, O. P., S. T. D., O. P. M., *A Companion to the Summa* (1938–1942; domcentral.org: The Walter Farrell Institute) http://op.org/farrell/companion/comp205.htm

140. Kevin White, "The Passions of the Soul (Ia IIae, qq. 22–48)," in *The Ethics of Aquinas*, ed. Stephen J. Pope (Washington, D.C.: Georgetown University Press, 2002), p. 106.

141. Ex eo enim quod diversimode dispositi sumus secundum concupiscentiam, iram et timorem, et alias passiones, diversimode nobis aliquid bonum vel malum videtur. *Compendium*, I:128. See also *Summa theologica*, Ia IIae, q. 77, a. 2, ad. 2: "the fact that something appears good in particular to the reason, whereas it is not good, is due to a passion: and yet this particular judgment is contrary to the universal knowledge of the reason."

142. [Omnis] cognitio perficitur per assimilationem cognoscentis ad rem cognitam, ita quod assimilatio dicta est causa cognitionis. Thomas Aquinas, *De Veritate*, Fundación Tomás de Aquino (http://www.corpusthomisticum.org), 2008–2009: q. 1, a. 1, resp.

143. Veritas quae est in anima causata a rebus, non sequitur aestimationem animae, sed existentiam rerum: quoniam eo quod res est vel non est, dicitur oratio vera vel falsa. Ibid., q. 1, a. 2, ad. 3.

144. *Summa theologica*, Ia IIae, q. 49, a. 1, resp.

145. Ibid., q. 51, a. 1, ad. 3.

146. See ibid., q. 77, a. 7 and 8.

147. Ibid., q. 51, a. 2, resp.

148. See ibid., q. 1, a. 1, resp.

149. Ibid., q. 49, a. 4, resp.

150. Ibid., q. 55, a. 1, resp.

151. Ibid., ad. 1.

152. Ibid., a. 2, resp.

153. *Nicomachean Ethics*, 1102a.34–1102b.12, pp. 28–29.

154. Ibid., 1102b.14, p. 29.

155. Ibid., 1103a.4–6, p. 30.

156. *Summa theologica*, Ia IIae, q. 58, a. 2, resp.

157. *Nicomachean Ethics*, 1177a.11–14, p. 270. Further on the intellectualist bias shared by Aristotle and Thomas: Anthony Kenny notes in his discussion of Thomas's commentary on the Ethics: "it is common ground among commentators on the *Nicomachean Ethics* that happiness is there defined as the exercise of virtue. Modern interpreters do not agree, however, whether to take it as the exercise of a single dominant virtue, or as the inclusive exercise of all of the virtues of the rational soul. Probably a majority of writers in English at the present time favor the inclusive interpretation. Aquinas will have none of this" (Anthony Kenny, "Aquinas on Aristotelian Happiness," in *Aquinas's Moral Theory: Essays in Honor of Norman Kretzmann*, ed. Scott MacDonald and Eleonore Stump [Ithaca, NY: Cornell University Press, 1999], p. 16). For his part, Kenny says: "Aquinas's [more exclusivist] interpretation is preferable, it seems to me, to the alternative interpretations which have been canvassed by modern commentators" (ibid., p. 19).

158. *Summa theologica*, Ia IIae, q. 57, a. 1, ad. 2. See also the *Summa contra gentiles*, in which he describes wisdom as "more perfect [than other virtues] because, in so far as a man gives himself to the pursuit of wisdom, so far does he even now have some share in true beatitude (*Summa contra gentiles*, bk. I, chap. 2, sec. 1, p. 61).

159. Ibid., q. 55, a. 3, sed contra.

160. Zagzebski, p. 104. This "deep quality" is crucial: "entrenchment is a necessary feature of virtues because they are often needed the most when they encounter resistance."

161. Kent, p. 117; italics added.

162. *Summa theologica*, Ia, q. 83, a. 1, resp.

163. Stump, "Wisdom: Will, Belief and Moral Goodness," pp. 58–59.

164. *Summa theologica*, Ia IIae, q. 78, a. 2. See also q. 58, a. 1, arg. 3: "Cicero says (De Invent. Rhet. ii) that "virtue is a habit like a second nature (modum naturae), in accord with reason."

165. Judith W. Kay, "Getting Egypt out of the People: Aquinas's Contributions to Liberation" in *Aquinas and Empowerment: Classical Ethics for Ordinary Lives*, ed. G. Simon Harak, S.J. (Washington, D.C.: Georgetown University Press, 1996), p. 16.

166. *Summa theologica*, Ia IIae, q. 1, a. 7.

167. *Nicomachean Ethics*, 1112a.24–27, p. 60.

168. See *Summa theologica*, Ia IIae, q. 2, a. 8, and q. 3, a. 8.

169. *Nicomachean Ethics*, 1101a.18, p. 24.

170. Ibid., 1101b.3–5, pp. 25–26.

171. Ibid., 1117b.10–14, p. 74.

172. Torrell, *Saint Thomas Aquinas: Volume 2*, p. 345.

173. *Summa theologica*, Ia IIae, q. 2, a. 8, resp. As Bradley notes, Thomas makes the "paradoxical claim" that "an other-worldly vision of God is an end that is not natural, but nonetheless it is the only satisfying end of an intellectual nature" (Denis Bradley, *Aquinas on the Twofold Human Good; Reasoned Human Happiness in Aquinas' Moral* Science [Washington, D.C.: Catholic University of America Press, 1997], p. 423). For more on this dilemma, see Bradley, esp. Chapter 9, "A Paradoxical Ethic," pp. 424–481, in which he presents the history of its debate. His own conclusion: that Thomas "leaves an important issue unresolved. Does the conclusion reached in SCG, III, 25–21 (that only the vision of God can satisfy man's natural desire to know God), leave the philosopher [as opposed to the Christian blessed with the theological virtue of hope] 'wishing' for the impossible?" (ibid., p. 481).

174. *Summa theologica*, IIa IIae, q. 26, a. 2, resp.

175. See ibid., q. 62, a. 1, resp.

176. Ibid., q. 23, a. 8, ad. 3.

177. Ibid., q. 25, a. 1, resp.

178. Ibid.

179. See ibid., q. 26, a. 4, resp.

180. Ibid., q. 24, a. 12, ad. 5.

181. Ibid., a. 4, ad. 3.

182. See ibid., q. 31.

183. See ibid., q. 32. Note: the Fathers of the English Dominican province translate the term as "almsdeeds."

184. See ibid., q. 33.

185. See ibid., qq. 28, 29.

186. See ibid., q. 24, a. 10, resp.

187. Ibid., a. 12, resp.

188. Ibid., a. 8, ad. 3. See also Ibid., q. 23, a. 8, resp, in which he defines charity as the form of all the other virtues, and ibid., q. 23, a. 6, resp., where he says it is the most excellent of all the virtues.

189. Ibid., Ia IIae, q. 19, a. 10, resp.

190. *Summa theologica*, Ia IIae, q. 71, a. 4.

191. Ibid., Ia, q. 48, a. 5, ad. 1.

192. Ibid., Ia, q. 49, a. 3, resp.

193. *Nicomachean Ethics*, 114a.17–22, p. 63.

194. *Summa theologica*, Ia IIae, q. 63, a. 2.

195. Ibid., IIa IIae, q. 20, a. 3, resp.

196. Ibid., q. 21, a. 4, resp.

197. Ibid., q. 21, a. 2.

198. Ibid., a. 3.

199. Ibid., a. 4, resp.

200. Ibid., q. 21, a. 2.

201. Michael C. Kalton, "Extending the Neo-Confucian Tradition: Questions and Reconceptualization for the Twenty-First Century," in Mary Evelyn Tucker and John Berthrong, eds. *Confucianism and Ecology: The Interrelation of Heaven, Earth and Humans* (Cambridge: Harvard University Press, 1998), pp. 86–87.

202. Tu Weiming, "Beyond the Enlightenment Mentality," in Mary Evelyn Tucker and John Berthrong, eds. *Confucianism and Ecology: The Interrelation of Heaven, Earth and* Humans (Cambridge: Harvard University Press, 1998), p. 17.

203. 乾稱父, 坤稱母; 予茲藐焉, 乃混然中處。故天地之塞, 吾其體; 天地之帥, 吾 其性。民, 吾同胞; 物, 吾與也。 Zhang Zai, *The Western Inscription* (*Ximing*, 西銘), http://sangle.web.wesleyan.edu/etext/song-qing/zhang-zm.html

204. Philip J. Ivanhoe, "Early Confucianism and Environmental Ethics," in *Confucianism and Ecology: The Interrelation of Heaven, Earth and Humans*, ed. Mary Evelyn Tucker and John Berthrong (Cambridge: Harvard University Press, 1998), pp. 64–65.

205. 仁 木, 義 金, 禮 火, 智 水, 信 土 。*Yulei*, chap. 6, in *Zhuzi quanshu*, vol. 14, p. 243.

206. Rodney L. Taylor, "Companionship with the World: Roots and Branches of a Confucian Ecology," in *Confucianism and Ecology: The Interrelation of Heaven, Earth and Humans, ed.* Mary Evelyn Tucker and John Berthrong (Cambridge: Harvard University Press, 1998), p. 53.

207. Kohn, p. 39.

208. Tu Weiming, "Epilogue: Human Rights as a Confucian Moral Discourse," in *Confucianism and Human Rights*, ed. Wm. Theodore de Bary and Tu Weiming (New York: Columbia University Press, 1998a), p. 302.

209. Cua, "Chinese Moral Vision, Responsive Agency, and Factual Beliefs," in *Moral Vision and Tradition*, p. 70.

210. Tu, "Beyond the Enlightenment Mentality," p. 14.

211. *Summa theologica*, Prologue, Ia IIae.

212. Colman O'Neill, quoted in Nichols, p. 91.

213. Until the time that God shall appear, those still on earth may become more like their Maker through the gift not only of the theological virtues, which are directed to God Himself, but also to divinely infused virtues, directed to more purely human ends: "even as the natural light of reason is something besides the acquired virtues, which are ordained to this natural light, so also the light of grace which is a participation of the Divine Nature is something besides the infused virtues which are derived from and are ordained to this light, hence the Apostle says (Ephesians 5:8): 'For you were heretofore darkness, but now light in the Lord. Walk then as children of the light.' For as the acquired virtues enable a man to walk, in accordance with the natural light of reason, so do the infused virtues enable a man to walk as befits the light of grace" (*Summa theologica*, Ia IIae, q. 112, a. 1, resp).

214. *Summa contra gentiles*, bk. III, chap. 24, sec. 8. See also *Summa theologica*, IIIa, q. 1, a. 1, resp.: "it belongs to the essence of goodness to communicate itself to others."

215. Gilson, p. 407.

216. Richard J. Regan, S. J. *The Moral Dimensions of Politics* (New York: Oxford University Press, 1986), p. 14.

217. Ibid., pp. 97–98.

218. "人一能之，己百之。人十能之，己千之。果能此道矣，雖愚必明，雖柔必強。" Quoted in *The Doctrine of the Mean*, chap. 20, in Xie, p. 43.

219. See *Summa theologica*, IIa IIae, q. 24, a. 2, resp.

220. Ibid., q. 23, a. 7, resp.; italics added.

Chapter 4. Exercising Authority

1. Regan, p. 45.

2. Ibid., p. 96. While Regan disagrees with this basic thesis, he readily concedes that "libertarians do well to remind us that freedom itself is a moral goal of organized society."

3. 文化产业作为一个新兴产业对经济的促进作用越来越大。Liu Wei (刘蔚), "The Function of Government in the Cluster Development of the Culture Industry" (政府在文化产业集群发展中的作用," *Journal of China Executive Leadership Academy* (中国井冈山干部学院报告) 1, no. 2 (第1 卷, 第2 期) (March 25, 2008 年3 月): 91.

4. 文化产业集群政策属于产业政策的一部分，是促进经济发展和结构调整的一种方法，也是使用文化经济繁荣区城和城市的手段。Ibid., p. 92.

5. 政府应该通过在专业化培训，基础设施和其他改善商业环境方面促成集群的形成。在产业集群的升级中，政府的角色是鼓励竞争而非扭曲竞争。政府投资的中心，应该方在改善产业集群内的产业环境，鼓励那些影响产业集群发展的公共物品或准公共物品的发展。Ibid., p. 92.

6. Sandra Tsing Loh, "I Choose My Choice!" *Atlantic Monthly*, July/August 2008, http://www.theatlantic.com/doc/200807/working-moms

7. Joseph Chan, "Giving Priority to the Worst Off: A Confucian Perspective," in *Confucianism for the Modern World*, ed. Daniel A. Bell and Hahm Chaibong (Cambridge, UK: University of Cambridge Press, 2003), p. 237.

8. Charles E. Curran, "Roman Catholic Christianity" in *God's Rule: The Politics of World Religions*, ed. Jacob Neusner (Washington: Georgetown University Press. 2003), p. 72.

9. Henry Rosemont, Jr., "Two Loci of Authority: Autonomous Individuals and Related Persons," in *Confucian Cultures of Authority*, ed. Peter D. Hershock and Roger T. Ames (Albany: State University of New York Press, 2006), p. 12.

10. See Curran, p. 71.

11. *Summa theologica*, IIa IIae, q. 32, a. 3, resp.

12. *Yulei*, chap. 106, sec. 1, translated in Chan, *Chu Hsi: New Studies*, p. 6.

13. Curran, pp. 70–71, nn. 28–29.

14. Peerenboom, p. 244.

15. John Kekes, "Pluralism and Moral Authority," *The Moral Circle and the Self: Chinese and Western Approaches*, in ed. Kim-chong Chong, Sor-hoon Tan, and C. L. Ten (Chicago: Open Court, 2003), p. 75.

16. Ibid., p. 76.

17. Cua, "Confucian Vision and Experience of the World," in *Moral Vision and Tradition*, p. 27.

18. This idea is not limited to the two traditions under discussion here. René Goldman notes that the *zaddik* in Jewish society traditionally played a role very similar to that of the Confucian sage or superior person: "the *zaddik*, like the *junzi* and even more the *shengren*, is an exceptional man whose calling is to set before the people an example of virtuous conduct" (Goldman, p. 336). However, according to Goldman, the manner in which these paradigmatic individuals provided those around them with moral example is profoundly different: "notwithstanding the intimate bond that we occasionally discover in the relationships between teachers and disciples (the finest example of which is the bond between Confucius and Yan Hui), Confucian paternalism seems somewhat aloof; the Confucian classics do not set before the *junzi* patterns of relationship with the people marked by the kind of intimacy that Judaism, particularly Hasidism, prescribes—intimacy without which, we are told by Yaakov Yosef, the *zaddik* would not only fail to spiritualize the people, but might even be corrupted by their materialism. . . . One could not imagine a *zaddik* uttering, as did Confucius (even though he was a humble man): 'Do not befriend those who are not like you' (*Analects* 9/24)" (ibid., p. 338).

19. Richard Madsen, "Confucian Conceptions of Civil Society" in *Confucian Political Ethics*, ed. Daniel A. Bell (Princeton, NJ: Princeton University Press, 2008), p. 10.

20. Regan, pp. 94–95. In an insightful aside, Regan notes that the picture is more complicated than generally made out to be: "pessimists are wont to speak of a descending curve of public morality. And in many areas, indeed, agreement on principles of public morality is obviously more indifferent than even a generation or two ago on such issues as extra- and premarital sexual behavior and abortion. Yet, in many other areas, agreement on principles of public morality has expanded; the public today is more concerned than previous generations with moral imperatives on such issues as war and peace, racial and sex discrimination, business practices, and the conduct of public officials. The resulting contemporary status of the public consensus of moral principles may be described summarily with respect to the proximate past as weaker in the area of personal and familial responsibilities and stronger in the area of social and political morality" (ibid., p. 95).

21. Ibid., pp. 67–68.

22. Mary M. Keys, *Aquinas, Aristotle, and the Promise of the Common Good* (New York: Cambridge University Press, 2006), p. 14.

23. Ibid., p. 12.

24. Ibid., p. 13. See also Regan, pp. 4–5, for his discussion of the prevalence of this mode of thinking in the political sphere, and his criticism of the same in religious contexts.

25. Sor-hoon Tan, "Can There Be a Confucian Civil Society?" in Kim-chong Chong, Sor-hoon Tan, and C. L. Ten, eds. *The Moral Circle and the Self: Chinese and Western Approaches* (Chicago: Open Court, 2003), p. 198.

26. Regan, pp. 67–68.

27. Tan, p. 198.

28. Tu Weiming, "The Way, Learning and Politics in Classical Confucianism," in *Way, Learning and Politics: Essays on* the Confucian Individual, Tu Weiming, ed. (Albany: State University of New York, 1993), pp. 5–6.

29. Regan, p. 39.

30. Curran, p. 81.

31. David B. Wong, "Rights and Community in Confucianism," in *Confucian Ethics: A Comparative Study of Self, Autonomy and Community*, Kwong-loi Shun and David B. Wong, eds. (Cambridge, UK: Cambridge University Press, 2004), p. 46.

32. 以氣言之, 則知覺運動人物若不異; 以理言之, 則仁義禮智之稟, 非物之所能全也。*Yulei*, chap. 4, in *Zhuzi quanshu*, vol. 14, p. 186; italics added.

33. 能盡其性, 則能盡人之性。能盡人之性, 則能盡物之性。能盡物之性, 則可以贊天地之化育。可以贊天地之化育, 則可以與 天地參矣。*Doctrine of the Mean*, Chapter 22, in Xie, p. 48.

34. Cua, "Confucian Vision and Experience of the World," in *Moral Vision and Tradition*, p. 26.

35. Ibid., p. 25.

36. 如人, 頭圓象天, 足方象地, 平正端直, 以其受天地之正氣, 所以識道理, 有知識。物受天地之偏氣, 所以禽獸橫生, 草木頭生向下, 尾反在上。*Yulei*, chap. 4, in *Zhuzi quanshu*, vol. 14, p. 194.

37. [人] 無 不 知, 無 不 能 。Ibid.

38. Yung-sik Kim, *The Natural Philosophy of Chu Hsi* (1130–1200). Philadelphia, PA: Memoirs of the American Philosophical Society Held At Philadelphia for Promoting Useful Knowledge, Volume 35, 2000), p. 320.

39. Benjamin I. Schwartz, "The Ethical and the Meta-Ethical in Chinese High Cultural Thought" in *Confucian Spirituality: Volume* One (Volume 11A of World Spirituality: An Encyclopedia of the Religious Quest), ed. Tu Weiming and Mary Evelyn Tucker (New York: The Crossroad Publishing Company, 2003), p. 59.

40. Kohn, p. 39.

41. 子曰, 人能弘道, 非道能弘人。*Analects* 15.28, in Xie, p. 251.

42. 問:「如何見天地之情? 」曰:「人正大, 便也見得天地之情正大。天地只是正大, 未嘗有些子邪處, 未嘗有些子小處。」 *Yulei*, chap. 4, in *Zhuzi quanshu*, vol. 14, p. 188.

43. Michael Nylan, "Boundaries of the Body and Body Politic in Early Confucian Thought," in *Confucian Political Ethics*, ed. Daniel A. Bell (Princeton, NJ: Princeton University Press, 2008), 92.

44 不以嗜欲累其心, 不以小害大, 末喪本焉爾。*Jinsilu* 5.33, in *Zhuzi quanshu*, vol. 13, p. 224.

45. Cf. *Doctrine of the Mean*, Chapter 26: "So large and deep, [sincerity] is the companion of Earth. So high and brilliant, it is the companion of Heaven. So far-reaching and long-continuing, it is without limitations (博厚配地, 高明配天, 悠久無疆)" (in Xie, p. 50).

46. 聖人與天地同*體*。Zhu Xi's Commentary on the *Doctrine of the Mean*, chap. 26, in *Zhuzi quanshu*, vol. 6, p. 52; italics added.

47. 聖人與天地同*用*。Ibid.; italics added.

48. Gen 1:28.

49. Nichols, pp. 85–86.

50. *Summa theologica*, Ia, q. 22, a. 1, ad. 2.

51. Ibid., a. 3, resp.

52. *Summa contra gentiles*, bk. III, chap. 77, sec. 5, pp. 259–260.

53. Ibid., chap. 71, sec. 3, p. 238; italics added.

54. *Summa theologica*, IIIa, q. 9, a. 1, ad. 1.

55. *Summa contra gentiles*, bk. III, chap. 64, sec. 11, p. 213. Such a view enables him to fully embrace the agency of creatures in themselves: a move that helps in current interreligious dialogue, for "without some concept of a natural moral order, Christians risk having nothing of relevance to say to the millions of people who are not Christians" (Regan, p. 6).

56. Ibid., chap. 78, sec. 3, p. 260.

57. *Summa theologica*, IIa IIae, q. 104, a. 1, resp.

58. *Summa contra gentiles*, bk. III, chap. 73, sec. 2, p. 244. See also *Summa theologica*, Ia, q. 103, a. 6, resp.: "since things which are governed should be brought to perfection by government, this government will be so much the better in the degree the things governed are brought to perfection." Again, the dynamism of Thomas, who is often categorized as a substance rather than

process philosopher, may be seen in his conception of a thing's 'perfection': "If each thing tends toward a likeness of divine goodness as its end, and if each thing becomes like the divine goodness in respect of all the things that belong to its proper goodness, then the goodness of the thing consists not only in its mere being, but in all the things needed for its perfection. . . . It is obvious, then, that things are ordered to God as an end, not merely according to their substantial act of being, but also according to those items which are added as pertinent to perfection, and even according to the proper operation which also belongs to the thing's perfection" (*Summa contra gentiles*, bk. III, chap. 20, sec. 8, pp. 80–81).

59. See *Summa theologica*, Ia IIae, q. 102, a. 6, ad 8.

60. Regan, p. 22.

61. See *Summa theologica*, IIa IIae, q. 184, a. 5.

62. See ibid., a. 4.

63. 天地之大也，人猶有所憾。*Doctrine of the Mean*, chap. 12, in Xie, p. 31.

64. 下焉者雖善不尊，不尊不信，不信民弗從。Ibid., chap. 29, in Xie, p. 56.

65. 下焉者，謂聖人在下，如孔子雖善於禮，而不在尊位也。Zhu Xi's Commentary on the *Doctrine of the Mean*, chap. 29, in *Zhuzi quanshu*, vol. 6, p. 55.

66. Wenshan Jia, "The Wei (Positioning)-Ming (Naming)-Lianmin (Face)-Guanxi (Relationship)-Renqing (Humanized Feelings) Complex in Contemporary Chinese Culture," in *Confucian Cultures of Authority*, ed. Peter D. Hershock and Roger T. Ames (Albany: State University of New York Press, 2006), p. 55. See pp. 60–61 for his argument that the state of affairs is much the same today, even in egalitarian communist China.

67. 非天子，不議禮，不制度，不考文。*Doctrine of the Mean*, chap. 28, in Xie, p. 54.

68. Tao Jiang, "Intimate Authority: The Rule of Ritual in Classical Confucian Discourse," in *Confucian Cultures of Authority*, ed. Peter D. Hershock and Roger T. Ames (Albany: State University of New York Press, 2006), p. 36.

69. *Summa theologica*, Ia, q. 96, a. 4.

70. Aliis enim animalibus natura praeparavit cibum, tegumenta pilorum, defensionem, ut dentes, cornua, ungues, vel saltem velocitatem ad fugam. Homo autem institutus est nullo horum sibi a natura praeparato, sed loco omnium data est ei ratio, per quam sibi haec omnia officio manuum posset praeparare, ad quae omnia praeparanda unus homo non sufficit. Nam unus homo per se sufficienter vitam transigere non posset. Est igitur homini naturale quod in societate multorum vivat. Thomas Aquinas, *De regno ad regem Cypri*, http://www.corpusthomisticum.org/, Fundación Tomás de Aquino, 2008–2009, lib. 1, cap. 1. Note on this text: entitled *On Kingship: To the King of Cyprus*, Thomas is understood to have composed it as a gift for the King of Cyprus while at the papal court in the 1260s. While the whole of the work was traditionally credited to Thomas, it is now believed that he wrote only the first of its four books, and

chapters 1–4 of the second. See Ronald W. Truman, *Spanish Treatises on Government, Society, and Religion in the Time of Philip II: The "De Regimine Principum" and Associated Traditions* (Boston: Brill, 1999), p. 17.

71. Keys, p. 78.

72. In the *Summa theologica,* he defines the city as "a perfect community" (*Summa theologica,* IIa IIae, q. 65, a. 2, ad. 2), and identifies the household as "a mean between the individual and the city or kingdom" (IIa IIae, q. 3, a. 3, resp.), but he does not engage in such a sustained discussion of the community as such as he does in the *Politics* commentary. A note on the text: Thomas's reverence for Aristotle, and his desire to engage with the latter and make his texts intelligible for a contemporary audience (discussed above in the Introduction), led him to comment on the Aristotelian corpus. Thomas began commentaries on eleven of Aristotle's works, several of which remained unfinished at his death, the *Commentary on the Politics* among them. Boyle quotes Tolomeo of Lucca, who had been Thomas's friend and confessor in Naples between 1272 and 1274, as saying that Thomas "expounded almost all of the philosophical works of Aristotle, whether natural or moral, while in charge of the studium at Rome (1265–1268), and wrote his lectures up in the form of a scriptum or commentary on each work, particularly on the *Ethics* and the *Metaphysics*" (Boyle, 4). As Boyle points out, "while this might suggest that Thomas taught these books to his students, Tolomeo does not say so. He confirms only that while Thomas was in charge of the studium at Rome, he lectured on certain aspects of Aristotle. In fact, it is highly unlikely that the immediate audience of Thomas at these lectures was his young and presumably untried bunch of students. Some of these may have been bright enough to audit without undue stress Thomas's learned and lengthy expositions of Aristotle, but the majority would likely have needed basic instruction in the fundamentals of Christian teaching" (ibid.).

73. Primo ostendit ex quibus sit civitas. Quia sicut vicus constituitur ex pluribus domibus, ita et civitas ex pluribus vicis. Secundo dicit, quod civitas est communitas perfecta: quod ex hoc probat, quia cum omnis communicatio omnium hominum ordinetur ad aliquid necessarium vitae, illa erit perfecta communitas, quae ordinatur ad hoc quod homo habeat sufficienter quicquid est necessarium ad vitam: talis autem est communitas civitatis. Est enim de ratione civitatis, quod in ea inveniantur omnia quae sufficiunt ad vitam humanam, sicut contingit esse. Et propter hoc componitur ex pluribus vicis, in quorum uno exercetur ars fabrilis, in alio ars textoria, et sic de aliis. Unde manifestum est, quod civitas est communitas perfecta. Tertio ostendit ad quid est civitas ordinata: est enim primitus facta gratia vivendi, ut scilicet homines sufficienter invenirent unde vivere possent: sed ex eius esse provenit, quod homines non solum vivant, sed quod bene vivant, inquantum per leges civitatis ordinatur vita hominum ad virtutes (*Comm. Pol. I*, n. 23, http://www.corpusthomisticum.org/cpo.html). Translation in Keys, pp. 78–79.

74. *Summa theologica,* Ia, q. 96, a. 4, resp. See also De regno, lib. 1, cap. 1–2, for detailed discussion of his thoughts on this issue.

75. Ibid., IIa IIae, q. 104, a. 1, resp.

76. See also ibid., Ia, q. 109, a. 2. resp.

77. Curran, p. 70. See *Summa theologica*, Ia, q. 108, a. 1–6.

78. Regan, pp. 70–71.

79. *Summa theologica*, Ia, q. 96, a. 4.

80. Ibid., q. 92, a. 1, ad. 2.

81. 子欲善, 而民善矣。君子之德風, 小人之德草。草上之風, 必偃。Analects 12:19, in Xie, p. 204. Herbert Fingarette famously claimed that the process by which this occurred was "magical." See Fingarette, esp. pp. 3–5 for his discussion of the power of the king.

82. 有是君, 有是臣, 則有是政也。Zhu Xi's Commentary on the *Doctrine of the Mean*, chap. 20, in *Zhuzi quanshu*, vol. 6, p. 44.

83. 為政在人,家語作「為政在於得人」, 語意尤備。人, 謂賢臣。言君為政在於得人, 而取人之則又在脩身。Ibid., in *Zhuzi quanshu*, vol. 6, pp. 44–45.

84. 天下至誠, 謂聖人之德之實, 天下莫能加也。盡其性者, 德無不實, 故無人欲之私, 而天命之在我者, 察之由之, 巨細精粗, 無毫髮之不盡也。Ibid., Chapter 22, in *Zhuzi quanshu*, vol. 6, p. 50. See "Zhu Xi's Human Being: In Need of Communal Assistance" in my Chapter 2 for further discussion of this issue.

85. Tu, *Centrality and Commonality*, p. 50.

86. 天之生民, 必 有出類之才,起而君長之。治之而爭奪息, 導之而生養遂, 教之而倫理明, 然後人道立, 天道成, 地道平。 *Yulei*, chap. 3, in *Zhuzi quanshu*, vol. 13, p. 202, quoting from Cheng Yi's Commentary on the Spring and Autumn Annals (春秋傳序).

87. 是 氣 清 明 純 粹, 而 無 一 毫 昏 濁。。。不 待 學 而 能, 如 堯 舜 是 也 。Ibid., chap. 4, in *Zhuzi quanshu*, vol. 14, p. 194.

88. 必 學 而 後 知, 必 行 而 後 至 。Ibid.

89. Jiang, p. 35.

90. Tu, "The Structure and Function of the Confucian Intellectual in Ancient China," in *Way, Learning and Politics*, p. 27.

91. Ibid.

92. 能盡之者, 謂知之無不明而處之無不當也。Zhu Xi's Commentary on the *Doctrine of the Mean*, ch. 22, in *Zhuzi quanshu*, vol. 6, p. 50; italics added.

93. 聖人能使無實之人不敢盡其虛誕之辭。蓋我之明德既明, 自然有以畏服民之心志, 故訟不待聽而自無也。關於此言, 可以知本末之先後矣。Zhu Xi's *Commentary on the Great Learning*, chap. 4, in *Zhuzi quanshu*, vol. 6, p. 20.

94. 子曰: 「聽訟, 吾猶人也。必也, 使無訟乎! 」*Analects* 12.13, in Xie, p. 202.

95. Kim-chong Chong, "Autonomy in the Analects," in *The Moral Circle and the Self: Chinese and Western Approaches*, ed. Kim-chong Chong, Sor-hoon Tan, and C. L. Ten (Chicago: Open Court, 2003), p. 277. Chong points out, "this allows us to make sense of the fact that although choices can be severely restricted by poverty and adversity, paradigmatic individuals are still able to express their autonomy."

96. Hahm Chaihark, "Constitutionalism, Confucian Civic Virtue, and Ritual Propriety" in Daniel A. Bell and Hahm Chaibong, eds. *Confucianism for the Modern World* (Cambridge, UK: University of Cambridge Press, 2003), p. 33.

97. 一家仁, 一國興仁; 一家讓, 一國興讓; 一人貪戾, 一國作亂。此謂一言僨事, 一人定國。*Great Learning*, Chapter 9, in Xie, p. 13.

98. 此言教成於國之效。Zhu Xi's *Commentary on the Great Learning*, Chapter 9, in *Zhuzi quanshu*, Vol. 6, p. 23.

99. "The man [in the text] is the junzi (一人, 謂君也)" (ibid.).

100. 此三者, 上行下效, 捷於影響, 所謂家齊而國治也。亦可以見人心之所同, 而不可使有一夫之不獲矣。是以君子必當因其所同, 推以度物, 使彼我之間各得分願, 則上下四旁均齊方正, 而天下平矣。Ibid., chap. 10, in *Zhuzi quanshu*, vol. 6, p. 24. The text on which he is commenting reads: "that which is meant by 'pacifying all under heaven is in governing the nation' [is as follows]: when those above treat the old as the old should be treated, the people will flourish in filial piety, when those above treat their elders as they should be treated, the people will flourish in brotherliness, and when those above treat the helpless with compassion then the people will not be differentiated. This is the measure of the Way used by the superior person (所謂平天下在治其國者: 上老老而民興孝, 上長長而民興弟, 上恤孤而民不倍, 是以君子有絜矩之道也)" (ibid.).

101. Mark Csikszentmihalyi, "Confucianism," in *God's Rule: The Politics of World Religions*, ed. Jacob Neusner (Washington: Georgetown University Press, 2003), p. 218.

102. 仁者, 仁之本體; 禮者, 仁之節文; 義者, 仁之斷制; 知者, 仁之分別。*Yulei*, chap. 6, in *Zhuzi quanshu*, vol. 14, p. 249.

103. *Summa theologica*, IIa IIae, a. 2, resp.

104. Ibid., Ia IIae, q. 92, a. 2,ad. 3.

105. Ibid., IIa IIae, q. 64, a. 3, resp.

106. Seu forma, praelationis in omnibus bonus est: consistit enim in quodam ordine alterius tamquam regentis, et alterius tamquam subjacentis . . . simpliciter dicendum est, omnem praelationem a Deo esse. Thomas Aquinas, *Scriptum super sententiis*, Fundación Tomás de Aquino (http://www.corpusthomisticum.org), 2008–2009: lib. 2 d. 44 q. 1 a. 2 co. See note 57 in Chapter 1 about the place of the *Sentences* in the medieval curriculum.

107. Aliquas praelationes non esse a Deo: quia scilicet abusus earum non est a Deo, vel quia etiam injusta actio per quam ad praelationem pervenitur, a Deo non est. Ibid.

108. *Summa theologica*, IIa IIae, q. 153, a. 3, ad. 3.

109. Ibid., resp.

110. Ibid., a. 2, resp. See also *Compendium*, II:194: "inordinate movements of passion overflow in the lower appetites, and at the same time the light of wisdom, which divinely illuminated the human so long as his will was subjected to God, is by consequence subdued by sensible things (abundantibus enim in appetitu inferiori inordinatis motibus passionum, simul etiam et in

ratione deficiente lumine sapientiae, quo divinitus illustrabatur voluntas dum erat Deo subiecta, per consequens affectum suum rebus sensibilibus subdidit)."

111. *Summa theologica*, IIa IIae, q. 57, a. 4, resp.

112. Ibid., a. 3, ad. 2.

113. Ibid., a. 11, resp. Nor is humanly acquired prudence the only useful element in reining and redirecting human passions. See my Chapters 2 and 3 for discussions of how divine grace also plays a role in increasing wisdom and other relevant intellectual virtues through conferring theological and divinely infused virtues.

114. Ibid., a. 12, resp.

115. See ibid., Ia IIae, q. 19, esp. a. 3, 5, 6.

116. See ibid., q. 42., a. 2, ad. 3.

117. *Summa contra gentiles*, bk. III, chap. 81, sec. 4, p. 273. See also *Summa theologica*, IIa IIae, q. 104, a. 1, resp.: "in virtue of the divinely established natural order the lower natural things need to be subject to the movement of the higher." See also Ia, q. 109, a. 2, resp., in which he explains, "since action follows the nature of a thing, where natures are subordinate, actions also must be subordinate to each other."

118. *Summa contra gentiles*, bk. III, chap. 81, sec. 5, p. 273. See also ibid., chap. 78, sec. 3, p. 260. See also *Summa theologica*, Ia, q. 96, a. 4 and *Summa theologica*, Ia, q. 96, a. 4, both quoted above in this chapter.

119. Mark C. Murphy, "Consent, Custom, and the Common Good in Aquinas's Account of Political Authority," *The Review of Politics* 59, no. 2, (Spring 1997): 330–331.

120. Ibid., p. 331.

121. Ibid., p. 329.

122. Ibid., bk. I, chap. 1, sec. 1, p. 59. Quoting Aristotle's *Topics*, II, 1 (102a 30) and *Metaphysics*, I, 2 (982a 18).

123. *Summa contra gentiles*, bk. III, chap. 81, sec. 6, pp. 273–274.

124. Ibid.

125. Daniel Daly, "From Nature to Second Nature: The Relationship of Natural Law, Acquired Virtue, and Moral Precepts in Thomas Aquinas' *Summa theologiae*" (PhD diss., Boston College, 2008), p. 139.

126. *Summa theologica*, IIa IIae, q. 99, a. 1, ad. 1.

127. Ibid., q. 90, a. 2, resp.

128. Ibid., q. 96, a. 6, ad. 3.

129. Ibid., Ia IIae, q. 95, a. 2, resp.

130. Keys, p. 211.

131. *Summa theologica*, Ia IIae, q. 92, a. 2, sed contra.

132. Ibid., resp.

133. Keys, p. 211.

134. Curran, p. 70.

135. See *Summa theologica*, IIa IIae, q. 64, a. 3, resp., and q. 40, a. 1, resp.

136. Ibid., q. 45, a. 2, resp.

137. Tucker, p. 1.

138. 小德者，全體之分；大德者，萬殊之本。。。此言天地之道。Zhu Xi's Commentary on the *Doctrine of the Mean*, Chapter 28, in *Zhuzi quanshu*, vol. 6, p. 56.

139. 然後人道立, 天道成, 地道平。 Ibid., Chapter 3, in *Zhuzi quanshu*, vol. 13, p. 202, quoting from Cheng Yi's *Commentary on the Spring and Autumn Annals* (春秋傳序).

140. *Summa contra gentiles*, bk. III, chap. 64, sec. 9, p. 213.

141. Ibid., bk. III, chap. 64, sec. 9, p. 213. See also *Summa theologica*, Ia, q. 103, a. 6, resp.: "since things which are governed should be brought to perfection by government, this government will be so much the better in the degree the things governed are brought to perfection." Since one thing's perfection is not the perfection of another's, given the diversity of the created beings in the universe, order must be established between them that cooperative communal perfection may be reached.

142. Helgesen, p. 164. He is referencing the work of Zygmunt Bauman, a sociologist who studies the human consequences of globalization.

143. Regan, p. 45.

144. I am using globalization in the sense summarized by Helgesen: "increasing convergence and interdependence of national economies and of the international scope and availability of markets, distribution systems, capital, labor, and technology" (Helgesen, p. 164).

145. Letter to Christopher Tolkien, November 29, 1943, in Carpenter, pp. 63–64.

Chapter 5. Limiting Authority

1. Ayn Rand, *Atlas Shrugged* (New York: Plume, 1999), p. 974.

2. Seligman, *Modernity's Wager*, p. 39.

3. Cooley, p. 209. See "Self-Interested Actors and Selfless Comrades" in my Chapter 2 for discussion of Samuel Coleman's similar theory.

4. Brian Daley, quoted in Lisa Fullam, "The Virtue of Humility: A Reconstruction Based in Thomas Aquinas" (PhD diss., Harvard University, 2001), p. 112.

5. He Zhen, "Women's Revenge" ("女子復仇論"), translated in *Sources of Chinese Tradition, Volume Two: From 1600 to the Twentieth Century*, 2nd ed., ed. Wm. Theodore de Bary and Richard Lufrano (New York: Columbia University Press, 2001), p. 394.

6. 問: 或有孤孀貧窮無托者, 可再嫁否？ 曰: 只是後世怕寒餓死, 故有是說。然餓死事極小, 失節事極大。 *Jinsilu* 6:13, in *Zhuzi quanshu*, vol. 13, p. 229.

7. See *Jinsilu* 6:17, in *Zhuzi quanshu*, vol. 13, pp. 230–231.

8. He, p. 393.

9. Fullam 2001, p. 43.

10. Ibid., p. 113.

11. As she explains, "humility is most often used as a check to appetites that might otherwise take powerful control: the self-lowering associated with humility is best understood not as the end of the virtue itself, but as a counterbalance toward a normal human tendency to self-celebration. Humility acts to regulate the appetite of the self for self-aggrandizement. For most people in most circumstances, the task of humility in perfecting that appetite is to limit or restrain the appetite from excess" (ibid., pp. 4–5).

12. "Humility in its epistemological dimension is exactly the pursuit of a morally accurate self-understanding" (ibid., p. 136).

13. In a Screwtapian manner, Fullam sardonically raises the possibility that "[perhaps] to be truthfully humble would require that you avoid doing anything remotely praiseworthy, and that you never utilize your talents" (ibid., p. 7). In truth, however, as will be discussed further below, in the Christian tradition, "humility is about seeing and revering God's gifts in others, while not failing to recognize our own defects" (ibid., p. 53).

14. 八九岁读到《孟子》"圣人与我同类," 为成圣的希望激动得 "喜不可言"。 Chen Lai (陈来). *Zhu Xi zhexue yanjiu* (*朱熹哲学研究*) (Beijing: Zhongguo shehui kexue chubanshe (北京: 中国社会科學出版社), 1988), p. 1.

15. G. K. Chesterton, *Saint Thomas Aquinas* (New York: Sheed and Ward, Inc., 1933), pp. 56–57.

16. See note 1 of the Introduction.

17. 性只是仁義禮智。*Yulei*, chap. 4, in *Zhuzi quanshu*, vol. 14, p. 192. See "Zhu Xi and Socialization" in my Chapter 3 for a brief discussion of how Zhu's account of the virtues differs from Mencius's.

18. 仁木, 義金, 禮火, 智水, 信土。Ibid., chap. 6, in *Zhuzi quanshu*, vol. 14, p. 243.

19. 或問 : 「仁義禮智, 性之四德, 又添『信』字, 謂之『五性』, 如何 ? 」曰: 「信是誠實此四。」Ibid., chap. 6, in *Zhuzi quanshu*, vol. 14, p. 243.

20. See *Yulei*, chap. 6, in *Zhuzi quanshu*, vol. 14.

21. 子曰: 「中庸其至矣乎! 民鮮能久矣! 」*Doctrine of the Mean*, chap. 3, in Xie, p. 25.

22. 子曰: 「道之不行也, 我知之矣: 知者過之, 愚者不及也。道之不明也, 我知之矣: 賢者過之, 不肖者不及也。」Ibid., Chapter 5, in Xie, p. 25.

23. 子貢問: 「師與商也孰賢? 」子曰: 「師也過, 商也不及。」曰: 「然則師愈與? 」子曰: 「過猶不及。」*Analects* 11:15, in Xie, p. 187.

24. 必學而後知, 必行而後至。 *Yulei*, chap. 4, in *Zhuzi quanshu*, vol. 14, p. 194.

25. Tu, "Pain and Suffering in Confucian Self-Cultivation," in *Way, Learning, and Politics*, p. 55.

26. 子曰: 「君子義以為質, 禮以行之, 孫以出之, 信以成之。君子哉! 」*Analects* 15.17, in Xie, p. 248. Italics added.

27. *Doctrine of the Mean*, Chapter 13, in Xie, p. 32.

28. Jane Geaney, "Guarding Moral Boundaries: Shame in Early Confucianism," *Philosophy East and West* 54, No. 2, (Apr., 2004): 113.

29. Ibid., p. 133.

30. [君子] 居上不驕。 *Doctrine of the Mean*, chap. 27, in Xie, p. 53.

31. Joseph Chan, "Confucian Attitudes Toward Ethical Pluralism," p. 124. See Virginia Suddath, "Ought We Throw the Confucian Baby Out With the Bathwater?: A Critical Inquiry into Lu Xun's Anti-Confucian Identity," in *Confucian Cultures of Authority, ed.* Peter D. Hershock and Roger T. Ames (Albany: State University of New York Press, 2006), p. 224, for a similar argument.

32. 朱子曰: '存一份天理, 去一份人欲。' *此语是针对士大夫而言, 非对一般百姓。因为士大夫是未来的政治社会领袖的, 必须了解利、义之分。* 朱子的这一段话并不要老百姓不要 "利," 不要吃饭, 而是针对士大夫说的。 Yü Ying-shih, *Xiandai ruxue*, p. 69; italics added.

33. Pei-Yi Wu, "Self-Examination and Confession of Sins in Traditional China," *Harvard Journal of Asiatic Studies* 39, no. 1 (Jun., 1979): 15.

34. 鄭問「何有於我哉」。曰: 「此語難說。聖人是自謙, 言我不曾有此數者。聖人常有慊然不足之意。衆人雖見他是仁之至熟, 義之至精, 它只管自見得有欠闕處。」 *Yulei*, chap. 34, in *Zhuzi quanshu*, vol. 15, p. 1205.

35. A. S. Cua, "Li and Moral Justification: A Study in the Li Chi," *Philosophy East and West* 33, no. 1 (Jan., 1983): 5, http://www.jstor.org

36. A compatible reading of humility is put forward by Norvin Richards, who muses, "never to appreciate one's good qualities might conceivably be endearing, like a tendency to get flustered easily, but for it to be morally estimable is something else again" (Norvin Richards, "Is Humility a Virtue?" *American Philosophical Quarterly*, vol. 25, No. 3 [Jul., 1988], 253). Richards, who does consider it to be morally estimable, goes on to note: "very often, it might be the hero who is right to think our reaction excessive, rather than we who are right to think him too modest. Perhaps he knows better than we how hard or easy the deed was for him, or what his motivation was, or how clearly he understood what he was doing. (He needn't be particularly articulate about these things in order to be in that position—he knows by having been the one who did it.) . . . Those who truly are underestimating themselves aren't expressing humility, on my view, but those who simply reject attention certainly can be" (Richards, pp. 256–257).

37. 火 中 有 黑, 陽 中 陰 也。。。 陰 以 陽 為 質, 陽 以 陰 為 質 。 水 內 明 而 外 暗, 火 內 暗 而 外 明 。 *Yulei*, chap. 1, in *Zhuzi quanshu*, vol. 14, p. 125.

38. 看來夫子平日不曾如此說, 往往多謙抑, 與此不同。」先生笑云: 「此卻是真箇事急了, 不覺說將出來。」 Ibid., chap. 36, in *Zhuzi quanshu*, vol. 15,p. 1333.

39. 天下未嘗有性外之物。仁則為慈愛之類; 義則為剛斷之類; 禮則為謙遜; 智則為明辨 。Ibid., chap. 20, in *Zhuzi quanshu*, vol. 14, p. 705.

40. 問: 「或人問伊川曰: 『「孝弟為仁之本」, 此是由孝弟可以至仁否?』伊川曰: 『非也。』不知如何。」曰: 「仁不可言至。仁者, 義理之言, 不是地位之言, 地位則可以言至。又不是孝弟在這裏, 仁在那裏, 便由孝弟以至仁, 無此理。。。程先生便只說道: 『盡得仁, 斯盡得孝弟; 盡得孝弟, 便是仁。』又曰: 『孝弟, 仁之一事。』」Ibid., chap. 6, in *Zhuzi quanshu*, vol. 14, p. 256.

41. 皆作「衣錦尚絅」。古之學者為己, 故其立心如此。衣錦, 故有日常之實。淺, 簡, 温, 絅之襲於外也, 不厭而文且理焉, 錦之美在中也。小人反是, 此暴於外而無實以繼之。Zhu Xi's Commentary on *Doctrine of the Mean*, chap. 33, in *Zhuzi quanshu*, vol. 6, pp. 57–58.

42. Sara Rushing has a complementary reading: that humility is a "disposition of strength" in that it frees up energy that might be have been spent in self-promotion for the development and exercise of social and political virtues. See Rushing, "What is Confucian Humility?" in Stephen Angle and Michael Slote, eds., *Virtue Ethics and Confucianism* (New York: Routledge, 2013), pp. 173–181.

43. François Jullien, "The Chinese Notion of 'Blandness' as a Virtue: A Preliminary Outline," trans. Graham Parkes, *Philosophy East and West*, 43, No. 1, (Jan., 1993): 107.

44. Tu, "The Way, Learning and Politics in Classical Confucianism," in *Way, Learning, and Politics*, p. 6.

45. Cua makes somewhat of the same point, but in language I do not use: "humility may be regarded as a general Confucian virtue" (Cua, "Li and Moral Justification," p. 5).

46. *Summa theologica*, IIa IIae, q. 81, a. 1.

47. Ibid., q. 151, a. 1.

48. Ibid., q. 30, a. 3.

49. For example, for a discussion of how he departs from Aristotle's notion that one should not feel pity toward the blameworthy, see Anthony Keaty, "The Christian Virtue of Mercy: Aquinas' Transformation of Aristotelian Pity," *Heythrop Journal*, 46 (2005): 181–198.

50. *Summa theologica*, IIa IIae, q. 161, a. 1, obj. 5.

51. Ibid., ad. 5.

52. Fullam, p. 161.

53. Ibid., p. 141.

54. *Summa theologica*, IIa IIae, q. 129, a. 3, ad. 4.

55. Ibid.

56. Fullam, p. 206.

57. Ibid., p. 237.

58. *Summa theologica*, Ia IIae, q. 94, a. 4, resp.

59. While Aristotle's texts were largely unavailable in early medieval Europe, they were highly influential in Muslim philosophy during the same period. The recovery of Aristotle in the Latin West in the period immediately before and during Thomas's lifetime was in great part due to the role Muslim scholars played in preserving and promoting the Aristotelian corpus.

60. Ibid., ad. 3.

61. Ibid., IIa IIae, q. 129, a. 3, ad. 4.

62. Ibid., q. 161, a. 1, ad. 3.

63. Ibid., q. 129, a. 6, ad. 1. N.B.: the translation of the Dominican Fathers has "since man is naturally a social animal, for he is sufficient by himself to provide for his own life," which seems to be a typographical error: I have added the "not" as the original Latin reads "quia homo est naturaliter animal sociale, eo quod sibi *non* sufficit ad vitam."

64. Ibid., q. 21, a. 1. Against Thomas, Fullam believes that presumption consists in "defective humility" as opposed to defective magnanimity, arguing provocatively—and persuasively—that Thomas's own personal shortcomings led him to his contrary thesis: "Magnanimity to excess, I suggest, involves rather an inordinate connection to a particular gift: one example of magnanimity to excess is workaholism: a successful workaholic takes a single capacity and subsumes the rest of his or her life to that gift. . . . The gift, in such a case, controls the person, rather than the person using the gift. Thomas did not recognize this as a vice—he also (at least apparently) worked himself to death" (Fullam, p. 181).

65. Keys, p. 156.

66. See *Summa theologica*, IIa IIae, q. 145, a. 1, as well as Ibid., Ia IIae, q. 65, a. 1, sed contra and resp. for his position that all of the virtues are interconnected and mutually dependent.

67. Fullam, p. 132.

68. Ibid., p. 136.

69. For citations of such studies, see Rowatt, Wade C., Alison Ottenbreit, K. Paul Messelroade, Jr., Paige A. Cunningham, "On Being Holier-Than-Thou or Humbler-Than-Thee: A Social Psychological Perspective on Religiousness and Humility," in *Journal for the Scientific Study of Religion*, vol. 42, no. 2 (Jun., 2002): 228.

70. [君子之道]及其至也，雖聖人亦有所不知 焉。*Doctrine of the Mean*, chap. 12, in Xie, p. 30.

71. 聖人與天地同體。Zhu Xi's Commentary on the *Doctrine of the Mean*, chap. 26, in *Zhuzi quanshu*, vol. 6, p. 52.

72. 聖人與天地同用。Ibid., in *Zhuzi quanshu*, vol. 6, p. 52. As discussed elsewhere, one who is not of the same substance and function as Heaven and Earth is not a sage. To go back to the ancient era for evidence of similar thinking, Confucius's famous doctrine of the rectification of names provides a formulation of this same basic principle: "if names are not rectified, then what is said cannot be followed. If what is said cannot be followed, then work cannot be carried out. If work is not carried out, then ritual and music will not flourish. If ritual and music do not flourish, then criminal punishments will not be suitable. If criminal punishments are not suitable, the people will not [know how to] direct hand or foot. Therefore, the superior person will [use] names that can be spoken, and his speech will accord with his actions (名不正，則言不順；言不順，則事不成；事不成，則禮樂不興；禮樂不興，則刑罰不中；刑罰不中，則民無所措手足。故君子名之必可言也，言之必 可行也)" (*Analects* 13.3, in Xie, p. 208).

73. 《詩》云: 「穆穆文王, 於緝熙敬止! 」為人君, 止於仁; 為人臣, 止於敬; 為人子, 止於孝; 為人父, 止於慈; 與國人交, 止於信。*Great Learning*, chap. 3, in Xie, p. 6.

74. 引此而言聖人之止, 無非止善。五者乃其目之大者也。學者於此, 究其精微之蘊, 而又推類以盡其餘, 則於天下之事, 皆有以知其所止而無疑矣。Zhu Xi's Commentary on the *Great Learning*, chap. 3, in *Zhuzi quanshu*, vol. 6, p. 19.

75. 子曰: 「吾十有五而志於學, 三十而立, 四十而不惑, 五十而知天命, 六十而耳順, 七十而從心所欲, 不踰矩。」*Analects* 2:4, in Xie, p. 75.

76. *Summa theologica*, IIa IIae, q. 163, a. 1, resp.

77. Ibid., a. 2, resp.

78. Ibid., IIa IIae, q. 2, a. 6, resp.

79. Pinckaers, p. 21.

80. *Summa theologica*, Ia IIae, q. 2, a. 8, ad. 1.

81. Ibid., q. 1, a. 7, resp.

82. Ibid., q. 3, a. 8, ad. 2. See also *Compendium*, I:106: "we will never understand God as He understands Himself . . . His brilliance and truth are infinite, while our intellect is finite (non comprehendamus ipsum sicut ipse se comprehendit . . . eius claritas seu veritas sit infinita, intellectus autem noster finitus).

83. *Summa theologica*, IIa IIae, q. 161, a. 1, resp.

84. Ibid., a. 2, resp.

85. See ibid., q. 2, a. 4, ad. 1: "The researches of natural reason do not suffice mankind for the knowledge of Divine matters, even of those that can be proved by reason." See also *Compendium, II*:8: "knowledge of God's glory and goodness cannot come to men except through the grace of divine Revelation (cognitio divinae magnitudinis et bonitatis hominibus provenire non potest nisi per gratiam revelationis divinae)."

86. 子曰: 「三人行, 必有我師焉: 擇其善者而從之, 其不善者而改之。」*Analects* 7:21, in Xie, p. 141.

87. 人多以老成则不肯下问, 故终身不知"。*Jinsilu* 2:98, in *Zhuzi quanshu*, vol. 13, p. 190.

88. Stephen C. Angle, *Sagehood: The Contemporary Significance of Neo-Confucian Philosophy* (Oxford, UK: Oxford University Press, 2009).

89. Tu, "The Structure and Function of the Confucian Intellectual in Ancient China," in *Way, Learning, and Politics*, p. 26.

90. 子曰: 「參乎! 吾道一以貫之。」曾子曰: 「唯。」子出。門人問曰: 「何謂也? 」曾子曰: 「夫子之道, 忠恕而已矣」*Analects* 4:15, in Xie, 102.

91. 如不欲上之無禮於我, 則必以此度下之心, 而以不敢以此無禮使之。不欲下之無忠於我, 則必以此度上之心, 而以不敢以此不忠事也。至於前後左右, 無不皆然, 則身之所處, 上下四旁, 長短廣狹, 彼此如一, 而無不方矣。Zhu Xi's *Commentary on the Great Learning*, chap. 10, in *Zhuzi quanshu*, vol. 6, p. 24. The chapter on which he is commenting reads as follows: "What a man hates in those above him, let him not display in the treatment of his

inferiors; what he dislikes in inferiors, let him not display in the service of his superiors; what he hates in those who are before him, let him not therewith lead those behind him; what he hates in those who are behind him, let him not bestow on those whom he follows; what he hates to receive on the left, let him not bestow on the right; what he hates on the right, let him not bestow on the left: this is what is called 'the measuring square with which to regulate one's conduct' (所惡於上, 毋以使下; 所惡於下, 毋以事上; 所惡於前, 毋以先後; 所惡於後, 毋以從前; 所惡於右, 毋以交於左; 所惡於左, 毋以交於右。此之謂絜矩之道)" (*Great Learning*, chap. 10, in Xie, 15).

92. Kevin Shun-Kai Cheng, "The Social Dimension of Liberation in Early Confucian Tradition" in *Ching Feng*, 36, nos. 2–3 (1993): p. 67.

93. Terry Woo, "Confucianism and Feminism" in *Feminism and World Religions*, ed. Arvind Sharma and Katherine K. Young (Albany: State University of New York Press, 1999), p. 115. A feminist scholar, Woo adds, "Confucius could not have supported infanticide, and bound feet would not have been accepted."

94. "The way has its beginnings in the relation between women and men (君子之道, 造端乎夫婦)" (*Doctrine of the Mean*, chap. 12, in Xie, p. 30).

95. 夫婦之愚, 可以與之焉。。。夫婦之不肖, 可以能行焉。*Doctrine of the Mean*, chap. 12, in Xie, p. 30.

96. Tu, "The Confucian Sage: Exemplar of Personal Knowledge," in *Way, Learning, and Politics*, p. 29.

97. Lk 10:21.

98. Chesterton, *Saint Thomas Aquinas*, p. 37.

99. *Summa contra gentiles*, bk. I, chap. 4, sec. 3–6, pp. 66–68.

100. Nichols, p. 97.

101. Ibid., pp. 96–97.

102. *Summa theologica*, Ia IIae, q. 58, a. 4, ad. 2.

103. Ibid., IIa IIae, q. 161, a. 3, ad. 2.

104. Keys, p. 162.

105. Josef Pieper, *The Four Cardinal Virtues* (Notre Dame, IN: University of Notre Dame Press, 1968), p. 98.

106. See *Summa theologica*, IIa IIae, q. 50, a. 1, ad. 2.

107. Fullam, p. 187.

108. Ibid., p. 168.

109. Ibid., pp. 221–222.

110. 賊仁者謂之賊, 賊義者謂之殘; 殘賊之人, 謂之一夫。聞誅一夫紂矣。未聞弒君也。Mencius 1B8, in Xie, pp. 343–344.

111. Csikszentmihalyi, p. 229.

112. 道得眾則得國, 失眾則失國。*Great Learning*, chap. 10, in Xie, 15.

113. 有天下者, 能存此心而不失, 則所以而與民同欲者。 Zhu Xi's *Commentary on the Great Learning*, chap. 10, in *Zhuzi quanshu*, vol. 6, p. 25.

114. 好善而惡惡, 人之性也。 Zhu Xi's *Commentary on the Great Learning*, chap. 10, in *Zhuzi quanshu*, vol. 6, p. 26.

115. For further discussion of this issue, see Jongryn Mo, "The Challenge of Accountability," in *Confucianism for the Modern World, ed.* Daniel A. Bell and Hahm Chaibong (Cambridge, UK: University of Cambridge Press, 2003), p. 56.

116. Suddath, p. 223. A similar set of practices and values was to be found in imperial Korea, where the role of censor, or advisor to the king, was both multi-faceted and prominent. For a discussion of the censor's responsibilities, and the implications of his sometimes spotty success rate in influencing government policy, see Mo, esp. pp. 58–60.

117. For a discussion of the ruler as judged by responsive performance rather than by holding fast to a rigidly conceived mandate, see Tu, "The Way, Learning and Politics in Classical Confucianism," in *Way, Learning, and Politics*, p. 6.

118. Ibid. Indeed, as Tu points out, "to use Confucianism as a mechanism for social control turned out to be a double-edged sword for the Han regime. The establishment of the authority of the ruler, the father and the husband may have been an effective way to ensure the stability of the society under the domination of autocracy and patriarchy. Yet the Confucian ideology, with its emphasis on exemplary teaching and mutual responsibility, also required that the ruler live up to the ideal of kingship, that the father live up to the ideal of fatherhood, and that the husband also live up to the ideal of householder" (Tu, "The Structure and Function of the Confucian Intellectual in Ancient China," in *Way, Learning, and Politics*, p. 27).

119. Regan, p. 39. See Daly, p. 47, for a similar argument.

120. Ibid., p. 43.

121. *Summa contra gentiles*, bk. III, chap. 69, sec. 16, p. 230.

122. *Summa theologica*, Ia IIae, q. 92, a. 1, ad. 4.

123. Ibid., q. 96, a. 4, resp.

124. Defectum in ipso modo acquirendi, quia scilicet per violentiam vel per simoniam, vel aliquo illicito modo acquirit. *Scriptum super sententiis*, lib. 2 d. 44 q. 2 a. 2 co.

125. Qui enim per violentiam dominium surripit non efficitur vere praelatus vel dominus; et ideo cum facultas adest, potest aliquis tale dominium repellere. Ibid.

126. *Summa theologica*, Ia IIae, q. 105, a. 1, ad. 1.

127. Ibid.

128. Ibid.

129. Ibid., IIa IIae, q. 42, a. 1, resp.

130. See Ibid., Ia, q. 96, a. 4, and Ia, q. 92, a. 1, ad. 2.

131. Si ad ius multitudinis alicuius pertineat sibi providere de rege, non iniuste ab eadem rex institutus potest destitui vel refrenari eius potestas, si potestate regia tyrannice abutatur. Nec putanda est talis multitudo infideliter agere tyrannum destituens, etiam si eidem in perpetuo se ante subiecerat: quia hoc ipse meruit, in multitudinis regimine se non fideliter gerens ut exigit regis officium, quod ei pactum a subditis non reservetur. *De regno*, lib. 1, cap. 7.

132. McInerny, *Ethica thomistica*, p. 66.

133. Wing-tsit Chan, "Chu Hsi's Appraisal of Lao Tzu," *Philosophy East and West* 25, no. 2 (Apr., 1975): 132.

134. *Summa theologica*, IIa IIae, q. 129, a. 3, ad. 4.

135. Fullam, p. 116.

136. Other people are approaching the virtue of humility in complementary ways. For example, Mark Button seeks to recast humility, with its traditionally religious overtones, as a fundamentally political and social virtue that can be embraced by people from different faith traditions in pluralistic societies, arguing that "humility needs to be reconceived as an active, other-regarding civic virtue and public ethos, and not as an interior, self-referencing quality indexed to an external standard of the good or a singular scale of value. Thus, I define democratic humility as a cultivated sensitivity toward the incompleteness and contingency of both one's personal moral powers and commitments, and of the particular forms, laws and institutions that structure one's political and social life with others" (Mark Button, "A Monkish Kind of Virtue? For and against Humility," in *Political Theory*, vol. 33, no. 6 (Dec. 2005): 841.

137. Keys, pp. 98–99.

Conclusion. The Virtue of Humble Authority

1. Moreover, we tend to distrust people who wholly identify themselves with one pursuit or role; see the "Roles" section in Chapter 3 for a brief discussion of this issue.

2. Michael Sandel, *What Money Can't Buy: The Moral Limits of Markets* (New York: Farrar, Strauss and Giroux, 2012).

3. See Wilson's *The Social Conquest of Earth* (New York: Norton Press, 2012), Haidt's *The Righteous Mind: Why Good People Are Divided by Politics and Religion* (New York: Pantheon Books, 2012), and Douthat's *Bad Religion: How We Became a Nation of Heretics* (New York: Simon and Schuster, 2012).

4. Alain de Botton, *Religion for Atheists: A Non-believer's Guide to the Uses of Religion* (New York: Pantheon Books, 2012), p. 279.

5. Ibid., p. 18.

6. De Botton is well aware of this problem, and his solution is practical or functional. Throughout his book, he draws the attention of the more skeptical members of his readership to what he considers to be the matchless efficiency and endurance of religious institutions.

7. Quoted in Timothy Radcliffe, O. P., *What is the Point of Being a Christian?* (New York: Burns and Oats, 2005), p. 121. The novelist Marilynne Robinson would agree: "There was a time when people felt as if structure in most forms were a constraint and they attacked it, which in a culture is like an autoimmune problem: the organism is not allowing itself the conditions of its own existence. We're cultural creatures and meaning doesn't simply generate

itself out of thin air; it's sustained by a cultural framework. It's like deciding how much more interesting it would be if you had no skeleton: you could just slide under the door" (Marilynne Robinson, interview with *Paris Review*).

8. Luke 16:19–31.

9. James Keenan, *Moral Wisdom: Lessons and Texts from the Catholic Tradition* (New York: Sheed and Ward, 2004), 51–52.

10. See Matthew 26:73–75, Mark 14:66–72, Luke 22:54–62, and John 18:13–27.

11. Matthew 16:18.

12. Michael Nylan and Thomas Wilson, *Lives of Confucius: Civilization's Greatest Sage Throughout the Ages* (New York: Doubleday, 2010), p. 3.

13. Ibid.

14. *Analects*, 5:11.

15. Ibid., 6:8.

16. Tu Weiming makes a similar case in his discussion of human perception and cognition, urging his readers to recognize the several components of human intelligence, each uniquely important in its own right: "data is simply not the same as information, information is simply not the same as knowledge, and knowledge is not the same as wisdom (材料(datum) 決不等同于信息, 信息決不等同于知識, 知識又不等同于智慧)" (Tu Weiming (杜維明), "史華慈叙事的人文主義視界 在纪念史华慈追思会上的讲话 (Shi Huaci xushide renwenzhuyi shijie zai jinian Shi Huaci nianhui zhuisihuishangde jianghua)," 世界汉学 (*World Sinology*) January 2003 (2003年 01期): 98, http://cnki.net. In this paean to his former teacher, Benjamin Schwartz, Tu does not see a problem with new methods of interacting with the world per se, but rather with the way in which they have effectively replaced earlier approaches: "as computers opened up completely different methods of communication and storing knowledge, they prioritized these forms of experience and knowledge. [In this new situation, it seems] the printed word must be more efficacious than face-to-face communication; quantifiable data must be more obviously important than narrative; and the methods of individuals who make judgments and decide issues on their own must be treasured more than the wisdom of elders. According to Benjamin Schwartz's way of thinking, these statements can all be problematical. Benjamin Schwartz tells us that the methods of narrative, [of listening to the] elderly, of face-to-face communication and contextualized knowledge—the methods of concrete knowledge—are vibrant (隨着計算機開發出了截然不同的溝通與信息存儲方式, 它們強化了這種經驗與知識的形式: 印刷文字要比面對面的交流更有效力, 數據要比叙事顯重要, 以個人為中心的判斷與解決問題的要比年長著的智慧更爲寶貴; 按照史華慈的想法, 這些説法都可以質疑的 (problematical) 。史華慈向我們講説, 叙 事, 長者, 面對面的交流與語境化的認知方法 (具體化的認知方式) 是有活力的)" (ibid.).

17. William Scott Green, "Introduction: Religion and Politics: A Volatile Mix" in Neusner, Jacob, ed. *God's Rule: The Politics of World Religions* (Washington: Georgetown University Press, 2003), p. 2.

18. The accuracy of Seligman's reading is supported by the fact that the language of rights is so pervasive—and persuasive—in American society, so much so that it is a truism that Americans feel entitled to choose their own happiness, and how best to pursue it, on their own terms. Such persons are liable to exercise obedience—to law, custom, or other people—as a tactic rather than a virtue, and to conceive of authority as virtuous in inverse proportion to its exercise.

19. Seligman, *Modernity's Wager*, p. 63. Philip Rieff's reading of the process of secularization is compatible with Seligman's. From Rieff's more Freudian point of view, what arises in secularized society is "therapeutic man," who "no longer believes he is suffering from sin, but from the disease of too elevated a faith" (Rieff, "For the Last Time Psychology!" p. 360). Such a person may well seek a quasi-medical, practical set of relations with the world, seeking for more therapeutically effective positions and outcomes for him- or herself. On the other hand, Jeffrey Stout offers the wholly alternative case that secularization is not an inherently irreligious process (see Stout, especially pp. 97–99, for his argument that secularization merely removes the assumption that everyone has the same religious views, rather than the views themselves). Such an argument is intriguing, but leaves untouched the issue of the universality and claimed objectivity of many religious truth claims, and how these may be threatened—or be perceived to be threatened—by an explicitly pluralistic environment. While recognizing that some of the claims discussed here are simply incompatible, this book seeks to identify points of congruence and contact between two great traditions, and to avoid conflating either tradition into the other.

20. Seligman, *Modernity's Wage*, p. 85. On a similar note, Rieff points out: "a man can be made healthier without being made better—rather, morally worse. Not the good life but better living is the Freudian standard" (Philip Rieff, "Reflections on Psychological Man in America," in *The Feeling Intellect*, p. 7).

21. Fullam, p. 223, n. 52. She draws attention to James Keenan's proposed new list of cardinal virtues—of justice, prudence, fidelity and self-care—as an example of this latter tendency.

22. Yearley, "Two Strands of Confucianism," p. 139.

23. Ibid., p. 140.

24. Wm. Theodore de Bary, "Epilogue: Why Confucius Now?" in *Confucianism for the Modern World*, ed. Daniel A. Bell and Hahm Chaibong (Cambridge, UK: University of Cambridge Press, 2003), p. 367.

25. Keys, p. 237. She asks the question: "Should politics, understood as humans' own government, be suffused with pride in human virtue, or should it be humbled by the realization of human dependence on God and interdependence with others?" (p. 143). Answering it in a very Thomistic way, she says, "reflection on the totalitarian experiences of the twentieth century reveals the humanity and nobility of a magnanimity informed by humility" (p. 144).

26. *Summa theologica*, IIa IIae, q. 50, a. 1, ad. 2.

27. Curran, p. 81.

28. Abraham Cohen, *Everyman's Talmud: The Major Teachings of the Rabbinic Sages* (New York: Schocken Books, 1995), p. 212.

29. Ibid., p. 249.

30. G. K. Chesterton, *Heretics* (1919; Gutenberg.org: Project Gutenberg, 2008), chap. 3, http://www.gutenberg.org/files/470/470-h/470-h.htm

31. "'Blessed are Thou, O Lord our God, King of the Universe, Who hast formed man in wisdom and created in him many orifices and vessels. It is revealed and known before the Throne of Thy Glory, that if one of these be opened, or one of those closed, it would be impossible to exist and stand before Thee. Blessed art Thou, O Lord, Who healest all flesh and doest wondrously'" (Quoting Ber. 60b, in Cohen, p. 243).

32. Ibid., p. 375.

33. Former Master of the Order of Preachers (Dominicans) Timothy Radcliffe makes a similar point about our deeply entrenched faith in the rational/empiricist principles and skeptical values of the Enlightenment. While Radcliffe is certainly not advocating a rejection of this modern tradition of thought, he is uneasy about people's often unskeptical acceptance of its fundamental assumptions: "our society understands truth almost exclusively in terms of the tradition of the Enlightenment . . . It is hard to identify this tradition because it colours all that we say. The ruling ideology is, Alain de Botton writes, 'like a colourless, odourless gas' which saturates the atmosphere and which we inhale at every moment without noticing" (Radcliffe, 119–120). The work of Charles Taylor, John Milbank, and others to make us more aware of the intellectual air we breathe is important in helping us to understand more clearly the kinds of biases that influence even our efforts at unbiased thinking. On the Confucian side, the work of Tu Weiming calls our attention to the problems of the anthropomorphic worldview associated with Western modernity, and our tendency to equate data with knowledge (see note 16 above for more discussion of this latter trend).

34. Nor is this reductionist vision limited to those who work in the physical sciences: there is also a popular movement to understand everything from an economic point of view. See Sandel, *What Money Can't Buy*, esp. pp. i-I.

35. Dennis Wrong, "The Oversocialized Conception of Man in Modern Sociology," in *American Sociological Review* 26, no. 2 (Apr., 1961): 190.

36. For example, a common trope of popular movies is the gradual awakening of a work-obsessed protagonist to the value of love, friendship, and family, and the promise of his or her development into a more well-rounded person.

37. A similar case can be made for a liberal arts education, which is currently under fire for not being directly linked to earning power. In this era of exploding higher education costs and an imploding economy, many parents are asking, what in the world does a degree in medieval French poetry, or in the sociology of knowledge, have to do with getting a job upon graduation? Responding to this trend that prioritizes the natural sciences, particularly the applied sciences which help to produce new technology, over all other intel-

lectual concerns, William Deresiewicz writes: "Indeed, technology creates the future. But it is not enough to create the future. We also need to organize it, as the social sciences enable us to do. We need to make sense of it, as the humanities enable us to do" ("Faulty Towers: The Crisis in Higher Education," *The Nation*, http://www.thenation.com/article/160410/faulty-towers-crisis-higher-education?page=full, May 23, 2011; accessed July 25, 2011).

38. So, for example, we find the Archbishop of Canterbury working to accommodate people with different social values in the Anglican church. When confronted with the question of whether he is paying "too high a price for keeping together people who believe different things about gender, priesthood and sexuality" together in one communion, replies, "I've no sympathy for that view. I don't want to see the church so balkanised that we talk only to people we like and agree with" (David Hare, "Rowan Williams, God's Boxer," for the archbishop of Canterbury's statements with regard to this issue (*The Guardian*, http://www.guardian.co.uk/uk/2011/jul/08/rowan-williams-interview-david-hare, July 8, 2011; accessed July 11, 2011). In a similar vein, see Eli Pariser's TED talk on the dangers of the customized Internet experience (http://www.ted.com/talks/eli_pariser_beware_online_filter_bubbles.html; posted May 2011, accessed May 31, 2012), or, for a more in-depth discussion of technologically encouraged close-mindedness, see Jeffrey Stout's *Democracy and Tradition* (esp. p. 114).

39. Suddath, p. 220.

40. Rosemont, "Two Loci of Authority: Autonomous Individuals and Related Persons," in *Confucian Cultures of Authority*, pp. 18–19. He adds in a stinging critique, "rather does the wrongness lie in the belief that we—especially in the United States—are already fully in the possession of those values in the proper order, and therefore feel justified, backed by superior economic might and a military juggernaut, in foisting that particular order on everyone else."

41. Nor are they the only two figures who may be put into fruitful conversation on such issues. For those who do not subscribe and do not wish to subscribe to the fundamental assumptions of Thomas and/or Zhu, I note here that this discussion has also made room for other views to be added to the mix by asking the formal, fairly bare, questions raised in the Introduction—with more time and space, the harmony developed here could become very complex indeed.

42. See, for example, *Summa Theologica*, Ia, q. 71, obj. 1 and ad. 1, as well as q. 84, a. 4, resp.

43. See, for example, ibid., q. 88, a. 1, obj. 4 and ad. 4, as well as Ia, q. 4, a. 2, resp.

44. 義理儘無窮, 前人恁地說, 亦未必盡。 *Yulei*, chap. 9, in *Zhuzi quanshu*, vol. 14, p. 309.

45. Herbert McCabe, *God, Christ and Us*, Brian Davies, O. P., ed. (New York: Continuum, 2003), p. 11. The sermon in question was delivered in 1986 (see p. x of the Introduction).

46. William Scott Green makes a similar point: "religions exhibit a tendency to totalize, to extend their reach to all dimensions of experience. [They]

come to expression not only in speech and writing, but also in art, music, and dance, in smell and taste, in ethics and intellect. They have cosmologies (stories of the origin of the world) and eschatologies (stories of the end of the world), theories of nature, birth, morality, sexuality, marriage, suffering, and death. The comprehensiveness of religion allows it to touch all the transition points of life, both collective and individual" (Green, p. 2).

47. Madeleine L'Engle, *And It Was Good: Reflections on Beginnings* (Wheaton, IL: Harold Shaw Publishers, 1983), p. 26.

48. Rom 8:22.

49. President Barack Obama's first inaugural speech provides an example of humble authority that's explicitly open to all (see http://www.cnn.com/2009/POLITICS/01/20/obama.politics/index.html for the text). His speech began with the words, "I stand here today humbled by the task before us." Such humility was accompanied by unabashedly authoritative proclamations about the tasks facing Americans all throughout the country: "Starting today, we must pick ourselves up, dust ourselves off, and begin again the work of remaking America. For everywhere we look, there is work to be done. The state of the economy calls for action, bold and swift, and we will act—not only to create new jobs, but to lay a new foundation for growth. We will build the roads and bridges, the electric grids and digital lines that feed our commerce and bind us together. We will restore science to its rightful place, and wield technology's wonders to raise health care's quality and lower its cost. We will harness the sun and the winds and the soil to fuel our cars and run our factories. And we will transform our schools and colleges and universities to meet the demands of a new age. All this we can do. And all this we will do." The two themes of humility and authority came together in his reflection on those far away and those who came before him, as he called on his listeners to boldly engage in *service to a cause*: "as we consider the road that unfolds before us, we remember with humble gratitude those brave Americans who, at this very hour, patrol far-off deserts and distant mountains. They have something to tell us today, just as the fallen heroes who lie in Arlington whisper through the ages. We honor them not only because they are guardians of our liberty, but because they embody the spirit of service; a willingness to find meaning in something greater than themselves. And yet, at this moment—a moment that will define a generation—it is precisely this spirit that must inhabit us all." Significantly, he was careful to reach out to the un- or a-religious: "we are a nation of Christians and Muslims, Jews and Hindus—and nonbelievers." This speech crystallizes many of the attributes of humble authority: realistic about the difficulties of the tasks at hand, and open to the messages that may be taught by others, Obama stated his goals and his instructions without reservation, and invited all people of all and no religious persuasions to join him.

50. Taylor, *A Secular Age*, p. 727. On the same note, he muses, "the secular age is schizophrenic, or better, deeply cross-pressured. People seem at

a safe distance from religion; and yet they are very moved to know that there are dedicated believers, like Mother Teresa . . . It's as though many people who don't want to follow want nevertheless to hear the message of Christ, want it to be proclaimed out there . . . Such are the strange and complex conditions of belief in our age" (ibid.).

Bibliography

Aertsen, Johannes Adrianus. *Nature and Creatures: Thomas Aquinas' Way of Thought*. Brill Academic Publishers, 1997.

Alighieri, Dante. *The Divine Comedy*. Translated by C. H. Sisson, and edited, with introduction, by David H. Higgins. Oxford, UK: Oxford University Press, 1998.

Ames, Roger T. "*Li* and the A-theistic Religiousness of Classical Confucianism." In *Confucian Spirituality: Volume One* (Volume 11A of *World Spirituality: An Encyclopedia of the Religious Quest*), edited by Tu Weiming and Mary Evelyn Tucker, 165–182. New York: The Crossroad Publishing Company, 2003.

Angle, Stephen C. *Sagehood: The Contemporary Significance of Neo-Confucian Philosophy*. Oxford, UK: Oxford University Press, 2009.

Aquinas, Thomas. *Compendium theologiae*. http://www.corpusthomisticum.org, Fundación Tomás de Aquino, 2008–2009. http://www.corpusthomisticum.org/iopera.html

Aquinas, Thomas. *De regno ad regem Cypri*. http://www.corpusthomisticum.org, Fundación Tomás de Aquino, 2008–2009. http://www.corpusthomisticum.org/iopera.html

Aquinas, Thomas. *De veritate*. http://www.corpusthomisticum.org, Fundación Tomás de Aquino, 2008–2009. http://www.corpusthomisticum.org/iopera.html

Aquinas, Thomas. *Scriptum super sententiis*. http://www.corpusthomisticum.org, Fundación Tomás de Aquino, 2008–2009. http://www.corpusthomisticum.org/iopera.html

Aquinas, Thomas. *Summa Contra Gentiles*. Translated by Anton C. Pegis, James F. Anderson, Vernon J. Bourke, and Charles J. O'Neil. Notre Dame, IN: University of Notre Dame Press, 1992.

Aquinas, Thomas. *Summa Theologica*. Translated by the Fathers of the English Dominican Province. Online Edition Copyright 2003 by Kevin Knight. *Imprimatur* + F. Beda Jarrett, O. P., S. T. L., A. M., Prior Provincialis Angliæ. http://www.newadvent.org/summa/

Aquinas, Thomas, and Fra Rainaldo da Piperno. *Supplement to the Third Part of the Summa Theologica*. Fathers of the English Dominican Province, trans. Online Edition Copyright 2003 by Kevin Knight. *Imprimatur* + F. Beda Jarrett, O. P., S. T. L., A. M., Prior Provincialis Angliæ. http://www.newadvent.org/summa/.

Aristotle. *Nicomachean Ethics*. Translated by J. A. K Thomson, edited by Hugh Tredennick, and introduction by Jonathan Barnes. New York: Penguin Classics, 2004.

Augustine. *Handbook on Faith, Hope and Love*, translated by J. F. Shaw, edited and revised by Kevin Knight. 1887. Newadvent.org, The Fathers of the Church: 2008. http://www.newadvent.org/fathers/1302.htm

Augustine. *On Nature and Grace*, translated by Kevin Knight. Newadvent.org, The Fathers of the Church: 2008. http://www.newadvent.org/fathers/1503.htm

Augustine. *The City of God*. Translated by Marcus Dods, and with an introduction by Robert Merton. New York: The Modern Library, Random House, 1950.

Barker, Eileen. "The Scientific Study of Religion? You Must Be Joking!" *Journal for the Scientific Study of Religion* 34, no. 3 (Sep. 1995): 287–310.

Bell, Catherine M. *Ritual: Perspectives and Dimensions*. New York: Oxford University Press, 1997.

Bell, Daniel A., and Hahm Chaibong. "Introduction: The Contemporary Relevance of Confucianism." In *Confucianism for the Modern World*, edited by Daniel A. Bell and Hahm Chaibong, 1–28. Cambridge, UK: University of Cambridge Press, 2003.

Berry, Thomas. "Affectivity in Classical Chinese Tradition." In *Confucian Spirituality: Volume One* (Volume 11A of *World Spirituality: An Encyclopedia of the Religious Quest*), edited by Tu Weiming and Mary Evelyn Tucker, 96–112. New York: The Crossroad Publishing Company, 2003.

Berthrong, John H. *All Under Heaven: Transforming Paradigms in Confucian-Christian Dialogue*. Albany: State University of New York Press, 1994.

Berthrong, John H. *The Divine Deli: Religious Identity in the North American Cultural Mosaic*. Maryknoll, NY: Orbis Books, 1999.

Berthrong, John H. "Boston Confucianism: The Third Wave of Global Confucianism." In *Confucianism in Dialogue Today: West, Christianity and Judaism*, edited by Liu Shu-Hsien, John Berthrong, and Leonard Swidler, 26–47. Philadelphia: Ecumenical Press, 2004.

Black, Alison Harley. *Man and Nature in the Philosophical Thought of Wang Fu-chih*. Seattle: University of Washington Press, 1989.

Blau, Peter. *Exchange and Power in Social Life*. New York: J. Wiley, 1964.

Bloom, Allan. *The Closing of the American Mind*. Simon & Schuster: New York, 1988.

Blumenthal, Ralph. "Evolution's Backers in Kansas Start Counterattack." *New York Times*, August 1, 2006, http://www.nytimes.com/2006/08/01/us/01evolution.html

Blumer, Harold. *Symbolic Interactionism: Perspective and Method.* Englewood Cliffs, NJ: Prentice Hall, 1969.

Bol, Peter. *This Culture of Ours: Intellectual Transitions in T'ang and Sung China.* Stanford, CA: Stanford University Press, 1992.

Boyle, Leonard E., O. P. "The Setting of the *Summa Theologiae* of Saint Thomas; Revisited." In *The Ethics of Aquinas*, edited by Stephen J. Pope, 1–16. Washington, D.C.: Georgetown University Press, 2002.

Bradley, Denis. *Aquinas on the Twofold Human Good; Reasoned Human Happiness in Aquinas' Moral Science.* Washington, D.C.: Catholic University of America Press, 1997.

Brown, Richard Harvey, and Elizabeth L. Malone. "Reason, Politics, and the Politics of Truth: How Science is Both Autonomous and Independent." *Sociological Theory* 22, no. 1 (Mar. 2004): 106–122.

Bruce, J. Perry. *Chu Hsi and His Masters.* New York: AMS Press, 1973.

Burrell, David. *Aquinas, God and Action.* Notre Dame, IN· University of Notre Dame Press, 1979.

Button, Mark. "A Monkish Kind of Virtue? For and against Humility." In *Political Theory*, vol. 33, no. 6 (Dec. 2005): 840–868.

Calhoun, Craig. "The Problem of Identity in Collective Action" in *Macro-micro Linkages in Sociology*, edited by Joan Huber, 51–75. Newbury Park, CA: Sage Publications, 1991.

Carpenter, Humphrey, ed. *The Letters of J. R. R. Tolkien.* With the assistance of Christopher Tolkien. New York: Houghton Mifflin, 2000.

Cates, Diana Fritz. *Choosing to Feel: Virtue, Friendship and Compassion for Friends.* Notre Dame, IN: The University of Notre Dame Press, 1997.

Central Committee of the Chinese Communist Party (中国共产党中央委员会). "Decision Concerning the Great Proletarian Cultural Revolution (The Sixteen Points) (《关于无产阶级文化大革命的决定［即"十六条"］》)." Public document promulgated August 8, 1966. http://www.wyzxsx.com/Article/Class10/200803/34610.html

Chaihark, Hahm. "Constitutionalism, Confucian Civic Virtue, and Ritual Propriety." In *Confucianism for the Modern World*, edited by Daniel A. Bell and Hahm Chaibong, 31–53. Cambridge, UK: University of Cambridge Press, 2003.

Chan, Joseph. "Confucian Attitudes Toward Ethical Pluralism." In *Confucian Political Ethics*, edited by Daniel A. Bell, 113–138. Princeton, NJ: Princeton University Press, 2008.

Chan, Joseph. "Giving Priority to the Worst Off: A Confucian Perspective." In *Confucianism for the Modern World*, edited by Daniel A. Bell and Hahm Chaibong, 236–253. Cambridge, UK: University of Cambridge Press. 2003.

Chan, Wing-tsit. *Chu Hsi: New Studies.* Honolulu: University of Hawaii Press, 1989.

Chan, Wing-tsit. "Chu Hsi's Appraisal of Lao Tzu." *Philosophy East and West* 25, no. 2 (Apr., 1975): 131–144.

Chan, Wing-tsit. "Introduction." In *Chu Hsi and Neo-Confucianism*, edited by Wing-tsit Chan. Honolulu: University of Hawaii Press, 1986.

Chan, Wing-tsit, trans., ed. *Neo-Confucian Terms Explained: The Pei-hsi Tzu-i*. New York: Columbia University Press, 1986a.

Chan, Wing-tsit, trans., ed. *Reflections on Things At Hand: the Neo-Confucian Anthology*, Compiled by Chu Hsi and Lü Tsu-chien. New York: Columbia University Press, 1967.

Chan, Wing-tsit, trans., comp. *A Sourcebook in Chinese Philosophy*. Princeton, NJ: Princeton University Press, 1963.

Chang, Carsun. *The Development of Neo-Confucian Thought*. New York: Bookman Associates, 1957.

Chang, Jung. *Wild Swans: Three Daughters of China*. New York: Doubleday, 1991.

Chen Lai (陈来). *Zhu Xi zhexue yanjiu (朱熹哲学研究)*. Beijing: Zhongguo shehui kexue chubanshe (北京: 中国社会科學出版社), 1988.

Cheng, Chung-ying. "Chu Hsi's Methodology and Theory of Understanding." In *Chu Hsi and Neo-Confucianism*, edited by Wing-tsit Chan, 169–196. Honolulu: University of Hawaii Press, 1986.

Cheng, Kevin Shun-Kai. "The Social Dimension of Liberation in Early Confucian Tradition." *Ching Feng* 36, nos. 2–3 (1993): 61–81.

Cheng Yi and Cheng Hao. "Selected Sayings of Cheng Yi from the *Waishu*, or Remaining Documents of the Masters Cheng." In *A Source Book in Chinese Philosophy*, translated and edited by Wing-tsit Chan, 551–571. New York: Columbia University Press, 1963.

Chenu, M. D., O. P. *Toward Understanding Saint Thomas*. Translated by A.-M. Landry, O. P., and D. Hughes, O. P. Chicago: Henry Regnery Company, 1964.

Chesterton, G. K. *Heretics*. 1919. Gutenberg.org: Project Gutenberg, 2008. http://www.gutenberg.org/files/470/470-h/470-h.htm

Chesterton, G. K. *Saint Francis of Assisi*. New York: Doubleday, 2001.

Chesterton, G. K. *Saint Thomas Aquinas*. New York: Sheed and Ward, Inc., 1933.

Ch'ien Mu (錢 穆). *Chu tzu hsin hsueh-an (朱 子 新 學 案)*. Taipei: San min (台 北: 三 民), 1971.

Ch'ien Mu. "Historical Perspectives on Chu Hsi's Learning." In *Chu Hsi and Neo-Confucianism*, edited by Wing-tsit Chan, 32–42. Honolulu: University of Hawaii Press, 1986.

Chilton, Bruce D. "Primitive and Early Christianity." In *God's Rule: The Politics of World Religions*, edited by Jacob Neusner, 37–59. Washington: Georgetown University Press, 2003.

Ching, Julia. "Chu Hsi on Personal Cultivation." In *Chu Hsi and Neo-Confucianism*, edited by Wing-tsit Chan, 273–291. Honolulu: University of Hawaii Press, 1986.

Ching, Julia. *Confucianism and Christianity: A Comparative Study*. New York: Kodansha International, 1977.

Ching, Julia. *The Religious Thought of Chu Hsi.* New York: Oxford University Press, 2000.

Chong, Kim-chong. "Autonomy in the *Analects*." In *The Moral Circle and the Self: Chinese and Western Approaches*, edited by Kim-chong Chong, Sor-hoon Tan, and C. L. Ten, 269–282. Chicago: Open Court, 2003.

Chung Tsai-chun. *The Development of the Concepts of Heaven and of Man in the Philosophy of Chu Hsi.* Taiwan: Institute of Chinese Literature and Philosophy, Academia Sinica, 1993.

Cohen, Abraham. *Everyman's Talmud: The Major Teachings of the Rabbinc Sages.* New York: Schocken Books, 1995.

Coleman, James Samuel. "Collective Decisions." In *Individual Interests and Collective Action: Selected Essays*, 15–32. New York: Cambridge University Press, 1986.

Coleman, James Samuel. "Individual Interests and Collective Action." In *Individual Interests and Collective Action: Selected Essays*, 305–318. New York: Cambridge University Press, 1986.

Collins, Randall. *Interaction Ritual Chains.* Princeton Studies in Cultural Sociology. Princeton, NJ: Princeton University Press, 2004.

Cooley, Charles Horton. *Human Nature and the Social Order.* New York: Schocken Books, 1964.

Copleston, Frederick. *History of Philosophy, Volume II: Medieval Philosophy from Augustine to Duns Scotus.* New York: Random House,1993.

Copleston, F. C. *Aquinas.* Baltimore: Penguin Books, 1967.

Csikszentmihalyi, Mark. "Confucianism." In *God's Rule: The Politics of World Religions*, edited by Jacob Neusner, 213–232. Washington, D.C.: Georgetown University Press, 2003.

Cua, A. S. "Basic Concepts of Confucian Ethics." In *Moral Vision and Tradition: Essays in Chinese Ethics* (Studies in Philosophy and the History of Philosophy, Volume 31), edited by A. S. Cua, 267–302. Washington, D.C.: The Catholic University Press, 1998.

Cua, A. S. "Chinese Moral Vision, Responsive Agency, and Factual Beliefs." In *Moral Vision and Tradition: Essays in Chinese Ethics* (Studies in Philosophy and the History of Philosophy, Volume 31), edited by A. S. Cua, 59–80. Washington, D.C.: The Catholic University Press, 1998.

Cua, A. S. "Competence, Concern, and the Role of Paradigmatic Individuals (Chun tzu [Junzi]) in Moral Education." In *Moral Vision and Tradition: Essays in Chinese Ethics* (Studies in Philosophy and the History of Philosophy, Volume 31), edited by A. S. Cua, 138–155. Washington, D.C.: The Catholic University Press, 1998.

Cua, A. S. "Confucian Vision and Experience of the World." In *Moral Vision and Tradition: Essays in Chinese Ethics* (Studies in Philosophy and the History of Philosophy, Volume 31), edited by A. S. Cua, 19–36. Washington, D.C.: The Catholic University Press, 1998.

Cua, A. S. "The Ethical and Religious Dimensions of *Li*." In *Confucian Spirituality: Volume One* (Volume 11A of *World Spirituality: An Encyclopedia of the Religious Quest*), edited by Tu Weiming and Mary Evelyn Tucker, 252–286. New York: The Crossroad Publishing Company, 2003.

Cua, A. S. "Li and Moral Justification: A Study in the Li Chi." *Philosophy East and West* 33, no. 1 (Jan., 1983): 1–16. http://www.jstor.org

Curran, Charles E. "Roman Catholic Christianity." In *God's Rule: The Politics of World Religions*, edited by Jacob Neusner, 61–84. Washington, D.C.: Georgetown University Press, 2003.

Dahrendorf, Ralf. "*Homo Sociologicus*." In *Essays in the Theory of Society*, comp. Ralf Dahrendorf, 19–87. London: Routledge and Kegan Paul, 1968.

Dahrendorf, Ralf. "Sociology and Human Nature." In *Essays in the Theory of Society*, comp. Ralf Dahrendorf, 88–106. London: Routledge and Kegan Paul, 1968.

Daly, Daniel. "From Nature to Second Nature: The Relationship of Natural Law, Acquired Virtue, and Moral Precepts in Thomas Aquinas' Summa theologiae". PhD diss., Boston College, 2008.

Damasio, Antonio. *Descartes' Error: Emotion, Reason, and the Human Brain*. New York: Penguin, 2005.

Damasio, Antonio. *The Feeling of What Happens: Body and Emotion in the Making of Consciousness*. Harvest Books: Fort Washington, PA, 2000.

Davies, Brian. *The Thought of Thomas Aquinas*. Oxford: Clarendon Press, 1992.

Dawkins, Richard. *The God Delusion* New York: Houghton Mifflin, 2006.

de Bary, Wm. Theodore. "Epilogue: Why Confucius Now?" In *Confucianism for the Modern World*, edited by Daniel A. Bell and Hahm Chaibong, 361–372. Cambridge, UK: University of Cambridge Press, 2003.

de Bary, Wm. Theodore. *The Liberal Tradition in China*. New York: Columbia University Press, 1983.

de Bary, Wm. Theodore. *Neo-Confucian Orthodoxy and the Learning of the Mind-and-Heart*. Neo-Confucian Studies sponsored by The Regional Seminar in Neo-Confucian Studies, Columbia University. New York: Columbia University Press, 1981.

de Bary, Wm. Theodore. "Preface." In *Confucianism and Human Rights*, edited by Wm. Theodore de Bary and Tu Weiming, ix–xx. New York: Columbia University Press, 1998.

de Bary, Wm. Theodore. "Some Common Tendencies in Neo-Confucianism." In *Confucianism in Action*, edited by David S. Nivison and Arthur Wright, 25–49. Stanford, CA: Stanford University Press, 1959.

de Bary, Wm. Theodore. "Zhu Xi's Neo-Confucian Spirituality." In *Confucian Spirituality: Volume Two* (Volume 11B of *World Spirituality: An Encyclopedia of the Religious Quest*), edited by Tu Weiming and Mary Evelyn Tucker, 72–98. New York: The Crossroad Publishing Company, 2004.

de Bary, Wm. Theodore, and Irene Bloom, ed. *Sources of Chinese Tradition, Volume One: From Earliest Times to 1600*. 2nd ed. New York: Columbia University Press, 1999.

de Bary, Wm. Theodore, and Richard Lufrano, ed. *Sources of Chinese Tradition: Volume Two: From 1600 to the Twentieth Century*. 2nd ed. New York: Columbia University Press, 2001.

Dell'Olio, Andrew J. "Zhu Xi and Thomas Aquinas on the Foundations of Moral Self-Cultivation." In *Proceedings of the American Catholic Philosophical Association* 77 (2003): 235–246.

de Wulf, Maurice. *History of Mediaeval Philosophy*. Translated by Ernest C. Messenger. London: Nelson, 1952.

de Botton, Alain. *Religion for Atheists: A Non-believer's Guide to the Uses of Religion*. New York: Pantheon Books, 2012.

Douthat, Ross. *Bad Religion: How We Became a Nation of Heretics*. New York: Simon and Schuster, 2012.

Dumont, Louis. *Essays on Individualism: Modern Ideology in Anthropological Perspective*. Chicago: University of Chicago Press, 1986.

Dumont, Louis. *From Mandeville to Marx: The Genesis and Triumph of Economic Ideology*. Chicago: University of Chicago Press, 1977.

Durkheim, Emile. *The Division of Labor in Society*, translated by George Simpson. Glencoe, IL: Free Press, 1933.

Eagleton, Terry. *Reason, Faith & Revolution: Reflections on the God Debate*. New Haven: Yale University Press, 2009.

Ebrey, Patricia Buckley, trans., ed. *Chu Hsi's Family Rituals: A Twelfth Century Chinese Manual for the Performance of Cappings, Weddings, Funerals and Ancestral Rites*. Princeton, NJ: Princeton University Press, 1991.

Edinburgh Creation Group. "Edinburgh Creation Group," http://edinburghcreationgroup.org/

Farrell, Walter, O. P., S. T. D. O. P. M. *A Companion to the Summa*. 1938–1942. Domcentral.org: The Walter Farrell Institute. http://www.domcentral.org/farrell/companion/default.htm

Fay, Sarah. "Marilynne Robinson, The Art of Fiction No. 198: Interview." *Paris Review*, Fall 2008, No. 186. Online at http://www.theparisreview.org/interviews/5863/the-art-of-fiction-no-198-marilynne-robinson; retrieved October 8, 2012.

Fingarette, Herbert. *Confucius: The Secular as Sacred*. New York: Harper and Row, 1972.

Finke, Roger, and Rodney Stark. *The Churching of America 1776–2005: Winners and Losers in Our Religious Economy*. 2nd ed. Rutgers, NJ: Rutgers University Press, 2005.

Flannery, Kevin L. *Acts Amid Precepts: The Aristotelian Logical Structure of Thomas Aquinas' Moral Theory*. Washington, D.C.: Catholic University of America Press, 2001.

Flescher, Andrew. *Heroes, Saints and Ordinary Morality*. Washington, D.C.: Georgetown University Press, 2003.

Fu, Charles Wei-hsun. "Chu Hsi on Buddhism." In *Chu Hsi and Neo-Confucianism*, edited by Wing-tsit Chan, 377–407. Honolulu: University of Hawaii Press, 1986.

Fullam, Lisa. "The Virtue of Humility. A Reconstruction Based in Thomas Aquinas." PhD diss., Harvard University, 2001.

Fung Yu-Lan. *The Spirit of Chinese Philosophy*, translated by E. R. Hughes. Boston: Beacon Press, 1967.

Gardner, Daniel K. "Attentiveness and Meditative Reading in Cheng-Zhu Neo-Confucianism." In *Confucian Spirituality: Volume Two* (Volume 11B of *World Spirituality: An Encyclopedia of the Religious Quest*), edited by Tu Weiming and Mary Evelyn Tucker, 99–119. New York: The Crossroad Publishing Company, 2004.

Gardner, Daniel K., trans, ed. *Chu Hsi and the Ta-hsueh: Neo-Confucian Reflection on the Confucian Canon*. Cambridge, MA: Harvard University Press, 1986.

Geaney, Jane. "Guarding Moral Boundaries: Shame in Early Confucianism." *Philosophy East and West* 54, no. 2 (Apr., 2004): 113–142.

Gilson, Etienne. *Thomism: The Philosophy of Thomas Aquinas*, translated by Laurence K. Shook and Armand Maurer. 6th ed. Toronto: Pontifical Institute of Medieval Studies, 2002.

Goffman, Erving. "On Face-Work." In *Interaction Ritual: Essays in Face-to-Face Behavior*, introduction by Joel Best, 5–46. New Brunswick, NJ: Transaction Publishers, 2005.

Goffman, Erving. *The Presentation of Self In Everyday Life*. Garden City, NY: Doubleday, 1973.

Goffman, Erving. "Where the Action Is." In *Interaction Ritual: Essays in Face-to-Face Behavior*, introduction by Joel Best, 139–259. New Brunswick, NJ: Transaction Publishers, 2005.

Goldman, René. "Moral Leadership in Society: Some Parallels between the Confucian 'Noble Man' and the Jewish 'Zaddik.'" *Philosophy East and West* 45, no. 3 (Jul. 1995): 329–365.

Graham, A. C. "The Background in the Mencian Theory of Human Nature." In *Studies in Chinese Philosophy and Philosophical Literature*, by A. C. Graham, 7–66. In SUNY Series in Chinese Philosophy and Culture. New York: State University of New York Press, 1986.

Green, William Scott. "Introduction: Religion and Politics: A Volatile Mix." In *God's Rule: The Politics of World Religions*, edited by Jacob Neusner, 1–9. Washington, D.C.: Georgetown University Press, 2003.

Gross, Neil, and Solon Simmons. "The Religiosity of American College and University Professors." *Sociology of Religion* 70, no. 2 (Summer 2009): 101–129.

Haidt, Jonathan. *The Righteous Mind: Why Good People Are Divided by Politics and Religion*. New York: Pantheon Books, 2012.

Hall, David L., and Roger T. Ames. "Sexism, With Chinese Characteristics." In*The Sage and the Second Sex: Confucianism, Ethics and Gender*, edited by Chenyang Li, 77–95. Chicago: Open Court, 2000.

Hawking, Stephen. *A Brief History of Time*. New York: Bantam Books, 1988.

He Zhen. "Women's Revenge (女子復仇論)." de Bary, Wm. Theodore, and Richard Lufrano, ed. *Sources of Chinese Tradition: Volume Two: From 1600 to the Twentieth Century*. 2nd ed. New York: Columbia University Press, 2001, 393–395.

Hechter, Michael. "From Exchange to Structure." In *Macro-micro Linkages in Sociology*, edited by Joan Huber, 46–50. Newbury Park, CA : Sage Publications, 1991.

Helgesen, Geir. "The Case for Moral Education." In *Confucianism for the Modern World*, edited by Daniel A. Bell and Hahm Chaibong, 161–177.Cambridge, UK: University of Cambridge Press, 2003.

Hirschman, Albert O. *The Passions and the Interests: Political Arguments for Capitalism before Its Triumph*. Princeton, NJ: Princeton University Press, 1977.

Hui-neng. "The Platform Scripture." In *A Source Book in Chinese Philosophy*, translated and edited by Wing-tsit Chan, 430–440. New York: Columbia University Press, 1963.

Hume, David. "A Treatise of Human Nature." In *Hume's Ethical Writings: Selections from David Hume*, edited by Alasdair MacIntyre, 216–235. Notre Dame, IN: University of Notre Dame Press, 1980.

Ikara, Craig C. "Are Individual Rights Necessary? A Confucian Perspective." In *Confucian Ethics: A Comparative Study of Self, Autonomy and Community*, edited by Kwong-loi Shun, and David B. Wong, 11–30. Cambridge, UK: Cambridge University Press, 2004.

Ing, Michael. *The Dysfunction of Ritual in Early Confucianism*. Oxford, UK: Oxford University Press. 2013.

Ivanhoe, Philip J. *Confucian Moral Self Cultivation*. 2nd ed. Indianapolis: Hackett Publishing Company, Inc., 2000.

Ivanhoe, Philip J. "Early Confucianism and Environmental Ethics." In *Confucianism and Ecology: The Interrelation of Heaven, Earth and Humans*, edited by Mary Evelyn Tucker and John Berthrong, 59–76. Cambridge: Harvard University Press, 1998.

James, William. *The Varieties of Religious Experience*. Introduction by Reinhold Niebuhr. New York: Touchstone, 2004.

Jerolmack, Colin, and Douglas Porpora. "Religion, Rationality, and Experience: A Response to the New Rational Choice Theory of Religion." *Sociological Theory* 22, no. 1 (Mar. 2004): 140–160.

Jia, Wenshan. "The *Wei* (Positioning)-*Ming* (Naming)-*Lianmin* (Face)-*Guanxi* (Relationship)-*Renqing* (Humanized Feelings) Complex in Contemporary Chinese Culture." In *Confucian Cultures of Authority*, edited by Peter D. Hershock and Roger T. Ames, 49–64. Albany: State University of New York Press, 2006.

Jiang, Tao. "Intimate Authority: The Rule of Ritual in Classical Confucian Discourse." In *Confucian Cultures of Authority*, edited by Peter D. Hershock and Roger T. Ames, 21–47. Albany: State University of New York Press, 2006.

John Paul II. *Fides et Ratio: The Relationship Between Faith and Reason (Encyclical Letter)*. Washington, D.C.: United States Catholic Conference, 1998.

Jullien, François. "The Chinese Notion of 'Blandness' as a Virtue: A Preliminary Outline." Translated by Graham Parkes. *Philosophy East and West* 43, no. 1 (Jan., 1993): 107–111.

Kalton, Michael C. "Extending the Neo-Confucian Tradition: Questions and Reconceptualization for the Twenty-First Century." In *Confucianism and Ecology: The Interrelation of Heaven, Earth and Humans*, edited by Mary Evelyn Tucker and John Berthrong, 77–103. Cambridge: Harvard University Press, 1998.

Kasulis, Thomas P. "The Strata of the Japanese Self." In *Self As Person in Asian Theory and Practice*, edited by Roger T. Ames, Wimal Dissanayake and Thomas P. Kasulis, 87–106. Albany: State University of New York, 1994.

Kant, Immanuel. *Critique of Pure Reason*. In *Classics of Western Philosophy*, 6th ed. Edited by Steven M. Cahn, 878–953. Indianapolis: Hackett Publishing Company, 2002.

Kay, Judith W. "Getting Egypt out of the People: Aquinas's Contributions to Liberation." In *Aquinas and Empowerment: Classical Ethics for Ordinary Lives*, edited by G. Simon Harak, S. J., 1–46. Washington, D.C.: Georgetown University Press, 1996.

Keaty, Anthony. "The Christian Virtue of Mercy: Aquinas' Transformation of Aristotelian Pity." In *Heythrop Journal*, 46, no. 2 (2005): 181–198.

Keenan, James. *Goodness and Rightness in Thomas Aquinas' Summa Theologiae*. Washington, D.C.: Georgetown University Press, 1992.

Keenan, James. "The Problem with Thomas Aquinas's Concept of Sin." *The Heythrop Journal* 35, no. 4 (1994): 401–420.

Keenan, James F., SJ. "Proposing Cardinal Virtues." *Theological Ethics* 56 (1995): 709–728.

Kekes, John. "Pluralism and Moral Authority." In *The Moral Circle and the Self: Chinese and Western Approaches*, edited by Kim-chong Chong, Sor-hoon Tan and C. L. Ten, 75–92. Chicago: Open Court, 2003.

Kenny, Anthony. "Aquinas on Aristotelian Happiness." In *Aquinas's Moral Theory: Essays in Honor of Norman Kretzmann*, edited by Scott MacDonald and Eleonore Stump, 15–27. Ithaca, NY: Cornell University Press, 1999.

Kenny, Anthony. "The Irrevocability of Faith," October 22, 2007, http://entertainment.timesonline.co.uk/tol/arts_and_entertainment/the_tls/article2717498.ee

Kent, Bonnie. "Habits and Virtues (Ia IIae, qq. 49–70)." In *The Ethics of Aquinas*, edited by Stephen J. Pope, 116–130. Washington, D.C.: Georgetown University Press, 2002.

Kerr, Fergus. *After Aquinas: Versions of Thomism*. Malden, MA: Blackwell Publishing, 2002.

Keys, Mary M. *Aquinas, Aristotle, and the Promise of the Common Good*. New York: Cambridge University Press, 2006.

Kim, Yung-sik. *The Natural Philosophy of Chu Hsi (1130–1200)*. Philadelphia, PA: Memoirs of the American Philosophical Society Held At Philadelphia For Promoting Useful Knowledge. Volume 35, 2000.

Knitter, Paul F. *Introducing Theologies of Religions*. Maryknoll, NY: Orbis Books, 2003.

Koehane, Joe. "How Facts Backfire." *Boston Globe*, July 11, 2010 (http://www.boston.com/bostonglobe/ideas/articles/2010/07/11/how_facts_backfire/

Kohn, Livia. "Chinese Religion." In *The Human Condition: A Volume in the Comparative Religious Ideas Project*, edited by Robert Cummings Neville, 21–47. Albany: State University of New York Press, 2000a.

Kotva, Joseph J. "Transformed in Prayer." In *Practice What You Preach: Virtues, Ethics, and Power in the Lives of Pastoral Minister and Their Congregations*, edited by James Keenan and Joseph J. Kotva, 147–155. Franklin, WI: Sheed and Ward, 1999.

Kupperman, Joel. "Tradition and Community in the Formation of Character and Self." In *Confucian Ethics: A Comparative Study of Self, Autonomy and Community*, edited by Kwong-loi Shun and David B. Wong, 103–123. Cambridge, UK: Cambridge University Press, 2004.

Kwasniewski, Peter A. Introduction to *On Love and Charity: Readings from the Commentary on the Sentences of Peter Lombard*, by Thomas Aquinas, translated by Peter A. Kwasniewski, Thomas Bolin, O.S.B. and Joseph Bolin, xv–xxx. Washington, D.C.: The Catholic University of America, 2008.

Kwok, D. W. Y. "On the Rites and Rights of Being Human." In *Confucianism and Human Rights*, edited by Wm. Theodore de Bary and Tu Weiming, 83–93. New York: Columbia University Press, 1998.

Lai, Karyn. "Confucian Moral Self-Cultivation: Some Parallels with Musical Training." In *The Moral Circle and the Self: Chinese and Western Approaches*, edited by Kim-chong Chong, Sor-hoon Tan and C. L. Ten, 107–133. Chicago: Open Court, 2003.

Langan, John P. "Augustine on the Unity and the Interconnection of the Virtues." In *The Harvard Theological Review* 72, no. 1/2 (Jan.–Apr. 1979): 81–95.

Lee, Peter H., and Wm. Theodore de Bary, ed. *Sources of Korean Tradition, Volume One: From Earliest Times to the Sixteenth Century*. New York: Columbia University Press, 1996.

Legge, James, ed., trans. *Confucius: Confucian Analects, The Great Learning, & The Doctrine of the Mean*. New York: Dover Publications, (1895) 1970.

Legge, James, ed., trans. *The Shoo King, or The Book of Historical Documents*. 2nd ed. Taipei: Chin-hsüeh shu-chu, (1893–1895) 1969.

Lehrer, Jonah. "The Future of Science Is . . . Art?"*Seed Magazine*, January 16, 2008, http://seedmagazine.com/news/2008/01/the_future_of_scienceis_art.php (accessed March 2, 2009).

L'Engle, Madeleine. *And It Was Good: Reflections on Beginnings*. Wheaton, IL: Harold Shaw Publishers, 1983.

Li, Huey-li. "Some Thoughts on Confucianism and Eco-Feminism." In *Confucianism and Ecology: The Interrelation of Heaven, Earth and Humans*, edited by Mary Evelyn Tucker and John Berthrong, 293–312. Cambridge: Harvard University Press, 1998.

Li Yuli. *The Unity of Rule and Virtue: A Critique of a Supposed Parallel Between Confucian Ethics and Virtue Ethics*. Singapore: Eastern Universities Press, 2004.

Lipka, Michael. "God is Alive and Well in America." Report released by Pew Research Center, September 13, 2013, http://www.pewresearch.org/fact-tank/2013/09/13/what-surveys-say-about-worship-attendance-and-why-some-stay-home/

Liu, James T.C. *China Turning Inward: Intellectual-Political Changes in the Early Twelfth Century*. Cambridge, MA: Council on East Asian Studies, Harvard University, 1988.

Liu Wei (刘蔚). "The Function of Government in the Culture Industry's Cluster Development (政府在文化产业集群发展中的作用)." *Journal of China Executive Leadership Academy* (中国井冈山干部学院报告) 1, no. 2 (第1 卷, 第2 期) (March 25, 2008 (2008 年3 月)): 91–94. www.cnki.net

Loh, Sandra Tsing. "I Choose My Choice!" *Atlantic Monthly*, July/August 2008. http://www.theatlantic.com/doc/200807/working-moms

Louie, Kam. *Critiques of Confucius in Contemporary China*. New York: St. Martin's Press, 1980.

Luther, Martin. *The Table Talk of Martin Luther*. Translated by William Hazlitt, and with introduction by Alexander Chalmers. 1872. Books.google.com: Google Books, 2008. http://books.google.com/books?id=ZUAuAAAAYAAJ&client=firefox-a

MacIntyre, Alasdair. *After Virtue: A Study in Moral Theory*. Notre Dame, IN: University of Notre Dame Press, 1981.

MacIntyre, Alasdair. *Whose Justice? Which Rationality?* South Bend, IN: University of Notre Dame Press, 1989.

Madsen, Richard. "Confucian Conceptions of Civil Society." In *Confucian Political Ethics*, edited by Daniel A. Bell, 3–19. Princeton, NJ: Princeton University Press, 2008.

Mandeville, Bernard. *The Grumbling Hive, 1705*. http://andromeda.rutgers.edu/~jlynch/, Jack Lynch: 2009. http://andromeda.rutgers.edu/~jlynch/Texts/hive.html

Manent, Pierre. *An Intellectual History of Liberalism*, translated by Rebecca Balinski. Princeton, NJ: Princeton University Press, 1995.

Mao Zedong (毛泽东). "Combat Liberalism (《反对自由主义》). Speech delivered September 7, 1937. http://www.marxists.org/chinese/17/marxist.org-chinese-mao-19370907.htm

Mao Zedong (毛泽东). "On the Correct Handling of Contradictions Among the People" (《关于正确处理人民内部矛盾的问题》). Speech delivered February 27, 1957. http://www.marxists.org/chinese/17/marxist.org-chinese-mao-19570227.htm

Maritain, Jacques. *St. Thomas Aquinas*. 1958. Nd.edu, Jacques Maritain Center, University of Notre Dame: 2009. http://www2.nd.edu/Departments//Maritain/etext/thomas.htm.

McCabe, Herbert. *God, Christ and Us*. Edited by Brian Davies, O. P. New York: Continuum, 2003.

McInerny, Ralph. *Aquinas*. Cambridge, UK: Polity Press. Malden, MA: Distributed in the USA by Blackwell Publishers, 2004.

McInerny, Ralph. Ethica Thomistica: *The Moral Philosophy of Thomas Aquinas*. Revised ed. Washington, D.C.: The Catholic University of America Press, 1997.

Merton, Robert King. "The Role-Set." In *On Social Structure and Science*, edited and with an introduction by Piotr Sztompka, 113–122. Chicago: University of Chicago Press, 1996.

Merton, Robert King. "The Self-Fulfilling Prophecy." In *On Social Structure and Science*, edited and with an introduction by Piotr Sztompka, 183–204. Chicago: University of Chicago Press, 1996.

Merton, Robert King. "Social Dysfunctions." In *On Social Structure and Science*, edited and with an introduction by Piotr Sztompka, 96–100. Chicago: University of Chicago Press, 1996.

Merton, Robert King. "Social Structure and Anomie." In *On Social Structure and Science*, edited and with an introduction by Piotr Sztompka, 132–152. Chicago: University of Chicago Press, 1996.

Metzger, Thomas A. *A Cloud Across the Pacific: Essays on the Clash Between Chinese and Western Political Theories Today*. Hong Kong: Chinese University Press, 2005.

Metzger, Thomas A. *Escape from Predicament: Neo-Confucianism and China's Evolving Political Culture*. New York: Columbia University Press, 1977.

Milbank, John. *Theology and Social Theory: Beyond Secular Reason*. 2nd ed. Malden, MA: Blackwell Publishing, 2006.

Mo, Jongryn. "The Challenge of Accountability." In *Confucianism for the Modern World*, edited by Daniel A. Bell and Hahm Chaibong, 54–68. Cambridge, UK: University of Cambridge Press, 2003.

Moulaison, Jane Barter. "'Our Bodies, Our Selves?' The Body as Source in Feminist Theology." *Scottish Journal of Theology* 60, no. 3 (2007): 341–359.

Munro, Donald J. *The Concept of Man in Early China*. Stanford, CA: Stanford University Press, 1969.

Murphy, Mark C. "Consent, Custom, and the Common Good in Aquinas's Account of Political Authority." *The Review of Politics* 59, no. 2 (Spring 1997): 323–350.

Nagel, Thomas. "Moral Luck." *Proceedings of the Aristotelian Society* (Supplementary Volumes) 50 (1976): 137–151.

Needham, Joseph, Ling Wang, and Peter J. Golas. *Science and Civilisation in China*. Cambridge, UK: Cambridge University Press, 1954.

Nelson, Benjamin. "*Conscience* and the Making of Early Modern Cultures: Beyond Max Weber." In *On the Roads to Modernity: Conscience, Science and Civilizations*, edited by Toby Huff, 67–79. Totowa, NJ: Rowman and Littlefield, 1981.

Nelson, Benjamin. "Epilogue: Priests, Prophets Machines, Futures: 1202, 1848, 1984, 2001." In *On the Roads to Modernity: Conscience, Science and Civilizations*, edited by Toby Huff, 244–258. Totowa, NJ: Rowman and Littlefield, 1981.

Neville, Robert Cummings. *Boston Confucianism: Portable Tradition in the Late-Modern World*. With a foreword by Tu Weiming. Albany: State University of New York Press, 2000.

Neville, Robert C., ed. *The Human Condition:* The Comparative Religious Ideas Project. Albany: State University of New York Press, 2000a.

Neville, Robert C. *Ritual and Deference: Extending Chinese Philosophy in a Comparative Context*. New York: State University of New York Press, 2008.

Neville, Robert C., ed. *Religious Truth: The Comparative Religious Ideas Project*. Albany, NY: State University of New York Press, 2000b.

Neville, Robert C., ed. Ultimate Realities: The Comparative Religious Ideas Project. Albany, NY: State University of New York Press, 2000c.

Newcomb, Theodore, Ralph H. Turner, and Philip E. Converse, ed. *Social Psychology: The Study of Human Interaction*. New York: Holt, Rinehart and Winston, Inc., 1965.

Newton, Isaac. *Newton's Philosophy of Nature: Selections from His Writings*. Whitefish, MT: Kessinger Publishing, 2003.

Nichols, Aidan, O. P. *Discovering Aquinas: An Introduction to His Life, Work and Influence*. Grand Rapids, MI: William B. Eerdmans Publishing Company, 2002.

Niou, Emerson. "Local Self-Governance with Chinese Characteristics." http://74.125.95.132/search?q=cache:ME7qat1d6AAJ:140.109.171.199/1010meeting/1-2.pdf+%22lu+family+compact%22&hl=en&ct=clnk&cd=1&gl=us&client=firefox-a

Nivison, David S. "Introduction." In *Confucianism in Action*, edited by David S. Nivison and Arthur Wright, 3–24. Stanford, CA: Stanford University Press, 1959.

Norris, Kathleen. *Amazing Grace: A Vocabulary of Faith*. New York: Penguin Riverhead Books, 1998.

Norton, David L. "Moral Minimalism and the Development of Moral Character." *Midwest Studies in Philosophy* XIII (1988): 180–195.

Nussbaum, Martha C. *The Fragility of Goodness: Luck and Ethics in Greek Tragedy and Philosophy*. New York: Cambridge University Press, 1986.

Nylan, Michael. "Boundaries of the Body and Body Politic in Early Confucian Thought." In *Confucian Political Ethics*, edited by Daniel A. Bell, 85–110. Princeton, NJ: Princeton University Press, 2008.

Obama, Barack. Presidential inauguration speech. Delivered January 20, 2009. http://www.cnn.com/2009/POLITICS/01/20/obama.politics/index.html

O'Meara, Thomas Franklin, O. P. *Thomas Aquinas: Theologian*. Notre Dame, IN: University of Notre Dame Press, 1997.

Owen, Richard. "The Ratzinger Effect: more money, more pilgrims—and lots more Latin." *The Times*, July 7, 2006, http://www.timesonline.co.uk/tol/comment/faith/article2039932.ece

Parsons, Talcott. *The Social System*. Glencoe, IL: Free Press, 1951.

Pasnau, Robert. *Thomas Aquinas on Human Nature: A Philosophical Study of Summa theologiae Ia 75–89*. Cambridge: Cambridge University, 2002.

Patt-Shamir, Galia. "Moral World, Ethical Terminology: The Moral Significance of Metaphysical Terms in Zhou Dunyi and Zhu Xi." *Journal of Chinese Philosophy* 31, no. 3 (Sept. 2004): 349–362.

Peerenboom, Randall. "Confucian Harmony and Freedom of Thought." In *Confucianism and Human Rights*, edited by Wm. Theodore de Bary and Tu Weiming, 234–260. New York: Columbia University Press, 1998.

Peng Guoxiang (彭国翔). *Rujia chuantong: zongjiao yu renwenzhuyi zhi jian* (儒家传统: 宗教与人文主义之间). Beijing: Beijing daxue chuban she (北京: 北京大学出版社), 2007.

Pinckaers, Servais-Theodore, O. P. "The Sources of the Ethics of Thomas Aquinas." Translated by Mary Thomas Noble, O. P. In *The Ethics of Aquinas*, edited by Stephen J. Pope, 17–29. Washington, D.C.: Georgetown University Press, 2002.

Pieper, Josef. *The Four Cardinal Virtues*. Notre Dame, IN: University of Notre Dame Press, 1968.

Pinker, Steven. "The Moral Instinct." *The Times Magazine*, January 13, 2008 http://www.nytimes.com/2008/01/13/magazine/13Psychology-t.html?pagewanted=1&_r=1

Pinker, Steven. *The Blank Slate: The Modern Denial of Human Nature*. New York: Penguin Books, 2002.

Pope, Stephen J. "Overview of the Ethics of Thomas Aquinas." In *The Ethics of Aquinas*, edited by Stephen J. Pope, 30–53. Washington, D.C.: Georgetown University Press, 2002.

Popper, Karl. *Conjectures and Refutations: The Growth of Scientific Knowledge*. New York: Routledge, 2002.

Popper, Karl. "Back to the Pre-Socratics: The Presidential Address." *Proceedings of the Aristotelian Society*, New Series, 59 (1958–1959): 1–24.

Porter, Jean. *Natural and Divine Law: Reclaiming the Tradition for Christian Ethics*. Grand Rapids, MI: Wm. B. Eerdmans Publishing, 1999.

Porter, Jean. *Nature as Reason: A Thomistic Theory of the Natural Law*. Grand Rapids, MI: Wm. B. Eerdmans Publishing, 2005.

Prothero, Stephen. *God Is Not One: The Eight Rival Religions That Run the World—and Why Their Differences Matter*. New York: HarperCollins, 2010.

Puett, Michael. "Innovation as Ritualization: The Fractured Cosmology of Early China." *Cardozo Law Review* 28, no. 1 (2006): 23–36.

Radcliffe, Timothy, O. P. *What is the Point of Being a Christian?* New York: Burns and Oats, 2005.

Rand, Ayn. *Atlas Shrugged*. New York: Plume, 1999.

Regan, Richard J., *The Moral Dimensions of Politics*. New York: Oxford University Press. 1986.

Reichburg, Gregory M. "The Intellectual Virtues (Ia IIae, qq. 57–58). In *The Ethics of Aquinas*, edited by Stephen J. Pope, 131–150. Washington, D.C.: Georgetown University Press. 2002.

Ren Jiyu. "Chu Hsi and Religion." In *Chu Hsi and Neo-Confucianism*, edited by Wing-tsit Chan, 355–376. Honolulu: University of Hawaii Press, 1986.

Richards, Norvin. "Is Humility a Virtue?" *American Philosophical Quarterly*, vol. 25, no. 3 (Jul., 1988), pp. 253–259.

Rieff, Philip. "For the Last Time Psychology!" *The Feeling Intellect: Selected Writings*, edited by Jonathan Imber, 351–366. Chicago: University of Chicago Press, 1990.

Rieff, Philip. "The Impossible Culture: Wilde as a Modern Prophet." *The Feeling Intellect: Selected Writings*, edited by Jonathan Imber, 273–289. Chicago: University of Chicago Press, 1990.

Rieff, Philip. "On Religion and Power." *The Feeling Intellect: Selected Writings*, edited by Jonathan Imber, 160–163. Chicago: University of Chicago Press, 1990.

Rieff, Philip. "Reflections on Psychological Man in America." *The Feeling Intellect: Selected Writings*, edited by Jonathan Imber, 3–9. Chicago: University of Chicago Press, 1990.

Rosemann, Philipp W. *The Story of a Great Medieval Book: Peter Lombard's "Sentences."* Peterborough, Ontario: Broadview Press, 2007.

Rosemont, Henry, Jr. "Civil Society, Government, and Confucianism: A Commentary." In *Confucian Political Ethics*, edited by Daniel A. Bell, 46–57. Princeton, NJ: Princeton University Press, 2008.

Rosemont, Henry, Jr. "Two Loci of Authority: Autonomous Individuals and Related Persons." In *Confucian Cultures of Authority*, edited by Peter D. Hershock and Roger T. Ames, 1–20. Albany: State University of New York Press, 2006.

Rosemont, Henry, Jr. "Whose Democracy? Which Rights? A Confucian Critique of Modern Western Liberalism." In *Confucian Ethics: A Comparative Study of Self, Autonomy and Community*, edited by Kwong-loi Shun and David B. Wong, 49–71. Cambridge, UK: Cambridge University Press, 2004.

Rowatt, Wade C., Alison Ottenbreit, K. Paul Messelroade, Jr., Paige A. Cunningham. "On Being Holier-Than-Thou or Humbler-Than-Thee: A Social Psychological Perspective on Religiousness and Humility." *Journal for the Scientific Study of Religion*, vol. 42, no. 2 (Jun., 2002), pp. 227–237.

Rushing, Sara. "What is Confucian Humility?" In *Virtue Ethics and Confucianism*, edited by Stephen Angle and Michael Slote, 173–181. New York: Routledge, 2013.

Sandel, Michael. "The Lost Art of Democratic Debate," available at http://www.ted.com/talks/lang/eng/michael_sandel_the_lost_art_of_democratic_debate.html

Sandel, Michael. *What Money Can't Buy: The Moral Limits of Markets*. New York: Farrar, Strauss and Giroux, 2012.

Schockenhoff, Eberhard. "The Theological Virtue of Charity (IIa IIae, qq. 23–46). Translated by Grant Kaplan and Frederick G. Lawrence. In *The Ethics of Aquinas*, edited by Stephen J. Pope, 244–258. Washington, D.C.: Georgetown University Press, 2002.

Schwartz, Barry. *The Paradox of Choice: Why More is Less*. New York: Harper-Collins Publishers. 2005.

Schwartz, Benjamin I. "The Ethical and the Meta-Ethical in Chinese High Cultural Thought." In *Confucian Spirituality: Volume One* (Volume 11A of *World Spirituality: An Encyclopedia of the Religious Quest*), edited by Tu Weiming and Mary Evelyn Tucker, 56–61. New York: The Crossroad Publishing Company, 2003.

Schwartz, Benjamin I. *The World of Thought in Ancient China*. Cambridge, MA: Bellknap Press, 1985.

Seligman, Adam. *Modernity's Wager: Authority, the Self, and Transcendence*. Princeton, NJ: Princeton University Press, 2000.

Seligman, Adam. "Role Complexity, Risk, and the Emergence of Trust." *Boston University Law Review* 81, no. 3 (June 2001): 619–634.

Seligman, Adam B., Robert P. Weller, Michael J. Puett, and Bennett Simon. *Ritual and its Consequences: An Essay on the Limits of Sincerity*. New York: Oxford University Press, 2008.

Shen-hui. "Recorded Conversations." In *A Source Book in Chinese Philosophy*, translated and edited by Wing-tsit Chan, 440–444. New York: Columbia University Press, 1963.

Shippey, Tom. *The Road to Middle-Earth: How J.R.R. Tolkien Created a New Mythology*. New York: Houghton Mifflin, 2003.

Sim, May. *Remastering Morals with Aristotle and Confucius*. New York: Cambridge University Press, 2007.

Smith, Huston. *The World Religions: Our Great Wisdom Traditions*. San Francisco: HarperCollins, 1991.

Sommer, Deborah. "Ritual and Sacrifice in Early Confucianism: Contacts with the Spirit World." In *Confucian Spirituality: Volume One* (Volume 11A of *World Spirituality: An Encyclopedia of the Religious Quest*), edited by Tu Weiming and Mary Evelyn Tucker, 197–219. New York: The Crossroad Publishing Company, 2003.

Stalnaker, Aaron. "Comparative Religious Ethics and the Problem of Human Nature." *Journal of Religious Ethics* 33, no. 2 (June 2005): 187–224.

Stalnaker, Aaron. *Overcoming Our Evil: Human Nature and Spiritual Exercises in Xunzi and Augustine*. Washington, D.C.: Georgetown University Press, 2006.

Stout, Jeffrey. *Democracy and Tradition*. Princeton, NJ: Princeton University Press, 2004.

Stump, Eleonore. *Aquinas*. London: Routledge, 2003.

Stump, Eleonore. "Wisdom: Will, Belief, and Moral Goodness" in *Aquinas's Moral Theory: Essays in Honor of Norman Kretzmann*, edited by Scott

MacDonald and Eleonore Stump, 28–62. Ithaca, NY: Cornell University Press, 1999.

Suddath, Virginia. "Ought We Throw the Confucian Baby Out With the Bathwater?: A Critical Inquiry into Lu Xun's Anti-Confucian Identity." In *Confucian Cultures of Authority*, edited by Peter D. Hershock and Roger T. Ames, 215–245. Albany: State University of New York Press, 2006.

Sweeney, Eileen. "Vice and Sin (Ia IIae, qq. 71–89)." In *The Ethics of Aquinas*, edited by Stephen J. Pope, 151–168. Washington, D.C.: Georgetown University Press, 2002.

Takehiko, Okada. "Chu Hsi and Wisdom as Hidden and Stored." In *Chu Hsi and Neo-Confucianism*, edited by Wing-tsit Chan, 197–211. Honolulu: University of Hawaii Press, 1986.

Tan, Sor-hoon. "Can There Be a Confucian Civil Society?" In *The Moral Circle and the Self: Chinese and Western Approaches*, edited by Kim-chong Chong, Sor-hoon Tan and C. L. Ten, 193–218. Chicago: Open Court, 2003.

Taylor, Charles. *A Secular Age*. Cambridge, MA: The Belknap Press of Harvard University Press, 2007.

Taylor, Charles. *Sources of the Self*. 2nd ed. Cambridge, MA: Harvard University Press, 1992.

Taylor, Rodney L. "Companionship with the World: Roots and Branches of a Confucian Ecology." In *Confucianism and Ecology: The Interrelation of Heaven, Earth and Humans*, edited by Mary Evelyn Tucker and John Berthrong, 37–58. Cambridge: Harvard University Press, 1998.

Taylor, Rodney L. "The Religious Dimensions of The Confucian Tradition." *Philosophy East & West* 48, no. 3 (January 1998): 80–108.

Tillman, Hoyt. *Confucian Discourse and Chu Hsi's Ascendancy*. Honolulu: University of Hawaii Press, 1992.

Thompson, Kirill Ole. "How to Rejuvenate Ethics: Suggestions from Chu Hsi." *Philosophy East and West* 41, no. 4 (October 1991): 493–513.

Thrower, James. *Marxism-Leninism as the Civil Religion of Soviet Society: God's Commissar*. Lewiston, New York: The Edwin Mellen Press, 1992.

Tolkien, J. R. R. *The Fellowship of the Ring: Being the First Part of THE LORD OF THE RINGS*. New York: Houghton Mifflin, 1994.

Tolkien, J. R. R. *The Tolkien Reader*. New York: Ballantine Books, 1966.

Torrell, Jean-Pierre, O. P. *Saint Thomas Aquinas: Volume 1. The Person and His Work*. Translated by Robert Royal. Washington, D.C.: The Catholic University of America Press, 1996.

Torrell, Jean-Pierre, O. P. *Saint Thomas Aquinas: Volume 2. Spiritual Master*. Translated by Robert Royal. Washington, D.C.: The Catholic University of America Press, 2003.

Toulmin, Stephen. "Rationality and Scientific Discovery." *Philosophy of Science Association: Proceedings of the Biennial Meeting of the Philosophy of Science Association* 1972 (1972): 387–406.

Trilling, Lionel. *Sincerity and Authenticity*. Cambridge, MA: Harvard University Press, 1997.

Truman, Ronald W. *Spanish Treatises on Government, Society, and Religion in the Time of Philip II: The "De Regimine Principum" and Associated Traditions*. Boston: Brill, 1999.

Tu Weiming (杜維明). "*Shi Huaci xushide renwenzhuyi shijie zai jinian Shi Huaci nianhui zhuisihuishangde jianghua* (史華慈叙事的人文主義視界 在纪念史华慈追思会上的讲话)," 世界汉学 (*World Sinology*), January 2003 (2003年 01期): 98, http://cnki.net

Tu Weiming. "Beyond the Enlightenment Mentality." In *Confucianism and Ecology: The Interrelation of Heaven, Earth and Humans*, edited by Mary Evelyn Tucker and John Berthrong, 3–22. Cambridge: Harvard University Press, 1998.

Tu Weiming. *Centrality and Commonality: An Essay on Confucian Religiousness*. Albany: State University of New York Press, 1989.

Tu Weiming. "The Confucian Sage: Exemplar of Personal Knowledge." In *Way, Learning, and Politics: Essays on the Confucian Individual*, edited by Tu Weiming, 29–44. Albany: State University of New York, 1993.

Tu Weiming. "The Creative Tension Between *Jen* [*Ren*] and *Li*." In *Humanity and Self-Cultivation: Essays in Confucian Thought*, 5–16. Berkeley, CA: Asian Humanities Press, 1979.

Tu Weiming. "Epilogue: Human Rights as a Confucian Moral Discourse." In *Confucianism and Human Rights*, edited by Wm. Theodore de Bary and Tu Weiming, 297–307. New York: Columbia University Press, 1998.

Tu Wei-ming. "*Li* as Process of Humanization." In *Humanity and Self-Cultivation: Essays in Confucian Thought*, 17–34. Berkeley, CA: Asian Humanities Press, 1979.

Tu Wei-ming. "The Neo-Confucian Concept of Man." In *Humanity and Self-Cultivation: Essays in Confucian Thought*, 71–82. Berkeley, CA: Asian Humanities Press, 1979.

Tu Weiming. "Pain and Suffering in Confucian Self-Cultivation." In *Way, Learning, and Politics: Essays on the Confucian Individual*, edited by Tu Weiming, 45–56. Albany: State University of New York, 1993.

Tu Weiming. "The Structure and Function of the Confucian Intellectual in Ancient China." In *Way, Learning, and Politics: Essays on the Confucian Individual*, edited by Tu Weiming, 13–28. Albany: State University of New York, 1993.

Tu Weiming. "The Unity of Knowing and Acting: From A Neo-Confucian Perspective." In *Humanity and Self-Cultivation: Essays in Confucian Thought*, 83–101. Berkeley, CA: Asian Humanities Press, 1979.

Tu Weiming. "The Way, Learning, and Politics in Classical Confucianism." In *Way, Learning, and Politics: Essays on the Confucian Individual*, edited by Tu Weiming, 1–12. Albany: State University of New York, 1993.

Tucker, Mary Evelyn. "Introduction." In *Confucian Spirituality: Volume One* (Volume 11A of *World Spirituality: An Encyclopedia of the Religious Quest*), edited by Tu Weiming and Mary Evelyn Tucker, 1–38. New York: The Crossroad Publishing Company, 2003.

Turner, Ralph H. *Collective Behavior*. Englewood Cliffs, NJ: Prentice-Hall, 1972.

United States Conference of Catholic Bishops. "Faithful Citizenship: A Call to Catholic Responsibility." USCCB statement promulgated November 2006. http://www.usccb.org/faithfulcitizenship/bishopStatement.html

Van Norden, Bryan W. "Mengzi and Virtue Ethics." In *Confucianism in Dialogue Today: West, Christianity and Judaism*, edited by Liu Shu-hsien, John Berthrong, and Leonard Swidler, 120–136. Philadelphia: Ecumenical Press, 2004.

Wang Juntao. "Confucian Democrats in Chinese History." In *Confucianism for the Modern World*, edited by Daniel A. Bell and Hahm Chaibong, 69–89. Cambridge, UK: University of Cambridge Press, 2003.

Wansbrough, Henry, ed. *The New Jerusalem Bible*. New York: Doubleday, 1999.

Warren, Rick. *The Purpose Driven Life: What On Earth Am I Here For?* Grand Rapids, MI: Zondervan, 2002.

Weber, Max. *The Religion of China*. Edited and translated by Hans H. Gerth. Glencoe, IL: The Free Press of America, 1951.

Weinandy, Thomas Gerard, Daniel A. Keating, John Yocum. *Aquinas on Scripture: An Introduction to His Biblical Commentaries*. New York: Continuum International Publishing Group, 2005.

Weishipl, James A. *Friar Thomas D'Aquino: His Life, Thought, and Work*. Garden City, NY: Doubleday, 1974.

Westberg, Daniel. "Good and Evil in Human Acts (Ia IIae, qq.18–21)." In *The Ethics of Aquinas*, edited by Stephen J. Pope, 90–102. Washington, D.C.: Georgetown University Press, 2002.

White, Kevin. The Passions of the Soul (Ia IIae, qq. 22–48)." In *The Ethics of Aquinas*, edited by Stephen J. Pope, 103–115. Washington, D.C.: Georgetown University Press, 2002.

White, Lynn, Jr. "The Historical Roots of Our Ecologic Crisis." *Science* 155 (March 1967): 1203–1207.

Wieland, Georg. "Happiness (Ia IIae, qq. 1–5)." In *The Ethics of Aquinas*, edited by Stephen J. Pope, 57–68. Washington, D.C.: Georgetown University Press, 2002.

Williams, B.A.O. "Moral Luck." *Proceedings of the Aristotelian Society* (Supplementary Volumes) 50 (1976): 115–135.

Wilson, E.O. *The Social Conquest of Earth*. New York: Norton Press, 2012),

Wong, David B. "Reasons and Analogical Reasoning in Mengzi" in *Essays on the Moral Philosophy of Mengzi*, edited by Xiusheng Liu, and Philip J. Ivanhoe, 187–220. Indianapolis, IN: Hackett Publishing Co., 2002.

Wong, David B. "Rights and Community in Confucianism." In *Confucian Ethics: A Comparative Study of Self, Autonomy and Community*, edited by

Kwong-loi Shun and David B. Wong, 31–48.Cambridge, UK: Cambridge University Press, 2004.

Woo, Terry. "Confucianism and Feminism." In *Feminism and World Religions*, edited by Arvind Sharma and Katherine K. Young, 110–147. Albany: State University of New York Press, 1999.

Wrong, Dennis. "The Oversocialized Conception of Man in Modern Sociology." *American Sociological Review* 26, no. 2 (Apr., 1961): 183–193.

Wu, Pei-Yi. "Self-Examination and Confession of Sins in Traditional China." *Harvard Journal of Asiatic Studies* 39, no. 1 (Jun., 1979): 5–38.

Xie Bingying (謝冰瑩), ed. *Xin yi sishu fuben (新譯四書讀本)*. Taibei: San min shu ju (臺北: 三民書局), 1967.

Xunzi (荀子). *Xunzi (荀子)*. Sangle.web.wesleyan.edu/etext/, Chinese Philosophical E-Text Archive—Pre-Qin Texts, 1996. http://sangle.web.wesleyan.edu/etext/pre-qin/xunzi.html.

Yao, Xinzhong. *Confucianism and Christianity: A Comparative Study of Jen and Agape*. Brighton, UK: Sussex Academic Press, 1996.

Yearley, Lee H. *Mencius and Aquinas: Theories of Virtue and Conceptions of Courage*. Albany: State University of New York Press, 1990.

Yearley, Lee. "Two Strands of Confucianism." In *Confucian Political Ethics*, edited by Daniel A. Bell, 139–143. Princeton, NJ: Princeton University Press, 2007.

Yearley, Lee H. "Virtues and Religious Virtues in the Confucian Tradition." In *Confucian Spirituality: Volume One* (Volume 11A of *World Spirituality: An Encyclopedia of the Religious Quest*), edited by Tu Weiming and Mary Evelyn Tucker, 134–162. New York: The Crossroad Publishing Company, 2003.

Yü, Ying-shih. "Between the Heavenly and the Human." In *Confucian Spirituality: Volume One* (Volume 11A of *World Spirituality: An Encyclopedia of the Religious Quest*), edited by Tu Weiming and Mary Evelyn Tucker, 62–80. New York: The Crossroad Publishing Company. 2003.

Yü, Ying-shih (余英时). *Xiandai ruxue de huigu yu zhanwang* (现代儒学的回顾与展望). Beijing: Sanlian shudian (北京: 三联书店), 2004.

Zagzebski, Linda. *Virtues of the Mind: An Inquiry into the Nature of Virtue and the Ethical Foundations of Knowledge*. Cambridge Studies in Philosophy. Cambridge, UK: Cambridge University Press, 1996.

Zhang Zai (張載).*The Western Inscription (Ximing,西銘)*. Sangle.web.wesleyan.edu/etext/, Chinese Philosophical E-Text Archive—Pre-Qin Texts, 1996. http://sangle.web.wesleyan.edu/etext/song-qing/zhang-zm.html

Zhu Xi (朱 熹). *Zhuzi quanshu* (朱子全書). Shanghai: Shanghai guji chubanshe. Hefei shi: Anhui guji chubanshe (上海: 上海古籍出版社: 合肥市: 安徽教育出版社), 2002.

Index